STAFFORDSHIRE GRITSTONE

The Roaches
The Definitive Guide

British Mountaineering Council
177–179 Burton Road, Manchester M20 2BB

Staffordshire Gritstone –
The Roaches
The definitive climbing guide to routes
and bouldering on Staffordshire grit

Copyright © 2009 British Mountaineering Council

Published by:
British Mountaineering Council,
177–179 Burton Road,
Manchester M20 2BB.

All rights reserved. No part of this work covered by the copyright
hereon may be reproduced or used in any form or by any means –
graphics, electronic, or mechanised, including photocopying,
recording, taping, or information storage and retrieval systems –
without the written permission of the publisher.

First printed 2009

ISBN 978-0-903908-18-4

Cover photo: Leanne Callaghan on The Sloth, HVS 5a (page 88).
Photo: Mike Hutton.

Photo opposite: Hands, Ramshaw, by Matthew Thompson.

Designed and typeset by the BMC

Previous Editions
1913 **Some Gritstone Climbs**   John Laycock
1924 **Recent Developments on Gritstone**   Fergus Graham *et al*
1951 **Climbs on Gritstone Volume 3**   Allan Allsop
1957 **Climbs on Gritstone Volume 3**   Revised
1957 **Climbs on Gritstone Volume 4**   Eric Byne and Wilf White
1968 **Rock Climbs on the Roaches and Hen Cloud**   North Staffs MC
1968 **Guide to the Staffordshire Roaches and Hen Cloud**   John Smith
1973 **The Staffordshire Gritstone Area**   David Salt
1981 **Staffordshire Area**   Mike Browell *et al*
1989 **Staffordshire Area**   Gary Gibson
2003 **The Staffordshire Roaches** (*reprint*)   Gary Gibson
2004 **Staffordshire Grit: The Roaches**   Dave Garnett

BMC Participation Statement
The BMC recognises that climbing, hillwalking and mountaineering
are activities with a danger of personal injury or death. Participants
in these activities should be aware of, and accept, these risks
and be responsible for their own actions and involvement.

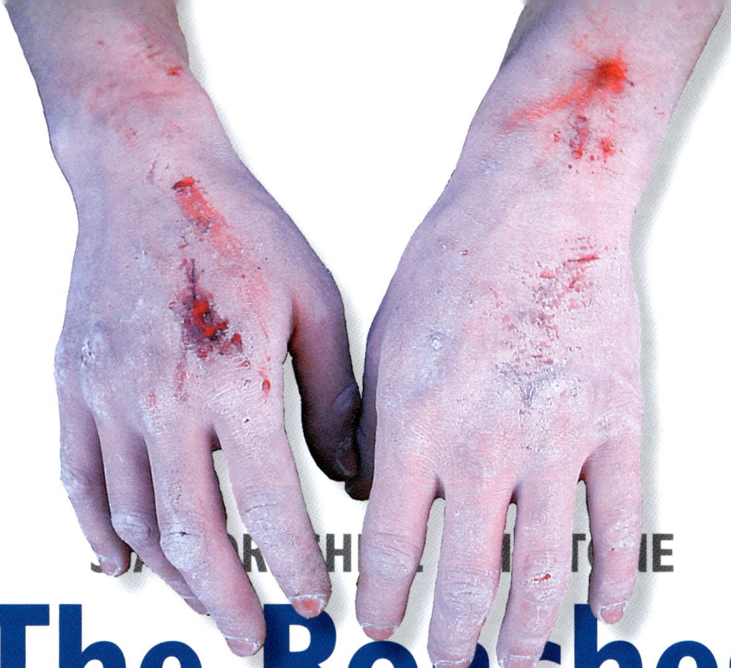

The Roaches
The Definitive Guide

BMC

Editor: Niall Grimes
Researched and compiled by
a team of guidebook volunteers

The BMC

The British Mountaineering Council (BMC) is the representative body for climbers, hillwalkers and mountaineers in England and Wales. It exists to promote their interests and to protect their freedom. Since its formation in 1944 it has worked, negotiated and acted in the many different aspects of outdoor life to ensure that the rights and freedoms that we share can continue in a responsible and sustainable way.

It has many core programmes that cover the broad spectrum of activities, which include: negotiating and securing access to hillwalking and climbing areas; promoting cliff and mountain conservation for the benefit of users and the environment alike; representing the interests of climbers, hillwalkers and mountaineers in the broader political world; promoting and advising on good practice in the worlds of training, equipment and facilities; promoting British climbing and British climbers throughout the world through international meets and the support of everything from bouldering competitions to Himalayan expeditions; supporting specialist programmes and events centred around youth, safety and excellence; organising and promoting events in the world of competitions; providing expert advice on all aspects of climbing wall use, design and management; support and advice to climbing, hillwalking and mountaineering clubs; providing the definitive record of climbs through its guidebook programme; giving up-to-date information on all aspects of work programmes; providing top class insurance cover for all members.

If you are not a member, and would like to support the work that the BMC does on your behalf, then contact us on the addresses below. If you would like to volunteer to help in one of the many projects the BMC are active in please visit the website and see what the BMC is involved in at the minute, then get in touch. For these, or any other inquiries, contact us at:

EMAIL: office@thebmc.co.uk **WEB:** www.thebmc.co.uk **TELEPHONE:** 0161 4456111

The BMC and Guidebooks

The BMC first became involved in publishing Peak District guidebooks in 1972 and has had a continued involvement ever since. Over those years, and even before, there have been trials and tribulations, dramas and controversies, much hair pulled out and much of it gone grey. However, what cannot be denied is that there has now been over 35 years of tremendous definitive guidebooks to one of the world's best climbing areas. The roll call of volunteers who are responsibe for this series of guides is too long to list, but they are heroes one and all.

Today, under the auspices of the current guidebook committee chaired by Ian Carr, this work carries on. The BMC guides being produced in 2009 continue to match the standard of what has gone before. Times may change, but quality, inspiration, innovation and dedication remain the same. Thanks to this the current series of BMC guides to the Peak and Pennine, with further guides for further afield planned, provide everything a climber could want from a guide, with definitive information to all routes and bouldering presented in a clear and enjoyable way.

British Mountaineering Council
177–179 Burton Road, Manchester M20 2BB

Table of Contents

Introduction	7
Acknowledgements	8
Climbing Notes	10
Bouldering Notes	12
Access and Conservation Notes	14
Other useful information	18
Mountain Rescue and First Aid	19
Geology	20
History	21

1 The Roaches — 32
- The Lower Tier — 38
- The Upper Tier — 72
- Roaches Green Circuit — 80
- The Skyline Area — 111
- The Five Clouds — 139
- Roaches Red Circuit — 148
- The Nth Cloud — 152

2 Hen Cloud — 162

3 Ramshaw Rocks — 196
- Circuit: The Ramshaw Rasher — 121

4 Newstones to Back Forest — 230
- Newstones — 234
- Baldstones — 242
- Royal Blue Circuit — 248
- Gib Torr — 251
- Gradbach Hill — 255
- Outlying Crags in the Gradbach Area — 261
- Wolf Edge — 262
- The Hanging Stone and Back Forest — 264

5 The Churnet — 274
- The Upper Churnet Valley — 276
- Sharpcliffe Rocks — 277
- Belmont Hall Crags — 280
- Harston Rocks — 285
- Garston Rocks — 289
- Oldridge Pinnacle — 290
- The Lower Churnet Valley — 292
- Dimmings Dale Area — 295
- Stoney Dale Quarry — 296
- Circuit: A Churnet Ramble — 300
- Ousal Dale — 302
  - Ousal Crag — 302
  - Cottage Rocks — 304
- Dimmings Dale — 307
  - Lord's Buttress — 307
  - Virgin Wall — 308
  - Gentleman's Rock — 308
- Wright's Rock — 310
- Peakstone Inn Amphitheatre — 318
- Rakes Dale — 320
- Peakstone Rock — 322
- Great Gate Buttress — 323
- Castle Crag — 324
- Park Banks Crag — 325
- Ina's Rock — 326
- Wootton Lodge Crags — 330

6 Outlying Crags — 336
- Windgather — 338
- Oldgate Nick — 348
- Castle Naze — 349
- Castle Naze – Surrounding Crags — 359
- Rudyard Pinnacle — 363
- Knypersley Area — 364
- Mow Cop — 367
- Bosley Cloud — 369
- Heighley Castle Quarries — 377

Graded List — 385

Route Index — 391

Big Country: Dave Garnett lost amidst the mightiness on Hen Cloud's bulging flanks, tussling with the deep joys of Second's Advance, HVS 4c (page 183). Photo: Niall Grimes.

Introduction

My association with Staffordshire, its climbs and its climbers, began a few years ago around a three-bar fire in a back room of the Wilkes' Head in Leek. A group of faces, Dave Garnett and his guidebook team, were sat round discussing every subject under the sun, from grades to grading to graded lists.

I had recently started as the BMC guidebook officer and this was to be one of the first projects I was involved in. Over the next couple of years I got to know the team very well – Andi, Justin, Gary, Mark, Luisa, Richie, Gus and Dave – and had a great time checking details, sweating blood and drinking beer together. From this team came, some time later, the 2004 Roaches guide, the first of the new series of full-colour, modernised BMC guides.

This rapidly became a favourite and really set the standard for BMC guides in the years to come. Thanks to that popularity it has now sold out, and the time came around for a reprint to be considered. Which brings us to the very volume you are holding in your hand right now.

Today I was on the blower to Andy, of Snap, Crackle and Andy Popp fame, Staffordshire loyalist and one-time guidebook worker himself, and the subject of the reprint came up:

"The old one wanted reprinting and it seemed like a good time to tweak it a little, slot in a couple of new routes, the odd new photo, you know. But it just grew and grew."

The Popp understood perfectly, and came up with the analogy of the amateur DIY enthusiast who notices a spot of wallpaper has peeled off in the living room. Deciding to fix it, he peels it off only to find a little loose plaster behind, and rationalising that he may as well repair that while he's at it, chips it out only to find that the entire wall is in need of replastering. Well you see where this is going. Before the DIYer knew, the room had been gutted, the wiring ripped out, the doors thrown in the skip and the old carpets chucked over the hedge of Mow Cop car park at midnight. All because of the little bit of wallpaper.

Well, as with most analogies, this is more fun than true. This is largely a drastic redecoration of Dave Garnett's fantastic 2004 guide. All the good stuff is still here, with plenty more besides. Maps are bigger, better and clearer; once-small crag topos now fill whole pages; errors have been ironed out and new ones introduced; grades rationalised; new routes and problems have been added; bouldering sections have been made loads clearer; the book now has five carefully selected bouldering circuits, a recent innovation for British guides; the Churnet Valley has had a total makeover to bring it the coverage it deserves.

Anyway, hope the guide brings you new joys, whether you are a first timer or an old timer, in this, the most beautiful of climbing counties.

Niall Grimes

Acknowledgements

This guide is based on Dave Garnett's fantastic 2004 edition, so most of the acknowledgements given below still stand, and the biggest acknowledgement of all is due, of course, to him.

Crag Writers (and everything else)
Dave Bishop, John H Bull, Dave Garnett, Gary Gibson, Niall Grimes, Chris 'Gus' Hudgins, Martin Kocsis, Robert Lavin, Stuart Millis, Richie Patterson, Paul Smith, Andi Turner, Sam Whittaker, Simon Wilson.

A special thanks to other people who gave constant support and input to the guide
Steve Clark, Justin Critchlow, Luisa Giles, Julian 'The Judge' Lines, Lynn Robinson, Mark Sharratt, Richard Taylor.

And all the people who made general input, by contributing written sections, route checking, advice and support
Clare Bond, Colin Foord, Peter Harding, Jon Read, Richard Wheeldon, Ken Wilson.

A very special thanks to all those involved in securing access to the crags in this book
Dave 'Rock On' Bishop, Catherine Flitcroft, Guy Keating, Andi Turner.

BMC Guidebook Committee
Les Ainsworth, Ian Carr, Brian Griffiths, Niall Grimes, Martin Kocsis, David Lanceley, Dave Turnbull, Richard Wheeldon.

A particular recognition is due to all those individuals involved in the production of volunteer-based guidebooks over the years, without whom the information would not exist.

For this edition

Steve Clark has been a checking machine, rummaging in the parts of the county where few dare to tread, unearthing and climbing neanderthal Churnet VSs, braving execution on banned crags as well as giving the popular areas a thorough going over. The accuracy of this edition is down to him. As an indicator of Steve's dedication to accuracy, he is the only person I know with a metre-marked rope, who will let you know that the HS on Knypersley is 7m long, not 5. Think about *that* for a while, it's mind blowing.

The local crew have supplied a lot of useful info to update and correct what errors there were in the last edition, and thanks go to Jon Fullwood, Martin Kocsis, Andy Lewandowski, Adam Long, Jon Read, Mark Sharratt and Andi Turner. A special mention to Stuart Brooks who showed a dedication to accuracy above and beyond the call of duty and thanks to him, along with Rob Mirfin and Mick Adams, the Churnet area, especially Dimmings Dale, is now a great piece of information for any visitor.

Illustrations

A massive thanks goes to the photographers who kindly supplied photos for this guide. The standard just keeps getting better, and Mike Hutton, Adam Long, Jon Read and David Simmonite in particular deserve a big fat medal: Nat Allen, John Beatty, Duncan Bourne, Stuart Brooks, Eric Byrom, Steve Clark, Justin Critchlow, Nigel Edley, Alex Ekins, Niall Grimes, Richard Harland, Paul Higginson, Mike Hutton, Simon Kincaid, Martin Kocsis, James Maddison, Alex Messenger, Ian Parnell, Dave Parry, Justin Pettifer, Paul Philips, Jon Read, Mark Sharratt, Nick Smith, Andi Turner and Al Williams.

Climbing Notes

Routes and bouldering
This is a guide to routes and boulder problems. To differentiate, routes are identified with a blue number, boulder problems with a red number.

Route grades
The system of grading for routes in this volume is the traditional British style, a combination of adjectival and technical grades, and assumes the leader has a normal rack, including standard camming devices, nuts, slings, quickdraws etc. The adjectival grade is the first part of the grade, and attempts to give a sense of the overall difficulty of a climb. This will be influenced by many aspects, including seriousness, sustainedness, technical difficulty, exposure, strenuousness, rock quality, and any other less tangible aspects which lend difficulty to a pitch. It is an open-ended system, and currently runs from Easy to Extremely Severe. Along the way, and in ascending order, are Moderate (Mod.), Difficult (D), Hard Difficult (HD), Very Difficult (VD), Hard Very Difficult (HVD), Severe (S), Hard Severe (HS), Very Severe (VS), Hard Very Severe (HVS) and Extremely Severe (E), the last category being split into E1, E2, E3 etc.

The second part of the grade, the technical grade, is there to give an indication of the hardest move to be found on the route, irrespective of how many of them there might be, how strenuous it is, or how frightened you are when you do it. They come onto the scale somewhere around 4a, a savage example of elitism that must have 3c merchants foaming at the mouth, and currently run thus; 4a, 4b, 4c, 5a, 5b, 5c, 6a, 6b, 6c, 7a, 7b.

Stars and daggers
For those who need them, stars (none, one, two or three) have been used in this guide to indicate quality. However, on Stanage, every route is worth doing. Where this is not true it will be clearly stated in the text. An un-starred route is by no means a bad route, and can give as good an experience as a three-star route. Route descriptions also point out the best features of any climb. Read through these and see what appeals to you. Try not to be too guided by stars alone.

Certain routes will have a dagger † symbol by them. This indicates a route where the guidebook team may have doubt about some aspect of the route, such as being unsure of the line, or having an unconfirmed grade due to insufficient repeats. It is not meant to cast doubt on a first ascent.

Ethics and style
The two most basic rules here are be honest, and don't damage the rock. Beyond that, it's entirely up to you, although in terms of style, some ascents are considered better than others. The best is still the on-sight flash, climbing the route first try with no falls and no helpful information. Few hard routes are done in this fashion, many higher grade routes being completed after some form of top-rope practise. However, this is currently acceptable, as long as the final result is a clean lead of the route, ideally placing protection *en route*. Many routes have also become established with side-runners for protection. Where this is so, it will be mentioned in the text, and the grade will reflect this fact. And finally, on a happier note, aid points and rest points have now disappeared from the areas covered in this book, and it is unlikely that a new route containing either would be seen as acceptable.

Fixed protection
Fixed protection – bolts, pegs, threads or hammered wires – is considered unacceptable on natural grit. Never, ever, think about placing any, be it on a new route or any subsequent ascent.

New routes, first ascents etc.
Details of first ascents, including name, grade, individuals involved, date and style of ascent, as well as contact details, should be sent to:
guides@thebmc.co.uk.

Gritstone – this precious rock
Climb the rock as it is. Do not be tempted to shape it to suit your inadequate skills or to gouge out

Introduction Climbing Notes

protection placements where none exist, so leave your wire brush and chisel at home. Brushing with anything other than a toothbrush to remove excess chalk is rarely necessary. Once the hard exterior layer is removed, the softer sandy interior erodes very rapidly. If you cannot do a route or problem in its existing state, go away and train harder or accept that you aren't good enough – yet! If new routeing please remember these ethics and in addition do not garden or remove vegetation.

Route Grades

UK adj.	UK tech.	French	US	Aust.	UIAA
M		F1/2	5.2	10	I
D		F1	5.3	11	II
VD	3c	F2	5.4	12	III
S	4a	F3	5.5	13	IV
HS	4b	F4	5.6	14	IV+
VS	4c	F4+	5.7	15	V- / V
HVS	5a	F5	5.8	16	V+
	5a	F5+	5.9	17	VI-
E1	5b	F6a	5.10	18	VI
E1		F6a+	5.10+	19	VI+
E2	5c	F6b	5.10++	20	VII-
E3	5c	F6b+	5.11a	21	VII
E3		F6c	5.11b	22	VII+
E4	6a	F6c+	5.11c	23	VIII- / VIII
E4		F7a	5.11d	23	VIII
E5		F7a+	5.12a	24	VIII+
E5	6b	F7b	5.12b	25	IX-
E6	6b	F7b+	5.12c	26	IX
E6		F7c	5.12d	27	IX
E7	6c	F7c+	5.13a	28	IX+
E7		F8a	5.13b	29	X-
E8		F8a+	5.13c	30	X
E8		F8b	5.13d	31	X
E9		F8b+	5.14a	32	X+
E9		F8c	5.14b	33	XI-
E999	7a	F8c+	5.14c	34	XI
E999		F9a	5.14d	35	XI

Bouldering Grades

V grade	UK technical grade	Font grade	Peak B grade
V0-	4c	3	
			B1
V0	5a	4	
V0+	5b	4+	B2
V1		5	
	5c	5+	B3
V2		6a	
	6a	6a+	B4
V3		6b	
			B5
V4		6b+	
V5	6b	6c	B6
		6c+	
V6		7a	B7
V7	6c	7a+	B8
V8		7b	B9
		7b+	
V9		7c	B10
V10	7a	7c+	
V11		8a	B11
V12		8a+	B12
	7b		
V13		8b	B13

Bouldering Notes

Bouldering grades
The V system is used in this guide, with problems running from V0-, V0, V0+, V1, V2, V3… V12. In addition, English technical grades are given in brackets after the V grade. This is more to help differentiate in the lower grades, and to help lower grade climbers who are unused to bouldering grades, and becomes more theoretical as technical grades exceed 6b. That being said, however, there is still a significant body who see the English technical grade as ideal for isolating single moves.

Highballs
If a boulder problem occurs with a full grade in brackets as opposed to just the technical grade, this means it is a highball problem, with aspects of a route about it. That is, you might not want to fall off! The definition between problems and routes has been who is most likely to do the climb. If it is a group of boulderers out with pads and spotters, a climb will probably be recorded as a boulder problem. If it is traditional climbers with a rope and rack, it will be recorded as a route. Use your sense.

Names and stars
Many of the problems in this guide have been given names. These names are in no way an attempt to 'claim' these problems, just a way of identifying them. A few first ascents have been recorded, but in general, trying to get first ascent information for problems would seem like more trouble than it is worth, and in a way, not in keeping with the spirit of the sport. Due to the subjective nature of quality, stars have not been used for boulder problems. A clear indication of how good an area is will be given in that area's introduction.

Environmental considerations for boulderers
All climbing has an environmental impact. However, boulderers may wish to bear some special points in mind. In a session, a problem can be climbed many more times than a route. This leads to an erosion rate greater than that seen on longer climbs. Try to do all you can to minimise the erosion. Brushing is the most obvious issue. Wire brushes can easily remove the tough outer skin of the rock, leaving the soft unprotected rock beneath to wear away. If you brush, use a soft, nylon-bristled brush. Always clean your feet before climbing, and climb well to avoid scratching about on the surface. Use as little chalk as possible. Never use Fontainebleau-style resin or 'pof'. It ruins problems. Never ever attempt to alter the rock in any way. Don't apply ugly tick marks to the rock. Use a bouldering mat if possible. Try to visit different areas.

Circuits

This guide sees the use of Fontainebleau-style bouldering circuits. These work by grouping together a series of boulder problems of somewhat similar difficulty into a linear circuit. You find the start, then use the map to go along the problems. If you follow the numerical pattern, then this should be a logical way to trace out the circuit. The idea is to do them all in a single session. However, this may just be the ultimate goal, and the first task might be to try to do them all individually, and then try to link them at a later point.

The map must then be used in conjunction with the main body of the guide in order to find the problems. Page numbers before the problems will tell you where to find them. In the list of problems, there is the problem number and name. The number after this refers to the number that is ascribed to the problem in the main text. It should all run like a dream. Also, in the main text, if a problem is on a circuit, it will have a small, correspondingly-coloured circled 'C' to indicate this: ●

Hopefully these circuits will provide a fun and unique way of visiting crags, taking the boulderer away from honeypots and seeing what crags have to offer.

Rik Battye stretching it out on one of the most classic problems in the guide, Joe's Arête, V3 (page 94). Photo: Norman Gilman.

Access and Conservation Notes

Our behaviour in the countryside is becoming more and more important, both for the continued survival of that countryside, and for our right to enjoy it. Please read these notes and act responsibly at all times.

Inclusion of a crag in this guide is not a guarantee of a right of access to it. That said, we are fortunate that the great majority of them are freely accessible with the co-operation of the landowner. In many cases access is now Open Access under The Countryside Rights of Way Act. Even then, restrictions on climbing to protect cliff-nesting birds and flora will continue to apply, as at present. In any case, do not cross drystone walls except at stiles provided and do not damage any stockproof fencing, but do close behind you any gates that you open.

Moorland, landowners and access agreements

Many of the gritstone crags in this guide are owned by public organisations. That is not the same as saying that the public have an undisputed right of access. A balance has to be struck between access, land management, and conservation interests.

The Peak District National Park Authority

(PDNPA, Aldern House, Baslow Road, Bakewell, Derbyshire DE45 1AE, 01629 816200, aldern@peakdistrict-npa.gov.uk), currently owns most of the crags on the Roaches Estate and their wide management responsibility includes, in priority order, to:

- Conserve and enhance wildlife habitat.
- Conserve features of geological, geomorphological, and cultural interest.
- Protect and enhance the landscape.
- Provide public access, recreation and education as far as is compatible with the above.
- Meet the proper needs of agricultural graziers compatible with the above.
- Provide for, wherever possible, the social and economic needs of the local community.
- Manage with maximum financial efficiency.

The PDNPA is reviewing its portfolio of landownership and there may be significant changes taking place in the way their estates are managed or owned in the years ahead. The BMC is actively involved on your behalf to ensure that access for climbing continues whilst helping to conserve the important moorland habitat.

The Staffordshire Wildlife Trust

(The Wolseley Centre, Wolseley Bridge, Stafford, ST17 0WT 01889 880100, www.staffs-wildlife.org.uk), owns Baldstones, Gib Torr, and moorland nearby, and their mission is to *'protect and enhance the wildlife and wild places of Staffordshire and to promote understanding, enjoyment and involvement in the natural world'*.

Other crags in this guide belong to private landowners who, with a few notable, not to say notorious, exceptions, are quite supportive of public access but many of them also have responsibilities and agreements covering wildlife protection. Climbers co-operation is therefore crucial to the continuing access we currently enjoy to the crags on the Staffordshire Moorlands and associated pasture land under voluntary agreements negotiated with the landowners by the BMC's full-time and voluntary access and conservation representatives. Our long-term interest as climbers and citizens is to continue this voluntary system of achieving a balance between responsible access, land management, and conservation. It is flexible and sensitive, and the relationships built up over time with most landowners are positive and supportive.

Access difficulties

Through much work, free access is granted to almost every crag in this guide. Please follow all instructions so as to keep that access for the future. If there are any special considerations, they will be

'Dave 'The Bish' Bishop, access legend, enjoying an evening's bouldering on the Yawning Stone. Gradbach Hill is one of the many quiet and sensitive crags in this guide where respect for the environment and an ability to tread lightly are necessities if climbers are to continue to enjoy the right to climb. Photo: Niall Grimes.

Staffordshire Grit

mentioned at the start of each section. Also, please make regular visits to the BMC's Regional Access Database (RAD) at www.thebmc.co.uk, and click on the RAD link for any up to date information regarding changes to access arrangements as for example for seasonal bird restrictions which are now becoming a fact of life on Western Grit and The Roaches and Hen Cloud in particular. This is a measure of the successful symbiosis between access and conservation interests. Please notify the BMC if you have any access difficulties, via the RAD comments form, or phone the BMC office on 0161 4456111. If you have any other local access queries, try the website or the BMC office, and find out the contact details for the local BMC access rep. They are all climbers, and are on your side.

Moorland & access

The heather and bilberry moorland is invaluable at all times to ground-nesting birds such as grouse, curlew, lapwing, and animals such as stoat, hare, shrew, common lizard etc., whilst the rocky outcrops and grazed fields attract our friend the ring-ouzel. So please stick to public footpaths and other designated means of access to the crags listed in this guide and keep disturbance to a minimum. Moorland, which is an internationally important biodiversity habitat, has been removed at an alarming rate and the damage done to its plant and wildlife is only just beginning to be reversed. Both the Peak National Park and Staffordshire Wildlife Trust are vital protagonists in this process and they both consult with the BMC access team so that our interests are taken into account.

Dogs

Dogs are good company, but running loose over the moors they are bad news for wildlife. They will cause birds to abandon their nests and animals to flee and thus probably bring about the avoidable death of a season's young. You probably wouldn't even know it had happened. So if you really can't leave Rover behind at home, then make sure your best friend is under control and preferably tethered whilst you are climbing. Farmers, landowners and tenants may shoot any dog worrying or disturbing their stock. You wouldn't want to have to explain that to your family when you got back home.

Top-roping

If overdone this can cause difficulties for other climbers and damage to the rock. It is worth

CRAG CODE
www.thebmc.co.uk

Access	Check the Regional Access Database (RAD) on www.thebmc.co.uk for the latest access information
Parking	Park carefully – avoid gateways and driveways
Footpaths	Keep to established paths – leave gates as you find them
Risk	Climbing can be dangerous – accept the risks and be aware of other people around you
Respect	Groups and individuals – respect the rock, local climbing ethics and other people
Wildlife	Do not disturb livestock, wildlife or cliff vegetation; respect seasonal bird nesting restrictions
Dogs	Keep dogs under control at all times; don't let your dog chase sheep or disturb wildlife
Litter	'Leave no trace' – take all litter home with you
Toilets	Don't make a mess – bury your waste
Economy	Do everything you can to support the rural economy – shop locally

BMC Participation Statement — Climbing, hill walking and mountaineering are activities with a danger of personal injury or death. Participants in these activities should be aware of and accept these risks and be responsible for their own actions and involvement.

Introduction Access Notes

remembering that all routes are graded for ascents from the bottom up placing your own protection as you go. If you really do feel the need to top-rope then please:

- Give priority to anyone who wants to lead the route from the bottom up.
- Do not occupy any area of rock for extended periods.
- Do not make continuous and repeated attempts at hard moves as this leads to rapid and unnecessary erosion of the holds, and they can't be replaced.

Sanitation

Another major environmental point to make is the one of sanitation. The sight of or proximity to rocks seems to excite peristalsis in some climbers with a consequent urgent need to find a secluded spot. The best advice is to 'Go before you go', i.e. before leaving home. If that fails, then please keep well away from the bouldering and climbing areas when leaving your mark and do not use or discard tissue as it takes weeks to disintegrate. Taking stones off walls to hide your contribution both damages the walls, which then have to be repaired at public, i.e. your, expense, and slows down the efforts of nature's scataphagous creatures who are keen to get stuck in to your waste offering. So help nature to help itself and leave it exposed. Sanitary towels, toilet paper and similar should be wrapped up and removed.

Litter

Finally, if you take a plastic bag with you, you can take home your litter and anyone else's that has been left around.

Guidance for Groups

Groups can vary from large organised climbing parties under the control of instructors to small gangs of friends and even groups such as management trainees whose use of the crag is instrumental in achieving some purpose other than climbing. Many groups are well organised and controlled, and operate with sensitivity both for the needs of other climbers and for the crag environment. However, the following advice will be helpful in reducing some of the unintended (we hope!) consequences of group use of the crags and for giving guidance to sustainable practice for all. To lessen ground and rock erosion, disturbance to wildlife, and friction between users, try these ideas and spread the word:

- Encourage leading climbs instead of top-roping.
- If you need to top-rope then keep both the time you occupy any route and the number of ascents to a minimum. Avoid placing multiple top-ropes and do not leave set-ups in place when you are not actively using them.
- Keep group sizes small and under control, and in particular cut down movement over the ground at the base by your group.
- Ensure that rucksacks and gear as well as group members do not block footpaths and access.
- Move on frequently to new locations. If you occupy a route or area for a long time, for example, all morning, all afternoon, all day, all week, or regularly use the same routes and locations, you hasten erosion and deny access to others.
- Running up and down boulders can be great fun but it erodes the ground, deposits dirt on the rock, and teaches unsustainable practice. Try simple bouldering instead.
- Consider abseiling at 'purpose built' locations such as Tegg's Nose Quarry and Miller's Dale Viaduct. Abseiling for its own sake should only take place on artificial structures and not on natural crags.
- Take litter away and encourage the cleaning of areas on leaving.
- Keep noise down and discourage yelling, cheering, and applause. Find other and quieter ways to encourage group members.

Other useful information

Maps
The most useful map for the gritstone area is Ordnance Survey 1:25,000 Outdoor Leisure Sheet 24: The Peak District White Peak Area. For detailed exploration of the Churnet Valley, Ordnance Survey 1:25,000 Pathfinder Sheet 810 (SK 04/14): Ashbourne and the Churnet Valley will be found handy. Ordnance Survey 1:50,000 Landranger Sheet 118 covers the outlying areas of Bosley Cloud, Mow Cop and Heighley Castle.

Public transport
For the main gritstone areas, the nearest railway stations are Buxton and Macclesfield (for info, phone 08457 484950). There is a regular bus service, the X18, between Sheffield and Hanley, via Bakewell, Buxton and Leek. It goes every couple of hours and gives access to Ramshaw and Upper Hulme (gateway to the Roaches and Hen Cloud), although you may wish to ask the driver to drop you as close as possible to your destination (for info, phone 0870 6082608). It has to be admitted that many of the other areas in this guide are inconvenient to reach by public transport.

Parking
Always use the designated parking area for any crag. The main Roaches and Hen Cloud area has limited parking and during the summer months. A fine usually results from parking outside designated areas in this vicinity.

Food & drink
During the summer months the Roaches Tearoom opposite Hen Cloud is extremely civilised. Tish's Teas beside the Newstones is another good brew stop.

There are the usual chippies and similar in Leek and, for a curry, the Bolaka on Stockwell Street (the Macclesfield road) is definitely a worth a visit.
The Lazy Trout at Meerbrook is friendly, good value and has a fine garden with a view of what you are missing on the crag. The Olde Rock Inn in Upper Hulme is within easy walking distance of the Hen Cloud campsite. After a visit to Ramshaw or the Newstones area, the Traveller's Rest (near the Flash turn off the main A53 Leek-Buxton road) is highly recommended. The Ship Inn, Wincle, is handy for the Hanging Stone, has good beer and is recommended for a slightly more up-market meal. Leek is packed with pubs, but the Wilkes' Head on St Edward's Street is favoured for its beer (and has been the very tolerant host to many guidebook meetings!).

Huts & camping
Don Whillans Memorial Hut, Rockhall Cottage, The Roaches. Owned by the BMC. Sleeps 12, mixed, in two rooms. Very good value. No dogs, smoking or camping. Contact the Booking Secretary: Michael Hunt, Vale Cottage, Foolow, Eyam, Hope Valley, S32 5QR (01433 639368).
There are several convenient Youth Hostels in the area. Meerbrook: Old School House, Meerbrook (01538 300174); Gradbach Mill, Quarnford, Buxton (01260 227625); Dimmingsdale, Little Ranger, Oakamoor (01538 702304). See www.YHA.org.uk.
There is a basic campsite below Hen Cloud. Contact Mr Day, The Holmestead, Upper Hulme, Leek (01538 300419). A more luxurious campsite may be found at the Camping and Caravanning Club, Blackshaw Grange, Blackshaw Moor (01538 300285).

Climbing shops
Mountain Fever, 25 Brunswick Street, Hanley, Stoke-on-Trent (01782 266137), www.mountainfever.co.uk

Jo Royle Outdoor, 6 Market Square, Buxton (01298 25824) www.jo-royle.co.uk

Camp Four, Pickford Street, Macclesfield, (01625 619204) www.campfour.co.uk

Climbing walls

The Stoke-on-Trent area seriously lacks a decent climbing wall. The nearest is:
Rope Race, Goyt Mill, Hibbert Lane, Marple, Stockport (0161 426 0226)

There is a small wall in Longnor but, although ideal for children, it isn't a serious venue for the hard core:
Upper Limits, Buxton Road, Longnor (01298 83149)

There is also a poor, decidedly old school, bouldering wall at:
Macclesfield Leisure Centre, Priory Lane, Macclesfield (01625 615602)

Wet weather entertainment

Alton Towers is the local centre of Babylonian excess and is conveniently adjacent to the lower Churnet crags. Ornithologists might try **Blackbrook Zoological Park** (Winkhill, on the Ashbourne road out of Leek, 01538 308293), whilst those with a bent for industrial archaeology might be interested in **Brindley's Mill**, Mill Street, Leek (weekends in the summer months only, 01538 483741). **Tittesworth Reservoir** has a pleasant visitors' centre. When the weather is too poor to see **Jodrell Bank** from the crag it might be worth a visit (just off the A535, between Holmes Chapel and Chelford, 01477 571339). Those struggling to entertain small children should try the narrow gauge steam railway in **Rudyard** (01995 672280) which runs during summer weekends. Finally, **Poole's Cavern** is guaranteed weatherproof (Green Lane, Buxton, 01298 26978). **Tourist Information Office** is on the Market Square in Leek (01538 483741).

Mountain Rescue and First Aid

Dial 999 and ask for Police – Mountain Rescue. Briefly describe the nature of the incident and give the crag name and OS map reference as listed at the start of each crag section.

The Police will co-ordinate the Mountain Rescue team and, if appropriate, the county air ambulance that is available for evacuations from the crag. The local team is based in Buxton. Although **they should not be contacted directly for call-outs**, they are very happy to hear from anyone wishing to support their voluntary efforts:
Buxton Mountain Rescue Team,
8a Halsteads, Dove Holes, Buxton, Derbyshire SK17 8BJ (01298 812232), www.buxtonmrt.org.uk

Likewise, anyone wishing to support the County Air Ambulance might like to contact them at:
Staffordshire County Air Ambulance,
Appeals Headquarters, Burton Road, Dudley, West Midlands DY1 3BB (01384 241133), www.county-air-ambulance.com.

FIRST AID in case of ACCIDENT

1. **If spinal injuries** or **head injuries** are suspected **do not move the patient** without skilled help, except to maintain breathing and circulation.
2. **If breathing has stopped**, clear airways and commence **CPR** (cardio-pulmonary resuscitation). **Do not stop until expert opinion diagnoses death.**
3. **Stop bleeding** by applying direct pressure.
4. **Summon help.**

These are the basic principles of first aid. If you climb at all regularly, you should seriously consider taking a first aid course. Learning enough to save a life isn't at all difficult and one day you might be very glad that you (or someone else) did.

Geology

by Clare Bond

The geology in the Staffordshire area is dominated by the great escarpments of the Roaches, Ramshaw and the Clouds – this is also, unsurprisingly, the best area for climbing.

In the carboniferous period, approximately 345 Ma (million years ago), the White Peak was just a sea of warm clear waters. Then, either due to the up-lift of land in Scotland and Scandinavia or faulting enable rapid subsidence, deepening the warm tropical sea, the conditions changed. Sediments – grits and sands – from the land were washed into the sea and deposited, and over the years, settled and compacted into what we now know as gritstone. Sedimentary structures, cross-bedding, which can be seen on many of the climbing crags as diagonal layers within individual beds (layers of sediment) suggest that the sediment was mainly washed into the sea from the north – maybe from a granite in Scotland.

The grits are inter-bedded (or layered with) marine shales, muds and coal. If it weren't for the deposition of these inter-layers of shale and mud, we might have substantially larger gritstone outcrops! The classic Roaches scenery is dependent on these inter-layers, which are far 'softer' and therefore much more easily eroded than the gritstone. The erosion of the shale layers leaves the gritstone outcrops prominent on the landscape, forming 'edges'.

Individual layers or beds of gritstone often contain layers of different sized pebbles and grains. The pebbles have been transported in a high-energy flow, whilst the smaller grains require less energy to be transported. The pebbles are smooth and round, the result of abrasion during transportation. Individual pebbles are often the key to, and the crux of, many gritstone climbs. If you find yourself at the Roaches on Catastrophe International, whilst pulling on the pebbles think about how they got there and how rounded they are – or may be you should just concentrate on pulling!

At the very end of the Carboniferous there was a period of compression that folded the rocks. The area of the Roaches, Ramshaw and the Clouds is part of a large syncline, a fold in the shape of a U, which trends north to south and plunges (is tilted) North. The core or centre of the fold contains coal deposits which lie on top of the layers of gritstone and shale. The structure is best seen from a distance with a pint in your hand at the Mermaid Inn. After several pints you may appreciate that the gritstone of the Roaches is in fact the same layer of rock that can be climbed on at Ramshaw – the layer is folded and outcrops on different limbs or sides of the fold.

Between the Permian and the Triassic (280–195 Ma), extensive erosion uncovered the limestone to the east. To the west a fault separates the Carboniferous sediments from those of the Triassic, but to the south-east the contact is an unconformity or erosion surface. In fact there are few Triassic rock outcrops and climbing is concentrated on those in the Churnet Valley. Here the Triassic sediments are thick beds of sandstone and conglomerate which are red in colour due to staining of iron oxides. The sediments are thought to have been deposited in shallow water lakes and seas, on the edge of vast deserts which covered most of the English Midlands. The conglomerates at Sharpcliffe Rocks, with pebbles as big as fists, show that local flooding did occur in the Triassic transporting quite large pebbles.

The rocks of Staffordshire have come along way from the Carboniferous tropical sea in which we started the story. When you're out on the moorland think that one day it may be back under the sea and future visitor to Staffordshire maybe dodging lava flows from volcanoes rather than bogs!

History

by Niall Grimes

> "Ramshaw Edge, a grotesque succession of ghoulish faces, bovine and porcine heads, and half-finished monsters springing from the parent rock. And beyond, where Hen Cloud extends its array of pinnacles, outlines that the camera may prove to be less than vertical or only slightly overhanging, but to the eye appear like curving horns, their points overweighted with threatening tons of rock. Then [the Roaches], another peak of strange shape that appears to be a loose accumulation of boulders of all sizes and the most extravagant forms, gnarled, rifted, fantastically weathered, and often perched in positions that seem to defy the laws of mechanics."

This flowery and doom-laden description of the three major Staffordshire crags comes from one of the area's first explorers, EA Baker, in his book *Moors, Crags and Caves of the High Peak*. Baker, originally from Derby, was a member of that great exploratory group of Peak District activists, the Kyndwr Club. Was it truly how the group saw this landscape, wayward and threatening, ready to pounce and devour at any time, or was it just a flight of Baker's fancy, combined with his prodigious poetic licence?

Perhaps a bit of both. The Kyndwr Club was formed in 1900, a collection of professional men who sought their adventures in the moorland around the Sheffield, Derby and Manchester areas. The key members were Baker, Sheffield's WJ Watson and the legendary JW 'Jimmy' Puttrell. This group, and Puttrell in particular had, since the late 1880s, roamed the entire district, adding rock climbs on every possible feature. The first entries of practically every crag's ascent list in the Peak bears Puttrell's name. However, it took the group a long time to ever venture Staffordshire's way, and when first they did, they famously spent a day wandering lost in the mist in an attempt to find Lud's Church (a rumour of rock had been heard, mumble, mumble). When they eventually happened upon it, it was found to be disappointing. Perhaps this hapless day is where Baker's early visions came from.

The group did return, however. They explored Ramshaw Rocks, and ventured to Hen Cloud where Baker again gives an account of 'a tussle with gloves on' in the Pinnacles area. It is not sure which route this was, although it is more likely to have been Chockstone Chimney than Mindbridge. They also made a visit to the Roaches, where, despite a healthy fascination with Rock Hall, they managed to record the first route on this beautiful crag, Raven Rock Gully.

> Some villagers were anxious to know if we had scaled this imposing crag [Raven Rock] which they evidently considered the finest climb about here, and were much disappointed to hear we had not attempted it. The rustic, being no climber himself, thinks nothing of impossibilities.
> **EA Baker**

Staffordshire Grit

> For many years the Roches have stood to the climber as an El Dorado, a glorious myth, whose wonders were known to exist, but were never explored due to their apparent difficulty, and it is only during the last few years that the rocks have been regularly visited.
>
> **Morley Wood, 1924**

Yet, despite the obvious potential the area possessed, it appears they made few further visits to the county, perhaps setting in motion one of the overwhelming characteristics of Staffordshire climbing, that of its slightly forgotten nature. Time and again through its history it can be seen that, while it has never lagged behind in terms of quality nor difficulty, its light has often been eclipsed by events further east, or northwards in Yorkshire. Why this should happen is not obvious, but the result has been a relative quietness and 'localness' that is one of the most endearing traits that this fine area has to offer.

Little activity took place on the cliffs for over 10 years (Laycock and Thompson's notable Hen Cloud epic aside, as well as a few minor routes here and on the Roches) until 1913. In this year, a new breed of gritstone 'tigers' hit the scene. New techniques and attitudes were in evidence. Rock-climbing was generally no longer viewed as an 'exercise for the Alps'. Clothing and footwear was such as it was no longer so restrictive on movement. Woollen stockings and heavy nailed boots gave way to rubber-soled gym-shoes. The 'grab and pull' of earlier generations was gone in favour of more open climbing, relying more on friction and balance, techniques that were to influence the direction of British rock-climbing until the arrival of the brutality of the Rock and Ice. Most notably of these tigers was the powerful trio of Stanley Jeffcoat, Siegfried Herford and John Laycock. They 'discovered' the Upper Tier of the Roches, adding Jeffcoat's Buttress and Chimney, as well as Hen Cloud's classic Great

Dave Noddings soloing Peter Harding's Valkyrie (page 59), as good today as it's ever been.
Photo: Adam Long.

Chimney. A testimony to their ability is Scafell's Central Buttress, Herford's mighty pioneering climb from 1914, recognised as the hardest lead in the country for some time. It has been argued that every major advance in British climbing has been instigated by climbers who have been trained on outcrops, and this example certainly supports that theory.

The bold and open climbing pioneered by this group was taken a stage further by climbers such as AS 'Fred' Pigott, Morley Wood and Lindlay Henshaw in the early '20s. Bachelor's Buttress, Pedestal Route, Black and Tans, Crack and Corner, Left-Hand Route – an ascent of any of these climbs, even with today's

> **The final overhang of Crack and Corner** was only overcome by the leader taking a shoulder. "The top must some day become an easy day for a lady, but at present it is no place for a gentleman."
>
> **Morley Wood**

equipment, will give an insight into what had been achieved by such climbers all those years ago, both in technical and psychological terms. However, the ultimate achievement of the era must still be Ivan Waller's mightily exposed Bengal Buttress. Waller was a dandy, fond of torturing passengers with excessive speed in his Alvis sports car. As revenge, one victim, Fred Pigott, led Waller to the Lower Tier and pointed the evil driver at an unclimbed slab. 'Waller', it is said, 'devoured the buttress very promptly.' So much for revenge. Even today this climb is renowned for its breakneck smearing and bold crux, and a real eye-opener to sticky-soled, pant-filling, leg-trembling leaders.

This was the era during which the use of the rubber shoe began to pay good dividends, and along with this came the development of the shoulder belay which at first was considered to be so secure that it was not always practice for a climber to anchor himself to the rock.
AS Pigott talking about the 1920s.

There followed, throughout the 1930s, another of Staffordshire's fallow periods. Little was added to any of the major or minor outcrops. It was a time of great depression in the cities, when the free time

Staffordshire Grit

of unemployment and the depressing frustration of bleak cities forced a wave of working class men out into their local countryside for recreation. Here, the landed class saw 'escape' as 'invasion', and strict and sometimes aggressive keepering was applied in protection of what was seen as a threat. In some areas this fearsome protection was greater than others, and while some areas of the eastern Peak continued to provide climbs, one must presume that the landed class were more successful in their ruling in Staffordshire. This sad time was rounded off in the bleakest of fashions by the outbreak of the Second World War in 1939, and from then until its end in 1945, the country had little appetite for activities on rock.

The Karabiner Club led the way with exploration of the Skyline area in 1945, but the first big event of the post-war period came in the sweeping beauty of Peter Harding's Valkyrie. At the time, Harding, a wiry and quick-minded engineer, with a healthy faith in his own abilities, was acknowledged as among the finest climbers in the land, and raised standards significantly, not only in his local area, but in the mountains of North Wales. His climbs such as Promontory Traverse and Demon Rib at Black Rocks, and Cratcliffe's Suicide Wall were his big additions to grit; fierce, technical climbs up steep terrain. But he is equally remembered for routes such as Valkyrie and Goliath's Groove at Stanage, climbs which were not at the limits of the possible, but which bore such a touch of class that they would be destined to become the favourite classics of their grade.

In the aftermath of the horrors and privations of the War, there was a shift in the whole social structure of the country. While rationing persisted until the '50s, the post-war period was noted for its full employment, and a renewed sense of hope sweeping through the land. Better transport allowed easier access to the moors surrounding the great cities. Value was being placed on the outdoors. The traditional strictures that served to keep the lower classes 'in their place' were lessening, as evidenced by the election of a new Labour government. The Peak District National Park was decreed, guaranteeing access for all. These factors served to allow a new breed of climber onto centre stage in British climbing, and onto the Peak District in particular, and with it came new and refreshing attitudes that would go on to produce an advance in climbing standards the like of which has not been seen before or since.

The Valkyrie Club was already a strong group soon after it was formed in 1947, but when Joe Brown joined it soon after, it was set to make history. Characterised by a rough, working-class toughness, the group swept all before them. Uncredited routes from the 1951 guide, such as Hedgehog Crack, Rainbow Crack and Central Climb Direct, all hint towards a new type of route: steep long cracks, often reliant on jamming and devoid of the safety of ledges. Yet when Joe Brown led Saul's Crack on the Upper Tier in 1947, something new had begun. The route is a ferocious and technical jamming crack, overhanging and uncompromising, the start of a new breed of super-route.

Brown's next big addition was Valkyrie Direct. He jammed easily up to the left of the great flake, and disappeared round the corner to top out. Slim Sorrell was not in a seconding mood, so when a passer-by asked for a go, he was allowed to tie on. The passer-by followed with ease, even continuing up the nasty upper crack that Brown had avoided, and joined the leader on the summit. The young lad was Don Whillans, and from this first meeting, the two combined and formed the most dynamic and fearsome partnership of theirs or any other day.

Many routes were to 'get the message' from these two. Matinee, Hen Cloud Eliminate, Delstree, Brown's Crack, Don's Crack, Crack of Gloom, Sloth: all, arguably, the best lines on the best crags. From reading their accounts, you are left with the impression that they just were not finding any of it difficult, wandering up the routes with ease. The climbing tends to be characterised by very technical and gymnastic climbing, usually jamming, in a very strenuous position. The age of the genteel balance climb had gone, with Whillans' ferocious fist swinging at its retreating back.

After this great time, which lasted well into the 1950s, there followed a lull in Staffordshire climbing. Perhaps the county was reeling from the onslaught, or perhaps the great surge of development on the newly-fashionable limestone cliffs had taken away the force. New route activity did take place, along with a surge of discovery. The Churnet valley yielded a great number of routes on its many crags, and renewed interest was shown in Mow

Introduction History

Different times. Someone, it might be Don Whillans, being belayed by a little fella who might be Joe Brown, questing up the fierce Hen Cloud testpiece, Bachelor's Left-Hand (page 184). However, why anyone would even bother to belay, or to own a rope for that matter, is a mystery, as it hangs unused from the back of the leader's waist. Talk about balls! Photo: Nat Allen Collection / Simon Kincaid.

Staffordshire Grit

Cop, Bosley Cloud and Gradbach Hill. But they were not routes of any great stature or historic significance. Mike Simpkins' bold Roaches challenges (Wombat, Walleroo, Elegy, and so on) kept the pot simmering, of course, along with interesting additions elsewhere: Chicken, Encouragement, The Untouchable, Rubberneck springing to mind. Still, the '60s will not be seen as one of the great decades of Staffordshire development.

But something new was in the air. Revolution, floral shirts, Led Zeppelin guitar solos, drugs and streaking. Denim shorts and EBs. The early years of the 1970s marked the beginning of the great Gritstone Renaissance sweeping Yorkshire, the Eastern Edges and Staffordshire. The Roaches were, once more, where it was at!

Looking at first ascents, one can see, from the early '70s, a huge explosion in the numbers of new routes being added in Staffordshire. The Roaches, Hen Cloud, Ramshaw, as well as all the lesser crags, were peppered with new climbs, many of them pushing the technical standards of the day. The great cracks had all been climbed by earlier generations, but this one found the walls in between covered in holds, and duly swarmed up them. These routes may have sometimes lacked in stature or maybe line, but that was less important. This was the era of 'the move'. Technical interest was prime, and this was frequently combined with sizzling boldness as sequences were often led away from the comfort of cracks.

An almost obsessional level of interest was shown by a good number of climbers. From the east, the cream team of John Allen and Steve Bancroft began their very fruitful raids, culminating in their four big 'C' routes on Hen Cloud. Other quality additions were found elsewhere at the Roaches and Ramshaw. However, Staffordshire had its own answer to the young Sheffield-based talents, in the shape of two curly haired rascals called the Woodwards.

Andrew and Jonny Woodward opened their account with the truly ground-breaking route, Ascent of Man. Not ground-breaking in terms of difficulty necessarily, but in style of climbing, for it was the first real pebble-puller to be added to the Roaches, a type of climbing for which that area of the crag would become renowned. From that point on, the two brothers, with Jonny becoming dominant, scorched the county's crags, reaping the yields of their prodigious talents. The Undertaker, National Acrobat, The Joker, Patient Weaver, all testify to their roving ability. However, it was at the Roaches where they really upped the bar.

On The Skyline, beauty and difficulty came together in near perfection. The year was 1977, and with San Melas the brothers realised that holds were a luxury, not a necessity. This was further proven with Wings of Unreason, with its ludicrous top move, and then Track of the Cat. This latter route was equal in quality to anything Bancroft and Allen were adding to the Eastern Edges. (A few years later Andrew matched this run with Entropy's Jaw, a route that completes a good Skyline tick-list of tough slab routes.)

The ultimate route, however, came on the Lower Tier, with Jonny's Piece of Mind. A route truly ahead of its time – totally holdless climbing on minimal smears in a position of utmost death, it was to wait almost 20 years for an on-sight ascent (although one hopeful did come dangerously close in 1986!). It was then rated E6 6c, and although not far off the mark today, this was seen as an extraordinary claim at the time, and attracted much criticism.

But then the Woodwards weren't above such criticisms. The era they were in, seems, more than most, to have been a particularly competitive one. With so many climbers with so much appetite, competition was fierce. The 1981 guide, following hot on the heels of this era, has a history section full of admonishments of greed and underhand tactics. The young brothers also were criticised for their heavy adoption of top-rope practice. This may have been slightly hypocritical, as this was, and had often been, a common tactic of the gritstone new-router. Perhaps it was just the level that they took this method to that in some way broke the subtle and unwritten rules of gamesmanship. They also attracted several cries of foul. Most notable was the Traveller in Time/Jumbo controversy on Ramshaw. Many simply put these infractions down to youthful over-enthusiasm, and it must also be remembered that they were seen as young upstarts by the established community. Ultimately, Jonny's ascent of Beau Geste on Froggatt in 1982, acknowledged as the hardest route of the day, silenced all who had doubted his talent.

The pace continued all through the '70s and '80s, where one name is notable in first ascents.

James Pearson on Traveller in Time / Jumbo, E3 5c (page 201) at Ramshaw. The route was claimed by local ace Martin Boysen in July 1977 but was later counter-claimed by notorious local upstarts Andrew and Jonny Woodward. The claim remained a bone of contention between the climbers. Photo: David Simmonite.

Staffordshire Grit

Gary Gibson, a local Stoke lad, is renowned throughout the British climbing scene for his near-manic obsession with new-routeing. He is, quite simply, a new route machine. Crags everywhere bear his name, but it was in Staffordshire that he acquired his taste. Bad Joke, Fast Piping, Knossos, Shortcomings and Licence to Run are just a few of the mountain of first ascents to his name.

Then in the early '80s, the climbing that was achieved in the '70s was taken to a new level, the result of a combination of training and incredible talent. This was the era of hard limestone sport climbing, climbing walls and dieting. Luckily, it was also an era of very high unemployment, a 'dole culture' and spare time. Three cheers for Mrs. Thatcher! The outcome was that standards surged. Nick Dixon was prime amongst a group of Stoke residents. Fiercely strong, and with very high levels of drive and application, it wasn't long before he was to make his impact on the area's climbing.

The beautiful A Fist Full of Crystals began his bold campaign on the pebbly Lower Tier. In the same area, he went on to add Pindles Numb, and with Catastrophe Internationale, shifted pebble-pulling to a new technical level. However, it was with his route, Doug, that this technical level was combined with a high level of danger, to bring a new grade to Staffordshire. The area's first E8 (arriving at almost the same time as Dawes' Gaia and Dunne's New Statesman) employed all the tricks: reports of pillars of glue to hold ramshackle pebbles in place, and a group of hecklers below holding a 'fireman's blanket' to protect a fall – a fact that reflects Dixon's theatrical style more than his preservation instincts. It remained, however, an extremely bold outing, and one of the most important ascents in Staffordshire's history.

Simon Nadin may not be one of the first names known to climbers. He is, however, the very definition of British climbing talent. A lanky blond, quiet and with an almost unbelievable modesty about his own abilities, he first came on the scene in the '80s known as the Buxton Stick Man. Unusual, as his early climbing was mostly spent on the Buxton climbing wall developing his strength and technique; however, when he made it to the rock, he wasn't slow in applying these skills.

At the time...

I was doing things like Paralogism and some of those other climbs at the Roaches, and I remember thinking that they weren't particularly hard routes really, and that I wasn't climbing that well. But then just after that I went to Europe and I won the World Championship and thought 'hmmmm…'.
Simon Nadin

The rarefied grades of E6 and E7 were churned out thick and fast by the Stick Man: Dangerous Crocodile Snogging, Never, Never Land, Master of Reality, B4XS, Barriers in Time, Art Nouveau, Painted Rumour, Paralogism. The list of three-star hard routes with his name on them could go on for a long time. All show his ability to keep it together on big bold leads. Climbs such as Thing on a Spring, Crystal Voyager, Who Needs Ready Brek? and Laguna Sunrise all demonstrate, if it were needed, the level of technical ability he had. Added to this is a host of unclaimed and undocumented (and probably unrepeated) boulder problems scattered around, victim of Nadin's modesty and amnesia.

What will be remembered, however, is by a long way the hardest and best set of additions in the history of Staffordshire climbing. Perhaps less known at the time than some of Dawes' creations around Sheffield, perhaps due to the isolation' of Staffordshire, or perhaps lacking Johnny's media-magnetic personality, Nadin's routes were the equal to what was being added anywhere in the country. Only, really, in the 1990s did many of his routes received repeats, (some are still unrepeated) and then rarely. Nadin was, without doubt, a tough buck.

Perhaps unsurprisingly, new route activity in the 1990s slowed down to an almost non-existent level when compared with what had taken place in the previous two decades. In the 'Hard Grit' resurgence of the mid-90s, methodical top-roping allowed many (but not that many) of the previous desperates to get repeats. A few harder routes were added to the area, a few of them landing in the E8 bracket. Seb Grieve, a Nottingham-based madman, who accounted for second ascents of many of Nadin's climbs, went on to add his own masterpiece, Clippety Clop, to the outrageous arête avoided by

Introduction History

Dougie isn't the only King of the Roaches. In the 1980s Simon Nadin, quietly and with hardly any fuss, sent the standard of Staffordshire climbing into outer space. He produced a series of simply dazzling leads combining a cool head with red-hot technicalities, seen here on perhaps the greatest of them all, Thing on a Spring, E6 7a (page 60). Photo: Al Williams.

Dangerous Crocodile, using knees, denim and lunacy to great effect; Julian Lines smeared dangerously up (and very quickly back down again) the slab left of Piece of Mind, due to an Obsession Fatale; the talented teenager, Justin Critchlow levitated up Ramshaw's blankest arête, to produce the ridiculously technical, but survivable Ultimate Sculpture, and Mark Katz bouldered riskily up Hen Cloud's shortest and hardest climb, The Young Pretender.

But what that decade will be remembered for most will be the bouldering revolution. The popularity of this sub-sport exploded in these years, the result of the dominance of 'power' as a climbing medium, accessibility, user-friendliness, fun, sociability, 'newness' and fashion. Not that it was anything new. Brown and Whillans obviously tried their hands at it, leaving Joe's Arête and Don's Crack (although the Joe Brown Pad and the Whillans Toothbrush never caught on). From the '60s onwards, crags such as Baldstones and Newstones were developed by climbers such as Martin Boysen, perhaps the foremost technician of his time, Jerry Peel, Hugh Banner and Tony Barley. Charlie's Overhang, Elephants Ear, Press Direct and Peel's Problem are all good examples here. In the '70s, the short technical nature of the climbing broke down

Staffordshire Grit

the barriers between what was considered bouldering and routes (The Fin, Tierdrop, The Ultra-Direct, Mantis). By the '80s, bouldering had achieved a status, with climbers such as Nadin, Allen Williams, Nick Dixon and Gary Cooper producing many of today's classic problems. Finger of Fate, Inertia Reel, Crystal Voyager, The Cube are just a few of those whose history is known.

Yet in the '90s, what we see are hordes of climbers who see bouldering, not as training for real routes, but as an end in itself. Paul Higginson, Justin Critchlow, Andi Turner, Mark Katz, Andy Brown and Dave Aucott among many others, were to scour the edges and boulders, and bring new levels of power to the sport. Tit Grip, Epilogue, Boba Fett, Undercut Dyno, Simple Simon, Gibbering Wreck, Higginson's Arm and Grand Theft, coupled with raids from Sheffield to produce Inertia Reel Traverse, Mushin' and Ram Air; all are top-notch problems of the highest order, that go a long way to make Staffordshire every bit as good a bouldering venue as Stanage or Almscliff.

In the years since the publication of the 2004 edition development has continued. While this has not matched earlier years in terms of quantity, it still carries things forward in terms of quality and difficulty. This development has been forced on by the fiercely loyal locals who had spent the time before the last edition repeating all the testpieces of earlier generations, now finally getting the chance to add their own mark.

The majority of this development, in the main Gritstone area at least, has taken place on the mighty Hen Cloud. It is no surprise that these have all been great powerful and bold climbs in every way a match for Hen Cloud's expectations. Mark Sharratt's Night Prowler and Jon Read's Mandatory and Justin Time were obvious gaps calling out for the required committment. Andi Turner's additions to the crag, Myxi, and more significantly, Catharsis, edges forward the upper limit of difficulty here, the latter climb featuring a 7a dyno to cover the stately wall to the right of Caesarian. These climbs are all masterpieces hung in a very exclusive gallery.

Meanwhile, across on the Roaches, while the Headless Horseman arête – perhaps the most noted project in the area – remains undone, Ben Bransby crossed over from the east to add what is probably the hardest lead in the area, Skin and Wishbones. This E8 7a combines very technical climbing with long runouts to solve a problem that has seen many suitors off in the past.

Away from the main area, the Churnet Valley has seen lots of activity both in terms of greater popularity and cutting-edge development with Wright's Rock and Ina's Rock seeing some very hard new routes. The bouldering at Wright's, and at many of the surrounding crags, is now firmly on the radar of those in the know, with many desperate, powerful and fingery problems, courtesy of climbers such as Mick Adams, Rob Mirfin and Stuart Brooks.

Nearby, bouldering has been taken to a new heights. Having repeated the existing routes at Ina's Rock, Andi Turner did the first ascent of Thumbelina, a hard and high wall climb of the highest quality. Subsequent ascents followed and used bouldering mats to pad the climb out into super highball territory. This outrageous approach caught on, and for a while the route was probably the most popular Extreme in Staffordshire. Rob Mirfin soon upped the ante somewhat by climbing the arête to the left of Thumbelina to give Cornelius. This E8 6c has now seen at least two ground-up ascents, and points the way to a new and very significant trend on routes this size.

So, where are we now? In the early years of the third millennium, it is hard to see what there is left. This may have been said by older generations, but the impact of the last few years' exploration has left us with no sense of the impossible. The list of Last Great Problems is short, for both bouldering and routes. Perhaps the combination of power and skill will result in a rise in on-sighting standards, which currently lags behind cutting-edge first ascents by many years. There have been notable flashes and on-sights in the last few years, but these are very rare occurrences, far from the norm.

What is certain is that Staffordshire climbing will continue. People will still come, thrash, smear, pull, jam, layback, and top-out. People will still have beautiful days and great climbing on some of the greatest routes anywhere in this or any other land, enriched by its great history, immersed in its legendsand great figures and epics.

Staffordshire. There is no finer climbing area.

Andi Turner unleashing on the 7a crux of Catharsis, E7, the hardest of the bunch of new routes at Hen Cloud (page 173). Photo: Jon Read.

Ed Hill on the second pitch of Peter Harding's 1946 masterpiece, Valkyrie (page 59). With the hardest climbing now behind him, the climber can enjoy the exposure of the final tower of the essential Roaches VS. Photo: James Maddison.

The Roaches 1

"I have generally found that things get better, the further west one goes..."

Oscar Wilde.

The Roaches

A gothic cathedral of a crag; a place of pilgrimage for disciples of fist-jamming and pebble-pulling, a site of ritual observance for devout boulderers. The Roaches is steeped in a history that reaches from the pioneers of gritstone climbing, through the Golden Age of jamming, to state of the art testpieces. It has enclosed misty cloisters and airy pinnacles and terrifying gargoyles; the sketchiest of nail-biting slabs, the most carnivorous of cracks and the wildest of roofs. This wealth of development and diversity of styles has resulted in classic routes over the full spectrum of grades. Here the most accessible and enjoyable of VDiffs may be found within metres of the most uncompromising E8s. All this with watercolour pastoral views, and all within an hour's drive of the Potteries and Manchester.

Access
The land is currently owned by the Peak District National Park Authority and there is generally open access to all climbing areas. However, access to areas of surrounding open moorland, especially to the east of the Upper Tier, Skyline, and Five Clouds is discouraged apart from using the obvious public footpaths. These areas are some of the few remaining quiet locations for wildlife, particularly ground-nesting birds between March and July in any year. This is relevant for access to the Cube, which should be approached via footpaths from the south-east (i.e. from the right-hand side of the Upper Tier), and not directly from the path to the Skyline. The other rule relates to bouldering on the Hard Very Far Skyline area. A local understanding has been arrived at that there should be no bouldering on the friable buttresses above the main path from Roach End. Occasional local bird restrictions may be in place at Five Clouds, Nth Cloud, and the Upper Tier. These will be clearly signposted on site as well as published in the BMC's. website (www.thebmc.co.uk) under the Regional Access Database which is amended immediately changes take place. Peregrines have occupied a ledge in the 'Humdinger' area in recent years before moving on to Hen Cloud. Any necessary restrictions will be placed on site and onto the BMC RAD site. If you speak Peregrine then encourage the birds to continue to use Hen Cloud as it is a lot less restrictive on climbing and bouldering.

Parking & approach
For the main areas of the Roaches and Five Clouds, park in the lay-bys on the road below the crag. Parking outside the marked areas (including in front

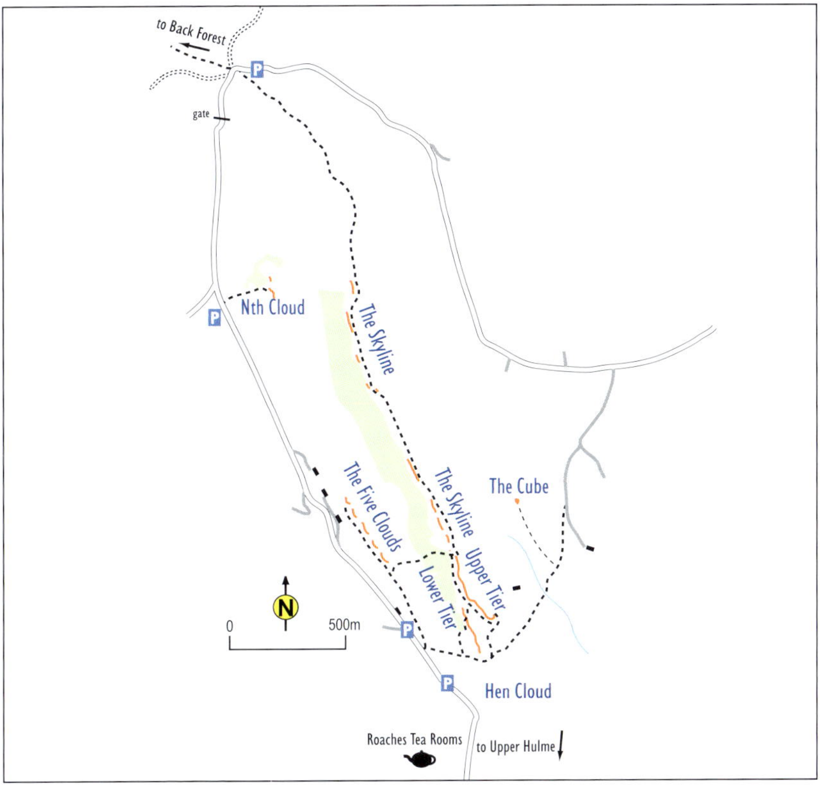

The Roaches Area Map

Climbers lost among the boulder backwash of the final spillings of the Lower Tier as the mighty bastions of Valkyrie Buttress and Kestrel Buttress diminish into the smaller slabbier buttresses beyond, and finally into the gentle Piece of Mind Boulders. Climbers can be seen on Commander Energy, while two lost souls pray for salvation. Photo: Jon Read.

The Roaches Tiers Map

of the cottage) will almost certainly result in a fine. The police do not tolerate any partial blocking of the highway and local residents are reporting contraventions. Access is needed for locals and emergency vehicles at all times. Theft from vehicles at the Roaches and other isolated parking locations is still a problem. Leave nothing on show. For The Very Far and Hard Very Far Skyline areas a quicker approach is to park at Roach End. Follow the lane north under the Five Clouds through a gate (please close behind you), and over a cattle grid to parking just north of the grid and round the bend. Do not park in the lanes leading west and north as this can impede the farmer's vehicles and animal movements. A well-engineered path leads up the ridge to the trig point (10 minutes). From here, the Hard Very Far Skyline and bouldering areas are within 5 minute's easy walk.

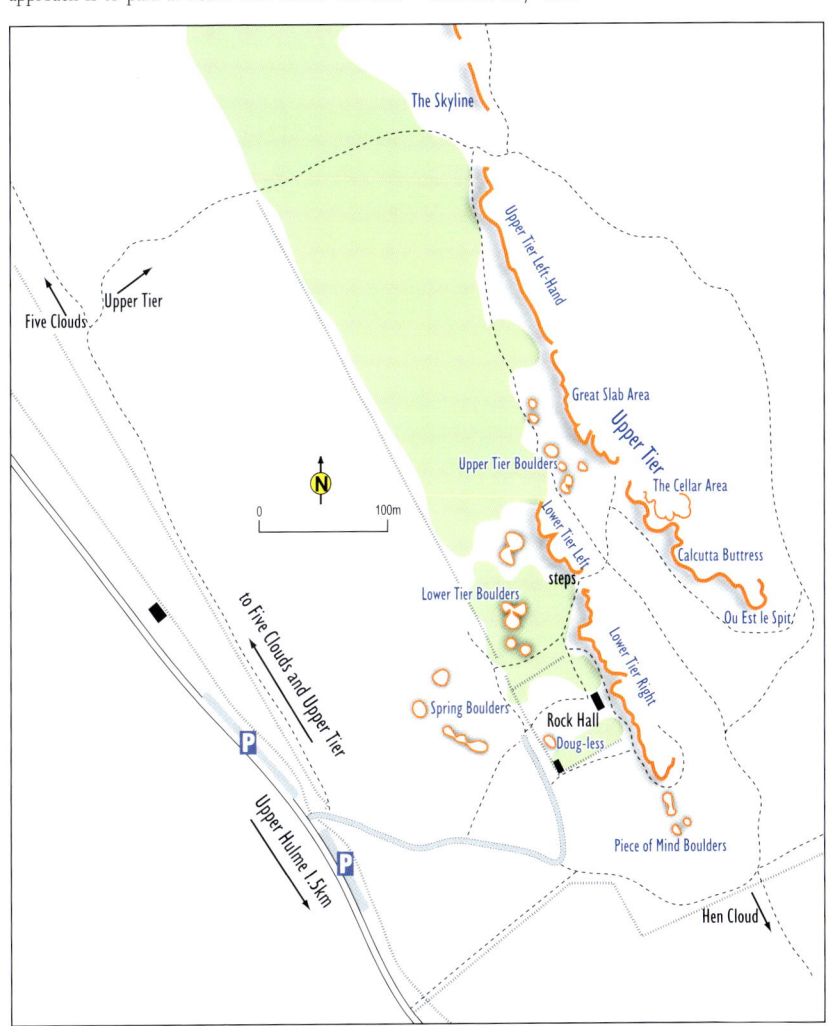

Spring Boulders

The first rock arrived at on the walk up is a collection of fine boulders on the left of the path. This is a fairly good circuit with a good mix of slabby pebble-pulling testpieces as well as the usual Roaches brutality. It tends to be very boggy under lots of the problems, and extremely boggy under some, in which case you may want to borrow a friend's bouldering mat. The slabs on Boulder F are a great place to learn to smear, while falling off the offwidth on Boulder C is a great place to learn to swim.

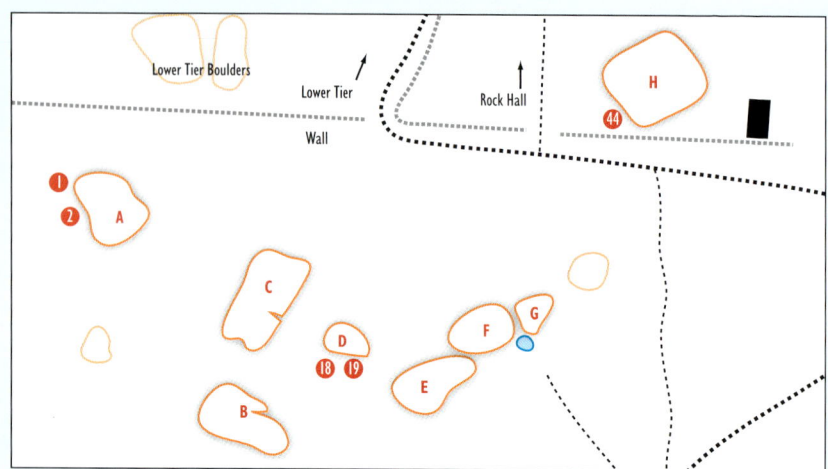

A: The Fly Boulder

1   The Fly V4 (6a)
The overhanging prow on the farthest boulder. Starting low on the flake is V7 (6c).

2   The Lurch V5 (6b)
Attain and ascend the hanging scoop right of the prow with all guns blazing.

B: The Ramp Boulder

3   The Ramp V1 (5c)

4   Ramphole of the Roaches V2 (6a)
Move up and mantel from the shallow hole.

5   Flakes V0 (5b)
The flaky arête.

6   Pod 'n' up V2 (5c)
Move up from the left end of the pod on the back of the boulder.

C: Shothole Boulder

7   Violence V2 (5c)
Scurry up the beautiful scoop.

8   Impotence V2 (5c)
The blunt nose direct.

Roaches Lower Tier Spring Boulders

9 Lout V1 (5b)
Ledge to slopey topout.

10 Seconds Out V1 (5b)
The offwidth will suit those with a strong work ethic. Climbing the left arête itself is V2 (5c).

11 Skinned Rabbit V6 (6b)
You will be. Move up from the shotholes to a rounded topout.

12 The Grind V4 (6b)
If you enjoyed the Skinned Rabbit… Hole, flake and topout. A sit-start makes it V6, mainly because of the weight of your wet pants.

13 Arête on Left V6 (6b)

14 Arête on Right V5 (6b)

15 Mr Nice V4 (6b)
Hurdle the dark sidewall to the right using a single chipped foothold.

16 Mr Left V5 (6b)
From the arête to the right, pull out left into the scoop and go up. A direct start to this looks impossible, but then again, they said that about time travel.

17 Arête on Left V3 (5c)
The arête all the way.

Sarah Warburton on Spring Slab, V7 (page 41). Photo: Adam Long.

Staffordshire Grit

D: Little Summit

18 Summit Arête V0− (4b)
The slabby arête of the small boulder.

19 Slab to Summit V0− (5a)
The slab to the right to the highest point.

E: Bog Boulder

A good boulder although some of the problems on the front have a sponge factor.

20 Bog Arête Left V0− (4a)

21 Bog Arête Right V3 (6a)

22 Pebbles and Seam V2 (6a)
Tinkle up the steep slab past a seam.

23 Bog Monster V2 (5c)
Climb the top features to a featureless top. Climbers who have fallen into the incredible sponge below this route have reappeared in Peking. ⊙

24 Bog Standard V1 (5c)
Layback the shallow flake to a rounded top. ⊙

On the back of the boulder:

25 Bog Slab V0− (4c)
Climb the slab to the finish of the next problem.

26 Poxy V0− (4a)
Follow the line of shallow pockles. ⊙

27 The Swinger V0 (5a)
Use a rounded hold to gain the fantastic porthole, then use this to swing left onto the slab.

28 Back Wall V1 (5b)
Climb the short wall using undercuts and sidepulls.

29 Boo Meringue V1 (5b)
A ramble. Step onto the arête of Problem 20 then make a smeary low-level traverse to the left arête. Swing up then hand traverse the top on deep holes to regain Problem 20. Move up or down from here. ⊙

Roaches Lower Tier   Spring Boulders

F: Spring Boulder
A super-classic slab with some of the best smearing problems at the Roaches. The landings are usually fairly dry, unless you fall into the spring, of course.

30 Spring Slab   V7 (6b)
The left side of the slab, on pocks 'n' pebbles, has become harder over the years: **see photo on page 39**. A very thin time can be had traversing the invisible seam from left to right: **Boba's Traverse** V7 (6c).

31 C3PO   V6 (6b)
Climb the slab to the right on buttery smears. **G**

32 Boba Fett   V8 (6c)
Climb the tallest part of the slab on nothings. A smearing masterpiece. Avoiding the arête completely earns you a V9 (7a) tick.

33 Bobarête   V7 (6b)
Skedaddle right to the arête and climb this. Worryingly placed above a watery hole.

On the back of the boulder is:

34 Sprung   V3 (6a)
From a sit start on the sidepull jug, move up and use the seam and the groove to gain the summit.

35 Sprat   V0+ (5a)
From the same sit start, groove up and right to the top of the boulder. **G**

36 Sprite   V0 (5a)
The layback arête to the right, on its left.

G: Little Boulder

37 Spring Roll Left   V2 (6a)
A quick shimmy over the left side of the blunt nose just right.

38 Spring Roll   V0 (5a)
Climb the short arête on its right.

H: The Dougless Boulder
A great big boulder just inside the walls of the cottage with a fistful of burly highballs. Some of the problems here may require brushing first.

39 Particle Exchange   V6 (E4 6b)
From the crack, step left on a brushed foothold and gain the arête. This will feel a lot harder if it is at all dirty, so it may be worth brushing first.

40 Doug-less   V4 (E3 6a)
Climb the crack to the horizontal feature, and mantel it. Getting on for being a route.

41 The Rumour   V7 (6c)
A bit of a neo-classic following the wall to the right of the crack past the ripples.

42 Sketchy Rib   V2 (5c)
The slabby rib to the right.

43 Slabby Arête   V0− (4b)
The more defined arête just right again.

On the opposite side of the boulder:

44 Scratchy Scoop   V3 (E1 6a)
The slabby scoop to the right of the chippy steps. **G**

Lower Tier Boulders

More boulders lie just across the wall in the form of the classic and popular Lower Tier Boulders, nestled among the larch trees below Teck Crack. A bit of everything at all grades. Good shelter and quick drying. Popular.

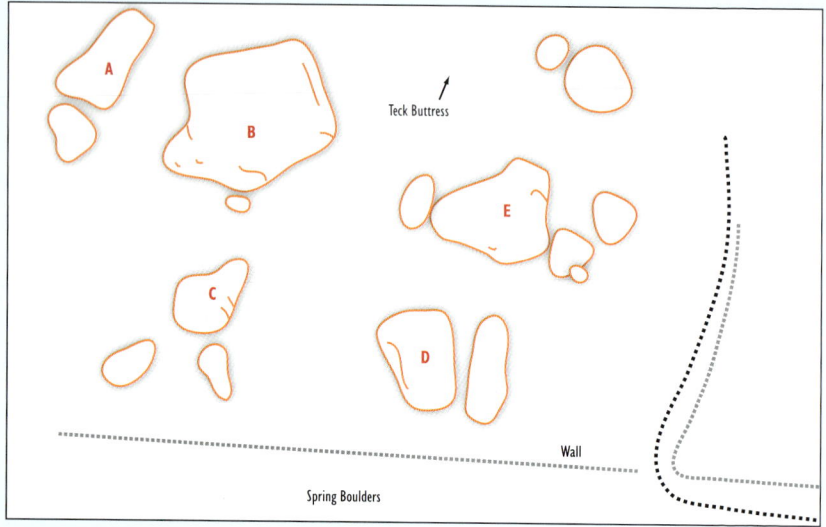

A: Blister Slab

1 Left Slab V0− (4c)
The left line on the slab. ☻

2 Slab 2 V0− (4a)
An easier, left-trending line.

3 Blister's Sister V0+ (5a)
A smeary line just left of the blisters.

4 Blister Slab V1 (5c)
Press it out on a sloping, chest-height hold to gain the protruding dimples above direct. Technical.

5 Back Slab Right V0− (4b)
The right-hand line.

B: The Big Block

6 Black Nook Slab V0− (4c)
The quick slab right of the damp groove.

7 Black Nook Arête V0− (5a)
The slabby, pebbly arête to the right.

8 Pockets Arête V0 (5b)
Climb the blunt end of the boulder. ☻

9 Three Pocket Slab V3 (6a)
Climb the slab on shallow pockets. A committing step up at the top rounds off a memorable classic. ☻

42 The Roaches

Roaches Lower Tier   Lower Tier Boulders

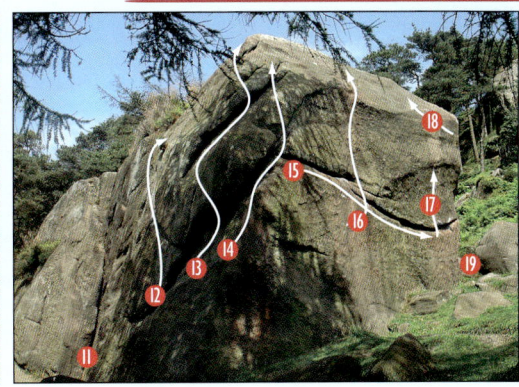

10 Parental Duties V8 (6c)
The steep slab directly above the first foot pocket, avoiding the foot-ledge out right.

11 Big Block Gully V0− (4a)

12 Bow Crack V2 (5c)
The diagonal crack with tricky laybacking and sketchy smearing.

13 Flake Arête V0 (VS 5a)
The mountaineers' route, with a big feel. Climb the big arête on its left with strenuous and smeary undercutting, technical all the way.

14 Big Block Arête V0 (4c)
An easier and less bold version swings onto the right side of the arête then up to good jams. ⊖

15 The Undercut Traverse V4 (6a)
Traverse the undercut rightwards. While it's not very hard, you will almost certainly skid off it.

16 Stretch and Mantel V5 (6b)
A beauty. Gaining the boss on the lip is the crux, but manteling out the top is a real test of confidence. ⊖

17 Undercut Dyno V7 (6b)
Some wild turbonics from the undercut to the boss on the lip.

18 Stretch Left V4 (6a)
From the arête, stretch left to the boss and mantel.

19 Classic Arête V0 (5a)
The flaky right arête. Lots of good variants are available by omitting holds. ⊖

The Full Girdle, V5 (6b), starts with a reverse of The Undercut Traverse and traverses the entire boulder leftwards, a few feet above the ground to finish up Black Nook Slab or Tarzanning across the hanging garden to complete the full link up.

C: Twin Flakes

20 Heinous Mantel V5 (6b)
Bust a move on the rounded sloping nose.

21 The Uppercut V4 (6a)
Tenuous undercutting of the thinner upper flake. A good V3 (6a) using the arête.

22 The Undercutter V3 (6a)
Tenuous uppercutting of the under flake. Starting low on the good hold is a wee bit harder.

The Roaches

Staffordshire Grit

23 The Grasper V0 (5a)
From the big flake, go up and left along the edge. ⓒ

D: Pine Tree Slab

24 Boss Slab V0 (5a)
The gentle slab. Good sport can be had jumping onto this one from the boulder behind and climbing no-handed; quite hard. ⓒ

25 Pine Slab V0+ (5a)
The thinner slab just left of the crack. Again, a good no-hander, and again, can be leapt onto from the boulder behind before climbing it handless. The 'touch-down' is not as hard as on Boss Slab. ⓒ

26 Pine Crack V0− (4a)

27 Up Chips V0− (4b)
The fun line of holds. The squeezy slab to the left is V2 (5c).

28 The Arch V0− (5a)
Climb through the centre of the arch.

29 Pine Arête V0− (4c)
The nice slabby arête.

30 Pine Arête Right V0 (5a)
It's a wee bit steeper on the right.

31 Green Slab V3 (6a)
The tallest part of the slab between the flake and the arête.

32 Pine Martin V0 (5b)
The flake. Try it one-handed. ⓒ

E: Greener Boulder

33 The Green Greenie V1 (5c)
Mantel out from the start of the traverse. ⓒ

34 The Greener Traverse V3 (5c)
Traverse the finger-rail from left to right, with a bit of a lunge at the end. A sitting start off the poor crimps is V4 (6b).

35 Greenerête V4 (6b)
The arête from a sit start.

Bouldering at the Roaches

Justin Critchlow on Inertia Reel Traverse, V12 (page 51). Photo: Niall Grimes.

The Lower Tier

by Andi Turner

O.S. Ref. SK006622   Altitude: 400m a.s.l.

Fiercely classic climbing with top notch routes of all grades. The crag is made up of a run of smooth pebble-dashed slabs on the left side, and a series of jutting prows on the main, right-hand side. The two are divided by a set of steps running to the Upper Tier.

Conditions & aspect

The Lower Tier tends to be fairly sheltered, not being as high up the ridge, and with many trees nearby to break the wind. This shelter also makes some of the faces slow to dry and sometimes green, although, surprisingly, this green doesn't always effect the climbing. Faces south-west, getting sun from afternoon onwards.

Approach

A horrendous 5 minute march is needed from the main car-park.

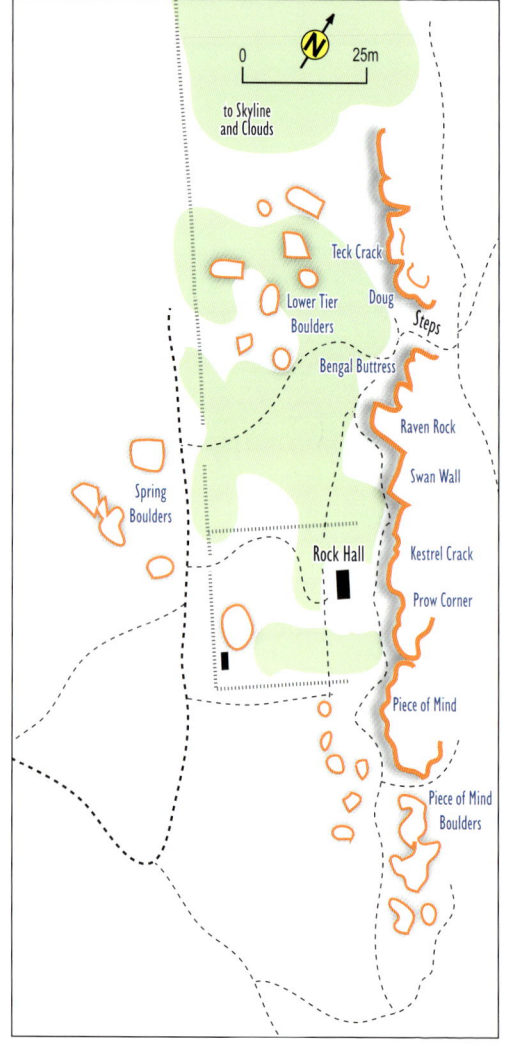

46 The Roaches

Climbers having a little damp green fun on Prow Cracks, HD (page 67). The right-hand end of the Lower Tier has a good array of well-protected cracks and corners in the low grades and is an excellent venue to hone leading skills. Photo: Niall Grimes.

The Left-Hand Section

The main path leads up through the larches towards the steps to the Upper Tier. To the left, above the popular bouldering circuit, stands an impressive set of buttresses, sometimes slabby above, but always fiercely steep at their base. Here is the highest concentration of hard routes to be found at the Roaches. This, combined with the popularity of this area with boulderers, means that the lower sections of many of the routes here are frequently well-chalked: the upper sections less so! The climbing offers a satisfying balance of the strenuous and the tenuous, with more than a dash of the bold.

About 20m beyond the left-hand end of the main wall is a small buttress consisting of a jumble of boulders, with a characteristic stunted tree growing at their base. This holds **Beware Coconuts** (VS 4b, 1995), climbing the arête and squirming between branches to reach the top. Just to the left of the edge proper is a small cave with an obvious prow above, providing two short routes. **Burrito Deluxe** (E3 5c, 1979) is quite a serious little climb up the green left-hand wall of the prow from a grassy ledge. **National Hero** (E2 5c, 1978) climbs out of the right-hand side of the cave and up the right-hand side of the prow. The left-hand end of the first main buttress is marked by a vigorous holly tree, which conceals a secret way to the top for the thick-skinned.

Above: Doug Moller, Lord and King of the Roaches – axeman, poet, royalty – stands before his one-time home, Rock Hall. Photo: John Beatty.

The Lower Tier The Left-Hand Section

1 Snap, Crackle and Andy Popp
E1 5c   1987
7m Climb the left-hand end of the wall, just to the right of the holly. Full leathers may be required to avoid being fatally mauled!

2 Apache Dawn E5 6c ★★   1993
8m From the middle of the pod, climb directly up on pebbles to a shallow divot and top out. Intimidating and intense: highball V7.

3 Catastrophe Internationale
E5 6b ★★   1985
8m Pure pebble climbing at an uncomfortable height. From the pod, choose your pebbles. The objective is a rounded boss on the right, just below the top followed by an entertaining pull over on trustworthy heather: highball V6.

4 Slippery Jim HVS 5a ★   1958
7m Climb the corner crack to its heathery conclusion. A Rock and Ice classic: *see photo on page 50.*

5 Bareback Rider E4 6b ★★   1980
8m Ron Fawcett's favourite E3! Try to avoid being thrown from the technical and bouldery arête before an awkward mantelshelf gains the sloping rib. Continue airily up the slab: highball V4.

6 K.P. Nuts E6 7a   1989
8m A technical, nerve-racking and, so far, unrepeated Nadin testpiece. Climb the wall and make a technical rockover to gain the slab above using the peanut-shaped pebbles. Compose yourself and float up the slab above to join Ascent of Man at the finish.

7 Traverse of Man V2 (5c)
Start in the cave below the next route and traverse left, into the corner, then all the way to the holly. The first section alone, into the corner, is V0+ (5a).

8 Ascent of Man E3 6a ★★★   1974
10m Welcome to pebble pulling. Make a hard move to reach a good break and then the fine flake above: a V2 in its own right. Place wobbly runners and make a committing step left onto the pebbly ramp. Mantel onto the top as soon as you dare.

An independent right-hand start slapping up the twin ribs (V4), combined with a direct finish using the (from this side) even wobblier runners, is the very worthwhile **Ascent of Woman** (E4 6a, trad).

9 Days of Future Passed E3 6b ★   1974
9m The arête of the buttress has a powerful start (or jump) and a belly-flop finish with baffling rounded side-pulls in between.

10 The Aspirant E3 5c   1978
8m From the pedestal at the base of the left wall of the gully, make a surprisingly committing move to the obvious hold and then exit carefully onto the rib above.

The Roaches

Today's image of Don Whillans often involves a flat cap, a pint of beer and a fat belly. It's easy to forget that he was one of the best climbers Britain ever produced. In this early image of a young Don on the first ascent of Slippery Jim (page 49), the athleticism, attitude and body magic that made him the climber he was are only too obvious. Go on Don, 'av it! Photo: Nat Allen Collection.

The Lower Tier Teck Buttress

11 Ackit HVS 5b ★★   1958
15m The hanging corner. A strenuous start and then some tough laybacking lead to a welcome rest below the tricky final bulge above, which often fails to get the deft technique it deserves. A great leveller!

12 Just for Today E6 7a †   1994
9m A desperate eliminate, starting as for Barriers then taking the slab just to the left, with runners in Ackit.

13 Barriers in Time E6 6b ★★★   1983
16m The impressive stepped arête marked a major breakthrough for its time and is still an unforgettable lead today. Climb the scalloped wall to the second break and protection. Proceed thoughtfully to the top via the rounded arête as the runners recede alarmingly. Traverse left into Ackit at the top.

14 Inertia Reel Traverse V12 (7a)
Moffatt's awesome traverse is as hard as they come, and sees few repeats. Traverse the all-sloping shelf from left to right: *see photo on page 45*.

15 Ant Lives V6 (6b)
A gruesome mantel off the lower shelf to gain the sloping ledge above. Originally topped out on the right, adding a grade or two.

16 Sunday at Chapel E6 6c ★   1988
9m The lower arête of Barriers in Time, climbed on its right-hand side starting from Ant Lives, via a crazed series of slaps, using a side runner in Ackit. Once on the ledge simply escape down towards the belay below the crack on Teck Crack.

Staffordshire Grit

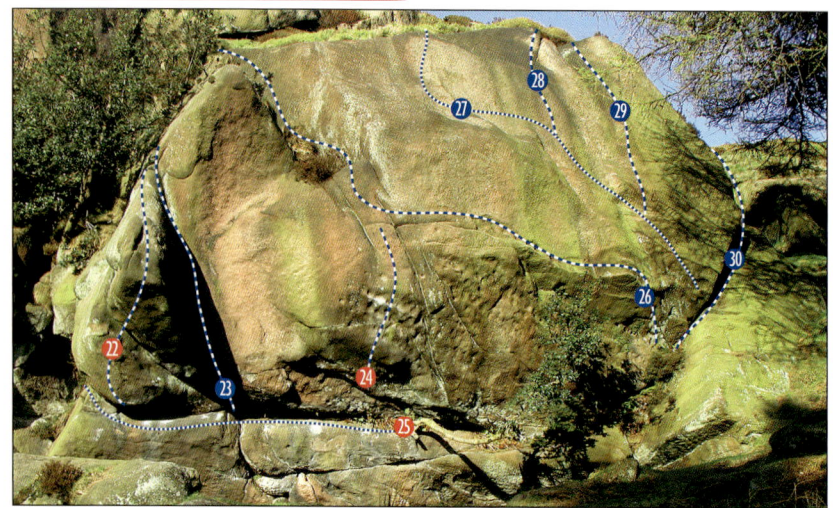

17 Inertia Reel V7 (6c)
A Dawes classic starting just left of the vague nose. Undercut, bridge, palm and dyno to gain the ledge. Desperate. The sit start, **Turbo**, is all too obvious and obviously all too hard: V10 (7a).

18 Teck Crack Direct V5 (6b)
Quick moves across the sloping shelf leads to desperate lunges to better holds by the blind crack. Up this to the terrace. ◐ **Thud** V8 (6c) is a unique low start. Pull on with hands in a low undercut and a round dish (feet on back wall), then swing up and gain the shelf of the direct with your feet. Do all you can to re-establish conventional mode and continue. Helmet advised.

19 Teck Crack Super-Direct V9 (6c)
Levitate up the cruel seam. Six-footers only need apply!

20 The Dignity of Labour V6 (6b)
Step off the boulder and traverse left until dynamic moves up lead to an intimidating mantel using a square pebble. An adventurous landing may mean the original E3 is still deserved.

21 Teck Crack HVS 5b ★★★   1958
26m A fantastic sandbag, with steep laybacking in an impressive situation; a Lower Tier classic. Start from the big ledge (best gained up the ramshackle gully below and right). Commit to the crack fully and it will succumb. Finish up the continuation crack to a historic bolt and seat belay.

22 Skydivin' V5 (6b)
Jump from the boulder and gain the nose. Continue up this. **A Modest Proposal** V6 (6b), gains the same finish by slapping out from the break below, via the left-hand prow. The roof crack has been climbed at E3 6a (V5), reputedly by Joe Brown.

23 Lightning Crack HVS 5b, 4c ★   1958
1. 8m After a puzzling entry, layback the crack to reach a tree.
2. 12m Move up behind the tree and climb the triangular wall behind. Climb up to the sloping ledge and either finish direct or, better still, by a leftward rising pod.

24 Mushin' V10 (7a)
Ben Moon's brutal direct start to Pindles Numb. Start from the break, move up to undercuts then power outwards on sloping dishes to a junction with Pindles. Most boulderers will jump off from here.

The Lower Tier Crystal Grazer Area

25 The Boozy Traverse V8 (6b)
From the holly, traverse left, finishing with a very pumpy sloping section.

26 Pindles Numb E4 6b 1984
11m Hand-traverse the handrail with increasing difficulty, until it is possible to pull desperately into the groove above: highball V5.

27 Crystal Grazer E5 6a ★ 1982
11m From the ramp, pull up left until standing on the lip of the overhang. Foot traverse past a shallow groove until it is possible to move up and gain the obvious hold directly above the holly. Unprotected.

28 A Fist Full of Crystals E6 6b ★★★ 1983
12m Brilliant, balancy and bold climbing on smears and pebbles. Start as for Crystal Grazer as far as the groove. Climb this and either step left onto a finishing foothold or continue direct. Surmounting the overhang to gain the groove directly is **Heredity** (E6 6c, 1989).

29 Doug E8 6c ★ 1986
12m A historic route, the country's first E8. Hard, blind and unprotected pebble-pulling up the shallow scoop at the right-hand side of the slab. Start as for the two previous routes but then climb immediately up the right-hand side of the front face of the buttress to finish up the hanging scoop.

30 Fred's Café VS 5a 1978
12m A green climb up the rightward-slanting crack at the right side of the buttress, finishing leftwards up flakes.

The Lower Tier steps

and the pathway along the ridge were built in 1860, along what is possibly a Roman causeway. On August 23rd, 1872, the steps were used by the Duke and Duchess of Teck and Prince Francis to gain the upper tier for a picnic. A seat was carved into the rock for the Duchess, and railings put in place for safety.

Neil Foster on the first ascent of Steps, E5 6b (page 57). Photo: David Simmonite.

The Roaches

The Roaches at its summer best, with a gentle warming sun and a cooling breeze to keep the rock sweet and the midges at bay. Tina Gardner satches it up on the crux section of Yong, HVD (opposite page) while Ana Jolly belays. Photo: Niall Grimes.

The Lower Tier Yong Area

The Right-Hand Section

The first route starts immediately right of the steps.

31 Yong Arête S ★   1957–68
7m An interesting route climbing the blunt rib. Protection arrives too late for the leader, but may be appreciated by the second.

32 Poisonous Python E2 5b   1978
8m The innocent-looking curving cracks through the overlap give some surprisingly difficult climbing. A good variation pulls out right to the arête, once over the overlap, to finish up this.

33 Yong HVD 4a ★   1957–68
9m The crack in the shallow corner is climbed on superb jams throughout, and is excellently protected. A perfect route for beginners: **see photo opposite**.

34 Something Better Change E2 5b   1978
9m The chipped slab right of Yong is climbed direct. Good. A side-runner reduces the grade to HVS.

35 Wisecrack VS 4c   1957–68
8m The slanting crack in the left side of the buttress.

36 Hypothesis E1 5b ★★   1968
10m The excellent cracked arête is technical, sustained and only just protectable.

37 Destination Earth E6 6b ★   1984
12m The centre of the front face is consistently hard, with a particularly testing crux at 7m.

38 Cannonball Crack S 4b   pre-1913
11m Slither up the crack in the left face, until a move left onto a boulder allows the top to be gained.

39 Graffiti E1 5b   1978
15m Climb the arête until a move left gains a slim corner, which is climbed to the crack above and then to the top.

40 Dorothy's Dilemma E1 5a ★★   1951
18m Climb the exposed arête in its entirety by a series of absorbing moves in a serious situation.

Niall Grimes on the crux of Northern Comfort, E6 6c (page 59) on the first ascent. Photo: Richard Harland.

The Lower Tier Raven Rock

41 Bengal Buttress HVS 4c ★★   1913–24
30m An inspired production from ancient times, being exposed, delicate and, even today, having dishearteningly protection. It takes a meandering, but logical line up the front of the buttress. Move up to a grassy ledge, then go right up to a break, runners. Move up to gain an airy position on the right of the arête where a trying move leads to the top of Raven Rock Gully. Step left and go up the short crack.

42 Schoolies E4 5c   1978
22m A scary and artificial line up the front of the buttress. Reachy roof moves gain a ledge. Continue boldly up the slab until crux moves gain easier-angled rock.

Raven Rock

To the right, a fine tower stands proud from the crag. It gives magnificent routes of all grades and although the climbs tend to be steep, by devious and inventive route-finding they usually manage to weave their wonderful ways upwards by guile rather than brute force.

43 Steps E5 6b ★   2003
23m Starting 2m left of Crack of Gloom, pull straight around the big roof, then climb to reach a break. Step left and climb a short left-facing corner, then traverse out along the lip of the big roof to gain the flake, which is followed to a wide shelf. Finish up the rib above: *see photo on page 53*.

44 Crack of Gloom E2 5b ★★   1958
23m A superb, dark and shadowy climb, with a character all its own, taking the mighty gloomy looming crack in the left wall of the recess, exiting left around the chockstone in a great position.

45 Raven Rock Gully Left-Hand VS 4b   1969
20m Ascend cracks and grooves in the left side of the gully, exiting through the skylight above. Good.

46 Raven Rock Gully D ★   1901
20m A filthy climb, popular with deviants for over a century. An absolute must! Follow the flakes in the back of the gully until it is possible to squirm through the manhole above. The steep crack in the wall to the right is **Swinger** (VS 4c, pre-1973) which can be used as a direct start to Via Dolorosa.

47 Sidewinder E5 6a   1980
25m A wild route up the hanging arête above the overhang. Possibly unrepeated. From the gully, hand-traverse right to climb the shallow groove in the blunt arête. Climb the left-hand side of the huge roof via the dubious protruding flake then make a long reach to gain a vertical flake on the wall.

Staffordshire Grit

Some years later...

...I went back to try to get some photos of the climb and was fortunate to find two young lads on the route. Meeting them at the top to congratulate them, I shyly mentioned that I had done the first ascent. At this they both went wide-eyed: the older one seized my hand, shook it vigorously and said: "You must be Joe Brown." Then, looking at me askance, he added: "But I always thought you were short and stocky with teeth like tombstones." Well, what else could I do but stay silent, try to look smaller, and give the toothiest smile I could muster?
Valkyrie pioneer, Peter Harding

The Lower Tier Raven Rock

48 Via Dolorosa VS 4c, 4a, 4c ★★★ 1913–24
33m A great historic climb, one of the very best of its grade in the area.
1. 8m Ascend a narrow glassy slab (hard, and almost becoming unpleasantly polished), then move up left through the holly to reach a ledge.
2. 10m Traverse left to the rib and follow a short crack, then a slab around to the left. Belay at a block.
3. 15m Climb boldly up right to a flake. Surmount this then move right round the arête and go up to the top. Sit down and enjoy the view.

49 Via Dolorosa Variations HS 4a ★★ traditional
By avoiding the polished corner (starting on the higher ledge on the right), and finishing left into Raven Rock Gully to avoid the last pitch, this superb climb can be enjoyed at a much lower standard.

Cold Bone Forgotten (E3 6b, 1988) climbs the lower roof left of Via Dolorosa with a runner in the tree.

50 Valkyrie Direct HVS 5b ★★ 1951
25m A superb climb in a supreme setting, taking a steep direct line through the parent route. A good gritstone fight. Force a steep line straight up to the left side of the Valkyrie flake. From here, step left, and finish up the obstinate crack to join Valkyrie.

51 The Gutter V7 (6b)
Start in undercuts at the back of the cave and come out to slap up the angular arête up and left.

52 Matinee HVS 5a,5b ★★★ 1951
23m A magnificent, and very testing, exercise in jamming, this climb takes the huge, beautifully ugly crack, which splits the right-hand face of Raven Rock.
1. 15m Climb the sometimes green crack on glorious jams to a belay on the fine ledge (The Crevasse).
2. 8m Continue up the widening crack to the final bulge. Technicians will elegantly side-step this, but for mortals much humiliating floundering awaits.

53 Valkyrie VS 4b, 4c ★★★ 1946
38m Simply one of the best routes on gritstone – intricate, exposed and varied, and while it is *only* VS, it definitely climbs through HVS territory.
1. 15m Follow the corner then traverse left to a fine belay on the Crevasse. A nondescript pitch, also

> **"At what is now the hard move**
> Peter paused for several minutes because the face was mossy and the finger holds were choked with soil and moss. He shouted for Veronica to pass him his penknife which was lowered down on a rope. He scratched the moss away, closed the knife, without more ado carried on to the top."
>
> Bowden Black on the first ascent of Valkyrie

quite polished, the start of Pebbledash making for a much more sustained and interesting beginning.
2. 23m Climb up and over and down the huge flake until an awkward move left (all very thrilling) brings generally easier climbing up the front of the buttress. Careful ropework advised, especially to protect the second: *see photo on page 32*.

The next routes all start from Valkyrie's Crevasse stance.

54 Northern Comfort E6 6c ★★ 1996
10m Technical and slappy climbing with a safe fall-out zone. From the crest of the Valkyrie flake, climb diagonally leftwards to reach a rounded notch on the arête (crux). Pull back right and follow the easier flake to the top.: *see photo on page 56*

55 Licence to Run E4 6a ★★★ 1980
10m A fingery wall climb with some obscure moves. Protection is good but exhausting to place. From the stance, climb up and right to follow a layback flake until it is possible to break out right to another flake. Tricky moves up and right gain a finishing jug.

56 Licence to Lust E4 6a ★ 1987
10m Climb the wall to the right of Licence to Run to its second smaller flake. Step left and follow the thin crack-line to the top. A direct line linking the start of Licence to Run to the finish of this route is **License to Kill**, E4 6b (2000).

57 Valkyrie Corner HS 4b ★ traditional
25m The major corner. Follow it all the way, or escape through the tunnel or, better, climb the flake on the left to the top. The ramp trending up and right also make a fine finish, easy but exposed.

Staffordshire Grit

The Swan Wall

The steep wall to the right features perfect grit and a collection of routes generally marked by fierce fingery cranking, usually with a bit of heart-fluttering thrown in as well.

58 Eugene's Axe E2 5c   1979
20m Climb the arête to the cracks above (very high side-runner in Pebbledash at this grade). Use these to gain a ramp, and finish up this.

59 Pebbledash HVS 5a, 4b ★   1969
1. 12m Climb the chimney and crack to a junction with the previous route. Scamper across the slab leftwards to the sanctuary of a belay ledge in the corner.
2. 9m The flake, corner or ramp above (or Valkyrie).

60 Secrets of Dance E4 6a ★   1984
20m Follow Pebbledash to the crack above. From here, gain and follow the finger-ramp above. Finish via pockets and breaks. Not overly protected once out of the crack, but the climbing does ease, a little.

61 Against the Grain E6 7a ★★★   1985
20m A stunning fingery sequence above a relatively safe fallout zone. Easy ground leads to good cracks. From the cracks, step leftwards and make a desperate sequence of increasingly difficult moves on tiny edges diagonally leftwards to gain the sloping ramp on Secrets of Dance. Finish up this.

62 Thing on a Spring E6 7a ★★★   1986
20m One of Simon Nadin's most technical creations with some of the hardest climbing in Staffordshire. From the cracks step right onto the ramp and foot traverse this to its end. Now compose yourself, and pop for the sloping break above. From here, romp confidently to the top: *see photo on page 29*.

63 The Swan E3 5c ★★★   1969
24m Manageable climbing in outrageous positions makes this a memorable lead. From the cracks (high runners), finger traverse out right. The footholds diminish as the handholds get bigger, culminating in a tough rockover to gain the rounded break. Follow the wide crack above to the top.

In an era when we have gone to the moon, to the poles, the highest mountain tops and the bottom of the ocean, it is still widely acknowledged that the loneliest place on earth is still right here in Staffordshire. Mark Sharratt poised between his past and his future in the middle of the slab of Elegy, E2 5c (page 64). Photo: David Simmonite. That's a brilliant photo, Dave.

A climber on Fledgling's Climb, S 4a. This is one of the easier classics of the Lower Tier although, with its bold and sloping lower section, one that's best enjoyed in nice dry conditions (page 64).
Photo: Niall Grimes

The Lower Tier Smear Test

64 Up The Swanee E4 5c ★   1971
22m As for The Swan, but using the handholds for footholds across the traverse. Delicate.

65 The Mincer HVS 5b ★★★   1951
20m Steep jamming with a tough reputation. Climb the crack through the stepped overhangs. The overhang is the crux and will reduce all but the most adept to a flailing display of appalling technique. All that remains is the wide crack above.

66 Swan Bank E4 5c   1981
20m From The Mincer, move left to a flake and then go directly up to the wide crack above. Not well-protected, and involving the hard move up on The Swan.

Smear Test Slab

Thin smearing test-pieces mark out the climbing on this beautiful hanging slab, although the routes tend to be eliminates.

67 Smear Test E3 6a ★★   1977
11m A good introduction to the harder slabs hereabouts. From The Mincer, traverse horizontally rightwards to finish up the bottomless crack. An independent start can be made up left from the start of Pincer joining The Mincer at the overhang.

68 Pincer VS 5a ★   1957–68
20m A good bouldery start, but the top lacks direction. Follow the groove (crux) into Guano Gully. Ascend this until it is possible to step back left onto the slab to reach the bottomless crack.

69 Bloodstone E5 6b ★★   1983
19m A good eliminate, with some exposed slab climbing. Climb Pincer, or the bouldery bulge to the right, to the roof and good gear. Make a hard move over the overlap, the 'kicking bird' move, then blast directly up the slab. Runners are placed low in The Mincer, and in the upper crack. **Kicking Bird** (E4 6a ★ 1978) is an earlier version that avoided the lower section of slab by climbing The Mincer.

70 Bloodspeed E6 6b ★★   1984
19m Probably the best line on this beautiful slab. From the ledge, smear up to the salvation of the

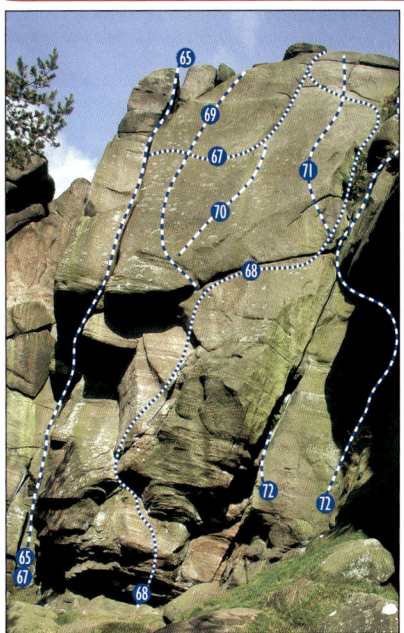

crack (to find it isn't a crack). Climb this or the slab on its right. Very blank and insecure throughout.

71 Cold Blood E5 6b ★★   2006
13m A recent route that fills a gap as good as any on the slab. From the junction of Guano Gully and The Pincer, place gear in the good slot then rock up and left onto the slab. Continue direct up the slab, following a line to the right of the hanging crack.

72 Guano Gully HS 4b   1927
13m Start in the corner under the overhang. Follow this then undercut leftwards to gain the main upper corner. The direct start up the lower crack is VS 5a.

73 Mousey's Mistake E2 5b   1978
15m Climb Guano Gully, or its direct start, then pass the boulder / overhang on its right. Climb the left side of the slab above. Bold.

Staffordshire Grit

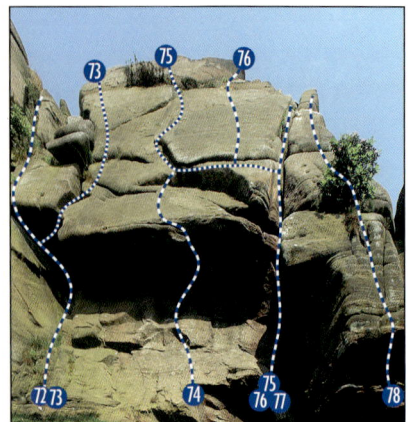

Elegy Slab

The hanging slab contains a gnarly classic and two contrasting desperates.

74 A Little Peculiar E7 7b ★   1993
16m Unique. Gain and cross the roof and make cherry popping moves to get established on the slab above. Finish up Elegy.

75 Elegy E2 5c ★★★   1960
16m An absorbing route of the utmost quality, with a tough crux followed by a sizzling runout. With high gear in The Bulger pull left around the bulge (technical crux). Follow the flake left to its end then climb the slab above on smears and slopers (psycho crux): *see photo on page 61*.

76 Clive Coolhead Realises the Excitement of Knowing You May Be the Author of Your Own Death is More Intense Than Orgasm E5 6b ★★   1983
16m Start as for Elegy, but once round the bulge establish yourself over the flake (crux) and climb the right of the slab above. Takes longer to memorise the name than to do the route! Gear is placed in The Bulger and the Elegy flake.

77 The Bulger VS 4c ★   1951
16m The crack climbed throughout. More difficult than would first appear and strangely rewarding.

78 Dirty Wee Rouge E3 6a   2003
13m A narrow journey up the front of the pillar, taking the overhang direct and avoiding The Bulger.

79 Fledgling's Climb S 4a ★   1927
13m A bold and balancy route. Good footwork is required to start the wall, which is followed first left, then back right, to finish up the arête above. Protection is awkward, and the route is precarious when damp, so fledglings beware: **photo on page 62.**

80 Wing Wing HS 4a   traditional
9m A bolder variation on the last climb follows the groove in the middle of the wall before a couple of pulls gain the diagonal flake. Rock right onto the triangular ledge above to finish. Poorly protected.

81 Little Chimney M   1949–51
9m The little chimney can provide a quick way down for the competent.

82 Battery Crack VS 4b   1968–73
10m The wide crack just right, with a taxing exit out of the sentry box. Finish up the chimney.

83 Lucas Chimney S 4a   1927
11m A good traditional thrutch up the wide chimney in the corner, swinging carefully left to finish.

"Routes like Elegy are easier to solo…

…because you know where you stand.
Although, there was that time in the 'seventies Phil Burke tried to solo it midweek. He got on the slab, got gripped, and just started screaming his head off, but, of course, there was nobody about. But then Dougie appeared at the top and looked over, and Burke was screaming, "Throw me a rope, quick!" Dougie disappeared, and when he came back, he tossed this loop of blue nylon rope down at Burke which tumbled down the slab and hit him – but Dougie hadn't tied it on to anything at the top, so the whole thing just snaked past Burke and fell to the ground, and so he just had to set off and shake his way to the top."
Ron Fawcett

The Lower Tier Kestrel Buttress

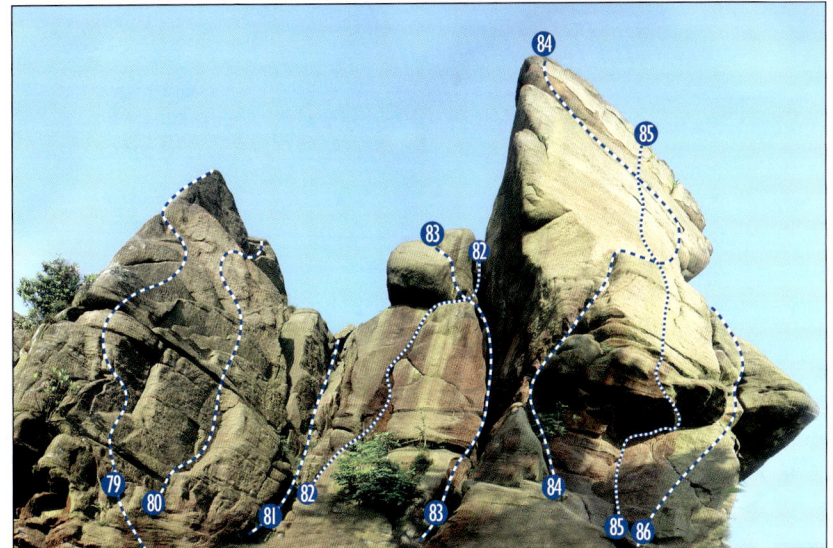

Kestrel Buttress

The attractive slim buttress to the right, and just above the roof of Rock Hall, with a powerful crack-line cleaving its centre.

84 Hawkwing E1 5b ★★ 1978
21m This weaves up the face giving reasonable, but sustained climbing, with protection that requires some care. Follow a curving crack-line rightwards onto the front face to join the wide crack (Kestrel Crack). Climb this for 2m then traverse back left via the parallel slanting cracks to finish up the left arête.

85 Carrion E3 5c ★ 1980
19m Good climbing, and while it is low in the grade technically, it has an exposed feel. Fun, protectable moves lead over the lower roof to gain the ledge on Hawkwing. Follow the centre of the face above via long stretches between nice rounded breaks. A meaner variation is **Poison Gift** (E4 6a, 1980). This follows Carrion to the ledge (where you might want to place a runner up and right). Gain the thin lower break, and crimp along this leftwards until a stretch gains the left arête (crux). Use this to get onto a good foothold, and a quick, easy finish.

86 Kestrel Crack HS 4b ★★ 1913–24
20m A great rounded gritstone tester, varied and well-positioned. Just right is an impressive groove. Climb this with stiff gymnastic moves (or a wedge and a squirm) to gain a ledge. (It is possible, but harder, to gain this coming in from the right.) The grand upper crack is made harder or easier depending on which way you face.

87 Headless Horseman E1 5b 1978
20m From the chockstone of Kestrel Crack, move out right to climb the striking arête on its left side. Poorly protected.

88 Logical Progression E7 6c ★★ 1998
18m An inventive solution to the challenge of the big blank wall. Make a desperate leftwards traverse of the lip to the obvious pockets (possible poor cam). Delicately rock up into these and finish more easily into Headless Horseman.

To the right of Logical Progression is a smooth wall which has so far only been breached by a 7a top rope problem up the blunt nose and arête below the small triangular roof. Watch this space...

Staffordshire Grit

89 Flimney S 4a   1957–68
18m Although somewhat overgrown, the jungle bashing proves to be great fun. Climb a large flake left of the bushes and finish up the crack and corner behind.

90 The Death Knell E4 5c ★★   1970
10m A bold route that deserves more attention. Climb the short arête until a good hold can be attained in the crack. Using this, get established on the upper wall (crux), then continue more easily using either the crack or the arête. The original version stepped left above the crux into cracks now choked with vegetation.

91 Rhodren HVS 5b ★★   1958
11m A great climb taking the stepped corner, with constricted undercutting making it a good warm-up for The Mincer.

To the right is a fallen flake forming an interesting arch, which marks the starts of the next two routes.

92 Flake Chimney D ★   1949–51
14m A great adventurous little route. Take the edge of the fallen flake, then 'walk the plank' into the corner on the right. The chimney leads to the top.

93 Straight Crack HS 4a   1957–68
10m Bridge against the flake to start, then climb the crack just right of Rhodren.

94 Punch E3 6b   1957–68
14m At the left end of the overhang to the right, behind an ominous rhododendron, is a short hanging groove, which is, unfortunately, often very green. Pull into this (crux) and climb the cracks above. Only for the gritstone thug.

95 Choka E1 5c ★   1958
12m The large roof 3m right of Punch is overcome by gymnastic finger-jamming. Only the small detail of the offwidth above remains.

96 Stolen Days E2 5c   1996
10m Start on the bottom slab of Circuit Breaker. Step left onto the slab and climb it, trending leftwards to the top.

97 Circuit Breaker E3 6a   1980
10m From the crack, move immediately left to the arête and pull over the bulge. Place protection then climb the flake in the arête above to a pull over onto the slab.

The Lower Tier Prow Area

98 Hunky Dory E3 6a ★★★ 1975
10m A steep Roaches classic that requires a bit of effort. Climb the snaking crack until it is possible to break out right onto the resting ledge. Continue up the bold wall to an easier-than-it-looks finish. It is also possible to finish left at the top of the crack by means of a less bold 6a mantel. **Fluorescent Stripper** (E3 6a, 1985), continues artificially up and rightwards from the resting ledge.

99 Prow Corner VD ★ 1957–68
12m The main corner is a good climb. Climb the tall crack and finish up the spectacular 'flying' crack.

100 Corner Cracks HVD 4a ★ traditional
10m A good variation on the last climb is to stick to the twin cracks on the right all the way, with a well-protected crux. All classic stuff.

101 Chalkstorm E 3 5c ★ 1977
10m A bold route requiring some concentration. Climb the centre of the slab on sloping holds and rockovers. Traditionally climbed with a side-runner, which reduces the grade to between HVS and E2 depending on how high you place it. The narrow slab just left has been climbed at 5c.

102 Prow Cracks VD ★ 1957–68
10m Ascend using both cracks and a variety of technique. If you can't jam, you'll need to bridge and if you can't bridge, then learn to smear. A good first lead. Either crack can be climbed independently at HVD. Both are good: *see photo on page 47*.

103 Voila 3 E4 6a 1989
8m An alarming route that gains the flying arête of the next route from the left, with a mighty span from Prow Cracks. Continue laybacking on the left to glory.

104 Commander Energy E2 5c ★★★ 1975
12m A route of tremendous exposure up the 'out there' arête. Climb the rounded right arête of the slab to the triangular roof. Pull over this on a good flake (spike runner) and layback dramatically up the flying arête above.

105 Sumo Cellulite E4 6a ★ 1989
12m For the same exposure, only without the holds, climb the upper slab to the right of Commander Energy's flying arête. From below the roof, teeter right up the curving crack, before a precarious step up gains a thin hold, then continue direct.

Staffordshire Grit

106 Rocking Stone Gully VD   traditional
8m The chunky corner to the right lives up to its name. Elegant semi-layback moves avoid the halfway grovel.

107 Captain Lethargy VD   traditional
8m Climb the well-formed crack right of the corner. Finish on the left.

108 Sifta's Quid HS 4c ★★   1968
9m An entertaining climb, with an entertaining history. Climb to the ledge. Now either climb out over the bulge, or for much more fun, squeeze through the tunnel by the huge boulder under the roof. The scene of much amusing thrutching, most of it 'on the spot'. A classic Roaches rite of passage. ◐ The roof just to the left is breached by **Dougie Returns Home** (E1 5b, 1992).

109 Obsession Fatale E7 6b ★   1992
11m The unprotected centre of the slab is climbed direct to its utterly blank and unforgiving crux at the very top. Regularly abseiled, frequently toproped and sometimes headpointed: however on-sight attempts have ended in North Staffordshire A&E on more than one occasion.

110 Piece of Mind E6 6b ★★★   1977
11m The blunt central arête is a very serious proposition demanding the cleanest of technique and the coolest of heads. Balance up via scoops until a precarious step right can be made onto a faith in friction foothold and so the top. One of the first routes of its type on gritstone, well ahead of its time. A direct finish has also been climbed at a similar grade, **The Emergency Exit**.

111 Final Destination E8 6c ★   2003
9m The steep slab, starting as for the next route and finishing just right of Piece of Mind. Like all the routes on this slab, it is utterly serious.

112 The Thin Air E5 6a ★★★   1980
9m Quality climbing on the right-hand side of the slab, above a serious landing. Starting in a scoop on the left, climb rightwards to a distinctive ripple whence an airy rockover gains the rounded and easily-fluffable top.

The Lower Tier Girdle Traverses

Lower Tier Girdle Traverses

The Golden Age of Girdle Traversing appears to have passed. In case it again becomes fashionable, the descriptions of three of the genre are included in all their original splendour.

113 The Girdle Traverse HVS 5a   1960
80m A wandering line but pleasant nonetheless. From almost the top of Bengal Buttress, traverse the chockstone and continue to join Valkyrie at the lip. Reverse this to the stance in the crevasse, then move right to the corner. Go up a short way, and move right across the great wall via high-level breaks. Descend into The Mincer and continue by a line almost at the top of the crag into The Bulger to finish.

114 The Underpass E1 5b   1968
50m A variant on the Girdle Traverse. From the end of the traverse on Bengal Buttress, reverse the crux of Crack of Gloom into the gully and pass rightwards beneath the chockstone into Raven Rock Gully. Continue the traverse round under the great overhang to meet Valkyrie Direct. Awkward moves gain Matinee which is followed almost to the top. Take the right-hand branch of the crack to finish.

115 The Super Girdle E4 5c, 6a, 5c ★   1980
45m Perhaps a hybrid, but still marvellous horizontal movement on the best of gritstone slabs.
1. 22m Follow The Swan, but continue at the same level to join The Mincer.
2. 11m Traverse Smear Test, place gear, then continue slightly downwards into Guano Gully by sustained tiptoeing.
3. 12m Move out again onto the Elegy slab, and traverse boldly across the slab horizontally to meet and finish up The Bulger. It is advised to step down and arrange protection in the flake of Elegy at halfway.

"Staffordshire was always a very important area for me.

I wasn't putting up the hardest routes there, but while I was doing my own first ascents around Sheffield, I would regularly go over to test myself against other peoples' routes, kind of like a gauge if you like, by which to measure myself, my own performance, my own routes. I remember one day doing Bloodspeed, Script for a Tear, A Fist Full of Crystals, Barriers, all E6s, all on-sight, then trying to finish off with Piece of Mind. I slipped off the last move and bounced all the way down the slab, then ran through the boulders, until my shoe lace caught on a tree root and stopped me. The lace probably saved my life."
Johnny Dawes

Piece of Mind Bouldering

A very quiet circuit with masses of problems. They mostly tend to be short and, while there is good variety, many tend to be of the 'rollover' type, although there's a good selection of slabs and arêtes as well as a few oddments. It gets the sun from first thing to last. Generally clean, but with the lack of traffic some of the surfaces can be a bit biscuity. The first problem is on a boulder down near the wall surrounding Rock Hall.

1 Cottage Arête
V2 (5c)
The square arête of the boulder just outside the wall, on its right-hand side. A nice V1 (5b) on its left.

2 Open Bum Cleft
V3 (6a)
The swooping groove on a boulder to the right, facing Hen Cloud, will feel harder for the short.

On a slab, 10m right:

3 Sail Slab V0– (4a)
The gentle left edge of the slab.

4 Mantel and Pocket V0– (4b)
Udge over the bulge and follow the slab 2m left of the arête.

5 Sail Arête
V0– (5a)
Start on the right and use a round hold to swing left onto the slab.

6 Sail Rib V0 (5a)
Pad up the vague arête.

7 Tittersworth Rib
V2 (5c)
The tall arête behind the slab, climbed on either side. Done from a sitter on the right is V4 (6b).

8 Chips Ahoy V1 (5b)
Sail directly up the slab from the first chip to a scary rounded top.

9 Ramp V0– (5a)
The wall facing Hen Cloud.

10 Potty V0– (4c)
Pull into the scoop.

11 Croissant Groove V2 (5c)
The groove on the low boulder facing Hen Cloud.

Way back again towards Piece of Mind is:

12 The Jams V2 (5c)
The highball, left-hand crack line.

13 The Teacup V1 (5b)
The hanging slab on round flakes.

14 Twisted Crack
V4 (6b)
The wide crack can be climbed on its left or right sides, or directly by deviants.

15 Off Work V2 (5c)
Surrender to the offwidth you swine!

16 Flake and Arête
V2 (5c)
The nice arête with a reachy top.

17 Wildy's Arête
V2 (6a)
The arête on its left. The sit-start is V5 (6b).

The Lower Tier Piece of Mind Bouldering

18 Wildy's Right
V3 (6a)

A fine problem following the arête on its right. ☉

19 Slab and Crack
V0– (4c)

The slab and bulge above. ☉ Finishing left, using the crack to rock onto the slab, is a good V1 (5b).

20 Jobby V0– (4b)
The easy arête on the right side of the boulder.

21 Micky V0– (4a)
The thin crack on the back of the boulder.

In the chasm behind is:

22 Scab V2 (5c)
Climb the feisty crack in the chasm between the boulders from a sitting start.

23 Buster V4 (6b)
From the jams at the bottom of Scab, reach up and right to a blind flake. Move up and continue along the lip to make a rollover at the end.

The next problems are based around the collection of boulders up and behind Piece of Mind. that form a small square 'room'. They are sometimes a wee bit high. The first of these takes a very exposed rampline that leads leftwards around the leftmost boulder.

24 Dropsy V1 (5a)
Smear leftwards up the rounded groove in an exposed position.

25 The Blob V1 (5b)
Up the arête of the boulder to the blob.

26 Crinkles Wall
V5 (6b)

The very thin wall in the boulder room.

27 Rock Room Slab
V1 (5b)

A quaint little slab on the opposite side of the room.

28 Annie's Egg
V5 (E4 6a)

On the back of the boulder, jump across the gap to gain and climb the hanging scoop, and don't fall off.

The Upper Tier

by Chris 'Gus' Hudgins

O.S. Ref. SK005624 — Altitude: 425m a.s.l.

The biggest, most classic and most popular section of the Roaches, with a height and big feel rarely available on any other grit crag. The central sections are all very clean, and sometimes polished. Smaller sections to the left and right are a little quieter. One of the most impressive aspects is the stature of climbs from even the lowest grades, and for people operating up to HVS, some of the most memorable days out on grit are on offer here.

Conditions & aspect
Very exposed and quick drying apart from some climbs on the left-hand section that are sheltered by trees. Faces south-west and gets sun afternoon and evening.

Parking & approach
The Roaches parking. Approach is around 10 minutes.

The Upper Tier is usually approached from the steps through the Lower Tier, in which case the first area encountered is the right-hand end of Great Slab, easily recognised by the spectacular capping overhang and the boulders comprising the venerable Upper Tier circuit. Descriptions start at the left end of the crag, 200m away.

Left-Hand Section

The Upper Tier starts in a rather unspectacular fashion on the far left, among the larch trees. Its left-hand side is defined by a worn track leading to the top of the escarpment. The first climbs lie on the small slab a few feet above the level of the main path.

1 Rooster HVD 1957–68
12m Climb directly up sloping holds from the top of the leaning blocks to the ledge and tackle the jamming crack above.

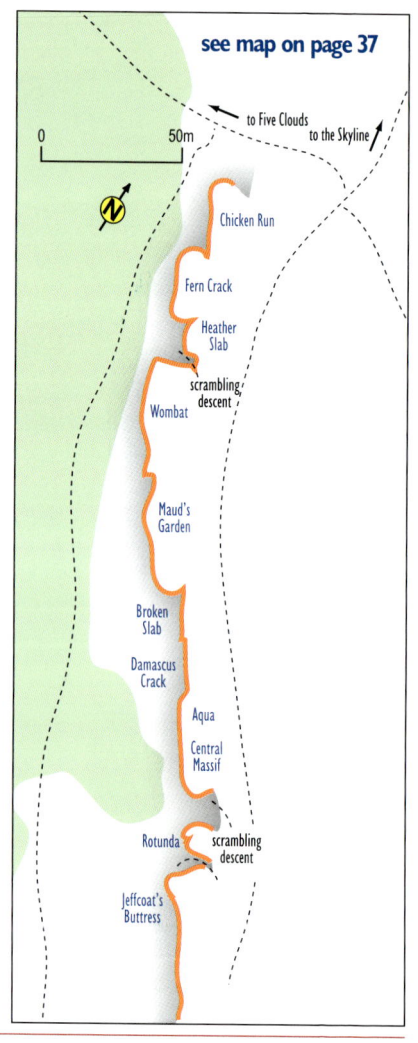

72 The Roaches

The Upper Tier Left-Hand Section

2 Chicken Run S 4a   1949–51
12m A bold route that turns very nasty if at all damp. From the blocks, gain the long pocket then climb up on worrying polished rock. From the right side of the large ledge, and gear, move left taking care with more polished holds to the top.

3 Freak Out E1 5b   1971
15m Follow the arête, around the bulge to gain the sloping ledge. Finish up the rounded arête above.

4 Fern Crack HVD 4b ★★   1931
18m A really good climb, which can be tackled in two pitches. A powerful start gains a crack and a flake. Use these to ascend to a thread and move left onto a ledge. A mantelshelf onto the next ledge remains before a possible belay is reached. Shuffle, or walk (depending on how comfortable you feel) leftwards round the corner, to follow sloping holds up the right wall of the recess. Bring lots of slings.

5 Demon Wall VS 4c   1945
15m Sensible rope work will enable the route to be climbed as a single pitch. Climb up to the left-hand end of an overhang and make a steep and committing pull into a sandy corner, leading to a large ledge. From here, scary moves on polished holds lead up the wall to the left of the chimney. **Heartbleed** (HVS 5b, 1979) pulls over the roof to the left to the ledge, followed by a direct finish.

6 Perverted Staircase VS 5a   1958
12m Well named. The steep crack leading to the left-hand side of the overhang provides an uphill struggle. Obscene entertainment.

7 Simpkins' Overhang E4 5c ★   1979
14m A route that stresses both arms and the mind in equal measure. Climb steeply to the flake in the roof. Hand-traverse this with your feet on the wall for as long as you can (but not long enough!), before cutting loose, and then desperately trying to re-establish contact with something. Finally, pull over with your heart racing. The **Fantasy Finish** is a possible final pitch up the thin runnel at the back of the sandy ledge, at E3 5c.

8 Inverted Staircase D ★★   1931
21m A friendly wander up the groove on the right-hand side of the overhang, beginning below and left at the lowest point. The groove leads to a huge party ledge on the left and a belay. From here the remaining squeeze through the small gap between the boulders provides a fun finale!

Staffordshire Grit

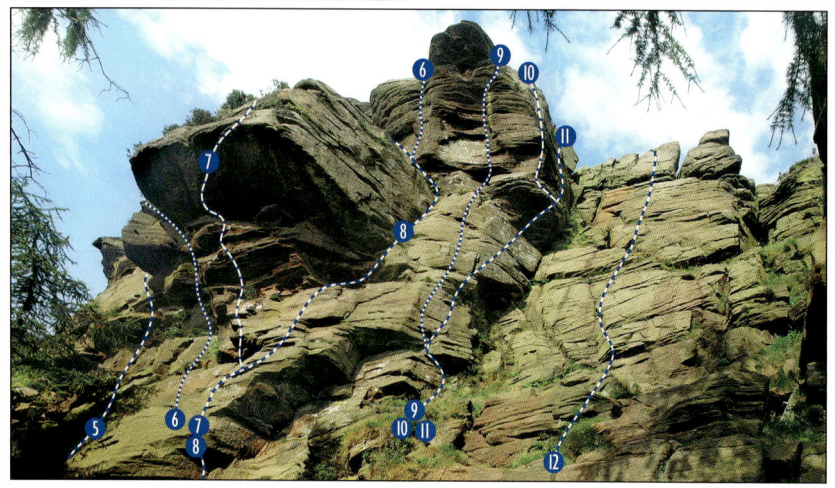

9 The Tower of Bizarre Delights
E3 5c ★   1978
16m This route follows the overhanging grooved tower and short crack above the corner of Inverted Staircase by intense and serious moves, until the short crack is reached.

10 The Sublime E2 5b ★   1979
16m High on the right is a triangular wall. Climb the rounded arête below this wall to a bulge. Burst over this, then power up the hanging arête.

11 Crenation E1 5a ★   1978
17m Follow The Sublime to the bulge. Move right from here round the corner to climb the triangular wall on hidden holds.

12 Heather Slab S 3c   1949–51
14m The recessed slab to the right is climbed centrally and directly. The short wide crack is avoided just to its left. The right arête of the slab gives a worthwhile Severe. The gully to the right gives a Moderate, finishing left.

Heather Descent: The gully to the right, taking the right fork in the upper setion, gives a handy scrambling descent. However the easiest descent is to skirt round to the left (facing in) of the crag.

West's Wallaby Area

To the right lies an area of dramatic overhanging territory, set in tree-enclosed surroundings. The wooded nature of this area affords shelter in windy conditions, the price being some dampness after wet weather.

13 Capitol Climb HS 4a   1954
14m A miniature mountain route. Climb the short corner near the left-hand side of the buttress. Step right between the roofs to gain the protruding nose, crux. Move round this to follow the crack on its right then the slab above.

14 Wombat E2 5b ★★   1960
20m A rapid approach will pay dividends on this, the hard classic of the area. Attain the break below the roof. Good protection is available here, and in the flake early on, but is more dubious further out. Climb to the lip, and pull round on reasonable holds to the wide crack and easy slab above. **Wrong Way Round** (E2 5b, 1979) is a dirty route avoiding the roof on the left.

15 Live Bait E4 5c   1981
20m To the right is a tiny flake on the wall. With difficulty, climb past this to reach the break. Move right to the hanging block, then explode leftwards

74 The Roaches

The Upper Tier Maud's Garden

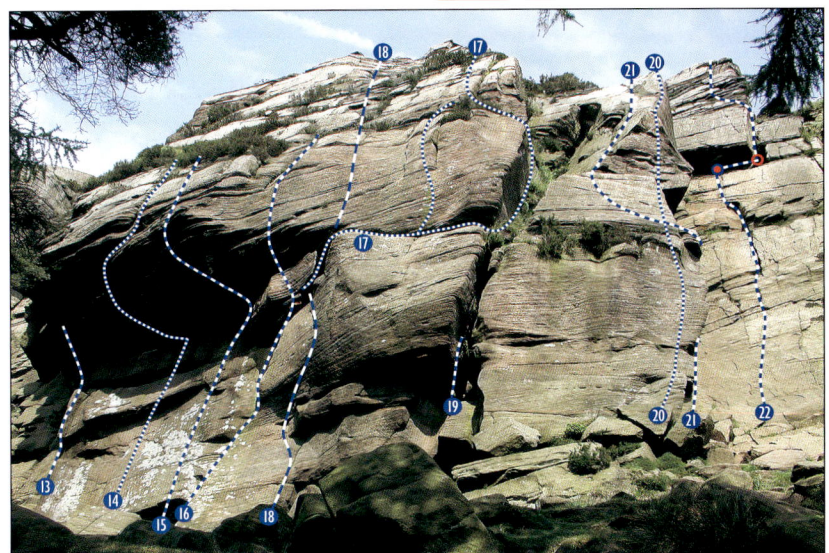

across the roof at its widest point. An alarming reach then gains easier ground.

16 Walleroo E2 5c ★★ 1960
20m More inverted pleasure. Neatly layback the crack to the great block. From the right side of this, difficult, fingery moves lead leftwards through the bulge into a faint groove. Finish easily above.

17 West's Wallaby VS 4c ★★ 1960
23m A great climb that negotiates steep terrain at a modest standard. Climb to the block, then swing dramatically all the way to the gully. Move up and left from here to finish on slabby rock. A very good **Direct Finish** (5a) tackles the obvious steep challenge above the traverse, and is more satisfying, being much more in character with the rest of the route.

18 Between the Lines E4 6a 1986
20m Climb the thin crack and the arête on its right-hand side to the block. Move off the block to climb directly up the wall.

19 Late Night Final HVD 4a 1951–57
20m Squirm, curse, and grunt up the overhanging chimney, and continue up the stony gully.

Maud's Garden Area

Right of the overhanging terrain of the Wombat section, the rock once again turns gentle and inviting, with a series of recessing slabs. There is a wealth of climbing here for the lower grade climber, and the routes are never busy.

Descent: Skirt the crag in either direction, or use the gully by Heather Slab.

20 The Valve E4 5c ★ 1978
15m A bold route following the tower that looms over the gully. Start on the left side of the arête, left of Beckermet Slab. Gain the ledge, then pull up the short overhanging wall just right of the arête to the base of the tower. Move right across the curving rampline then break out left to finish up the arête.

21 Beckermet Slab VD 4a ★ 1945
15m From the foot of the gully, bridge out to gain the horizontal break on the left wall. Swing onto this with difficulty, then move left to the arête. Gain a ledge above and finish up the slabby arête.

The corner to the right is Diff.

Staffordshire Grit

22 Maud's Garden VD ★★ 1945
21m A tricky start that has been bold for nearly 60 years and a thrilling finale, with interesting climbing in between. Follow the well-trodden path up the centre of the slab. This leads to a crack and protection. Press on to the sandy alcove and a possible belay. Wriggle up the chimney then step out left onto the wall, where good holds lead to exposed territory and the top. The overhang direct is 5c. The right side of the slab is **Lybstep** (VS 4b, 1978).

23 Contrary Mary VS 4b ★ 1951–57
15m A tricky pull over the low overhang gains easier ground among a sea of heather. This leads to a break above where the angle changes (not for the better!) and a bold finish up the headwall.

24 Coldfinger VS 4b 1978
15m Climb the arête, stepping out right above the overhangs at the top.

25 Reset Portion of Galley 37 HS 4a 1958
12m Ascend the corner until forced awkwardly right below the roof. Finish up the crack.

26 Broken Slab VS 4b 1945
12m A bold start leads to easier climbing with spaced protection. Ascend the wall direct, then bear right to reach a crack. A difficult move starts the crack, which is then followed to the top. Alternatively, a groove to the right of the slab can be taken to a direct finish, VS 4b.

27 Dawn Piper HVS 5b ★ 1978
7m A worthwhile problem up the sharp arête, followed by easier climbing. **Skallagrigg** (HVS 5b, 1997) is the steep wall on the left, avoiding the crack.

28 Runner Route HS 4b ★ 1955
11m From the corner, pad delicately rightwards across the slab. Mantelshelf onto the break (good runner), then move left to the holly and continue up the crack behind it. **Jog**, (HVS 5b, 1996) climbs just left of Runner Route to the hanging slab. Climb this slab, artificially avoiding the left edge.

29 Ging E1 5c 1996
11m Climb the slab, heading for the 'headwall'. From there, layaway off the right edge to reach the horizontal break and so to the top, with a runner in the crack on the left

30 Damascus Crack HS 4b ★★ 1955
12m The polished crack provides excellent protection and good climbing. After reaching the ledge, follow slightly suspect flaky rock up the buttress above. A finish up the short crack in the tower up and left is VS 4b, making a superb exposed finish.

Twelve fine climbs in the lower grades on the Roaches

Jill Whittaker reaches the belay ledge on Maud's Garden, VD (opposite) Photo: Alex Messenger.

The list below is aimed at those emerging from the climbing walls, seeking a chance to improve, looking for adventure and a chance to develop their skills and ropework, will find these climbs to be a stepping stone to the fine portfolio of Roaches Severes... steps that are well worth observing in the process of fully learning key skills (most notably route finding, runner placement and belaying) before embarking on harder things.

Lower Tier

Raven Rock Gully looks uninviting but develops into quite a challenging slot with the crux (very safe) as the final move. Good fun at night with a headtorch and also in wet conditions when it gives a real speleological struggle; **Prow Corner** – straightforward crack work amidst impressive rock scenery.

Upper Tier

Left-Hand Route – steep entertaining jug pulling on a minor buttress. **Right Route** – well-protected and straightforward but in a fine position. Not hard for the grade. Don't miss out the final pitch; **Pedestal Route** – a journey amidst spectacular rock scenery. With the overhang of *Technical Slab* forming the dramatic exit this must be considered the top of its grade ... an exciting outing; **Black Velvet** – tough for its grade and replete with challenging but well-protected moves. Tails off at the finish which is more of a relief than a defect; **Jeffcoat's Chimney** – a big line up an impressive cliff. The final pitch offers great excitement and is often avoided. Another good headtorcher. **Beckermet Slab** or **Maud's Garden** – rather unprepossessing climbs that provide useful training at a steady standard. **Inverted Staircase** – an excellent test-piece at the grade amidst fine rock prows, technically harder than the more exposed *Right Route*.

Skyline

Lighthouse – Short but entertaining; **Perched Block Arête** – interesting climbing amidst problems of a far higher standard; **Karabiner Chimney** – a poor man's *Central Buttress of Scafell* complete with its imitation **Great Flake**.

Staffordshire Grit

31 Third Degree Burn E2 5b ★   1978
9m Unprotected climbing in as direct a line as possible up the wall.

32 Libra HVS 4c ★   1957–68
14m The technical crack-line becomes increasingly tricky near the top. From here, the route wanders left and up a small tower on some awesome pockets.

The Central Massif

The next section is a little steeper, but again, routes are marred a little by heather.

33 Joe Public HS 4a   1978
18m Just round right from the arête, start up a groove, or the wall just right (4b), or the wall just right again (4c) to gain the break. Take the best rock from here to finish up an enjoyable steep crack. **A Day at the Seaside** (VS 4b, 1982) is a poor route taking the centre of the wall and slab to the left, finishing over a small triangular roof, while **The Attempted Moustache** (VS 4c, 2000) is a counter line to that, gaining the ledge from the left using a pleasant rib, then finishing via heather and a short crack.

34 Lone Ascent HVS 5a   1951–57
18m Right again, just out of reach, is a good, but often green hold in the middle of a good, but often green wall. This is gained by delicate moves, a long reach, or a hoofing big jump. Move up and right in a rather intimidating position up the often green wall to the left of a crack, to a final wide, often green crack. Good if you like green things.

35 Little Perforations E2 6a   1985
15m Climb the vague scoop in the wall just right. Technical and reachy moves constitute the crux above a faint horizontal break. Finish easily straight up.

36 Central Massif HD   1945
15m Climb to a large protruding flake on the right, then go direct in the same line to the top. Better and easier than it looks. **Wipers** (VS 4b, 1978) takes a strict direct line up the wall 2m left and finishes up the right arête of the upper wall.

37 Aqua VS 4b ★★   1954
12m One of the better routes in the area. The obvious crack-line through the roof yields easily to finesse. The rest is often covered in an assortment of vegetation but is luckily a lot simpler.

38 Quickbrew E2 5c ★   1981
12m Stiff! A massive jug in the hanging right arête enables protection to be placed before a cunning move or a desperate pull round the roof on brick edges. **Public Enemy Number One** (HVS 5a, 1979) takes a parallel line 1m left.

39 Tealeaf Crack HS 4a ★   1957–68
12m Climb up to the square overhang. Move around this on the right to a crack. A difficult move up and a step left gain the pleasant arête above.

Cornflake (M, 1957–68) is the chimney up and right, which manages to avoid all vegetation to give some good climbing. **A Short Trip to a Transylvanian Brain Surgery** (HS 4b, 1978) is a pleasant route which climbs the front face of the buttress. A steep move near the top is fortunately well-protected.

Rotunda Descent: The best descent in this area is to come down the stepped rocky ramp to the left of the Rotunda, the next feature.

Jill Whittaker with the runout crux behind her on Fred Piggott's 1922 creation, Bachelor's Buttress, VS 4b (page 82). The exposed nature of this climb once made it the sole preserve of unmarried men; nowadays, as this picture shows, it can even be enjoyed by married mothers, although you still get the odd wobbling bachelor muttering about HVS. Never. Photo: Niall Grimes.

Spring Boulders page 38

Lots of classics here but only a couple in the circuit because of the usual boggy conditions. If you find it dry underfoot, add The Ramp (3), Seconds Out (10) and Violence (7) to your itinerary.

1	Bog Standard	(24)
2	Boo Meringue	(29)
3	Poxy	(26)
4	Sprat	(35)

Lower Tier Boulders page 42

Time to hoover up a few classics now on one of the more popular bouldering areas.

5	Green Greenie	(33)
6	Boss Slab	(24)

Try it no-handed.

7	Grasper	(23)
8	Pine Marten	(32)
9	Classic Arête	(19)
10	Big Block Arête	(14)
11	Pockets Arête	(8)
12	Left Slab	(1)

Lower Tier page 46

13	Traverse of Man	(7)

As far as the corner of Slippery Jim.

14	Sifta's Quid	(108)

By the squeeze route. You won't need your mat for this, as falling off is the least of your worries.

Piece of Mind Boulders page 70

15	Pocket and Mantel	(4)
16	Sail Rib	(6)
17	Chips Ahoy	(8)
18	Slab and Crack	(19)
19	The Teacup	(13)

Calcutta Problems page 108

20	Calcutta Rib	(9)
21	Bombay Overhang	(1)

Cellar and Attic page 102

22	Cellar Slab I	(12)
23	Scrack	(7)
24	The Squirm	(1)

Upper Tier Boulders
Roscoe's Wall page 98

25	Babbacombe Start	(61)
26	Crack Start	(60)

Great Slab page 98

27	Scallop	(54)
28	Cheesy Moon	(47)
29	Long Traverse	(49)

Upper Tier Boulders page 92

The crux of the circuit, as most problems require a fair amount of pulling. Make sure you save some energy for the last problem.

30	Juggy Groove	(43)
31	Flakes and Chips	(36)
32	Wing Wong	(30)
33	Don's Crack	(27)
34	Left Arête	(1)
35	Crimpy Wall	(8)
36	Nose Arête Right	(10)
37	Staircase	(23)
38	Mantel	(25)
39	Joe's Portholes	(17)
40	Joe's Arête	(14)

Roaches Green Circuit

A grand tour of the main Upper and Lower Tiers of the Roaches taking in 40 problems mainly in the V0 to V2 range. This is a great circuit for beginners as there are very few highballs, and tons of quality at the lower end of the difficulty range. It's also great for those new to the area for as well as visiting the honeypots of the Lower Tier and Upper Tier Boulders, it also visits the outer provinces, areas such as Piece of Mind, Calcutta Buttress and the Cellar and Attic. It also takes a fresh look at the popular areas, with a nice traverse on the wall above the Lower Tier problems as well as some tricky stuff on the crag below The Sloth. Of course there's tons more at the Roaches, with the Five Clouds and Nth Cloud and especially the Skyline holding further delights. But for now, here's plenty to be getting on with.

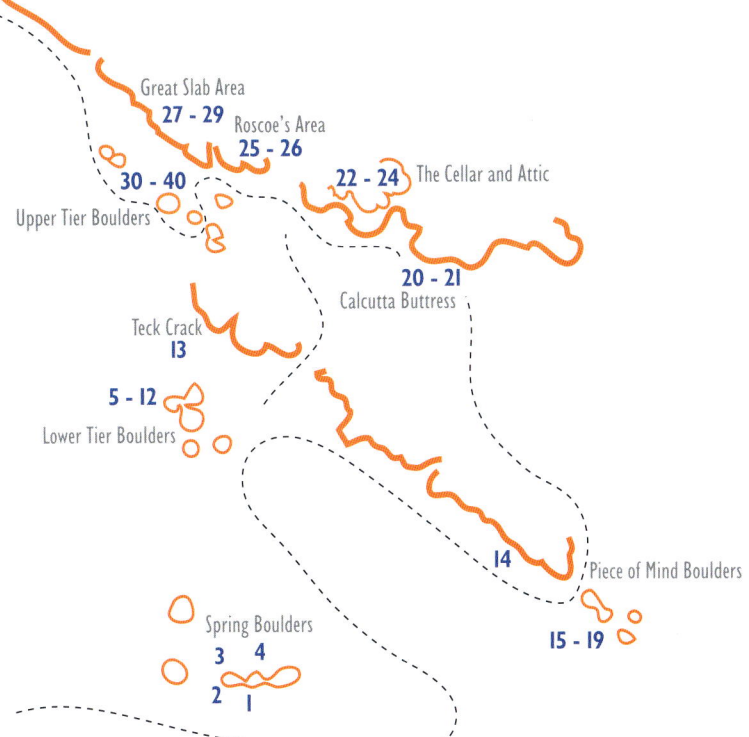

Staffordshire Grit

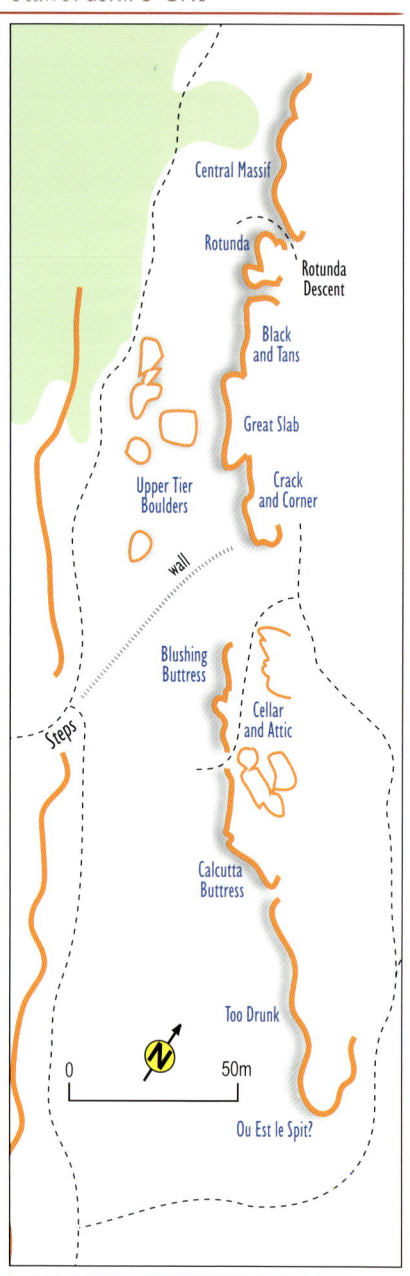

Black and Tans Area

The Upper Tier starts to flex its muscles from here on, giving lots of high quality, long climbs. The first couple of buttresses lie to the left of the towering smoothness of Great Slab, and give a good range of high quality lower grade climbs, with a few desperates thrown in for good measure.

Rotunda Descent: A steep, scrambly, but easy, descent leads down to the left of Rotunda Buttress.

40 Rotunda Buttress VS 4c   1945
18m Start at a wide crack left of the gully. Follow this for 3m before moving up and left with some concern to a ledge. Ascend rightwards, then left to another ledge below an arête. The steep final wall provides the punch.

41 Rotunda Gully M   4000BC
15m A bit of a non-climb. Climbing the crack in the left-hand face is a better option as an alternative finish at HVD, making the outing almost worthwhile.

42 Bachelor's Buttress VS 4b ★   1922
18m This ancient classic offers delicate mantelshelving in exposed situations. Climb the slab to the gully. Traverse the hanging slab up and right, past a nut placement. Summon your courage, then move up to a short crack and the top: *see photo on page 79.* A direct finish (VS 4c), goes directly up from the middle of the traverse.

The Upper Tier Black and Tans

43 Gypfast E4 5c ★★ 1979
18m The underside of the roof gives a very exciting ride. Follow the roof rightwards, to its widest point, on flakes that are better than they look (protection in the lip of Saul's Crack, and Bachelor's Buttress). A direct start up the centre of the slab is 5c.

44 Something Biblical E2 6a ★ 1987
18m Climb the slab to the roof. Using the protection offered by Saul's Crack, but not the holds, pull through the roof. Finish up the wall above.

45 Saul's Crack HVS 5a ★★★ 1947
18m The Master's first addition to the Roaches; perfectly protected, but it makes you work for it. Amble up the crack to a niche and make an easier-for-the-short move (at last!) to pass this. The corner above requires proficient jamming to ensure you have enough puff left for the final intimidating roof. Keep going, the holds are there.

46 Humdinger E1 5b ★ 1969
18m Follow the wall to a tiered overhang, and a jug on the lip. From here, a tormenting move gains (or doesn't) the obvious yet distant hold above.

Simply stunning. John Beatty's breathtaking aerial photograph of the Roaches showing the area in its true geological majesty. The twin ridge dominates all, with the precious boulders tossed before it, ejected in some Carbiniferous cataclysm. Behind, the August purples of Goldsitch Moss provide a soothing forgotten backdrop. Meanwhile, perched on the belay halfway up Pedestal Route, Andi Turner and Mark Sharratt enjoy their Friday evening fags. That's Pixie and Reg below.

Staffordshire Grit

47 Jeffcoat's Chimney Variations
HS 4a, 4c ★ traditional
1. 18m The unprotected left wall of the chimney is followed boldly to the cave. Gain the left arête and climb this and the left wall above to the ledge.
2. 6m Boulder up the wall from the right to escape left.

48 Jeffcoat's Chimney VD ★★ 1913
A historic and cavernous classic of considerable character, one of the Upper Tier's first climbs.
1. 18m The slippery chimney is followed past a cave to an accommodating belay ledge. Going right at 3m and regaining the chimney where the wall steepens is Diff.
2. 6m From the left hand edge of the ledge, move right by a long step and go up to the overlap. Move left from here to an easy finish.

49 Jeffcoat's Buttress HS 5a, 4a ★★★ 1913
A tremendous example of pre-War crackcraft, with consistently difficult, varied and enjoyable climbing.
1. 18m A technical fingery 5a start (avoidable by coming in from the chimney at 4b) leads to better holds and an easier corner. Follow this, then perform an impressive but straightforward traverse right above the roof to a belay beneath two cracks.
2. 9m Follow the cracks above the belay to finish.

50 Hanging Around HVS 5b 1978
24m Climb the bulging wall, then continue direct to reach the large cracked roof. Move strenuously right beneath the roof until technical moves gain the crack above.

51 Ruby Tuesday E2 5b, 4b, 5b ★★★ 1971
30m A big undertaking involving both bold and plain hard climbing. A fantastic route..
1. 12m Climb directly up to the overhang. Powerful moves over this lead to a niche. From here, delicate climbing on small holds leads rightwards to the belay.
2. 6m Move easily left and up to the next belay.
3. 12m Follow cracks, then forsake these for a bold traverse to gain and climb an overhanging arête and chimney. An alternative (should you for some strange reason want something harder and more committing) bisects the traverse midway by pulling directly through the roof and to the top, at E4 6a.

52 Black and Tans Variations
HVS 5a ★ traditional
26m Climb the wall directly to the first corner, then tackle the wall above the ledge to cross the upper overhang just left of Black Velvet.

53 Black and Tans S 4a, 3c ★★★ 1922
30m Fred Piggott's stylish swagger up this mighty slab is a righteous climb, classic in every sense, with a technical lower section and a psychological upper.
1. 12m Climb a shallow corner to a ledge (a runner hereabouts will be appreciated by the second), then shuffle left to belay in the next corner.
2. 18m Climb the corner above and follow a good break left onto the nose. Continue directly by means of exposed mantelshelves and good pockets.

54 Black Velvet HVD 4a ★★ 1957–68
27m Classy climbing taking a good direct line up some impressive terrain. Climb to the first hanging corner, as for Black and Tans. Pull steeply up the cracked wall above, and continue to pass the roof on the right.

55 Diamond Wednesday HVS 5a ★ 1978
26m A good, well-protected, if slightly artificial, climb. From the holly, follow the slim groove and crack to a small triangular roof. An awkward move round this leads to slabby breaks above.

The Roaches – The First Ten

For an interesting day out, try to tick off the first ten routes recorded at the Roaches, get yourself a little insight into the minds and abilities of Victorian and Edwardian crag rats. Raven Rock Gully from Puttrell and Watson's Kyndwr Club is a bit of filthy fun to get you going, and follow that up with the nearby Cannonball Crack. Buxton's Stanley Jeffcoat who, along with his partners, the powerful Seigfried Herford and noted night climber John Laycock, added his (Jeffcoat's) Buttress and Chimney to the Upper Tier in 1913. In 1922 Fred Piggott added the classy Black and Tans, but then upped the boldness factor a notch with Bachelor's Buttress (VS!). This was quite a year for the Upper Tier, as it also saw Morley Wood blitz the crag with Pedestal Route Left and Right, Right Route and the fantastic Crack and Corner. That'll be a nice day out.

The Upper Tier Great Slab

The Great Slab

To the right lies a towering bastion of top quality grit, giving routes up to 30m in height, where soaring slabs are punctuated by small ledges and unlikely overhangs. All the routes here have a big feel about them, with lots of splendid multi-pitch adventures, superb crack-lines and some of the most spectacular roof climbs to be had anywhere. Unsurprisingly, this quality has led to great popularity which, over 90 years of sport, has left a few of the routes quite polished, so beware. High and exposed, it catches the wind but dries quickly.

Descent: Rotunda descent is the most convenient.

56 Hollybush Crack HS 4b ★★ traditional
26m The major crackline is a fine big pitch with a straddling crux in a prickly situation. Shimmy up cracks left of the holly then step rightwards across (or onto) it. Continue to gain the crack then blast up this to an easier finish above the roof.

57 The Neb Finish VS 4b ★★ 1957–68
25m Reasonable though rousing climbing, crossing the hanging sidewall. Once over the overhang on Hollybush Crack, arrange a high runner. Step down again, and traverse rightwards on pockets, feet just above the lip, further and further away from that runner, to a finish near the arête. A logical conclusion to Technical Slab.

Staffordshire Grit

58 Technical Slab HS 4a ★★ 1945
23m A brilliant exposed route, high in the grade due to its technicality and seriousness. Ascend the slab, with delicate stretches between well-spaced holds, and distant protection, to the roof. From here, the Neb Finish makes for a three star combination (although be careful with the ropework).

59 Gillted E5 6a ★ 1979
30m The first of the big climbs crossing the Great Roof. From the corner on the left, follow the obvious handrail running rightwards to its end. Swing blindly round under the very lip of the overhang to reach the cave (large sling runner). Exit up and right via a pocket. This finish is desperate, and may be unrepeated, the only known repeat went up the arête on the left. Previously given E4, it is possibly harder than Painted Rumour.

60 Pedestal Route HVD 4a,3c ★★★ 1922
27m Engrossing for the grade and a good day out.
1. 12m Climb by any means to the large ledge at 4m. From the centre of this, layback either side of the flake to a dainty mantel onto the pedestal, and belay.
2. 15m Shuffle leftwards and use the break awkwardly to gain a standing position. Continue left into the corner, before moving over a small roof by bridging the gap. Finish steadily up the corner.

(**Hint:** A runner in the crack out left can keep the rope from getting jammed in the back of the roof.)

61 Painted Rumour E6 6a ★★★ 1985
26m This mighty route attacks the gigantic overhang at its widest, wildest point by some strenuous and scary yarding. Stuff in some gear before climbing out to the cave where a spike runner and a lie-down rest in the cave. This is not a particularly relaxing kind of rest. Pull leftwards out of the cave and move up the headwall on sharp rugosities (crux) to finish. Most climbers use a tensioned rope on the sling to keep it from falling off the spike. Imagine that happens when you're on the headwall!

62 Loculus Lie E5 6a ★★ 1983
28m One word: exposure. From the lip of The Sloth, make a breathtaking traverse leftwards in the middle of nowhere. Excitement builds to near-unbearable levels until the cave is gained by a blind reach. Finish as for Painted Rumour. The original line reached left from the cheeseblock onto suspect flakes before moving back to the lip of The Sloth. This is rarely climbed and the route is just as superb without.

63 The Sloth HVS 5a ★★★ 1953
24m Superb, intimidating and steeped in legend – a route to bring out the Whillans in you. Climb to The Pedestal. Move up to the 'cheeseblock' (sling runner), and launch out across the juggy flakes to the lip and wide crack above. Protection is available on the way but have you the strength to place it? *See photo on front cover*.

64 New Fi'nial E6 6b ★★ 1985
28m The meat of this route is a powerful rightwards traverse from The Sloth, in a mega 'out there' position along the very lip of the roof. Sloping holds, heel-hooks, and a cool, cool head are pressed into service to pass the crucial short crack 5m along before heading for the top.

> **"Joe Brown made the second ascent, with myself as second**
>
> **when I was his Gentleman's Gentleman. When I was out on the roof he tied off the rope to the belay and came down to watch me, giving me the shock of my young life. When I asked if he was holding the rope because of all the slack, up from the deck floated the reply**
> **'Of course I am.'"**
>
> Dennis Gray talking about The Sloth

The Upper Tier The Great Slab

65 Central Route VS 4b ★★   1949–51

15m Serious climbing on small, and rather shiny, holds. Follow the slab directly, then traverse under the overhang to the belay ledge of Right Route. High in the grade, and remember the second when placing gear.

66 99% of Gargoyles Look Like Bob Todd
E5 6b ★   1986

24m An obscure classic with some hard and bold climbing. Arrange protection in a suspicious collection of brittle breaks and flakes above Central Route. Pull desperately into the groove and continue with care.

Staffordshire Grit

67 Right Route VD ★★ 1922
24m Morley Wood's early addition is one of the most popular routes on the crag, although novices may be unnerved by some of the frictionless footholds.
1. 15m Follow a line of pockets to the roof (take care not to jam protection). Make nervous moves left and then up more easily to the large ledge.
2. 9m Balance leftwards over the void to reach the crack which leads to the top. Initially precarious, the climbing soon eases.

68 Right Route Right VS 4b ★ 1957-68
15m As for Right Route to the roof. Thrutch over this to gain the corner and the top. **Kelly's Connection** (HVS 5a, 1957-68) takes a strenuous traverse line from the roof to the large pocket on Kelly's Direct.

69 Kelly's Direct E1 5b ★ 1968-73
15m Climb the thin crack to a ledge. Taking some care to place protection here, move precariously up, right and out to reach a thin flake before making an impressive lunge to a large pocket. Take further pockets from here in a direct line to the top.

70 Laughing all the way to the Blank
E4 6a 1993
14m Follow Kelly's Direct to the ledge and then move directly up the groove above to the large vegetated break. Pull out confidently onto the scary headwall and proceed thoughtfully to the top.

71 Kelly's Shelf S 4a ★ 1924-49
17m Using excellent handholds, make an elegant step or graceless flop (delete as appropriate) onto the shelf, then caterpillar along it to a finish up a crack. A fun alternative finish over the bulge to gain pockets is HS 4a.

72 Skin and Wishbones E8 7a ★★ 2007
23m From the good flake hold in the roof, trend out and rightwards along the bedding plane (runners) to the hanging triangular feature on the lip. Turn the roof with a spectacular sequence *see photo on page 107*.

73 Paralogism E7 6c ★★★ 1987
15m Awesome! This Nadin masterpiece is widely acclaimed as one of grit's hardest roofs, featuring blind slappy bouldering in a position of great danger. Starting at the right arête, make committing moves to gain the hanging coffin. A blind slap gains small holds on the left, before crossing the roof leftwards on better holds. From the lip, move right to a careful finish: *see photo on page 109*.

74 Antithesis E5 6c ★★ 1980
15m An overlooked technical masterpiece. From the ledge up right, desperate, intricate moves lead leftwards to an outstanding position on the nose and a direct finish. A cheeky runner high in Bed of Nails protects a swooping winger, not forgetting to keep your feet high!

75 Bed of Nails E2 5b ★ 1978
12m From the gully above the ledge, traverse the break leftwards to the base of the wide slanting crack. Climb this awkwardly to a niche before finishing easily up the left arête.

The Upper Tier The Great Slab

The Upper Tier Boulders

The ultra-classic Roaches circuit. Hard rock, hard problems and good landings combined with shelter and quick drying make this the most popular of the Roaches areas.

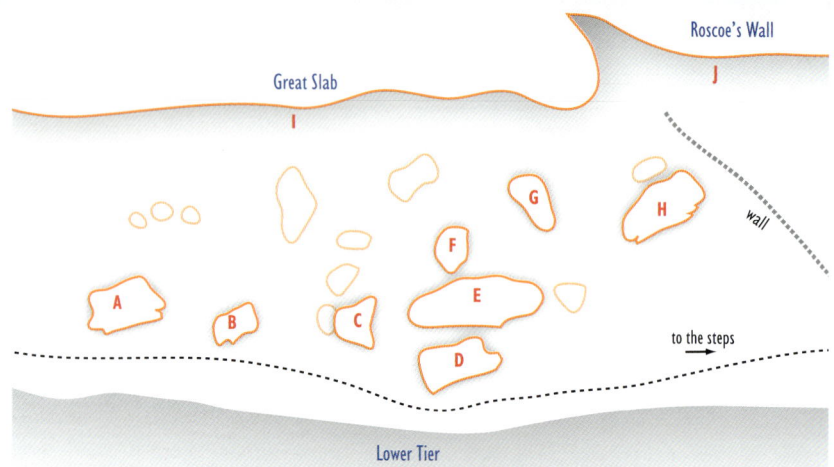

A: The Ripple

1 Left Arête V0 (5b)
Climbed on its right. C

2 Grand Theft
V9 (6c)
The classic lip traverse from the left arête to finish up The Boss.

3 Rippler V3 (5c)
Use the ripple to get onto the slab. A tricky sit start using the pinches and undercuts is V6 (6b).

4 The Boss V5 (6b)
Over the lip using the boss. Careful with those shins, now. C

5 Ripple Arête
V2 (5c)
Climb the short arête. The super low sit start involves a variety of techniques and usually results in you knee-barring your hand in place: V3 (6a).

B: Little Boulder
The boulder just right.

6 Nosy V0– (4c)
Climb up over the nose.

7 Upright V0– (4b)
Move up and right.

92 The Roaches

Strictly hardcore: Martin Dearden cranking through the crux on Nadin's Traverse, V7 (page 95).
Photo: David Simmonite.

Staffordshire Grit

C: The Nose

8 Crimpy Wall V0– (5a)
Up the left wall of the boulder. ○

9 Nose Arête Left V0 (5a)
Layback the nose on the left.

10 Nose Arête Right V0+ (5b)
A layback buckaroo leads over the bulge. ○

11 Nose Scoop V2 (5c)
Start from a crouch and mantel through the scoop.

12 Nose Mantel V0– (4a)

D: Joe's Boulder

13 Big 'Oles V0– (4b)
Rock up the massive holes to the very top.

14 Joe's Arête V3 (6a)
Doff your cap to the master by climbing the polished arête. The cleanest of technique is needed to unlock the key, but once done, it all falls into place. Variations possible, including one-handed ascents. ○ ○ (a double tick!!)

15 Pink Wall Eliminate V7 (6c)
A hard eliminate following the wall with the aid of a poor left hand sidepull and avoiding the better flakes on the right.

94 The Roaches

The Upper Tier Upper Tier Boulders

16 Pink Wall V1 (5b)
Climb the wall left the portholes on flakes, avoiding the holes.

17 Joe's Portholes V0− (5a)
Climb (don't jump) to the hole and thence the top. ⓒ A desperate eliminate, **Mean Ol' B'stard** V8 **(6c)**, starts in the low hole and sidepull to the right, snatches the micro-gaston right of the porthole, and finishes left. **Apocalypse Now** dynos from good opposing sidepulls on either side of the bottom hole to top at a lanky V4 (6b).

E: Long Boulder

18 Jug Up V1 (5b)
Go up on bumper holds from the low jug.

19 Glued Up V6 (6c)
Dyno from the glued hold to the top.

20 Reg V6 (6c)
Hoist up to the top from the sloping finger rail.

21 Pixie V1 (5c)
From the sidepull flake to the top.

22 Nadin's Traverse V7 (6c)
From big holds at the left side, traverse right and finish up 21. Or, keep going and finish with Staircase at V8, or keep traversing, with hands just below the top and finish with Cooper's Traverse: harder V8: *see photo on page 93*.

23 Staircase V1 (5c)
The chunky flake from a sit-start. A lot more strenuous than the size of the holds would suggest. ⓒ

24 Cooper's Traverse V3 (5c)
Monkey rightwards along the lip.

25 Mantel V1 (5c) ⓒ

26 Long Boulder Mantel V4 (6b)
Sit-start on two sidepulls. Slap upwards and grovel over the lip. ⓒ

F: Don's Boulder

27 Don's Crack V0+ (5b)
The crack. ⓒ Climbing between the crack and the right arête is V4 (6a).

28 Don's Arête V0− (4b)
The right arête of the block.

G: The Wing

29 Winger V1 (5c)
Traverse right past diagonal breaks, around the nose, to finish up the far arête.

30 Wing Wong V1 (5c)
A hard lock from the lower break gains the next, then the top. ⓒ

31 Broken Wing V7 (6b)
From a hanging start, with both hands in the slot on The Beak, swing left under the roof and powerfully up to gain the arête. Use this to udge for the break and finish as for Wing Wong.

32 The Beak V4 (6b)
Climb the nose from a hanging start.

Staffordshire Grit

H: The Grooves Boulder

33 Slippery Groove V0 (5a)
The polished groove.

34 Arête on Left V1 (5b)
The smooth edge with the aid of the thin crack.

35 Easy Groove V0– (4c)
A chunky ramble, to be sure.

36 Flakes and Chips V0+ (5b)
A great problem following the flake and rounded holds above ◉: *see photo opposite*. Without the chips it is V4 (6b), and a sit-start is V4 (6b).

37 Bancroft's 6b V7 (6b)
Think denim; think EBs and pale white legs. From standing in the first chip step out rightwards to hang the poor crimps and grind for the top: *see photo on page 389*. The direct start to this is project known as One Inch Punch. Hold-wise, if you can see it, it's not in.

38 Higginson's Arm V8 (6c)
An eliminate traverse starting under Left Groove, one hand on an undercut under the roof, another on the lip, and traversing the lip rightwards to finish up The Nose. Ask a local for full details.

39 Left Groove V4 (6b)
Classic, and a bit worrying. Spotter advised ◉. Eliminating the chipped foothold is V5, and the sit-start is a tough project.

40 Right Groove V2 (6a)
Layback into the shorter slanting groove. The low start is V6 (6c).

41 Vague Arête V1 (5c)
Now, where did I put that arête?

42 The Nose V5 (6b)
Start from the low beak and grasp up on rounded holds. The standup version is V4 (6a). ◉

43 Juggy Groove V2 (5c)
Fine fun up the rightmost groove. ◉

Despite numerous desperates hereabouts, the essential Upper Tier bouldering experience is still getting there of a summer evening after work and flowing through some of your favourite problems, the world all about you. Dave Garnett on Flakes and Chips, V0+ (opposite). Photo: Niall Grimes.

Staffordshire Grit

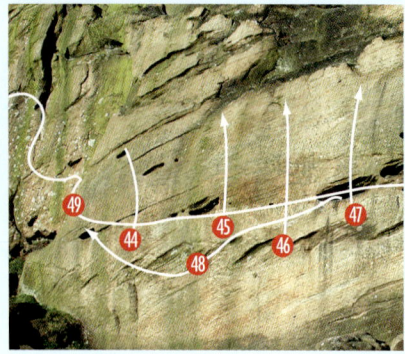

I: Great Slab Bouldering
The slabby walls below The Sloth have lots of previously undocumented bouldering on very nice rock. Lots of variations exist to what's listed here.

44 Popper   V0−   (4b)
Lovely moves up the pockets on the left of the slab. The line to the left, going from the big pocket, up the fingery, flaky rib, is V2 (5c).

45 Flap Dancer   V8   (6c)
Split your tips up the wall, starting from the bullet hole. No big slot.

46 The Lintel   V2   (5c)
Get your hands and feet on the ledge and move upwards. Without using the pocket you're more likely to fall off a V3 and smash your teeth out on the ledge on the way past.

47 Cheesy Moon   V0   (4b)
The wall has better holds than would first appear and is a classy way to start any of the routes above. ◉

48 No name   no grade neither
Never mind too hard to grade – this one's too hard to even name. Traverse left from the big pocket, onto The Lintel then drop down to the slopers and across to finish back on the Long Traverse. Desperate.

49 Long Traverse   V0+   (5b)
Pack your sandwiches and ramble leftwards across the wall. Continue around the corner onto the next wall and continue all the way to Hollybush Crack. ◉

50 Goats Gruff   V0+   (5a)
Start in the low pocket and swing up to better pockets above.

51 The Break   V2   (6a)
Take the crimps and go straight up. ◉ Eliminating the middle rail will make people think you're 'rangey'. Starting on the pocket down and left is Goat's Eye, V4 (6b).

52 Micro Diddy 'Ole AKA The Monodoigt   V9   (7a)
Take the tiny left ear and make progress to the doigt, continue to the top. Variations exist but all are around the same grade and have the same name. Proper English 7a!

53 The Flake Museum   V2   (5c)
Rock out to the flat holds in the face above the niche moving back onto hollow flakes; bad landing. ◉

54 Scallop   V0−   (4b)
Layback flakes at the right end of the wall. ◉

J: Roscoe's Wall Bouldering
This lies at the base of the next buttress up and round to the right. For the first two you'll need to have the start or finish of Roscoe's Wall sorted as this is the escape.

55 Magic Crossing   V1   (5b)
From the incut flake find the hidden dink in the left-facing mini-prow and pirouette up to good edges and across to the deep eye.

The Upper Tier Upper Tier Boulders

56 Toucan V6 (6c)
An incut edge starts this diabolical problem. Finding the crux hold is the first issue, committing to it is the next – gulp – up for jug.

57 Lichenthrope V7 (6c)
Crouching from the low slot, reach the shallow finger pod and rock out left using the tiny edge for the poor rail, and lay one on for Roscoe's jug. A project would be to keep going left instead of joining Roscoe's.

58 Crack Indirect V2 (5c)
A problem which some find easier than the original start to Crack and Corner. Start in the back of the cave and work out along its interior lip until joining the slot and up to the large bowl above without using the crack. Avoiding the slot makes for a mean, blind problem – V3 (6b).

59 Spandau Ballet Reachy
From the top of the last problem, try and fall onto the Roscoe jug from the pocket sidepull.

60 Crack Start V2 (5b)
The jammy crack from the back of the cave. ⊙

61 Babbacombe Start V1 (5b)
Delectable climbing up the pink flakes. ⊙ The improbable sit start using little crimpy breaks and useless undercuts is **Polish**, V7 (6c).

62 Sheep Shit V8 (6c)
From the central finger rail, get your feet on and get up.

63 Sheep Shit Crack V5 (6b)
Make a technical move up and right from hanging the rail into the thin flake line. ⊙

64 Oik V3 (6a)
From a hanging start beneath the roof, move quickly out on bendies to the jug and wham for the top up and right. ⊙

Andi 'Pobface' Turner on Lichenthrope. Photo: Florence bloody Nightingale.

Staffordshire Grit

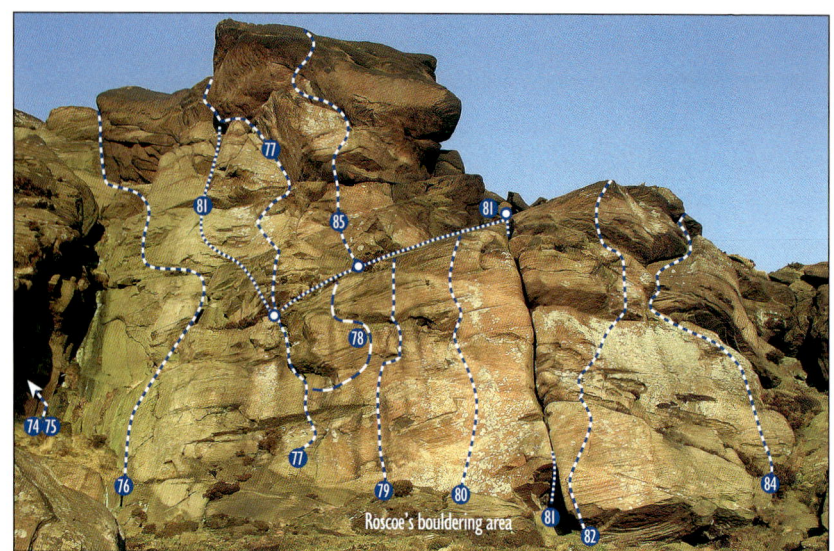

76 Easy Gully Wall S 4a   1957–68
21m Bold, technical climbing leads to a sandy ledge. Trend rightwards to a short layback crack and a bulge. Move up and traverse left below the overhang to finish up a wide crack.

77 Jelly Roll VS 4b, 4a ★   1957–68
Another good route that reaches the whole height of the crag.
1. 8m Climb the thin crack to belay on the block.
2. 15m Boldly follow the wall to a spectacular hanging groove. Follow this to finish as for Crack and Corner.

78 Magic Child HVS 5a   traditional
7m Gain holds leading right to the large pocket. Hand-traverse the ledge above leftwards before moving up, and right again to finish.

79 Ped X-ing HVS 5c   1997
11m Nice climbing weaving up the wall on good holds, a sort of Roscoe's on the cheap.

80 Roscoe's Wall HVS 5b ★★   1955
11m Impressive but amenable once the bouldery start is solved. A stiff pull above a worrying landing gains a niche. Swing right and up on fantastic holds and wish that there were more. Round Table makes a superb continuation pitch for the unsatisfied.

81 Crack and Corner S 4c, –, 4a ★★   1922
35m A classic long expedition with a desperate start and a thrilling finish, where you should spare a thought for the original pioneers with tweeds, plimsolls, and no belays.
1. 12m Jam, layback and swear your way into the undercut crack, which will take more gear than you can possibly put in.
2. 8m Wander left along the ledge to a belay.
3. 15m Pockets above lead to a large ledge on the left. The corner then leads to a superb and thrilling final overhang and streeetch for a hidden jug!
Alternatively, **Bud Love** (E4 6a ★, 1996) moves left along the parallel cracks on the third pitch to an even more imposing view of the overhang. From here, a flake is used to surmount this (hopefully) rapidly: *see photo opposite*.

82 Babbacombe Lee E1 5b ★   1978
11m A broken line, but giving good exposure. Boulder up the left hand end of the undercut wall, and follow a short crack to a contorted rest and a bold, reachy finale over the nose.

The pioneers of rock climbing at the Roaches. Bold adventureres, gentleman eccentrics in jackknife laybacks dressed in tweeds and plimsolls. With ropes but no protection, with belayers, but no belays. Incredible people to whom we owe the depth of our sport. Morley Wood looks on as Fred Piggott climbs his route Crack and Corner, Severe (opposite page) in 1922. The belayer is unknown. Photo Eric Byrom / Rucksack Club.

Staffordshire Grit

83 Destination Venus HVS 5b   1979
24m A traverse of the lower wall from right to left. From the ledge on Babbacombe Lee, move into Crack and Corner. Step down before making difficult moves left into the niche on Roscoe's Wall. Traverse left passing the large pocket into Jelly Roll. An obscure line, but with great moves and rock: it makes for a fine solo for the competent.

84 Hangman's Crack S 4a   1949
11m An interesting climb. The right-hand side of the wall leads to a large black roof flake. Step left to attack the wide crack. Difficult to protect.

The next two routes start from the ledge above the lower buttress, and take imposing lines up the steep rock above.

85 Trebia E4 6a   1981
10m Difficult moves up the undercut rib lead to a niche below the final roof. Take this direct at a shallow hole.

86 Round Table E1 5a ★★   1974
11m A route of surprisingly low grade taking the impressive crack and finishing at the highest point of the buttress. Steep and committing moves lead into the wide crack. Swing right across the bulge to an easy finish.

The Upper Tier has three justly neglected girdle traverses: **The Girdle Traverse** (S, pre-1924) goes from Routunda Gully at a low level to gain and climb Kelly's Shelf. At the top of this carry on to finish as for Crack and Corner. **The High Crossing** (VS 4b, 1949-51) again uses Kelly's Shelf to gain height then follows the crag left beneath the roof. Continue in this line to eventually finish with a reverse of Bachelor's Buttress to eventually gain the gully. **The Waistline** (E1 5b, 1968-73) starts in Rotunda Gully and keeps below the three roofs to eventually pull up into the stance on Black and Tans. Move on and cross Great Slab beneath the roof and finish with Kelly's Connection.

Cellar and Attic Bouldering

A good collection of quiet problems.

1 The Squirm V0+ (5a)
Climb the thin crack, then squirm through the jaws above. **C**

2 The Finger V1 (5b)
Climb the arête then move left up the finger.

3 Handy Wall V0− (5b)
The short wall and scoop above.

4 Mounty V0− (4c)
Surmount the bulge above the crack.

5 Barley V1 (5b)
Gain the flake on the wall and make a precarious stand up to gain the top.

6 Chasm Arête V2 (6a)
Layback the awkward left arête of the chasm.

7 Scrack V0 (4c) **C**

8 Reachy Wall V2 (6a)
Make long stretches up the wall. **C**

9 Runnel Rouser V0+ (5a)
Move directly up the wall from the runnel.

10 Arête V0− (4b)

11 Risky Runnel V1 (5b)
A lovely problem following the open runnel to a harrowing top-out.

The Upper Tier Cellar and Attic

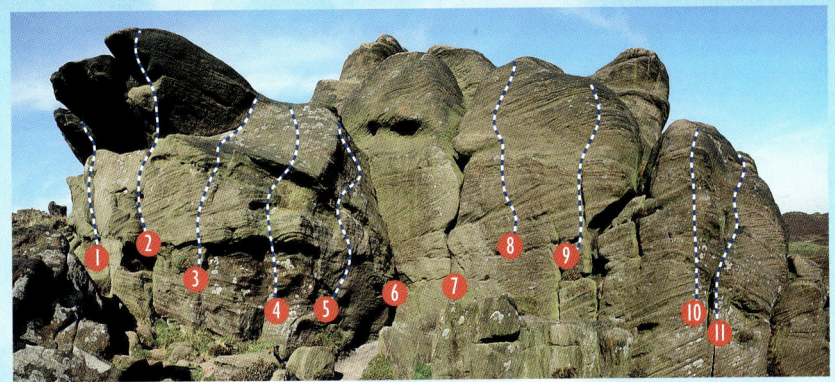

12 Cellar Slab 1   V1   (5b) ⓒ

13 Cellar Slab 2   V1   (5c)

14 Easy Groove   V0–   (3c)

15 Slab   V0–   (4c)

16 Tiny Groove   V0–   (4a)

17 Right Slab   V0–   (3c)

18 Cellar Dwella   V7   (6c)
A one move wonder using sidepulls to gain the top.

19 The Gates   V4   (6a)
The thin slab on the leaning boulder.

20 Crinkly Wall   V2   (5c)

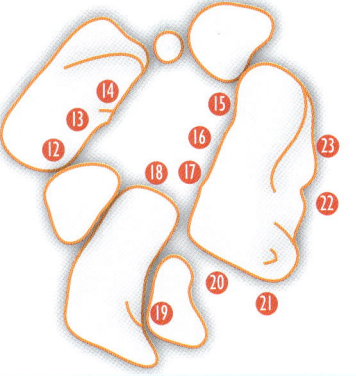

21 Ride My Pimp   V4   (6b)
Surmounting the bulging arête is remarkably similar to giving birth. Only harder. ⓒ

22 The Downpipe   V5   (6b)
Somehow try to ascend the angry pipeline on the front of the boulder.

23 Pipe Entry   V7   (6b)
From a sitting start on a blind flake, pull up to the lip. From here, go left to the pipe and up.

The Cellar

Calcutta Buttress

With the desperate start now below, a climber can relax and enjoy tremendous moves and rock scenery on Right-Hand Route, S 4b (opposite). Photo: Niall Grimes

The Upper Tier Blushing Buttress

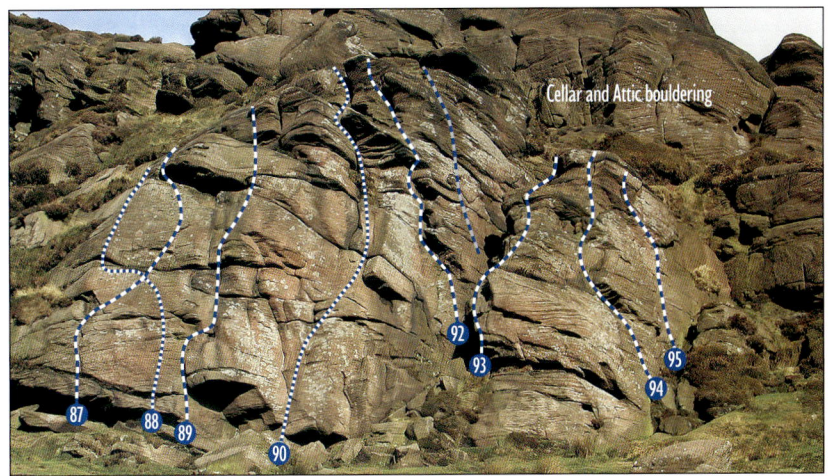

Blushing Buttress

Down and right is a fine compact buttress with good steep routes based on strong cracklines and friendly flakes. The rock is excellent, and it is a good escape from the hordes on Great Slab.

87 Scarlet Wall HS 4b   1949
11m Crank up the crack on the left of the buttress and move right to a large ledge. Move up carefully to a thread runner and precarious exit. The slab just left provides a bold HS 4a variant.

88 War Wound HVS 5c   1978
11m A difficult but very contrived start leads past a break to a large ledge. From the left edge of this, climb the bold, slabby arête.

89 Left-Hand Route HVD 4a ★   1924
13m Good climbing, steep at the start then delicate above. Layback the hanging flake past the left-hand end of a roof, then trend carefully ever upwards.

90 Right-Hand Route S 4b ★★   1924
13m An elegant line, steep and clean, and one of the earlier climbs at the Roaches. A hard layback start on shiny footholds (avoidable on the right) leads to a ledge. From here tackle the easier-than-it-looks roof crack above: *see photo opposite*.

91 Aperitif HS 4c   1968–73
25m A rising rightwards traverse of the buttress. Start low in a cave left of Scarlet Wall. Traverse right along the lip to the crack of Scarlet Wall, then hand-traverse into Left-Hand Route. Follow this for a few moves until it is possible to reach the ledge on Right-Hand Route. Swing right strenuously to reach the gully, then continue right across the next buttress.

92 Gully Wall VS 4b   1957–68
9m The large flakes lead steeply upwards to an awkward move left to gain the nose of Right-Hand Route. The wall to the right is **Grilled Fingers** (HVS 4c, 1979), finishing direct with long reaches.

93 The Rib M   1957–68
8m The right-hand rib of the gully, and started by coming in from the gully. HS 4b if started direct.

94 Rib Wall VD   1957–68
8m Climb the front wall of the buttress in a good position passing a niche and a large ledge in as direct a line as possible. The direct start left of the niche is a strenuous 5b.

95 Sparkle VS 4b   1978
8m Step off a block and use a variety of flakes and pockets to ascend, then traverse off leftwards. The direct finish is 4c.

Staffordshire Grit

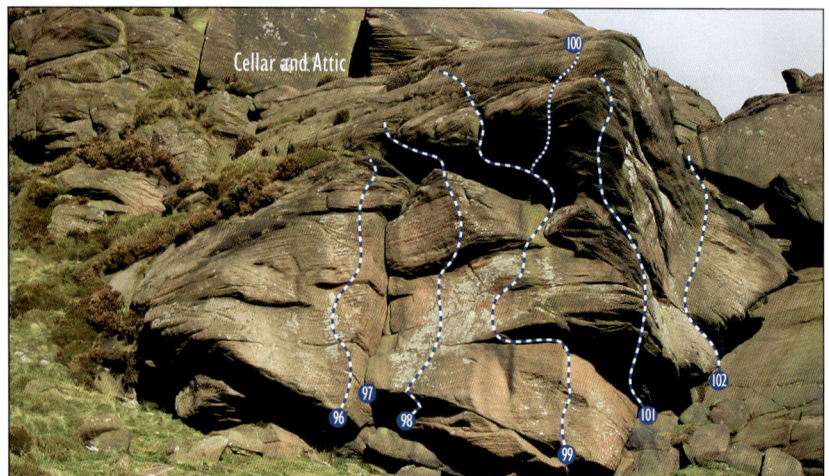

Calcutta Buttress

The next pert little buttress is again home to a clutch of fine steep routes on good rock, as well as some good bouldering, and like the last buttress, tends to be fairly quiet.

96 Sign of the Times El 5c   1979
6m A hard move on the arête leads to a break and good runners, before a small flake leads to a belly-flop climax.

97 Calcutta Crack S 4b ★★   1949
6m An awkward start, especially for the short, leads to steep satisfying climbing on ideal jams.

98 Mistral E2 6a ★   1987
6m A fierce boulder problem start leads to a short wall and bomber gear in a large break. From here tackle the small prow on small but improving holds.

99 Calcutta Buttress VS 5b ★   1957–68
11m Hard pulls up and then left gain a mantelshelf requiring great balance or a long reach. Continue right to a niche, then escape back left.

100 The Spectatorship of the Proletariat
E5 6b ★   2007
10m Climb directly up to an obvious spike and then straight through the middle of the roof on big flakes.

101 Genetix E3 6a   1979
11m Pull up to the suspicious flakes in the roof (now very brittle) and make an unprotected haul over to finish up the right side of the arête on green slopers.

102 Stop… Carry on! HVS 5a   2001
8m The hanging scoop in the right wall is unprotected. An awkward start leads leftwards onto a ledge, whence the scoop is climbed rightwards.

103 Calcutta Crab Dance HS 4c ★★ 2002
29m A right to left traverse taking in some hearty terrain. From the first moves of the previous route, continue leftwards with either protection or jugs, but never both. Follow the line around the nose to Calcutta Crack (possible belay), then finish more easily.

104 Between the Tiles HVS 5a   1979
25m A left to right girdle of the buttress at half height with an awkward section below the central prow and a tricky finish rightwards up the scoop.

Ben Bransby making the first ascent of one of the last great problems at the Roaches, Skin and Wishbones, E8 7a (page 90). This ranks as the hardest lead in the area, and will remain so until someone finally does the Headless Horseman arête. Photo: Adam Long.

Staffordshire Grit

Calcutta Buttress Bouldering

The base of Calcutta Buttress is home to a great handful of generally tricky and always fingery problems.

1 Bombay Overhang V1 (5c)
Round the bulging nose on good holds. Add an extra grade for traversing in from the right. ⏀

2 Calcutta Crimp V4 (6b)
Starting from a long fingerhold over the roof (or the jug below, harder and better), rock upwards towards the upper break. ⏀

3 Dirtnap V8 (6c)
Start as for Sleeping with the Flowers then scratch desperately leftwards to finish at the top of the nose.

4 Sign Start V2 (5c)
Some powerful locking-off leads up the arête to a good break.

5 Sleeping with the Flowers V5 (6b)
A sit start to the last problem going from the back of the roof and slapping out to eventually get good holds. Avoid the footblock on the right.

6 Mistral Start V3 (6a)
Crinkle over the roof on crisp crimps. ⏀ V4 from a low start.

7 Limbless Limbo Dancer V6 (6b)
Odder than a wallaby. From a low start, scurry up the vague rib.

8 Dish Grab V5 (6b)
Start low in the break, then hoist up and right for the positive dish.

9 Calcutta Rib V1 (5c)
The chirpy rib at the right of the buttress. ⏀

10 Calcutta Traverse V2 (5c)
Traverse the shelf from right to left, pulling into Calcutta Crack at the end. **The Black Hole Start,** **V7 (6b),** yields more bottom scraping by joining this from the crack on the right, on cruel crimps.

The Upper Tier Right-Hand End

Right-Hand End

In the last gasps of the Upper Tier, right of Calcutta Buttress, are a few final outcrops.

105 Pepper HVS 5a   1957–68
7m Twenty five metres right of Calcutta Buttress is another buttress. Climb the overhung front face to a ledge, then move left to finish up a crack.

106 Garlic HVS 5a   1979
7m From a short corner to the left move up before swinging right onto the ledge of Pepper. From here tackle the overhang on its right-hand side. **Dazed and Confused** (E3 6a, 2002) is essentially a direct start to this. Starting on the left of the buttress, under the roof, slap up the wall to finish as for Garlic.

107 Too Drunk V6 (6c)
Right of Pepper Buttress is a large boulder with a very overhanging front face. This is the central line on the overhang, from a sitting start, pulling onto the upper face on sloping pockets.

108 Drunk Enough V5 (6b)
The right arête, from a sitting start.

Behind these problems, more buttresses stretch off for 30m. On the last of these, a flat wall faces off towards Hen Cloud, with a few obscure routes to please the connoisseur. The left arête is **Shelty** *(HVS 5c, 1987), and an obscure wall left of this holds* **Dolly Mix, Mix** *(HVS 5a, 1987) via small pockets.*

109 Ou est le Spit? E5 6a ★   1986
5m A reclusive classic up the centre of the face, above a threatening boulder. Use some suspect sandy holds to reach the small grooved feature. Make use of this to move up to a better than it used-to-be hold (due to wire brushing; no more please) over the sloping top and use this to top out. Impressively dangerous, given its length. Just right, **Wolfman of the KGB** (E3 6b, 1987) is an extended boulder problem starting up the left-leaning ramp.

Fifteen metres in front of this is a boulder with a couple of problems. The prow facing Hen Cloud, starting low in the crack, is V3 (6a), and the sweet finger crack on the front is V0 (5a).

Ben Branchy on Paralogism, E7 6c (page 90). Photo: Adam Long

The Cube

Also known as Window Buttress and Back End Boulders, this small collection of blocks can be found 250m immediately behind the first buttress on the Skyline containing The Pugilist. First developed by Nick Dixon and Simon Whalley in 1986 as micro-routes (some can be led), their length, landing and climbing style lend them to be seen more as high (and not so high) bouldering, especially with a pad and spotter. Tackled this way, it is a superb venue, with a beautiful lonely setting overlooking wild moorland. Lots of sun, but quite exposed. **Access** is slightly sensitive, due to the natural value placed on the quiet surrounding moor by naturalists, so be discreet and approach from the right, not directly from the Skyline. At the right side of the Upper Tier, take the track running back from the crag, past old poles and 100m after a small stream, a vague sheep trod runs off this on the left, leading to the Cube. Takes under 10 minutes from the Upper Tier. See map on page 35.

1 Cube Traverse V4 (6b)
Traverse the three faces, with hands at the level of the mid-height break. Scenic.

2 Flakes V1 (5b)
4c to the break.

3 Cube Crack VD (4a)

4 Period Drama V2 (5c)
Traverse rightwards round the arête, and when the break fades, move up on edges by interesting moves. Can be led at E1.

5 Jump V4 (6b)
The square arête demands a dynamic approach. The **sit-start** is V7 (6c), and the blank wall to the right will eventually go at about V11.

6 The Cube V5 (6b)
A highball classic, with fingery wall climbing above a perfect landing. E3 as a route. The **direct start** up the scoop is V8 (6c).

7 The Pube V3 (6a)
Start as for the Cube, but continue up the arête on the left. Short and curly. The **sit start** is V9 (6c).

8 Right Pube V4 (6a)
The arête on the right.

9 Back Crack V1 (5b)
The crack and mantel. V2 (6a) for the sitting start.

10 Cave Exit V7 (6b)
Surmount the lip from the back of the grungy cave.

11 K2 V0− (4b)
Climbed on the steep side.

12 V0 (5a)
The slab from the slot. Avoid the ridge for as long as possible.

13 Summit Slab V2 (5c)
Thin smearing past the porthole.

14 Notch Slab V0+ (5a)
Another delicate passage.

15 2K V0− (4b)
Remember, in mountaineering, you're not up 'till you're down. Climb the right ridge on its steep side.

The Skyline Area
by Chris 'Gus' Hudgins

O.S. Ref. SK002634 — Altitude: 480m a.s.l.

The Skyline is effectively a continuation of the Upper Tier, although it offers a stark contrast to the situation offered by the rest of the Roaches. As opposed to the often bustling, sometimes noisy and crowded atmosphere which occurs on the lower and upper tiers, it is not uncommon to find peace and solitude among the short but perfectly formed buttresses, as well as awesome views. The lack of visitors, however, is definitely not an indication of the quality of climbing, and make no mistake about it, some of the best routes on gritstone at all grades can be found here. One only has to look.

Conditions & aspect
The crag itself consists of a number of bays of rock, rather than one continuous outcrop. These separate buttresses can offer surprising shelter from the wind due to the proximity of trees, but are otherwise very open to all other weather. When the sun does grace the rock, however, some of the best days climbing are on offer. Faces south-west, getting sun afternoon and evening.

Parking & approach
Park as for the Roaches or at Roach End, depending on where you are and where you are going (see maps on page 35, and next page). For getting between buttresses, it is usually best to return to the top path. Individual approach times given throughout the text and are, a) from the Upper Tier, (remember to add 10 minutes to get here), and b) from Roach End.

The climbs are described from **right** to **left**.

The first three routes are located on a seemingly insignificant, but attractive, little buttress just left of the ascent path. It is characterised by very pink rock at its base, and an overhang on the right, below a cracked arête.

1   The Pugilist   HVS 5c   ★   1957–68
7m A steep crack and groove give a punishing prelude to good hidden holds above the overhang which allow the arête and crack to be climbed. A poor route, **Stomach Punch** (VD 4b, trad), climbs up the right wall of the buttress.

2   In Passing   E2 5c   1976
8m The crack to the left provides another (reachy) fight to the death. Cower below the overhang before stepping left and pulling onto the slab above. Probably yet to receive a stylish ascent.

3   Southpaw   S 4b   1957–68
7m If the plant life is successfully avoided, the crack-line just left gives a good warm up. Just left again is a short-lived 4a problem.

Little Skyline Face
A little 4m high face lies 30m below the crag at this point, with a cutaway in its left arête. **Left Arête** features awkward laybacking, V1 (5b). **Centre Slab** is a tough classic, V5 (6b), climbing past very shallow pockets, all at a bit of a height. **Right Arête** is V1 (5c).

Staffordshire Grit

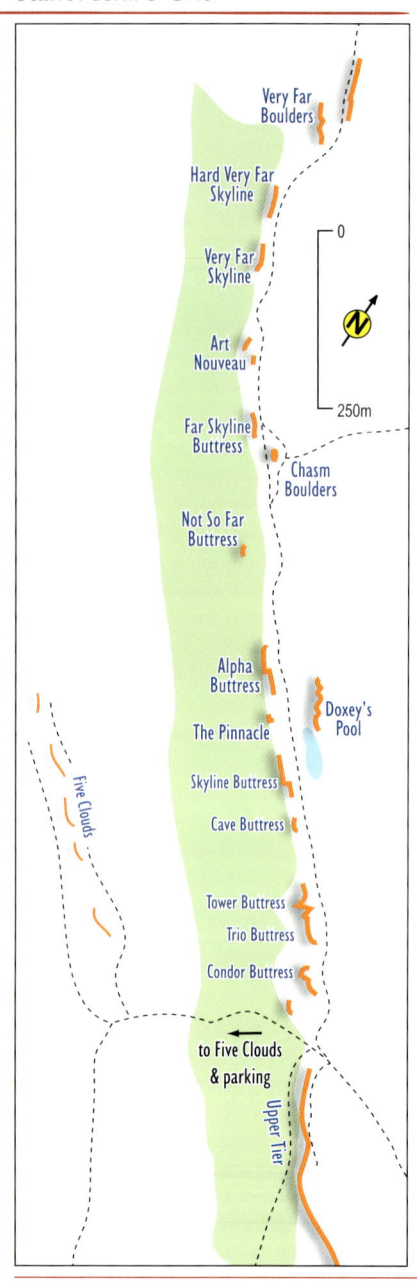

Condor Buttress

This lies 100m to the left and is named after the classic challenge hereabouts.

Approach from the clifftop path: a) 5 minutes, b) 25 minutes.

4 Lung Cancer S 4b   1977
7m Starting just right of a block, climb left under a roof. Move up, then go back right below another overlap using a crucial jam to contort through an awkward move. Moving right from the start of Lung Cancer and gaining the undercut arête via a good hold on the lip of the overhang is **Breathless** (HS 4a, trad).

5 Chicane S   1978
7m This is the clean, blunt arête. Very tough moves lead straight off the block (or, better, start up the crack just right at 4a) and pass to the left of a small roof. Finish past a shallow but useful pocket. **Chicanery** (HVD, trad) is the direct start up the crack just left.

6 False Chicane VD   traditional
7m Start at the small block a few metres left of the arête, to finish diagonally right up the slab. The line previously labelled as Chicane.

7 Navy Cut VD   1957–68
7m Climb the niche to the left to a chimney above. Either wedge yourself in and battle to make vertical progress or, for the claustrophobic, move slightly right and apply a somewhat more open approach.

8 Bruno Flake VS 4b ★   1957–68
7m The corner leads to steep, awkward, and sometimes powerful climbing through the roof/flake crack (large gear useful). Tough, but a good trophy.

9 Wheeze HVS 4c ★   1976
8m Climb the initial arête to a break and runners, then use both balance and reach to move onto the upper arête and into an impressive position. Not an easy climb to protect.

10 Tobacco Road VS 4c ★   1957–68
8m Take a direct line up the wall. Although inde-

Skyline Condor Buttress

pendent, the climbing is spookily similar to Wheeze, if less finely positioned.

11 Toxic Socks HVS 5b   1996
8m Another, rather claustrophobic, direct line just left.

12 Time to be Had VD   1978
8m Just right of the easy corner is a cracked wall.

13 Licensed to Fill HVS 4c   2002
8m From 3m up the easy corner, move left onto the steep side-wall to a long, sloping pocket. From here take a strict line up the centre of the wall. Protection arrives a little late.

14 Nosepicker HVS 5b ★   1975
8m Move delicately up to the overhang and, for once, take the easy way out avoiding it to the left by pleasantly delicate moves. Finish directly. The direct is **Johnny Pooh Poohed** (E2 6a, 1996), taken by altogether steeper moves. Hardcore!

15 Condor Chimney VD ★   1957–68
8m Although the deep chimney just left gives the impression of offering a deadly struggle, a confident approach transforms it into a pleasant bridging exercise.

16 Cracked Arête HVD 4a   1951–57
15m A pleasant two-tier route with some good smearing practice. Starting from a lower level, opposite the large boulder, climb the polished but still appealing arête, followed by the slab and flake crack above the ledge. Useful for developing those essential multi-pitch skills.

17 A.M. Anaesthetic VS 4c   1978
8m The precarious blunt arête. Testing climbing.

18 Condor Slab VS 4c ★★   1957–68
12m The top-notch VS of the buttress. A bold and very rewarding route requiring some faith in your ability. Start up a short crack and make tenuous moves up and left to the obvious hole, whence a trying move leads upwards to a ledge. Step right and finish centrally.

19 Chicane Destination VS 4c   1978
40m A rightwards horizontal outing beginning at the hole of the previous route. Your destination; Chicane!

Staffordshire Grit

Trio Buttress

The height of the crag now begins to increase and really gives an impression of what it has to offer. From now on the buttresses offer more continuous rock and have an excellent and concentrated selection of low-grade routes. Some of them have long runouts, so a cool head is often needed, while the longer routes on Tower Buttress will bring a smile to the face of jaded mountaineers.
Approach: a) 3 minutes, b) 25 minutes.

20 Ralph's Mantelshelves HVD 4a 1951–57
8m From the bottom right-hand end of the buttress, trend up and left by a series of ledges. The top one, in particular, is a full-on belly-flopper. A fine variation makes the hard start then continues up the right-hand wall of the buttress on surprising holds (**Ralph's Direct**, HVD 4a, 2002).

21 Lighthouse HVD ★ 1951–57
10m After a tricky start, follow a beckoning line of shallow grooves in the centre of the buttress from toe to top.

22 Substance VS 4c 1978
8m The left arête, climbed on its steep left-hand side, is tricky and quite intense.

The next four routes are based on, in and around the gloomy recess to the left: **Trio Chimney** (VD, 1951–57) is the short but enjoyable chimney in the right-hand corner. Start inside the cleft and remember to exit before it closes off. **Recess Wall and Arête** (HVS 4c, 2002) smears up the centre of the recess then the sharp arête above and left. **Square Chimney** (D, 1951–57) is the chimney in the left-hand corner, with a well-protected crux at the top. **Left Twin Crack** (HS 4a, 1951–57) begins 2m up Square Chimney, then follows a groove and crack to the left. Entertaining while it lasts.

23 Shortcomings E1 5c ★★ 1978
10m The attractive wall and beckoning flake provide a superb challenge. However, the route is well-named: the lower section is tricky and both making and protecting the crucial move to the flake are very height-dependent.

Skyline Trio Buttress

Rassp! (E2 5c, 1995) follows Shortcomings to the break then moves rightwards to finish up the wall. The climbing and rock are good, but it lacks the stature of its neighbours.

24 Safety Net E1 5b ★★★   1975
10m The blunt rib beneath an even grander roof is gained via a powerful, undercut, boulder problem start. A thought-provoking but well-protected move gains the roof. From here layback your way to glory!

25 Pebbles on a Wessex Beach E3 6a   1982
10m Ascend the centre of the short wall just to the left to the roof. With a runner in Safety Net, make a huuuge reach for the much wider and more flared flake crack above and left and storm up it. Quite low in the grade.

26 Paul's Puffer E4 6b   1989
7m Follow the crack just left directly up and over the roof, finishing up the wide crack above. This may also be reached more traditionally by an awkward traverse from the grim recess on the left (**Hank's Horror**, E1 5c, 1963).

Central Traverse (HS 4a, 1951–57), is a good problem that traverses this buttress, from Letter Box Gully to Square Chimney, using the half-height break.

27 Letter Box Gully M   1951–57
10m The slabs leading up to the huge jammed block couldn't be easier. From here, grovel your way through the gap under the block. Not for the big boned. The short crack on the right gives a VD with an awkward finish.

28 Letter Box Cracks VS 4c   1957–68
7m Choose either of the cracks beside the jammed block above the gully, or maybe both.

29 Topaz E2 5b ★★   1979
10m Just to the left, a rib leads straightforwardly enough to the roof. The crack above provides good holds leading rapidly up to the ramp and a suddenly rather exciting position. Fortunately, good protection in the crack and a safe fall-out zone provide the confidence needed to handle it. Usually.

30 Strain Station E4 5c   1981
12m A worrying proposition, climbing the roof and blunt arête to the left. It is gained direct or from the right. Difficult, and possibly unrepeated.

31 Rowan Tree Traverse VD   1951–57
15m From 5m up Topaz, ascend a long way leftwards to gain a ledge and a final layback crack.

32 Middleton's Motion VS 5a ★   1957–68
10m A character-building lead with a wild finish. Bisect the previous route at a small cave to finish via an obstinate crack.

33 Spectrum VS 4c   1977
8m Quite a technical route, which gains the finish of Rowan Tree Traverse via a faint groove.

34 Bad Sneakers E2 5c ★   1977
8m The beckoning slab to the left requires balance, bottle and actually quite good sneakers. Purists will climb direct up the middle (E3 5c), pragmatists will trend slightly left (and the floundering will veer rapidly to the arête).

Staffordshire Grit

Going to Extremes

One of the biggest barriers in climbing, is breaking into **Extreme** climbing. The magical E1 can seem off-putting. As a help, here are some routes of HVS that should prepare a leader for all the skills needed to climb E1, and then some good E1s to get started on. Some climbers may find the E1s easier than the HVSs, so don't be put off.

HVS
- **Delstree**, a steep and pumpy test in jamming;
- **Mantis**, good arête laybacking, an essential technique for harder grit;
- **Boysen's Delight**, as technical as they come, with perfect pro;
- **The Crippler**, get used to that brutality fella me lad;
- **Bengal Buttress**, bold and holdless, a feature of Extreme.

E1
- **Encouragement**, 2 pitches, spread the load;
- **Slowhand**, with a short bold section;
- **Safety Net**, a good fair climb;
- **Wild Thing**, a beautifully obscure test of boulder and bold.
- **Brown's Crack**, just in case you were starting to think E1s were easy; they're not!

35 Spare Rib VS 4b ★   1977
8m The rib left of the gully, started from its base on its left side, gives technical climbing requiring a bold head to reach and leave the mid-height protection.

36 The Black Pig VS 4c ★★   1957–68
8m Use the chimney to make initial vertical progress (the pedantic direct start is 5c) but forsake this as soon as possible in favour of the thin, rightwards-slanting crack. The VS climber's London Wall, but not as well protected!

37 Ogden Recess VD   1957–68
8m Follow the chimney in its entirety. Good fun.

38 Ogden Arête HS 4b ★★   1957–68
8m The left side of the clean-cut arête has a steep, technical and rather blind start and an airy finish.

39 Ogden HD   1951–57
10m The well-trodden path up the crack gives good practice for the harder lines in the area. **Cold Man's Finger** (E1 5b, 1992) is a direct up the slab to the left.

40 Oversight VD   1968–73
10m A good climb at the grade. The left arête of the stony gully, without sticking to any particular side. **Wad Man Slang** (S 4a, 2000) is a disappointing crack just to the right.

41 Bad Poynt D   1968
7m Start 3m to the left at a perched block and climb up it to a slab and crack.

Skyline Cave Buttress

Tower Buttress
This is the tall jutting buttress to the left.

42 Thrug VS 4c ★★ 1957–68
10m The steep crack splitting the right wall has escaped from Ramshaw. It gives a perfect test of jamming and definitely has a macho air about it.

43 Shrug E2 5b 1998
8m Climb the right arête of the first small pillar. From the top of the pillar climb directly up the wall passing two flakes, the second larger than the first.

44 Perched Block Arête VD 4a ★ 1951–57
15m A powerful line following the arête, climbed largely on its right, from its lowest point to the top block from where it becomes necessary to either gain a final chimney on the left or press straight on (VS 4b). Another alternative is to move right in search of a fine layback flake at HVS 4c.

45 Tower Chimney D ★ 1945
18m The flaky frontal chimney of the tower is a long, traditional treat. Starting up the right-hand groove is equally good. The bold may prefer to wander left along the top ledge to tackle the nose of the buttress at S.

46 Tower Face E1 5b ★★ 1977
15m A classic hard route. The flaky crack leads to a slanting break and crucial protection. The awkward short crack leads to a bold stretch to sloping holds. Finish directly up another flaky groove. Excellent, but not to be underestimated.

47 Curiosity Kitten E3 6a ★ 1999
15m Climb the arête left of Tower Face, over a roof to a break, and a meeting with Tower Eliminate, gear. Move right onto the face and follow the bold arête above.

48 Tower Eliminate HVS 5b ★ 1967
15m Around the arête to the left, a steep disjointed crack-line leads to a niche. From here, either finish up another crack or, better, move right onto the arête. Strangely gratifying. The wall to the left of this, past sloping ledges and a crack, is **Sorcerer's Apprentice**, E1 5b (1978).

Cave Buttress

About 25m left is the first of the connoisseur buttresses on the Skyline. The lack of traffic hereabouts is not justified and such route names as 'Cave Crack' and 'Cave Arête' ought to be irresistible! Approach: a) 5 minutes, b) 25 minutes.

49 Joiner HVD 3c 1951–57
9m An impressively clean, technical arête, taking the little groove on the right at the top. Quite bold. Even more so if finished direct.

50 Connector VS 5b traditional/1978
9m The flake in the wall to the left gives an excellent problem start followed by a poor finish.

51 King Swing VS 5b traditional/1978
7m Start at the right-hand edge of the cave. After placing a sensible high runner, swing immediately round the arête to the right. Steep pulls gain the excellent finishing slab.

52 Cave Crack HVS 5a ★ 1957–68
6m Essential practice for all contemplating The Sloth. Climb to and up the major feature. Two alternative and rather artificial starts are available; the left arête of the initial groove (5c), or the **Mousetrap Start**, which traverses in from the left (5b).

53 Stephen HVS 5a ★ 1957–68
7m Short but brutal. Climb the carnivorous crack and overhanging groove springing from the left edge of the cave. **Automatix** (E2 5b, 1981) starts just right and follows flakes rightwards to the finish of Cave Crack.

Staffordshire Grit

54 Cave Arête HVD 4a ★   1951–57
14m Another really good route. Starting from the lowest point of the buttress, follow the arête to a ledge. Take to the slab on the left for a while, before finishing, in a good position, back on the arête itself. A direct finish is possible at 4a. **Cave Buttress** (VD, 1951–57) gains the ledge from a short corner, then goes left to finish up a crack. Poor.

Battle through the jungle for 65m leftwards, or just walk pleasantly over the top, to reach a little buttress containing:

55 Capstan's Corner HD   1951–57
8m The pleasant right edge of the buttress.

56 Mistaken Identity S 4a   1951–57
10m To the left is a greasy groove with a slab to its left. Climb the slab then tackle the roof on either side (harder on the left).

57 Sally James VS 4c   1979
10m The left arête of the buttress, 10m further on. As pert as ever.

Skyline Buttress

A further 50m left is the most impressive face that the Skyline area has to offer. It has a good selection of long classics, guaranteed not to disappoint, but unfortunately a few routes that are now too overgrown to be enjoyable. It is best approached from above, descending steeply either side of the buttress.
Approach: a) 10 minutes, b) 20 minutes.

58 Slips E3 6b ★   1982
8m The undercut right arête of the buttress is begun from the slab below. Hard-as-nails moves are needed to reach the sloping crack further left, the upper arête, and the sanctuary of Slab and Arête. The Strapadictomy of western grit!

59 Skytrain E1 5b ★   1977
10m The leftwards-leaning crack provides a pleasantly technical outing leading onto Slab and Arête. Finish up this. The original continues rather artificially up the slab to a bold finish at E2.

60 Slab and Arête S 4a ★★★   1945
18m A classic route that builds to an exposed crescendo. At this grade, avoid the now-polished and desperate start up the pocketed slab by moving in from the left. Traverse the half-height break all the way to a memorable finish up the right edge of the buttress: *see photo opposite*.

61 Acid Drop E4 5c ★★★   1973
15m A gem that could have escaped from Bosigran. Climb above the traverse of Slab and Arête (which provides distant runners) to the arching overlap. From here make the famously height-dependent move to gain a good hold (6b for proficient shorties, and E5) to thank-God gear under the roof, which provides a baffling but enjoyable contrast.

62 Drop Acid E4 6a ★   1987
15m Follow a series of thin flakes up the slab just left of the arching overlap of Acid Drop to reach the roof. Pull over and finish direct. A side-runner in Abstract protects.

63 Karabiner Cracks M   1945
12m The cracks and chimney to the left. Finishing over the roof and up the crack just right is also a good exercise (**Abstract**, HVS 5a, 1957–68). Yet more adventure can be had by continuing the traverse all the way under the roof to the finish of Slab and Arête (**Poodle Vindaloo**, E2 5c, 1982).

64 Karabiner Slab VS 4c   1957–68
12m The central line on the slab left of the crack. Quite bold and high in the grade.

65 Karabiner Chimney HVD ★   1945
12m The chimney on the left is pleasant right to the very end.

Jon Barton on Slab and Arête, S (opposite page), one of the top ten easier leads at the Roaches. Photo: Adam Long.

Staffordshire Grit

66 Enigma Variation E1 5a ★★ 1976
10m A bold but well-behaved route. Balance across to the lovely right arête and follow it by straightforward moves in a bold position to a useful knobble and a gear placement a little too far round the arête for comfort. Move up and then break out left onto the slab.

67 Mantelshelf Slab VS 4b ★ 1947
10m A character-building slab climb. The central line up the slab involves a technical mantelshelf and continues into bolder and bolder (though easier and easier) territory.

68 Bilberry Traverse VS 4b 1945
35m A mid-height traverse from the gully bounding the buttress on the right to Mantelshelf Slab. Traverse left to the arête and reverse Slab and Arête to reach Karabiner Chimney. Precariously cross Enigma Variation (crux, runner above) to the ledge of Mantelshelf Slab. Finish up this.

69 Come Girl HVS 4c 1968–73
13m The blocky rib, 5m left of Mantelshelf Slab, finishing at a crack. Increasingly bold and currently rather dirty. **Go Girl** (HVD, 1968–73), allegedly climbs the very vegetated cracks 2m left leading to the finish of Come Girl, while **Lost Girl** (HVS 5a, 1999) starts as for Go Girl and cuts a swathe left to reach a pleasant undercut slab. Place protection on the left of the slab, then move across rightwards and tackle the bulge above by use of a flake.

The Pinnacle

This is an elegant pillar slightly lower and to the left.

70 Pinnacle Arête VS 4c ★ 1945
6m The right arête of The Pinnacle is a real beauty with one particularly perplexing, and not well-protected, move. **Pinnacle Slab** (HVD, 1951-57) is the undistinguished slab up and to the right, finishing at the top of the main edge.

There is reportedly 'some trivial fun to be had on the slab and thin crack just to the left' (**Split Personality**, E1 5b, 1979). However, if done at all directly, the steep slab is very much harder than this.

71 Pinnacle Crack D 1949–51
7m The wide crack bounding the left side of The Pinnacle's front face.

"Whilst never very difficult, the route offers no really positive straws for which the floundering may grasp."
Andy Popp, 1989 guide. Adam Long soloing San Melas, E3 5c (page 123). Photo: Mark Sharratt.

Staffordshire Grit

Alpha Buttress

Yet another fine buttress packed with quality lines lies 30m left. While the crag is not very tall, the routes here definitely pack a punch.
Approach: a) **10 minutes,** b) **20 minutes.**

72 Looking for Today HVS 5b   1976
7m Struggle up the blind crack and bulge to reach the useful thin flake and easy ground.

73 Right-Hand Route S 4a ★   1951–57
12m Climb the crack and chimney until a traverse left leads to the right-most of two flakes in the upper wall. Continuously interesting.

74 Definitive Gaze E1 5c   1979
10m Balance up into a scoop and make a tricky exit on the left. Finish direct avoiding the flakes of neighbouring routes. Leaving the scoop on the right and finishing directly is **Wicked Wind** (E3 5c, 1989).

75 Wallaby Wall S 4a   1951–57
10m An awkward start leads to an excellent series of moves up the wall to a ledge and then across to the left-hand of the two upper flakes.

76 39th Step E2 6a   1979
8m The shallow groove and slab 3m to the left, trending slightly rightwards and with a runner in the crack on the left.

77 Sennapod Crack VD   traditional
8m Hurry up the crack just right of the easy corner. It goes with less of a struggle than you might have been expecting.

78 Sennapod D   1978
7m The corner on the left.

79 Bounty Killer VS 5a   1996
7m Climb the flaky cracks in the side-wall of the next buttress, right of the arête.

Just left is an impressive slab divided at around half-height by a wide break. This provides welcome holds but scant protection for its routes.

80 Mantis HVS 5b ★★   1974
8m The clean arête is begun on its right by steep, technical laybacking above a gnarly landing. Protection arrives unhelpfully late and the upper arête, taken on its left, is more straightforward: highball V1. Starting the route by laybacking the arête on the left is a good alternative: E1 5c (V2).

81 Hallow to our Men E4 6b ★   1981
4m In the bottom centre of the slab, a shallow scoop provides the starting point for desperate climbing on the smallest of edges. Unfortunately, independence is lost at the break but continuing up San Melas gives a very sustained outing: highball V4.

Skyline Alpha Buttress

82 San Melas E3 5c ★★ 1977
8m Pebble-pulling up the lower slab, slightly to the left, gains the break. Place protection, take a deep breath, and commit yourself to a series of high steps and rockovers, with very little in the way of handholds. Pleasant balancy exercise for gritstone divas, but nail-ripping desperation for thugs: *see photo on page 121.*

83 Days Gone By S 4b 1978
7m The right-hand of three close parallel cracks. Quite hard if done strictly, but suffers from its interfering easier neighbour.

84 Breakfast Problem VD ★ 1951–57
7m The merging twin cracks to the left provide tons of protection, and good climbing as well. A popular first lead.

85 Formative Years E3 6a 1982
7m The cute slab to the left looks temptingly escapable. Oddly, it is an altogether different story when high up above the unfriendly landing!

86 Alpha Arête HVD 1957–68
7m The blocky left arête of the green corner. Sweet but bold.

87 Alpha D 1951–57
7m The small groove on the left. Hard work but well-protected.

88 Devotoed VS 4c ★ 1979
7m The crack leads to an silly sloping finish on the left wall of Alpha.

89 Rodeo E1 6a 1993
7m The blunt overhanging rib 2m left is ascended using a skin-ripping jam and leads to a mantelshelf directly above to finish.

90 Melaleucion VS 5a ★ 1976
7m Steep climbing over the bulges on the front face. A tough gem.

91 Omega S 4b 1957–68
7m Start just left and make a hard pull over a bulge to find yourself faced with a belly-flop on the right.

92 Bone Idol VS 4c ★ 1977
33m Yet another routine buttress traverse, but what a buttress to traverse! Start at Omega and finish on Right-Hand Route. Fun.

Thirty metres left of Alpha Buttress is a large broken and vegetated buttress. This has no routes but the weird pinnacles on the top tier and the slabs just left give some good low grade problems. The left-most slab is particularly good.

Staffordshire Grit

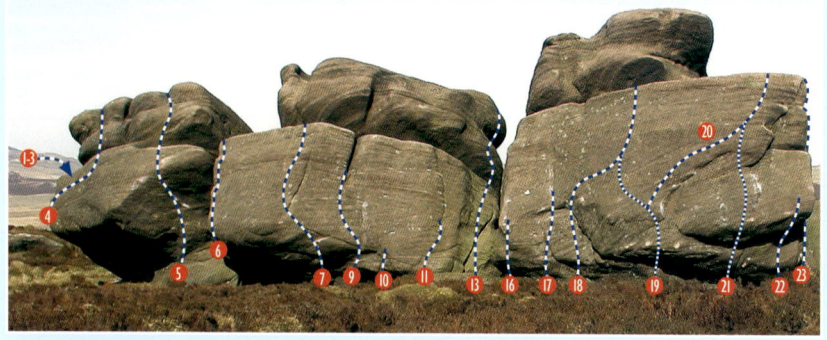

Doxey's Pool

A really classy venue, sat high on the Roaches ridge, with great views over miles of farmland towards the Cheshire plains in front, and wild lonely moorland behind. The climbing is good, powerful and rounded. Landings are perfect, although sometimes are boggy at the left side. The skin on the rock is thin, so treat it with respect, especially where brushing is concerned.

1 V5 (6b)
Up the bulging arête at the back to the roof. Traverse right. If you top out, then report yourself to the local police right away.

2 Left Cheek V1 (5a)
Climb the left arête of the crack.

3 Soggy Bottom Crack V4 (5b)
Overcome all odds and jam out from the back of the crack.

4 V5 (6b)
From a rounded hold by the crack, swing right to the front face and move up.

5 Staffordshire Flyer V4 (6a)
A Doxey's classic, crimping left to the steep arête.

6 The Arête V5 (6b)
Starting low from undercuts is V7.

7 Drowning Pool V7 (6c)
Start from a rounded hold down and right and somehow gain the blind flakeline above. From a standup it is V4.

8 Another Nadin Traverse V9(7a)
Holy moly, who the hell is this Nadin anyway? From the low start of 6, traverse the lip to finish up 7: see *photo on opposite page*.

9 Groovy Crack V0 (5b)

10 Chipped Wall V0- (4b)

11 Flake V1 (5b)

12 V1 (5b)
From the thin flake, delicately traverse the buttress to finish up 6.

13 V0– (4b)
Climb the slanting crack then up the wall.

14 V5 (6b)
Up the sloping sidewall past a pocket.

15 Arête on Left V4 (6b)

16 Arête on Right V2 (5b)
Use the flake. Avoiding the flake gives a V5 problem.

17 Blind Flake V2 (5c)
Climb without using the arête.

18 V6 (6b)
Squirm up and right to a small pocket on the slab.

19 V5 (6b)
Step up, then inch left to the same pocket.

20 V3 (6a)
Climb the feature rightwards to the top.

21 Little Flake V3 (6a)
Thugging into this from jams and undercuts is V5.

22 Bulging Arête V2 (5c)
Start on undercuts for an eye-popping V5.

23 V0– (4c)
Jam the nice crack then continue up the arête.

Skyline Doxey's Pool

24 Easy Arête V0− (4a)

25 Pancake V0- (4c)

26 Li'l Crack V0− (4a)
The arête to the right is similarly pleasant.

EA Baker and the Kyndwr Club
were walking the Skyline one hot summer day and happened upon Doxey's Pool. "The very picture of coolness. We could not resist." Two dived in and struck out for the middle. "Out there the bottom was spongy, and seemed to be covered with an oozy accumulation of decayed peat, which, on being stirred up, discharged a violent odour, as if some noisome explosion had gone off."
Moors, Crags and Caves, 1903

Doxey's Pool is a phenomenon

because it has no water coming in to it, it is on top of a hill, yet it never dries up. It is said the pool is bottomless, and it links up to the Blakemere several miles away by subterranean passages.

These pools are inhabited by a mermaid, one of the few inland mermaids in the country. The pool is named after Doxey, daughter of Bess of Rock Hall, who was renowned for her singing, which was said to be foreign and melancholy. She was taken away one night by men who were sheltering in the caves, was raped and then drowned in the pool.

Below: Martin Dearden on Another Nadin Traverse, V10 (opposite page). Photo: Niall Grimes.

Not So Far Skyline Buttress

About 100m beyond Alpha Buttress, twin stone gateposts will be found by the top path. Just beyond these, a faint path leads down under the trees and right (facing out) along to a small but steep buttress with a central green overhang at its base. The top of the buttress is marked by a large castellated boulder by the path.

At the right end **Three Tier Buttress** (VS 4b, 2003) starts off the flake and pulls up to a crack on the right. About 5m left is an attractive bouldery overhang with a huge jug that begs to be dangled from (**Monstrous Angel**, HS 4b, 2003). The highest part of the buttress is just about big enough for a couple of slightly more substantial routes.

93 Not So Fast VS 5a   2003
7m Start at the sculpted slab left of the big roof, below twin cracks through a small overhang. Pull through to a good break and then wobble up the awkward rounded finish.

94 Not So Steep VD   2003
7m Five metres left, a juggy prow leads steeply to a wide crack. From the ledge above, the deceptively short but ungradable offwidth provides an excellent comedy finish to either route. The left arête of the buttress gives a good climb on good holds (**Not Much Further**, VD, 2003).

Rugged individualists seeking an unusual adventure will make straight for the next routes. Approximately 150m beyond the stone gateposts, an overhanging prow of a boulder, engraved 'TH' will be found on the left of the path. From here descend 20m downhill, and the route is hidden 20m across to the left from this.

95 Don't Go Down to the Woods Today
HS 4b ★   1989
8m Or if you do, be sure to tell your mum where you're off to. Neat moves lead up the middle of the surprisingly clean slab to an angled break and a step left to the gap in the cornice. Good fun.

Thirty metres left, at the same level, is another buttress with a small cave.

96 Deep in Mystery E1 5b   1989
7m Pull over the overhang left of the cave and climb the pocketed slab to an unnerving mantelshelf.

Chasm Boulders

These boulders are to be found along the path in the region of Far Skyline Buttress, a couple of hundred metres beyond Doxey's Pool. They are slightly obscure, but are found in a spot just after the main track divides, in-between the two paths. It is a nice little clutch of short problems, although the surface can be a little crunchy. An interesting venue, one of the few areas in the Roaches where the rock will actually spot you. However, while it is also likely to encourage you and console you, it is unlikely to share the driving.

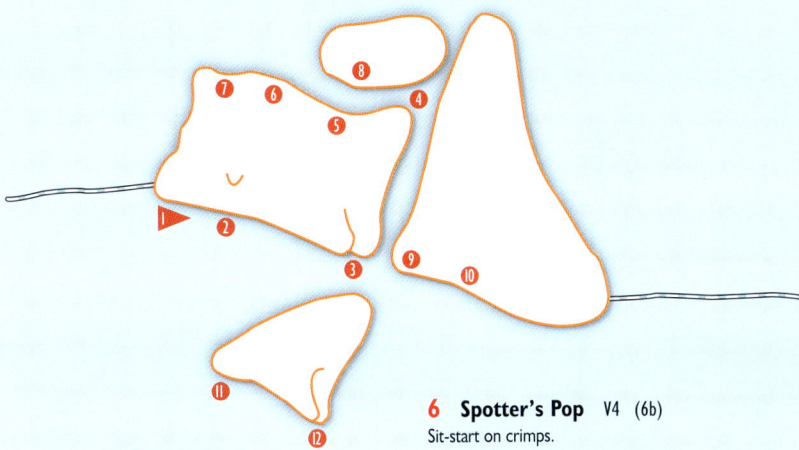

1   Chasm Crinkle Project
Traverse the lip from slopers on the left, along the beautiful crinkly feature, to the arête.

2   Gritstone Pimple   V4   (6a)
Pull over, aiming for the spot. Scary.

3   Ramp   V0   (5a)
Climb the ramp to the arête. The topout is escaped to the right. If you do the top direct, award yourself a medal.

4   Acne Arête   V6   (6c)
A tasty morsel up the hanging arête. If you are pumped, then lean back. The sit-start is V7 (6c), using a round hold and a heel-hook on the left, although you'll need to tuck your knees in to avoid resting on the side wall on the left, especially if someone is watching.

5   Squeezer's Spots   V5   (6b)
From a sit-start.

6   Spotter's Pop   V4   (6b)
Sit-start on crimps.

7   Pussin' Boots   V5   (6b)
Start sitting, with feet on the back flakes.

8   Spotter's Slop   V6   (6b)
Climb from the sloper to the top. Can be dynoed at V7 (6c).

9   Mantel   V1   (5b)

10   Harder Mantel   V3   (6a)
Totally holdless, unfortunately.

11   V0   (5a)
Climb past the round feature on the wall to the arête.

12   Triptych Groove   V7   (6b)
The groove and arête are climbed from a sit start. A real thuggy, technical classic.

Staffordshire Grit

Far Skyline Buttress

Just beyond the Chasm Boulders, the flat top of the crag can be found. An awkward descent reaches a steep buttress characterised by a roof at 2m height in its centre. The first route on the buttress is 5m right of this roof. Due to the proximity of trees and the lack of traffic, the starts of some of the routes can be somewhat vegetated. Despite the bushwhacking, the upper sections of most of the routes manage to justify the struggle. **Approach:** a) 15 minutes, b) 15 minutes.

97 The Black Ram S 4a   1970
11m The crack and square-cut groove 4m left of a small, leftwards slanting chimney has several green inhabitants. Fortunately there are steep cracks in good rock above.

98 Black Ram Arête VS 4c   1970
11m Start 3m left, by making a heroic mantelshelf onto a tiny ledge 1m off the ground. Step right to reach and climb a thin crack. All this leads to a vegetated ledge below the final attractive arête.

99 Dangler VS 4b ★   1970
11m From the same small ledge on Black Ram Arête, head directly up the almost non-existent crack on surprising holds to one of the more obvious runner placements in the area. After powering over the bulge, the hairline cracks in the slab above provide a satisfying prelude to topping out.

100 The Chimney VS 4b   1969
11m A powerful start involving muscular laybacking, or rubber limbs, enables the chimney right of the roof to be climbed. Currently rather choked with heather.

101 Entente Cordiale E3 6a ★   1981
12m After a dynamic start directly over the central roof, step left and climb the left arête by an engaging sequence of moves. From the wide break, smear boldly up the centre of the upper slab. A little wandering but with some memorable climbing.

102 Honky Tonk HS 4c ★★   1969
12m Thrash up the deep, V-cleft immediately left of the roof. Stretch tenuously right onto the lip of the overhang. Pausing only to savour the improbable exposure, head right for the arête which gives pleasant climbing before the top. **Steeplechase Crack** (HVD, 1970) is the dirty, vegetated crack that cuts through a square niche just left.

103 Dazzler S 4a ★   1970
8m The twin, thin cracks residing in another shallow niche provide another tricky start. Fortunately, sideways jug pulling, good protection and sinker jams await. **Mudhopper** (VD, 1970) is the grassy left-slanting groove on the left.

104 Slither HS 4b   1970
8m Climb the attractive slab and deceptive hanging groove 3m left of Mudhopper.

105 Steeplechaser D ★   1970
8m Climb an open corner to an overhang, which is hurdled on the left.

106 Tree Grooves HVD   1970
7m Climb the groove round the corner, or the slab to its left, to a second, easier, groove.

107 Tree Corner VD   1970
7m The corner and overhang behind the dead tree. This is often a bit dirty, a much better variant steps left and climbs the clean arête at the same grade

108 Chronicle VS 5b   1979
7m The overlap and slab just right of the end of the crag.

109 Flutterbye Grooves HS 4a 1969
7m From the left-hand end of the crag gain wispy cracks from the left or, better and harder, direct. Follow the cracks.

110 Microcosm HD 1979
7m A groove on the left moving right onto the front of the buttress at the top.

111 The Girdle Traverse HS 4a ★ 1970
30m A high, clean and exposed traverse of this buttress can be had. A poorer, low-level version is HS 4b.

The Very Far Skyline Area

The buttresses from this point onwards contain some of the finest routes in the area. While many are the preserve of the more experienced climber, there are several gems open to all comers. Approach: a) 15 minutes, b) 15 minutes.

Art Nouveau

A small clutch of boulders on the crag side of the path announce your arrival. These are the Art Nouveau Boulders (see next page). The slab below contains a hard classic and a filler-in. For a little relaxation, there is always **Transcendental Medication** *(D, 2001) on the slabby arête some 20m to its right.*

112 Pop Art HVS 5a 1989
7m From just right of Art Nouveau, step up right to stretch for a good hold near the arête. From here good holds lead straight to the top. Bold and smart moves, although easily escapable. **Coma Sutra** (HVD 4b, 2001) is the pocketed slab and scoop 5m left of the main slab.

Skyline Very Far Skyline

Gus' Slab Exams

The Roaches has long been seen as the capital of gritstone smearing, and rightly so. However, the holdless, and sometimes bold, nature of this style of climbing can sometimes terrify the uninitiated. For this reason, here's a little curriculum of slab test-pieces to help you along your way. Do 6 of them, and you are competent. Nine, and you are sticky. Do all 12, and you will never need another hold ever again.

Maud's Garden, VD – a pleasant introduction with a bold start; **Slab and Arête**, HS – a longer route to test you. But can you handle the exposure? **Technical Slab**, HS – flexibility always comes in handy on slabs. The holds are there, but how will you reach them? **Condor Slab**, VS – a good taster of the type of cerebral control needed to progress up the list; **Mantelshelf Slab**, VS – another example of the steadiness required for a runout; **Prelude to Space**, HVS – now you really are the proud owner of a cool head; **Hawkwing**, E1 – it's all coming together nicely now; **Elegy**, E2 – a tricky combination of faith in friction and a long runout to test your determination; **San Melas**, E3 – time to test that flexibility we talked about; **Wings of Unreason**, E4 – your slab skills will get you into an interesting position, but do you trust them enough to smear your way up. I'd just jump! **Counterstroke of Equity**, E5 – may require the ability to see footholds where others can't; **Obsession Fatale**, E7 – oh no! It's all gone wrong, you've gone mad!

Art Nouveau Boulders ▼

Chasm Boulders ▼

▲ Art Nouveau

▲ Far Skyline Buttress

Staffordshire Grit

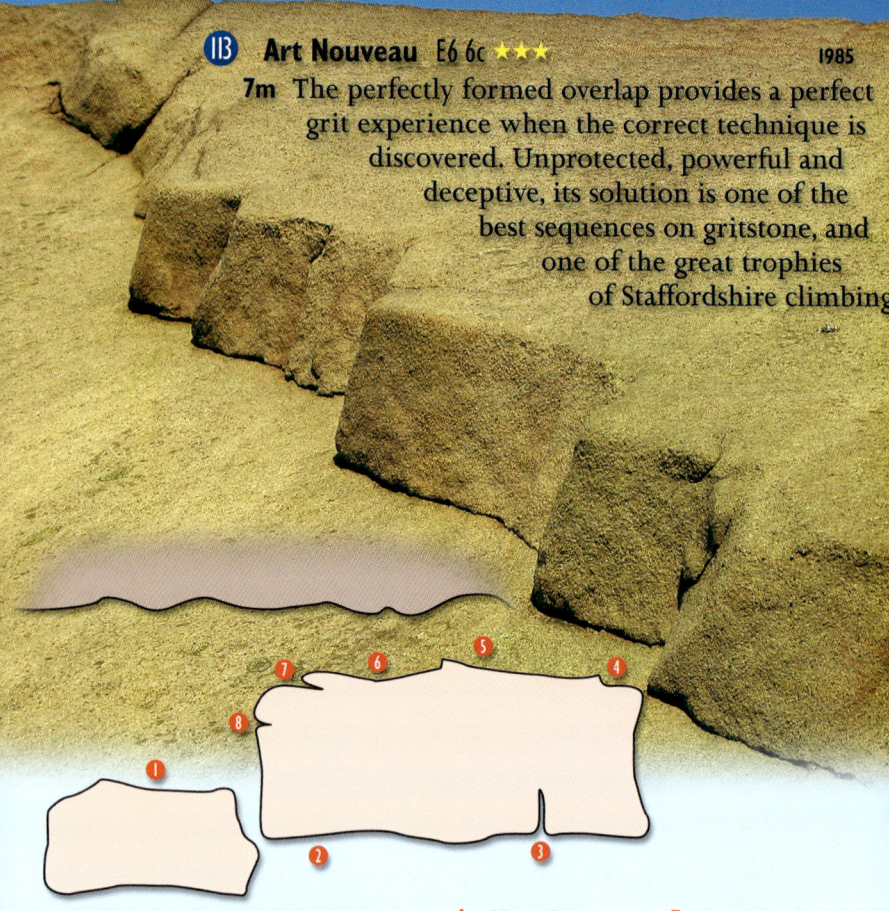

B **Art Nouveau** E6 6c ★★★ 1985
7m The perfectly formed overlap provides a perfect grit experience when the correct technique is discovered. Unprotected, powerful and deceptive, its solution is one of the best sequences on gritstone, and one of the great trophies of Staffordshire climbing.

Art Nouveau Boulders

Ah, Skyline grit. Is there anything finer? A limited number of good problems on very clean rock. A worthwhile venue on a longer circuit. The boulders are set on the crag side of the path right above Art Nouveau.

1 Mono Slab
V0− (4c)

2 Sidepull Wall
V7 (6c)

3 Crack V0− (4b)

4 Flaky Romp
V0 (5a)

5 Project
The wall left of the groove. Spotter advised.

6 Project
Open V-groove. 1 hold. 2 spotters.

7 Juggy Flakeline
V0+ (5a)

8 Crack and Arête
V3 (5c)

Skyline Very Far Skyline Buttress

Very Far Skyline Buttress

The final two buttresses are both similar, undercut at their base, above which perfectly formed slabs and grooves give sublime climbing. The first, and slightly smaller of the two, is 100m left of Art Nouveau.

114 Mild Thing D   1977
7m From the propped flake, climb the unsatisfying cracks above. Worth it for the name alone.

115 Script for a Tear E6 6c   1985
7m From the same starting point, step left onto the lip of the undercut slab and smear desperately upwards. This is made a much better route by smearing in along the lip from Wild Thing.

116 Wild Thing E1 5c ★★   1977
7m There are no such things as reach problems, just strength problems. From the large jug pocket, reach a distant edge by technical mastery and hydraulic arm strength, or a bunk up, and attain a standing position. A great V2. The groove that follows provides perfect delicate movement, where the confident can choose which pockets to eliminate.

117 Entropy's Jaw E5 6b ★★★   1982
7m From the standing position on the previous route, step delicately right to climb the thin seam by even thinner smearing, thumb sprags, and brilliant footwork. An RP may be placed en-route although the route is often soloed: *see photo on page 132*.

118 Triple Point E1 5c ★   1982
7m After the start of Wild Thing, step through onto the left arête and follow it by some great moves. A direct start up the left side of the arête is 6b.

119 The Calf Path E2 6b   1991
12m From the propped flake of Mild Thing, traverse left above the lip, finishing up Triple Point. Really just an excuse to climb more perfect rock.

120 Mr Decisive HVS 5b   1989
7m Five metres left of the slab is a jutting flake. The slabby arête is climbed on its left-hand side.

121 Curvature VS 4c   1979
6m About 5m left is an arête on a pointy boulder. Climb the arête on its left. Ten metres left again **The Parrot and the Balaclava** (HS 4b, 1989) takes the undercut slabby wall and **Very Connoisseurish** (E2 6a, traditional/1970s) takes the arête of this wall direct with blinkers (as a VS 4b variation start just left).

Simon Wilson questing into deep water on one of the most beautiful bits of friction climbing in the area, Entropy's Jaw. This tasty E5 6b (page 131) takes bouldering skills to a height where you'd definitely rather not fall off. Photo: Adam Long.

Some Staffordshire Highballs

With people going higher and higher above bouldering mats these days in search of thrill and spills, the line between boulder problems and routes is becoming ever more blurred. As such, here is a list of high boulder problems and micro-routes that fit into this blurred area. But be warned – just because something has a bouldering grade doesn't mean you can fall off it and walk away. Some of these are serious and still have high E grades despite low bouldering grades. To get an idea of the seriousness of any particular highball, subtract the square root of the E grade from the from the cube root of the V grade, throw yourself off the top and see how much it hurts. Good luck.

About E8
The Young Pretender V9 (HEN)
Ultimate Sculpture V9 (RAM)
Cornelius V9 (INA)

About E7
Cornelina V7 (INA)

About E6
Thumbeina V6 (INA)
Script for a Tear V7 (SKY)
Pie Hard V8 (WRI)
The Pride V6 (SDQ)
Art Nouveau V6 (SKY)

About E5
Apache Dawn V7 (RCH)
The Warp V7 (WRI)
Entropy's Jaw V4 (SKY)
Solitaire V5 (BOS)
Gibbering Wreck V8 (GIB)
Catastrophe International V6 (RCH)

About E4
Force Nine V6 (RAM)
Touch V7 (HEN)
Ina City Riot V4 (INA)
California Screamin' V8 (RAM)
Bareback Rider V4 (RCH)
Pindles Numb V6 (RCH)
Leather Joy Boys V8 (NST)
Particle Exchange V6 (RCH)
Always Dreaming V4 (5CL)

Crystal Voyager V8 (NTH)
Metaphysical Scoop V4 (NTH)
Hallow to our Men V5 (SKY)
Willow Farm V3 (SKY)
The Fatalist's Canoe V4 (OLD)

About E3
The Dignity of Labour V6 (RCH)
The Cube V5 (RCH)
This Poison V5 (HEN)
Ram Air V8 (RAM)
Tierdrop V6 (RAM)
Puffed Up V7 (NST)
The Gateless Gate V4 (OLD)
Qui Vive V4 (OLD)

About E2
Midge V3 (RAM)
Summit Arête V5 (BOS)
The Ultra Direct V5 (RAM)
Gib V5 (GIB)
Be Calmed V6 (RAM)
Milky Buttons V7 (5CL)
Stokesline V4 (HEN)
Charlie's Overhang V3 (NST)

About E1
Gully Arête V1 (RAM)
Sneeze V2 (RAM)
The Fin V5 (GIB)
Magic Roundabout Super Direct V2 (RAM)
Extended Torrture V4 (GIB)

Foord's Folly V3 (RAM)
Triple Point V2 (SKY)
Nutted by Reality V4 (HEN)
Teck Crack Direct V5 (RCH)
Finger of Fate V4 (5CL)
Wild Thing V2 (SKY)
Starlight and Storm V6 (HEN)
Slimline V1 (HEN)
Gain Entry to Your Soul V4 (SDQ)
Robin Hood V4 (SDQ)
High Speed Imp Act V6 (DD)

About HVS
Equilibria V1 (RAM)
Magic Roundabout Direct V0- (RAM)
Roscoe's Wall V1 (RCH)
Boysen's Delight V2 (5CL)
Mantis V0+ (SKY)
Prelude to Space V0 (SKY)
Pink Flake V1 (RAM)
Crocodile Slot V1 (RAM)
Mr Grogan V1 (SHP)
Charley Farley V0 (SHP)
The Sly Mantelshelf V1 (NST)
Sly Direct V1 (NST)
Gibbon Take V1 (GIB)
Gib Torrture V2 (GIB)

VS and under
Comminist Crack V1 (5CL)
Marxist Undertones V2 (5CL)
The Yawn V0+ (GRD)

5CL – Five Clouds
BST – Baldstones
BOS – Bosley
DIM – Dimmings
GBH – Gradbach
GIB – Gib Torr
HC – Hen Cloud
INA – Ina's Rock
NST – Newstones
NTH – Nth Cloud
OLD – Oldridge
RAM – Ramshaw
RCH – Roaches
SDQ – Stoney Dale Quarry Area
SKY – Skyline
WRI – Wright's
SHP – Sharpcliffe

Alicia Hudelson on Prelude to Space, HVS 4c (opposite). This is the easiest route on the slab, but with its impeccible rock and fine bold moves, it is one you will return to again and again. Photo: Nick Smith.

Skyline Hard Very Far Skyline Buttress

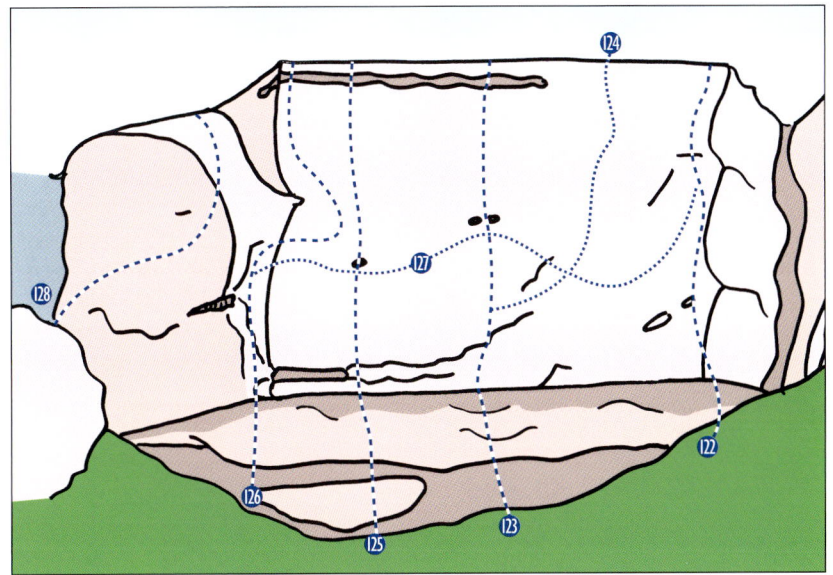

Hard Very Far Skyline Buttress

Forty metres on lies the centrepiece of the area. The rock on the fine slab is perfectly featured and provides a great choice of holds and means of ascent. Approach: a) 15 mins, b) 15 mins.

122 Prelude to Space HVS 4c ★★ 1977
10m A sample of the quality on offer hereabouts, at a more reasonable price. The right edge of the slab is unprotected and technical for the grade, involving excellent balancy moves: *see photo opposite*.

123 Wings of Unreason E4 6a ★★★ 1977
11m Brilliant, and appropriately named, taking the centre of the beautiful slab direct via unusual pockets. The powerful, undercut start probably constitutes the technical crux although the excitement undoubtedly lies above, involving an experience not available on any other route! Stretch monsters will have a significantly easier time than little people, but little people will, as usual, get to moan about it.

124 Counterstroke of Equity E5 6c ★ 1985
11m From the protection pocket on Wings, move back down, and right on a thin horizontal seam. From here, smear fiercely up the slab to a worrying top move, or a monster pendulum. For lovers of terror, **Counterstroke Direct**, E7 6c, climbs over the roof to gain the upper section directly, where you will sizzle like a fried egg, having avoided all holds and protection in Wings.

125 Nature Trail E5 6b ★★ 1985
11m To the left, a strenuous direct start through the roof leads onto the slab and protection in the pockets of the next route. From a standing position in these, smear directly to the top of the crag. Originally done with protection in Wings, easing the grade.

126 Track of the Cat E5 6a ★★★ 1977
12m One of the best routes at the Roaches, and for many people the best on grit, is based on the flying left arête of the slab. From around the corner slightly to the left, powerful moves lead into a groove and small protection. Careful climbing rightwards from here leads to a pull round onto the slab and twin pockets. The immaculate arête above culminates in a truly exhilarating final move, with the gear a distant memory.

Staffordshire Grit

127 Inspiration Point E2 5c ★   traditional
10m A great way to see this slab at a more reasonable grade starting up Track of the Cat, traversing the slab with hands in pockets, then down slightly to gain and finish up Prelude to Space.

128 Willow Farm E4 6a ★★   1977
10m To the left again the buttress is terminated by a neat little slab capped by a sloping gangway. Gain the right edge of this slab from the left and move up on tiny edges. A long reach over the top of the gangway may find a good hold, but some frantic yet precise footwork is required to reach easy ground. Worth three stars on any other buttress! *See photo on page 138.*

Very Far Boulders

Another classic set of boulders, good solid Skyline rock. The problems are seldom powerful, being more smeary and technical. Lower grade boulderers will find a lot to go at here. They are clearly visible from the top of hard Very Far Skyline Buttress.

1 V0 (5b)
The left arête of the small chasm behind the main boulders climbed direct. V0– (4c) starting from its left. A couple of dirty artificial lines lie to the right.

2 Rounded Arête V0– (4a)
Started from the left: V0 (5b) direct up the front.

3 Open Groove V0+ (5b)
Pull up the groove from its left, or take it more direct at V2 (5c).

4 Two Pocket Slab V2 (5c)
Climb past two small pockets to reach a short crack directly. Technical, demanding good footwork.

5 Lazy Trout V3 (6a)
Climb the tallest part of the slab to reach a deep pocket. A fine and natural variation trends right to the arête at V0 (5a).

6 V1 (5c)
Go up just left of the arête to reach the upper arête.

7 Max V2 (6a)
Clamp your way up the steep arête, full on. A tasty sit-start goes from the slot underneath, V7 (6b).

8 Crack V0– (4a)

136 The Roaches

Skyline Very Far Boulders

9 Harry Patch V1 (5b)
From the wide crack, pull left to deep pockets, and follow these over the bulge. Exciting, but positive.

10 Bernie V2 (6a)
Up the right side of the arête. Sitting starters can do a sit-start, V6 (6b)

11 Off-Fingers Crack V2 (5c)

12 Pinkies to Perkies V0– (4c)
Hell of a nice!

13 V0– (4a)
Pad up the delicate slab.

14 V1 (5c)
From beneath the arête, pull left and get established on the slab.

15 Inner Tube V4 (6a)
Sit-start. From hands in the big round hole, lurch upwards to the top.

16 Short Arête V0– (5a)

17 Wall and Rib V0– (4b)

18 Left Crack V0– (4c)

19 Right Crack V0– (4b)

20 Easy Ramp V0– (4a)

21 Flight Exam V1 (5c)
A peach. Climb the slab using the pocket for hands, feet and everything else. Essential practise for Wings of Unreason.

22 The Loner V2 (5c)
From the pocket, smear right and up, avoiding the top with your hands.

23 The Shepherd V5 (6b)
Technical and fingery climbing up the vague arête.

24 Leek Hills V4 (6a)
The right arête of the wall.

> The rocks above here have attracted climbers in the past. You are politely requested not to climb on these as they are friable and are eroding badly. Also, some of the area close by is sensitive for the protection of endangered species (wildlife, not human).

Crimps as crisp as diamonds, the rock the stuff of dreams. Another golden Staffordshire evening drinks down in the west while the snow that lingers in the shadows can do nothing to cool the glow you feel inside. Jon Fullwood savouring it all on Willow Farm, E4 6a (page 136). Photo: Adam Long

The Five Clouds

by Andi Turner

O.S. Ref. SK001625 | Altitude: 375m a.s.l.

The Five Clouds are the string of outcrops punctuating the subsidiary ridge below the Skyline area, clearly visible from the road leading to Roach End. These are little gems of crags that rank with the best to be found on the Skyline (from where it is clear that there are seven clouds, not five!). The grit is fine-grained, compact and sound, and formed into cracks, pockets, edges and scoops simply designed for climbing. The lines tend to be confident, straightforward challenges, often either steep forceful crack-lines or bald friction slabs. There is also a wealth of bouldering and a fine collection of micro-routes providing superb soloing for the competent. The setting gives the crags a delightfully peaceful and isolated ambience, heightened by almost guaranteed solitude, making the area feel a hundred miles from the hectic Roaches nearby.

Conditions & aspect

Very clean, compact rock. Quick-drying and relatively sheltered; climbing is possible all year round. Faces south-west, getting sun from midday untill sunset.

Routes

Only about 50, but with a high proportion of multi-starred classics including arguably the Peak's finest HVS.

Bouldering

Limited but superb. Some excellent mini-routes, and bouldering around the crag, including a couple of the area's hardest, and a classic free-standing boulder below the Fourth Cloud.

Parking & approach

Park as for the Roaches. Once inside the gate, turn immediately left along a quarry track. Where the track turns uphill into the quarry and towards the Upper Tier, follow a smaller track straight on towards the First Cloud (10 minutes). To approach from the Upper Tier, follow a well-worn path from its northern end down into the quarry to join the lower track (10 minutes). Please do not take short-cuts from the road: the dry-stone walls are daunting and precarious, and their demolition is guaranteed to sour access agreements.

Access

Occasional bird restrictions will be clearly signposted. Observe these restrictions. Generally, although nominally in the designated 'quiet area' exclusion zone, there have been no problems as long as the proper approach is used. Please respect the privacy of the nearby cottages and the atmosphere of the place by keeping the noise down.

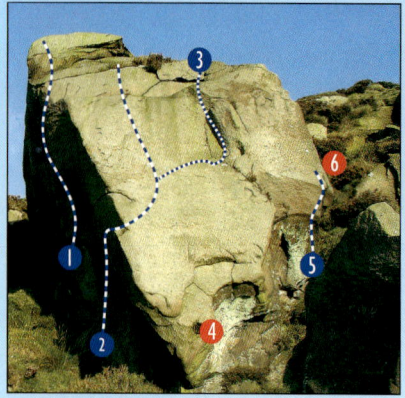

The Fifth Cloud

The furthest of the clouds, about 120m left of the first, has rock as good as any.

1 Foxy Lady MVS 4c   1977
7m The crack in the steep left face of the buttress, exiting right onto the front face. The overhanging arête to the left is **Ride the Lightning**, E2 6b (2002).

2 Cloud Nine E2 5b ★   1977
10m Definitely requires cumulative nimbleness. Swing up right to the ledge on the arête, move up and then make a committing reach/slap for a good little edge, just below the bigger ledge. Finish with ease.

3 Fifth Cloud Eliminate HVS 5a ★   1969
9m From the ledge on Cloud Nine, move across the slab to gain a shallow finishing scoop. This can be reached directly by the heathery crack below at the same grade.

4 Ninestein V2 (6a)
A shin-scraping direct start to Cloud Nine. Escape back down left again. **G**

5 Always Dreaming E4 6b   1993
6m Climb the hanging right-hand arête of the buttress. Start on the right, then swing left to climb the slabby arête on its left.

6 Dreamer V2 (5c)
The hanging arête climbed on its right side.

On the right side of the cloud, facing the Fourth Cloud, is a fine wee slab.

7 Matchbox Arête V3 (6a)
A beauty with a tricky undercut start. **G** Just as good is smearing leftwards along the lip from the next problem then moving up: V2 (6a).

8 Matchbox Slab V2 (5c)
Flawless smearing practice up the right side of the slab.

The Clouds Fourth Cloud

The Fourth Cloud

Just across the grass is the first of the big buttresses hereabouts. It offers fine technical climbs on the best of rock. Mostly, the landings are superb and therefore ideal for a picnic or for falling onto.

9 Static V0 (5b)
The left arête of the face.

10 Wander VD   pre-1968
5m The crack is a bit grassy on the easy sections.

11 Meander HVD ★   pre-1968
8m A pleasant route starting up the slab on its right-hand side, then move leftwards on the upper slab to the top. If only it were longer!

12 Meander Variation E1 5b   1977
9m From Meander, gain the centre of the short steep wall by means of the hold in the centre of the wall. Bold.

13 Stranglehold E1 5b   1979
10m Gain the upper crack of Smun steeply from the left via an undercut and a layback.

14 The Boston Strangler E2 5b   1991
11m Follow Stranglehold then swing left on to the rib, move up and leftwards to finish around a block.

15 Smun VS 4c ★   pre-1968
9m Climb the crack, bypassing the overhang on the left, and continuing up the corner above to a demeaning finish onto the grassy ledge.

16 Left Block Crack HS 5a   pre-1968
5m The left-hand twin. The unclimbed roof to the left has a nasty landing, but a few tempting holds.

17 Right Block Crack HS 4c   pre-1968
9m The right-hand twin.

18 Winter in Combat E1 5c   1985
9m The left edge of the slab to the right.

19 The Shining Path E6 6c   1997
9m The undercut slab is climbed by extremely thin smearing. Pull over the small roof to a horizontal

"Look, I drove over here, so no one leaves until I do this problem!" Sam Whittaker enjoying perfect conditions on Columns, V11 (page 144), while Harry Pennells and Neil Morris, awash in snow, chalk dust and snot, freeze their arses off. Photo: David Simmonite. The BMC wishes to point out that other indor climbing walls are available.

The Clouds Fourth Cloud

break (small cams), and continue up the bald slab above directly. Hard, but contrived.

20 Private Display E1 5b ★ 1970
9m An intimidating route; tough with obscure, absorbing moves. Start on the rock on the left and climb the vague rib and thin crack above.

21 Milky Buttons V7 (6c)
The fine scoop is climbed using a technical rockover. Brilliant, and slightly highball.

22 Boysen's Delight HVS 5c ★★ 1968
9m Getting into the groove is pleasantly tricky and the protection is guaranteed to make you smile. Finish up the crack above.

23 Mirror, Mirror E5 6b ★★ 1979
10m Definitive Five Clouds quality, with tough technical climbing throughout. Climb the sharp iron-rich rugosities to the sloping break (place nuts up and right here). Skip left into the undercut arch and gain the thin crack. Finish more easily.

24 Mantelshelf Route VD 4a ★ pre-1968
8m Rock up and up to the top via the ledges.

25 Chockstone Corner HD pre-1968
6m Every crag needs one!

26 Roman Candle HVS 5b 2002
7m Stride left off the block and pull into the well-protected thin crack.

27 Roman Nose E2 5b 1977
7m Bold and hairy. Step off the block and climb the middle of the slab on little bendy flakes to the top. Protection is minimal, and the holds might snap off.

> "All around lay the elements of a familiar landscape, each rendered special by the light that fell across them. Ahead, holding me transfixed, the sun fell down upon the earth, split, its contents spilling out. It appeared to me as though solid particles were raining down on distant streets and lying abundantly in fields. It was a place to which one could actually go, perhaps just ten miles away, across the plains of Cheshire."

Andy Popp, At the End of an Evening Climbing in Staffordshire

Staffordshire Grit

Fourth Cloud Boulder

Sat below the crag is one of the finest gritstone boulders, anywhere. Pure magic.

28 Fourth Arête V2 (5c)
The easier arête on the left of the flat face, using flakes on the front. ◐ A variation swings out right onto the face at the top: **Fourthright**, V3 (6a).

29 The Hard Arête V7 (6b)
Powerful full-bore slapping up the left side of the right arête gives one of the best problems of its grade on grit.

30 Tetris V9 (6c)
The sit start to the last problem is one of the Peak's hard classics. Slap up the rib to the lip, swing left and do battle with the still-desperate upper arête.

31 The Hanging Slab V6 (6b)
Rock desperately through the undercut scooped face and get stood on the slab above. The move from here to the top of the boulder gives one hundreth of a second of terror. Mega.

32 Columns VII (7a)
The last line on this boulder is a toughie. From the same sitting start as Tetris, gain the lip of the slab and hand traverse this to finish up the right arête. *See photo on page 142.* Omitting the sit start and traversing the lip rightwards from the scoop, gives a V8 (6c) version.

The Third Cloud

The largest and finest of the clouds, with an imposing sheer face and a clutch of excellent routes spread across a range of grades. Sunny, great climbs and perfect rock. Not bad. The first four routes are accessed across the ledge from the left or from one of the boulder problems below.

33 Glass Back HVD 4a   pre-1968
5m The steep crack above the left end of the terrace. A line up the arête, mainly on the right except to bypass the nose is HS 4c.

34 Squash Balls HVD 4a   2001
5m The impressively smooth and tight chimney.

35 Tip Toe HVS 4c   1993
5m The left side of the hour-glass wall is defined by a slabby scoop. Climb the slab using the arête and go directly over the bulge above. Easily escapable.

36 Sands of Time E4 6a ★   1993
5m A sustained and scary route up the hour-glass-shaped wall. Follow the blunt nose to the good hold in the middle of the wall. Pull up and leftwards to finish. Side-runners are of limited comfort.

37 Elastic Arm HVS 5b ★   pre-1968
5m Gain the wide crack from the left, then stretch, contort and squabble with this mighty fissure. Knee-pads advised.

38 Persistence V3 (6a)
The sweet and appropriately named problem based on the little flake. ◐

39 Who Needs Ready Brek? V9 (7a)
Persistence won't be enough to get you up this one; fingers of steel and outstanding technique are also required. Bounce out right from Persistence to the thin crack-line and glide to a reasonable hold 4m right. Levitate up to the next holds, where enlightenment is achieved.

40 Cloudbusting E4 6b ★   1986
8m A real boulder problem in the sky. Start as for Rubberneck, place a high runner, then climb the

The Clouds Third Cloud

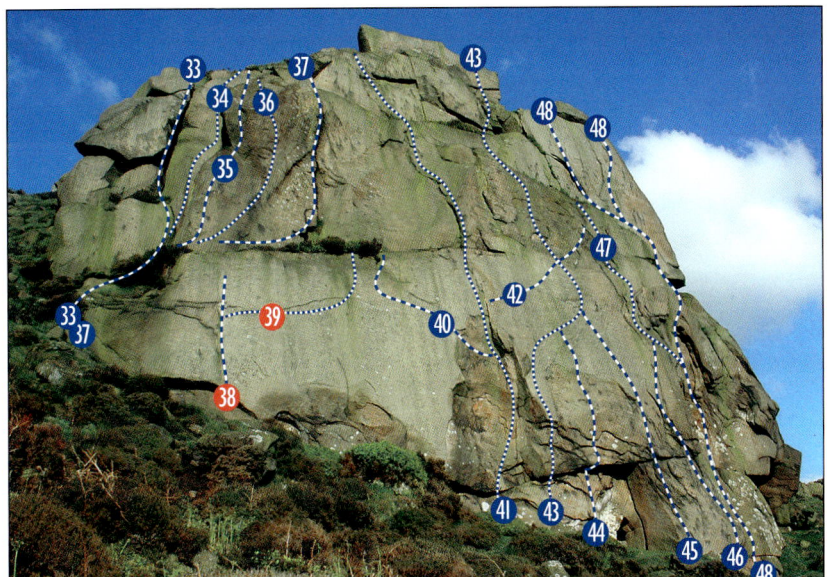

sickle-shaped flakes on the left to their termination. Sketch rapidly leftwards across the slab, mantel up and clutch at the grass. Run down to the ground and do it all over again.

41 Rubberneck HVS 5a ★★★   1967
15m An exemplary route, sustained, technical and well-protected; the classic of the crag. Start at the base of the scoop, dislocate your femur from your pelvis, and move up to the crack above (crux), where superb runners can be placed. Swarm up the crack and finish up the slab above, elated.

42 Walking on Sunshine E3 6b ★   1993
16m Forsake Rubberneck and foot traverse the Appaloosa handholds until an awkward move gains the jug. Continue into Crabbie's to finish.

43 Appaloosa Sunset E3 5c ★★★   1977
16m An exquisite solution to the 'blank' slab. Climb Rubberneck or the arête just right and, at 3m, launch rightwards along the diagonal line of holds, until a series of delicate and precise rockovers leads towards a jug. This is hard to gain and even harder to leave! Wander to the top past an obscure circular hole. Gear is placed high in Rubberneck at this grade, otherwise award yourself a hard E4. *See photo on page 147.*

44 The Eclipsed Peach E4 6b ★   1983
16m A technical and bold direct start to Appaloosa gaining the traverse from undercuts.

45 Laguna Sunrise E6 6c ★   1984/2007
15m An even harder and bolder start to Appaloosa. Clamber just right of the cave to stand in a break. Move up onto a flake, then scamper, scrape and slip up left to the Appaloosa jug. Originally done with side-runners, poor, marginal nuts and ground falls are now the way.

46 Bakewell Tart E2 5c ★   1991
15m A direct start to the next route, climbing the arête on the left of the start of Crabbie's with the aid of some thin flakes.

47 Crabbie's Crack Left-Hand
HVS 4c ★★   1968
16m A fine alternative to the mother crack follows flakes leftwards at the steepening, to easier ground.

Staffordshire Grit

48 Crabbie's Crack VS 4c ★★★ 1950s
15m Crack climbing of the utmost quality, at the upper limit of the grade. Climb the perfect jamming crack, to arrive, exhausted, on a ledge. Finish up a little crack or, for an excellent delicate contrast, climb up and right to finish up the arête – the **Flaky Wall Finish** (HVS 4c ★★★).

"The best gritstone climbing in Derbyshire actually lies in Staffordshire."

Paul Nunn, Mountain Magazine

49 Flower Power Arête E2 5c ★ 1968
15m From the rib left of the windy cave, climb to a small ledge. Balance up into the rounded flaky scoop, make a long move to a layback flake and follow it to the ledge above. Jam yourself in the tight chimney and squirm to the top.

50 Icarus Allsorts E4 6a ★★ 1977
15m A wonderful name for a wonderful climb. Purists will start by pulling through the roof of the cave to gain the top of the jutting block. From here step back across left to gain a flake and get onto the slab above the roof, and follow this to the ledge at the base of the wide corner crack. Step left and climb the arête in an exhilarating position, taking care not to fall off, as the gear leaves something to be desired.

51 Waxwing E1 5a 1979
10m The short bold arête gained easily from the right.

52 The Bender HS 4b ★ 1968-73
7m Thin curving cracks to the right, almost in the gully, left of the two flakes.

One of the best routes of its grade in Staffordshire with unforgettable move just on the right side of the safety margin – unless you're soloing, of course. Ben Bransby on Appaloosa Sunset, E3 5c (page 145). Photo: Adam Long.

53 Tim Benzadrino E3 5c   1979
7m The fat wall is spattered with tempting holds, but is positioned above a less than inspiring landing.

54 The Little Flake HVS 5a   pre-1968
8m Overcome the small overhang with a hard pull.

55 The Big Flake HS 4c   pre-1968
7m Wriggle, wiggle and writhe up the chimney. Superb. Laybacking the left side of the flake is E3 5b, **Geordie Girl** (1990s).

56 Pointless Arête HS 4b   1977
6m Well it is, as you can escape at almost any point.

57 Blue Bandanna E1 5b ★   1978
20m A pleasant girdle gobbling up much fine rock. From the block at the the base of Icarus Allsorts traverse left over the cave and into Crabbie's Crack. Continue to the Left-Hand Variant and across to Appaloosa Sunset. Nip across the hollow flakes to the refuge of Rubberneck. Finish up this.

Spring Boulders page 38

Lots of classics here but only a couple in the circuit because of the usual boggy conditions. If you find it dry underfoot, add Skinned Rabbit (11) and Mr Left (16) to your itinerary. Even as it is, Bog Mosnster will feel more like a deep mud solo.

1	C3PO	(31)
2	Bog Monster	(23)

Doug-less Boulder page 41

3	Scratchy Scoop	(44)

Lower Tier Boulders page 42

4	Pine Slab	(25)

Done with a jump from the boulder, and no hands, of course.

5	Stretch and Mantel	(16)
6	Three Pocket Slab	(9)

Lower Tier page 46

7	Ascent of Man start	(8)
8	Teck Crack Direct	(18)

Piece of Mind Boulders page 70

9	Open Bum Cleft	(2)
10	Wildy's Right	(18)
11	Off Work	(15)

Calcutta Problems page 108

12	Mistral Start	(6)
13	Calcutta Crimp	(2)

Cellar and Attic page 102

14	Ride My Pimp	(21)
15	Reachy Wall	(8)

Upper Tier Boulders page 92

16	Oik	(64)
17	Sheep Shit Crack	(63)
18	Flake Museum	(53)
19	The Break	(51)
20	The Nose	(42)
21	Left Groove	(39)
22	The Boss	(4)
23	Long Boulder Mantel	(26)
24	Joe's Arête	(14)

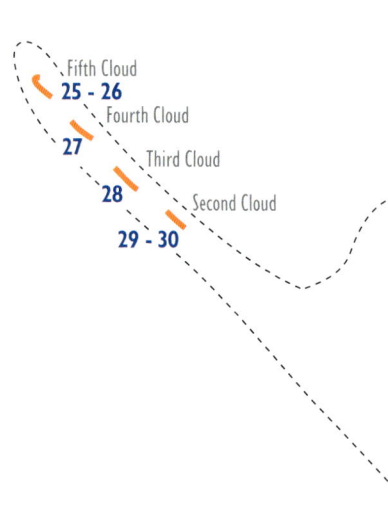

The Five Clouds page 139

From the Upper Tier, follow the path along to its end then follow the track down through the trees towards the Clouds. It is easiest to walk along the top of the cliffs until above the Fifth Cloud, and drop down here, but avoid cutting across the open moorland as it is environmentally sensitive.

25	Ninestein	(4)
26	Matchbox Arête	(7)
27	Fourth Arête	(28)
28	Persistence	(38)
29	Finger of Fate	(64)
30	Communist Crack	(66)

Roaches Red Circuit

Oh you lucky boulderers! What a lot of quality there is to be hoovered up in this circuit. This voyage doesn't contain many desperate problems, but most are tricky, and there are a lot of them. It spans the lower and upper tiers, then on to the Clouds. Of course there are problems all along the Skyline that are just as good, but would be best left for a day on their own. Problems 5, 6, 24 and 29 are some of the best in the county. There are a few highballs thrown in but these should be more than manageable if you can do the rest of the problems. Also here are a few obscurities designed to either give a totally different type of problem or to take you to an area you would otherwise not visit. Remember this is only a list of suggestions and if you don't want to do any of them, then don't. Have fun.

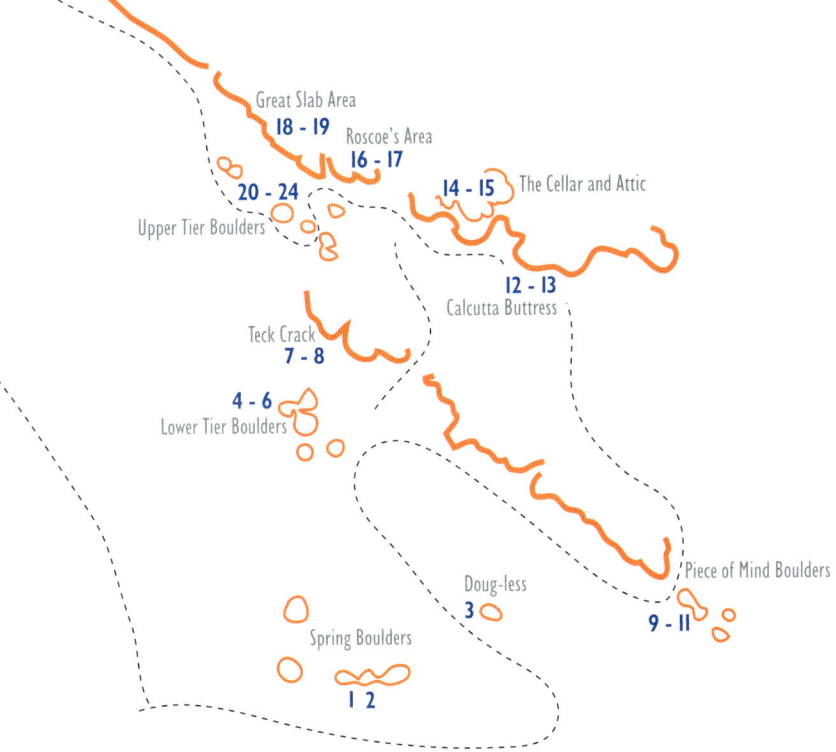

The clouds! The clouds! Photo: Dave Parry.

The Clouds Second Cloud

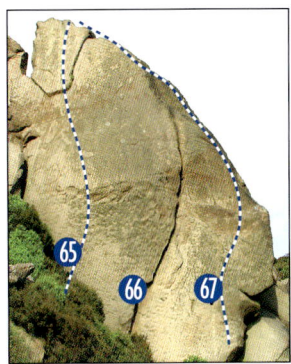

The Second Cloud

The next cloud provides a few good warm downs, some nice easyish cracks and a couple of great problems.

58 Jimmy Carter S   1973–80
6m Climb the amiable wall on flakes and protrusions.

59 Stalin HVD 4a   pre-1968
8m The crack to the right.

60 Legends of Lost Leaders E3 5c   1980
8m A bold proposition starting up the centre of the slab by an awkward mantel and a committing reachy finish up the right hand arête. Escapable.

61 Lenin HVD 4a   pre-1968
8m Pleasant climbing up the crack just right.

62 Yankee Jam HS 5a   1973–80
8m The crack protruding from the smelly cave.

63 Nadin's Secret Finger V9 (7a)
8m Swing onto the left edge of the finger at a very poor hold and aim for the diagonal break.

64 Finger of Fate V4 (E1 6a)
7m The perfect arête, climbed on its left, is a supreme test of barndoor laybacking. The situations are exciting, although difficulties decrease with height. ⊙ **KGB** (HVS 4c, 1977) avoids the low crux by swinging in from the right.

65 The Outdoor Pursuits Cooperative
E1 5a   1998
8m Short but committing, with a grisly landing. From the boulders gain the narrow ledge and move up on small holds to the U-shaped crack, and on to the top.

66 Communist Crack VS 5a ★   pre-1968
8m You know you want to. Easy for the confident but surprisingly steep and awkward to protect for the floundering: *see photo on page 16*. ⊙

67 Marxist Undertones VS 6a ★   1973–80
8m A delightful solo with a desperate low crux. From a deep pocket, dyno to the sloping ledge and mantel it. Continue up the arête on rugosities to the top: highball V2. Climbing the undercut right arête direct is a frisky V2 (5c), the crux being avoiding the wall on the right. Another sweetie goes up left from the pocket to a slim flake, then crank for the rail above: V2 (6a).

The First Cloud

Just past the small quarry the first Cloud is encountered up on the hillside – a large block with a cave at its base. There is some good slab climbing on this, and several routes have been done. However, in keeping with tradition, these routes continue to be un-named, un-graded, and un-recorded, so that it is still possible to have a true on-sight, not to say pioneering, experience.

The Nth Cloud

by David Garnett

O.S. Ref. SK998636   Altitude: 425m a.s.l.

Nth Cloud is rarely visited and small, with only a handful of routes. Yet here is a real little gem of a crag, with one of the finest slabs in the area (an extravagant claim given the competition) and top-class bouldering. The rock is sound, clean (despite the lack of traffic), peerlessly rough and beautifully textured with a variety of ripples, scoops and pockets. All this gives some delightful slab and crack climbing in what feels almost like a mountain crag in its solitude and outlook.

Conditions & aspect
The buttresses face south-west and the fine open slabs dry quickly, giving good climbing all year round. In blustery weather the crag can feel quite exposed, but even a hint of afternoon sun more than makes up for it.

Routes
Amongst barely a dozen routes are some real classics, including one of the boldest in the Peak and the superb Pillar of Judgement, worth the price of admission on its own. However, there is also easily enough in this splendid area to provide a quality day's climbing for an adventurous VS team.

Bouldering
The short clean walls to the left of the main buttress offer excellent bouldering, some of it very hard indeed.

Approaches & access
The road under the Roaches and Five Clouds leads round to Roach End meeting the lane rising steeply from Meerbrook at an acute-angled junction. Approaching from the Roaches, about 50m before this junction is an angled gate on the right with stone gate-posts, whence a track leads almost directly to the crag. There is space for two or three cars on the verge opposite the gate. However, please take care not to obstruct the gateway. The crag is on Open Access land in the ownership of a nearby farmer. The fields are managed both for farming and for wildlife conservation. Please help this program by ensuring all gates are kept closed and noise/disturbance is minimized. See map on page 35.

Left-Hand Rocks

From the road, some clean flat walls can be seen 150m to the left of the main crag. The first routes are to be found amongst the boulders in the trees, at a slightly lower level. The most obvious feature among the large boulders is a wide corner crack.

1 Josephina E4 5c   1998
6m Just left of the corner, an undercut start leads rightwards to a small ledge on the nose. Finish to the left on a slab and arête. Unprotected with a horrible landing.

2 Gromit HVS 5a   1997
8m The obvious corner crack. Good thrutchy jamming leads to a tricky exit.

3 Gromit Arête V2 (5c)
An exciting problem up the arête to the right, starting on the left-hand side. The sit-start is V7 (6c).

The Clouds Nth Cloud

Up and right is a flat wall with a couple of great problems and two tremendous projects.

4 Swivel Flakes V4 (6a)
The flakes at the left end of the wall are sustained and high above a sketchy landing. A good problem.

The steep unclimbed wall to the right holds what would be one of the best and hardest problems in the area.

5 Swivel Finger V3 (6a)
Excellent laybacking up the classic arête, with a tricky start and an awkward finish. A supreme problem. The **sit-start** is V5. **The Thrutch** is a full-bodied classic up the chasm right of Swivel Finger, V0 (4c). Another top-drawer project is up the very fingery flake right of The Thrutch.

Main Crag

Fifty metres to the right, a collection of outcrops holds the best concentrations of routes hereabouts.

6 Shaun's Other End HVS 5a   1997
12m Climb the flake to the ledge. Continue up the square face above on its left edge.

7 Grenadier HVD 4a ★   1960s
12m Climb into the obvious sentry box just right and exit to the ledge. Finish up the wide crack.

8 Happiness from Outer Space S 4a   2002
12m The right arête, via pleasant pockets. Nice.

9 Slanting Crack S 4b   1960s
12m The awkward wide crack just around the corner.

10 Mayhem VS 5a   1968
12m The even more awkward right-hand crack leading to an overhang. Move left and struggle on.

11 Green Chimney VD   1960s
11m The eponymous feature just right again, finishing round the chockstone. The corner, finishing left on the rib, is VD.

An angular boulder perched above the crag has a couple of steep problems, The **Leaky Traverse V2 (5c)** starts on the left beneath the little roof then traverses up past a couple of steps to finish on the shelf. Manteling leftwards through the steps in the lip is V1 (5c).

Staffordshire Grit

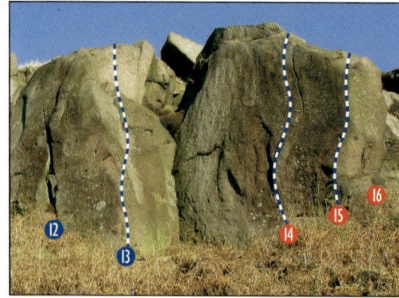

The buttress to the right gives a number of extended boulder problems.

12 Inexplicably Anonymous S 4b   traditional
5m The obvious crack gives good jamming.

13 Totally Unprecedented HVS 5a   1985
7m The left arête of the open corner, started on the left and finishing slightly to the right. Alternatively, start by climbing the left face of the corner directly. The corner itself is VD, but often dirty.

14 Crystal Voyager V8 (E4 6c)
Very technical climbing, almost too high to be a boulder problem, up the right wall of the corner. Reach the faint flake and continue on poor pockets.

15 Spankasaurus Does Chicago V3 (6a)
The arête to the right is a good problem.

16 Dreadful V0 (5b)
The edge of the buttress to a jug.

The Main Face

The main attraction is undoubtedly the superb main slab.

17 Little Crack VS 5a ★   1968
6m The brilliant finger crack at the left end of the main buttress. If only it were longer.

18 Rowan Tree Crack S   1968
9m The crack with the useful tree is now barely climbable.

Jon Fullwood about to make the crucial stretch into the wide crack on Pillar of Judgement. For climbers operating at E4 5c, one of the 3 great gritstone grades, this is an essential tick. Photo: Adam Long.

The Clouds Nth Cloud

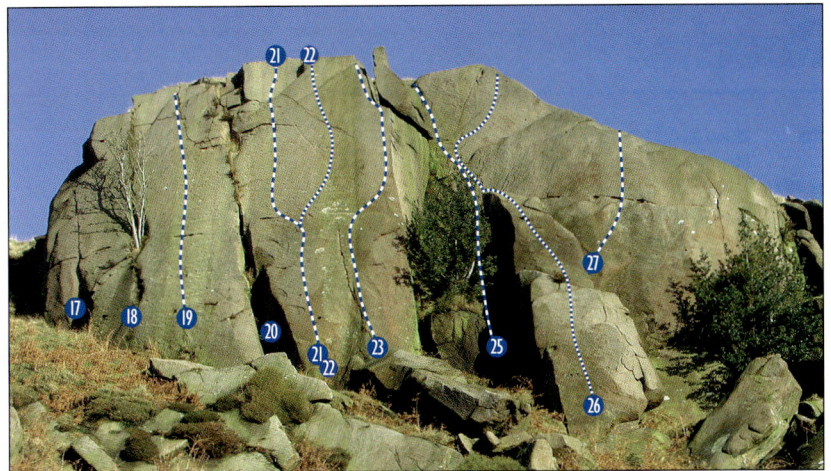

19 Ageing Adolescents E6 6c 1984
10m The slab to the right via shallow pockets. Normally climbed with a runner in the tree at E4.

20 Plumb-Line VS 4c 1968
12m The right-hand crack is rather vegetated.

21 Judge Jules E8 7a ★ 2003
15m painfully thin slab climbing with ludicrously low protection, squeezed into the left side of the slab. Gain the ledge as for Judge Dread. From its left-hand side, step up and left to gain a mono. Very thin climbing leads directly to the top of the slab.

22 Judge Dread E6 6b ★★ 1986
15m Bold and transparently thin climbing up the unforgiving main sweep of the buttress. Climb the pockety rib past a hole (wedged nuts) to the ledge. From its centre, gain an incut at the base of a diagonal seam (RPs), and climb this to the top.

23 Pillar of Judgement E4 5c ★★★ 1975
15m A elegant and bold climb and, despite a high, unprotected crux, a gift at the grade. Climb the pocketed crack, then step right and balance confidently up to reach the wide finishing crack. Remember to take something big enough to take advantage of it. The lower arête may be climbed direct at 6a. **See photo opposite**.

24 The Perp E2 5b 2002
25m Side-steps Judgement only to cross Judge Dread. Start behind the holly (on Barbecue Corners). Step awkwardly round the arête, hand-traverse the ledge and step delicately into Plumb-Line. Traverse pockets to Rowan Tree Crack. Climb this for a few feet until a foot-traverse into Little Crack can be made. Finish up this.

25 Barbecue Corners HVD ★ 1960s
18m Climb the corner to the right of the pillar. Masochists may wish to belay in the holly.

26 The Pinnacle Start and Shaun's End
HVS 5a ★ 1960s
18m Two variations on the last route combine to make an interesting and independent way up the cliff. Climb boldly up the front face of the pinnacle. Jump to the ledge in Barbecue Corners and then gain the scooped ledge in the right wall. Either continue rightwards along it or, better, climb the short awkward crack above.

27 Metaphysical Scoop E4 6b ★ 1987
9m Short but cerebral. Climb Barbecue Corners to reach the pocketed scoop on the right. Puzzling and committing moves up and right gain the line of large pockets. Finish philosophically via mantelshelves.

Staffordshire Grit

Roaches first ascents

1901	**Raven Rock Gully** Members of the Kyndwyr Club	1951	**Matinee** Joe Brown, Don Whillans AL *Matinee was called after the audience who sat on the boulders and watched the pioneering of Brown and Whillans on their through leads.*
pre-1913	**Cannonball Crack**		
1913	**Jeffcoat's Chimney, Jeffcoat's Buttress** Stanley Jeffcoat		
1922	**Bachelor's Buttress, Black and Tans** A S 'Fred' Pigott **Pedestal Route Left-Hand, Pedestal Route Right-Hand, Right Route, Crack and Corner** Morley Wood *'On Crack and Corner the leader took a shoulder from his second who was securely tied on to the block and it looked impossible without this.'* **Rucksack Club Journal.**	1949–51	**Little Chimney, Lucas Chimney, Flake Chimney, Central Route, Heather Slab, Chicken Run, High Crossing, Pinnacle Crack**
		1953 Jan	**The Sloth** Don Whillans, Joe Brown
		1954	**Aqua** Joe Brown, Don Whillans
		1954	**Capitol Climb** R Handley, Nat Allen
		early-1950s	**Crabbie's Crack** Bob Downes, Nea Morin Flaky Wall Finish added by Colin Foord in 1968.
1913–24	**Via Dolorosa, Kestrel Crack, Upper Tier Girdle**	1955 May 25	**Damascus Crack** G W S Pigott, W H Craster
		1955	**Roscoe's Wall** Don Roscoe
1913–24	**Bengal Buttress** Ivan Waller	1955	**Runner Route** Nat Allen, D Campbell
1924	**Left-Hand Route, Right-Hand Route** Lindlay Henshaw	1951–57	**Wallaby Wall, Alpha, Breakfast Problem, Mistaken Identity, Cave Arête, Joiner, Ogden, Ralph's Mantelshelves, Cracked Arête, Right-Hand Crack, Pinnacle Slab, Capstan's Corner, Rowan Tree Traverse, Square Chimney, Late Night Final, Central Traverse, Lighthouse, Trio Chimney, Left Twin Crack, Letterbox Gully, Perched Block Arête, Cave Buttress, Pinnacle Slab** John and Tony Vereker, Graham Martin and some members from North Stafford Mountaineering Club
1927	**Guano Gully** Originally named as **Dodo's Dilemma** but misplaced in the 1957 guidebook, this route has kept the former name.		
1927	**Fledgling's Climb, Lucas Chimney**		
1931	**Inverted Staircase, Fern Crack** A S Pigott		
1945	**Karabiner Chimney, Pinnacle Arête** R Desmond-Stevens **Karabiner Crack, Tower Chimney** A Simpson, R Desmond-Stevens **Slab and Arête, Central Massif** G Stoneley, R Desmond-Stevens **Bilberry Traverse** R Desmond-Stevens, G Stoneley		
		1951–57	**Lone Ascent, Contrary Mary**
		1958	**Crack of Gloom** Joe Brown, Don Whillans *'Brown and Whillans forced the dark and strenuous Crack of Gloom and stories were whispered of a couple of points of aid.'* 1981 Guidebook.
1945	**Demon Wall, Beckermet Slab, Maud's Garden, Broken Slab, Rotunda Buttress, Technical Slab** A Bowden Black		
		1958	**Teck Crack, Choka** (1 pt.), **Rhodren** Joe Brown.
1946 Oct 6	**Valkyrie** Peter Harding, A Bowden Black		
1947	**Mantelshelf Slab** Karabiner Club members	1958	**Ackit** (right-hand finish), **Slippery Jim** Don Whillans Ackit Direct Finish climbed by the Barley brothers on May 1, 1967.
1947	**Saul's Crack** Joe Brown		
1949	**Hangman's Crack, Scarlet Wall, Calcutta Crack** G W S Pigott, C Topping		
1924–49	**Kelly's Shelf** Harry Kelly	1958	**Reset Portion of Galley 37, Perverted Staircase** Geoff Sutton The former route was named after a printer's error that appeared in the 1957 guidebook.
1951	**Dorothy's Dilemma** Joe Brown, Merrick 'Slim' Sorrell, Dorothy Sorrell		
1951	**Valkyrie Direct, The Mincer, The Bulger** Joe Brown, Don Whillans	1958	**Lightning Crack** Don Whillans, Joe Brown
		1960	**The Girdle Traverse** Alan Parker, Paul Nunn, Bob Brayshaw

The Roaches   First Ascents

1960	**West's Wallaby** Graham West		1969	**The Chimney, Honky Tonk, Flutterbye Grooves** Steven and Brian Dale
1960	**Walleroo, Wombat, Elegy** (1 pt.) Mike Simpkins *Elegy was climbed free by John Yates in 1969.*		1960s	**Barbecue Corners, The Pinnacle Start, Grenadier, Green Chimney, Slanting Crack** North Staffordshire Mountaineering Club members *Shaun's End added in 2002 by Phil Hitchings and Richard Taylor.*

1963 Sep   **Hank's Horror**   Dave Salt, Colin Foord
1967 May 1   **Rubberneck**   Robin Barley, Tony Barley
pre-1968   **Communist Crack**   Hugh Banner
1967   **Tower Eliminate**   Colin Foord, Dave Salt
1957–68   **Lenin, Stalin, The Big Flake, The Little Flake, Elastic Arm, Glass Back, Chockstone Crack, Mantelshelf Route, Right Block Crack, Left Block Crack, Smun, Meander, Wander Yong Arête, Yong, Wisecrack, Pincer, Flimney, Straight Crack, Punch** (1 pt.), **Prow Corner, Prow Cracks, Pepper, Calcutta Buttress, Rib Wall, The Rib, Gully Wall, Jelly Roll, Easy Gully Wall, Kelly's Connection, Right Route Right, The Neb Finish, Black Velvet, Cornflake, Tealeaf Crack, Libra, Rooster, The Pugilist, Southpaw, Navy Cut, Bruno Flake, Tobacco Road, Condor Chimney, Condor Slab, Letter Box Cracks, Middleton's Motion, The Black Pig, Ogden Recess, Ogden Arête, Thrug, Cave Crack, Stephen, Abstract, Karabiner Slab, Alpha Arête, Omega**
   The first free ascent of Punch was made in 1978 by Jonny Woodward (solo).

1968   **Sifta's Quid**   John Amies   *The result of a bet by Dave Salt who claimed that everything that could be done, had been done. Amies never received the pound.*
1968   **Bad Poynt**   Ray Baddley, Terry Pointon
1968   **Crabbie's Crack Left-Hand**   John Yates
1968 Nov   **Plumb-Line, Little Crack, Rowan Tree Crack**   John Yates, Colin Foord
1968 Nov   **Mayhem**   Colin Foord, John Yates
   Hypothesis   Colin Foord, Dave Salt
1968   **The Underpass**   Dave Salt, Colin Foord
1968   **Boysen's Delight, Flower Power Arête**   Martin Boysen   *The latter named after the rather floral T-shirt worn by the first ascensionist.*
1969   **Fifth Cloud Eliminate**   John Yates
1969 Jul   **Humdinger**   Mick Guilliard
1969 Oct 12   **The Swan** (1 pt.)   John Gosling, Mike Simpkins   *The aid was a peg! FFA Ron Fawcett and Geoff Birtles, 1977.*
1969   **Raven Rock Gully Left-Hand, Pebbledash**   Dave Salt

1970 Apr   **The Black Ram, Black Ram Arête, Dangler, Steeplechase Crack, Dazzler, Mudhopper, Slither, Steeplechaser, Tree Grooves, Tree Corner, The Girdle Traverse of Far Skyline**   Steve Dale, Brian Dale
1970   **The Death Knell**   John Yates, Colin Foord   *Originally Death Knell finished up dirty cracks just left. The direct finish was added by Jonny and Andrew Woodward in 1977.*
1970   **Private Display**   John Yates
1971 Apr   **Up the Swanee**   John Yates
1971 Jun 22   **Ruby Tuesday**   Mick Guilliard, John Yates
1971   **Freak Out**   Steve Dale, Brian Dale
1973 Jun   **Acid Drop**   Jerry Peel, Tony Barley   *Named by Jonny Woodward in 1979, believing it to be a first ascent. Peel's name, Skytrain, along with the first ascent claim, was mistakenly transposed to a route further right. The names are being kept to avoid confusion.*
1968–73   **Swinger, Aperitif, Kelly's Direct, Waistline, Oversight, Go Girl, Come Girl, Battery Crack, The Bender**
1974   **Ascent of Man, Days of Future Passed, Mantis**   Andrew Woodward, Jonny Woodward
1974 Aug 17   **Round Table**   John Allen, Nick Colton, Steve Bancroft
1975 Mar 2   **Safety Net**   John Allen, Steve Bancroft, Tom Proctor
1975   **Nosepicker**   Jonny Woodward (solo)
1975   **Pillar of Judgement, Commander Energy**   John Allen, Mark Stokes
1975   **Hunky Dory**   Gabriel Regan and party
1976   **Melaleucion**   Steve Dale, Barry Marsden
1976   **In Passing, Wheeze, Looking for Today**   Jonny Woodward
1976 Sep   **Enigma Variation**   Andrew Woodward, Jonny Woodward
1977   **Mild Thing, San Melas, Wild Thing, Prelude to Space**   Andrew Woodward, Jonny Woodward   *The latter two routes were reputedly climbed in spring 1974 by John Allen and Steve Bancroft.*

Staffordshire Grit

1977	**Foxy Lady, Bad Sneakers** Dave Jones		

1977 **Foxy Lady, Bad Sneakers** Dave Jones

1977 **Wings of Unreason, Track of the Cat, Bone Idol, Spectrum, Spare Rib, Lung Cancer, Cloud Nine** Jonny Woodward, Andrew Woodward *Wings claimed to be the hardest route in the world (at HXS/E6 6c) due to the extensive amount of top-roping required before the ascent. 'Magnifying glass for aid'.*

1977 **Appaloosa Sunset, Roman Nose** Dave Jones, Ian Johnson, John Gilbert *On the former, a home-made protection device, for the hole at half-height, was measured for the ascent well in advance.*

1977 **Chalkstorm, KGB, Pointless Arête** Ian 'Hotshot' Johnson, Dave Jones

1977 Oct 15 **Piece of Mind** Jonny Woodward, Andrew Woodward *Dawes fell off the last move, on-sight, in 1986, and somehow survived. Flashed by Kevin Thaw in 1997, after watching top-ropers, and ground-up by Pete Robins in 2001. Pete also took the fall from the top move, but dusted himself off, and got back on again. The direct finish added in a panic by Niall Grimes in 1996: "More an emergency exit than a direct finish."*

1977 **Icarus Allsorts, Tower Face** Al Simpson, Dave Jones

1977 **Meander Variation, Willow Farm** Chris Hamper

1977 **Smear Test** Gabriel Regan and party

1977 **Skytrain** *Wrongly credited to Jerry Peel and Tony Barley. Their name, Skytrain, actually referred to their previously uncredited first ascent of what has become known as Acid Drop.*

1978 **Diamond Wednesday, Wipers, Short Trip etc, Something Better Change, Sparkle, War Wound, Shortcomings, Substance, Poisonous Python, Crenation, Coldfinger, Hanging Around, Fred's Café, Chicane Destination, Chicane, A.M. Anaesthetic, The Aspirant, Time to be Had, Sennapod, Days Gone By, Bed of Nails, National Hero, Graffiti, The Valve, Third Degree Burn** Gary Gibson, either solo, or with Ian Johnson, Nick Longland, Dave Jones, John Perry, Mark 'Ralph' Hewitt, Derek Beetlestone or Fred Cook

1978 **The Tower of Bizarre Delights, Joe Public, Babbacombe Lee, Mousey's Mistake, Sorcerer's Apprentice, Blue Bandanna** Dave Jones, either alone, or with Bob Cope, Tony Bristlin, Ian Johnston or Al Simpson

1978 Apr 6 **Schoolies** Phil Burke, Gary Gibson *Later climbed direct by John Codling*

1978 Apr **Dawn Piper** John Codling (solo)

1978 May **Lybstep** John Dodd

1978 May **Kicking Bird** Al Simpson, Dave Jones (AL), Nick Longland, Tony Bristlin *Strung together over two evenings. Where Jones failed on the first pitch Simpson used his knees. Most repeat ascensionists follow suit!*

1978 Oct 14 **Headless Horseman** Jonny Woodward

1978 **Hawkwing** Al Simpson, Dave Jones

1979 **Heartbleed, Destination Venus, Curvature, Between the Tiles, Definitive Gaze, Split Personality, The Sublime, Stranglehold, Topaz, 39th Step, Genetix, Public Enemy Number One, Wrong Way Round, Chronicle, Devotoed, Microcosm, Inspiration Point** Gary Gibson, either unseconded, or with Dave Jones, Ian Barker, John Perry or Phil Wilson

1979 **Gypfast, Garlic** Phil Gibson

1979 **Gillted, Simpkins' Overhang** Phil Burke, unseconded, or with George Cooper *Gillted named after Burke's ex-girlfriend. Mike Simpkins had top-roped the overhang over a decade earlier.*

1979 **Eugene's Axe, Waxwing** John Codling, Andy Fox, Dave Jones *Eugene's Axe named in honour of Rock Hall Cottage denizen Doug Moller who had erected a fence around The Lower Tier and fended off all-comers with an axe.*

1979 **Mirror, Mirror** Andrew Woodward (solo)

1979 **Grilled Fingers, Burrito Deluxe, The Fantasy Finish, Tim Benzadrino, Sign of the Times** Dave Jones, either unseconded or with John Codling or Gary Gibson

1979 **Sally James** Nick Longland (solo)

1973–80 **Marxist Undertones, Yankee Jam, Jimmy Carter**

1980 **Legends of Lost Leaders, Carrion, The Thin Air, Circuit Breaker, Poison Gift, Licence to Run** (1 pt.) Gary Gibson, either unseconded, or with Derek Beetlestone or Fred Crook *A controversial hanging rope was used on The Thin Air. Licence to Run was given a joke grade of E2 5c, which it retained. FFA by Pete O'Donovan and Gary Cooper in the same month.*

The Roaches First Ascents

1980 Sep	**Antithesis** Jonny Woodward Climbed in marked contrast to his previous first ascents, Woodward reluctantly took over the lead after Gibson had shown the sequence to everyone but failed to complete the lead.	
1980	**The Super Girdle** John Codling, Dave Jones	
1980	**Sidewinder** Phil Burke, Bob Toogood	
1980	**Bareback Rider** Dave Jones	
1981	**Trebia, Live Bait, Hallow to Our Men, Automatix, Strain Station, Entente Cordiale, Swan Bank** Gary Gibson, either solo, or with Derek Beetlestone, Mark Hewitt or Hazel Carnes, the future Mrs Gibson	
1981	**Quickbrew** Fred Crook, Ian Barker	
1982	**Pebbles on a Wessex Beach, Slips** Gary Gibson	
1982 Apr	**Entropy's Jaw** Andrew Woodward (solo)	
1982 Jul	**Formative Years** Howard Tingle (solo)	
1982	**Triple Point, Poodle Vindaloo** Jonny Woodward The direct start to Triple Point was added in 1983 by Nick Dixon.	
1982	**Crystal Grazer** Phil Burke	
1982	**A Day at the Seaside** Fred Crook, Ken Crook	
1983	**Loculus Lie, Bloodstone, Finger of Fate** Simon Nadin, Richard Davies An early start was made on Loculus Lie to avoid sweaty hands and to study for exams the following day.	
1983 Sep 25	**A Fist Full of Crystals** Nick Dixon Climbed in mistake for Crystal Grazer. Named from a top-rope ascent by Jonny Woodward who commented: 'Undoubtedly the hardest piece of climbing on the Roaches. It has three desperate moves involving an unlikely toe-jam move, a weird high sort of bridge and an all out crystal move. There are no runners and a fall would land you painfully in a holly tree. It will take me quite a time to pluck up the courage to lead it!' Climbed on-sight by Andy Popp and Johnny Dawes in 1985/86.	
1983 Oct 20	**Barriers in Time** Simon Nadin Climbed ground-up, with falls, by Allen Williams, headpointed by Nick Dixon, and flashed by Tony Ryan, all within a few months of the first ascent.	
1983	**Clive Coolhead...** Nick Dixon, Steve Lowe	
1983	**The Eclipsed Peach** Allen Williams	
1984	**Destination Earth, Secrets of Dance, Laguna Sunrise** Simon Nadin Destination Earth originally led with a side-runner by Phil Burke as Earthbound. Possible 2nd ascent by Sam Whittaker, 2002.	
1984	**Ageing Adolescents, Pindles Numb** Nick Dixon The former was led with a deviation into Rowan Tree Crack for holds and protection. Simon Nadin climbed without the crack for holds, but used the side-runners. Done without side-runners by Julian Lines in October 2003.	
1984 Sep 25	**Bloodspeed** Simon Nadin Climbed on-sight by Johnny Dawes in 1986.	
1985 Jan	**Winter in Combat** Richard Davies (solo)	
1985	**Against the Grain, Script for a Tear** Simon Nadin Second ascent of the former by Justin Critchlow, 3rd by Andi Turner, 1990s. Climbed ground-up by Leo Houlding in 2007. The latter climbed on-sight by Johnny Dawes in 1986.	
1985 Apr 23	**Totally Unprecedented** Gary Gibson (solo)	
1985 Jul 13	**New Fi'nial** Simon Nadin, Richard Davies, Gary Cooper Climbed on sight by Ben Bransby. He pissed it!	
1985	**Catastrophe Internationale, Fluorescent Stripper** Nick Dixon	
1985 Oct 13	**Painted Rumour** Simon Nadin, Martin Veale A loose flake was glued back to the roof! Climbed on-sight by Dave Thomas in 1998 and Ben Bransby in 1999.	
1985 Nov	**Nature Trail, Art Nouveau** Simon Nadin Art Nouveau on-sighted by Adam Long in 2001, and ground-up by Pete Robins in 2002.	
1985 Dec 27	**Counterstroke of Equity** Richard Davies	
1985	**Little Perforations** Gary Cooper, Fred Crook	
1986 Feb	**Ou Est Le Spit?** Nick Dixon, Simon Nadin Originally E6, holds being improved by wire-brushing.	
1986 Apr	**Judge Dread** Nick Dixon, Simon Whalley Top-roped first, and using a pre-placed runner complete with long extension to, essentially, top-rope the crux. The first proper ascent by Mark Sharratt in 2002, solo.	
1986 Apr	**Doug** Nick Dixon Only soloed after some optimistically glued pebbles had been pulled off during a top-roped ascent. A very major route. Second ascent by Justin Critchlow, aged 16!, 3rd by Julian Lines. Flashed on impulse by Nik Jennings in 2000, having seen a friend headpoint it, and having previously headpointed A Fist Full of Crystals. It remains, however, a supreme achievement.	

Staffordshire Grit

1986 Jun 12 **Thing on a Spring** Simon Nadin
Second ascent by Kevin Thaw, late '80s, and still a coveted prize.

1986 **99% of Gargoyles Look Like Bob Todd, Cloudbusting** Simon Nadin

1986 **Between the Lines** Gary Cooper, Fred Crook

1987 Feb 17 **Paralogism** Simon Nadin
One of the hardest roof climbs in Britain? 2nd ascent, Seb Grieve 1997. Soloed, virtually on-sight and totally on impulse, by Ben Heason in 2003, without mats or spotters. "I'd seen Seb Grieve do it on a video and thought, if he can do it, so can I."

1987 Feb 17 **Metaphysical Scoop**
Andy Popp, Steve Lowe, Gwion Hughes

1987 **Licence to Lust, Drop Acid, Shelty, Wolfman of the KGB, Dolly Mix, Mix** John Allen and party

1987 **Something Biblical, Mistral** Gary Cooper, Fred Crook **Snap, Crackle and Andy Popp** Fred Crook, Gary Cooper

1988 Feb **Sunday at Chapel** Nick Dixon, Allen Williams, G Cole, I Dunn, C Dunn Unrepeated?

1988 May **Cold Bone Forgotten** P Mitchell, P Evans

1989 **K.P. Nuts, Heredity** Simon Nadin
Some of the nuts have been eaten since the first ascent. Both unrepeated?

1989 **Paul's Puffer** Paul Mitchell A direct start was also rumoured at 5c in the 1981 guide.

1989 Apr 1 **Mr Decisive** Tim Twentyman (solo)

1989 Apr 14 **Don't Go Down to the Woods Today, Deep in Mystery, The Wicked Wind** Julian Lines (solo)

1989 May 18 **The Parrot and the Balaclava, Pop Art** Simon Alsop

1989 Jul 15 **Voila 3, Sumo Cellulite** John Allen

1991 Jan **The Boston Strangler**
Tom Nonis, Geoff Hornby, Suzi Sammut

1991 Jul **Bakewell Tart**
John Hudson, Keith Phizacklea

1991 **The Calf Path** Julian Lines

1992 **Cold Man's Finger, Dougie Returns Home,** Justin Critchlow, Tez Richardson

1992 Jul **Obsession Fatale** Julian Lines
Lines took a ground fall from high on the route prior to the first ascent. Second ascent Sam Whittaker, 1998. Kevin Thaw also fell off the last moves in 2002, on an amazing on-sight attempt. "I just looked down at it from above, saw the holds, and thought, Yeah, that'll work." Even considering the fall, this was still one of the best bits of on-sight climbing yet in Staffordshire.

1993 **Sands of Time, Tip Toe**
Richard Pickford, Sara Cummins

1993 **Apache Dawn, Rodeo, Walking on Sunshine, Always Dreaming** Julian Lines Apache flashed on-sight by James Ibbertson in 2003.

1993 **Laughing all the way to the Blank**
Gary Cooper, Fred Crook

1993 **A Little Peculiar** Paul Higginson Higginson had to train his already bumpy body specifically for the crux. Second ascent by Peter Whittaker in 2009.

1994 Aug **Just For Today** Paul Clarke Unrepeated?

1995 **Rassp** Richard Taylor, Kirsti Hicky

1995 Oct **Beware Coconuts** Phil Hitchings

1996 **Toxic Socks, Bounty Killer, Johnny Pooh Poohed** Mark Katz

1996 **Jog, Ging, Stolen Days** Graham Cole, Nige Bilby, Kenny Atherton

1996 **Northern Comfort** Niall Grimes, Alan Millar Second Ascent, Andi Turner ground up in 2008, a fantastic effort involving more the 30 whippers.

1996 **Bud Love** Justin Critchlow, M Bowyer

1997 **Ped X-ing** Gary Cooper, Fred Crook

1997 **Gromit, Shaun's Other End** Phil Hitchins, Richard Taylor

1997 **Skallagrigg**
Graham Cole, Kenny Atherton

1997 **Shining Path** Mark Katz

1998 **Shrug** Dave Bishop, John White

1998 **Logical Progression** Sam Whittaker
Repeated by Mike Lea, 2000.

1998 **Josephina** Richard Taylor

1998 **The Outdoor Pursuits Cooperative**
Pete Buswell, Roger Austin

1999 **Lost Girl** Steve Clark, Lynn Robinson

1999 **Curiosity Kitten** Graham Cole, Kenny Atherton, Alison Trinder, Dave Southan

1990s **Geordie Girl**
Geoff Hornby, Alex Sammutt

2000 **Wad Man Slang, The Attempted Moustache** John H Bull

2001 **Squash Balls**
Dave Garnett, Kate Garnett (aged 5)

2001 **Stop…Carry On** Mark Sharratt

The Roaches First Ascents

2001	**Transcendental Medication, Coma Sutra** John H Bull		2003 Aug 25	**Steps** Neil Foster, Clare Reading, Dave Simmonite *A special thanks to long-time Roaches Devotee, Fred Crook. Direct start added in September.*
2002	**Licensed to Fill** Chris Hudgins		2003	**Dirty Wee Rouge** Iain McKenzie
2002	**Dazed and Confused** Mark Sharratt, Justin Critchlow **Ride the Lightning** Mark Sharratt		2003 Oct	**Final Destination** Ben Heason
2002	**Roman Candle, Happiness from Outer Space, The Perp** John H Bull, Dave Garnett		2003 Oct	**Judge Jules** Julian Lines, Justin Critchlow *A last minute addition to the guide provided what is probably the hardest lead in the area. Several 'full length' falls were taken onto hopeful gear before the route finally fell to Lines. Second ascent by Alistair Robertson, 2009.*
2002	**Calcutta Crab Dance, Recess Wall and Arête** Steve Clark, Lynn Robinson		2006	**Cold Blood** Alastair Robertson, Will Harris
2003 Jun 11	**Not So Fast** Dave Garnett, John H Bull **Not So Steep** Ged O'Sullivan, John H Bull **Monstrous Angel** John H Bull, Ged O'Sullivan **Not Much Further** John H Bull **Three Tier Buttress** Steve Clark, Lynn Robinson		2007	**Skin and Wishbones** Ben Bransby
			2007	**The Spectatorship of the Proletariat** Ben Tetler
			2007	**Laguna Sunrise** Led without side-runners by Andi Turner

Roaches Bouldering First Ascents

A Modest Proposal Tom O'Rourke, 2002
Acne Arête Andi Turner, 2001
Acne Arête Sit-Start Justin Critchlow, 2001
Annie's Egg Nick Dixon, 1990s
Ant Lives Nick Dixon, April, 1987
Apocalypse Now Mark Sharratt
Boba Fett Simon Nadin
Boozy Traverse Simon Panton, 1994
Cellar Dwella Justin Critchlow
Columns Mick Adams
Crystal Voyager Simon Nadin, 1984
The Cube Nick Dixon, Allen Williams, Simon Oaker, Simon Whalley, March, 1986
Dignity of Labour Nick Dixon, 1983
Dirtnap Simon Willson
Don's Crack Don Whillans
Dreadful Dave Banks, 1989
Drunk Enough Simon Panton, 1994
Grand Theft Justin Critchlow, 2003
The Gutter Aussie Andy
Higginson's Arm Justin Critchlow, 2000
Inertia Reel Johnny Dawes, March, 1986
Inertia Reel Traverse Jerry Moffatt, 1998
Joe's Arête Joe Brown
Jump Simon Whalley, March, 1986
Limbless Limbo Dancer Paul Higginson, 1999
Mean Ol' B'stard, Milky Buttons Justin Critchlow
Milky Buttons Justin Critchlow, 2002
Mistral Start Gary Cooper, 1987
Mr Nice Justin Critchlow
Mushin' Ben Moon, 1996
Nadin's Secret Finger Simon Nadin, 1985
Open Bum Cleft Johnny Dawes
Particle Exchange Mark Katz, September, 1996
Period Drama John Bull, 2000
Pipe Entry Andi Turner, 2003
The Pube John Bull, 2000
Pussin Boots The Leek Lads, 2001
Skydivin' Justin Critchlow, Paul Higginson, 1999
Sleeping with the Flowers Justin Critchlow, Andi Turner, 2001
Spankasaurus Does Chicago Nik Jennings, 2000
Spotter's Dyno Justin Critchlow, Andi Turner, 2001
Spotter's Pop The Leek Lads, 2001
Squeezer's Spots Andi Turner, 2001
Swivel Finger Simon Whalley, Nick Dixon, 1986
Tetris Rupert Davies
Teck Crack Super-Direct Paul Higginson, 1990s
Thud Paul Higginson, 1997
Too Drunk Simon Panton, 1994
Triptych Groove Andi Turner, Justin Critchlow, 2001
Turbo Rupert Davies
Undercut Dyno Richard Williams, 1998
Who Needs Ready Brek? Simon Nadin, April 1986

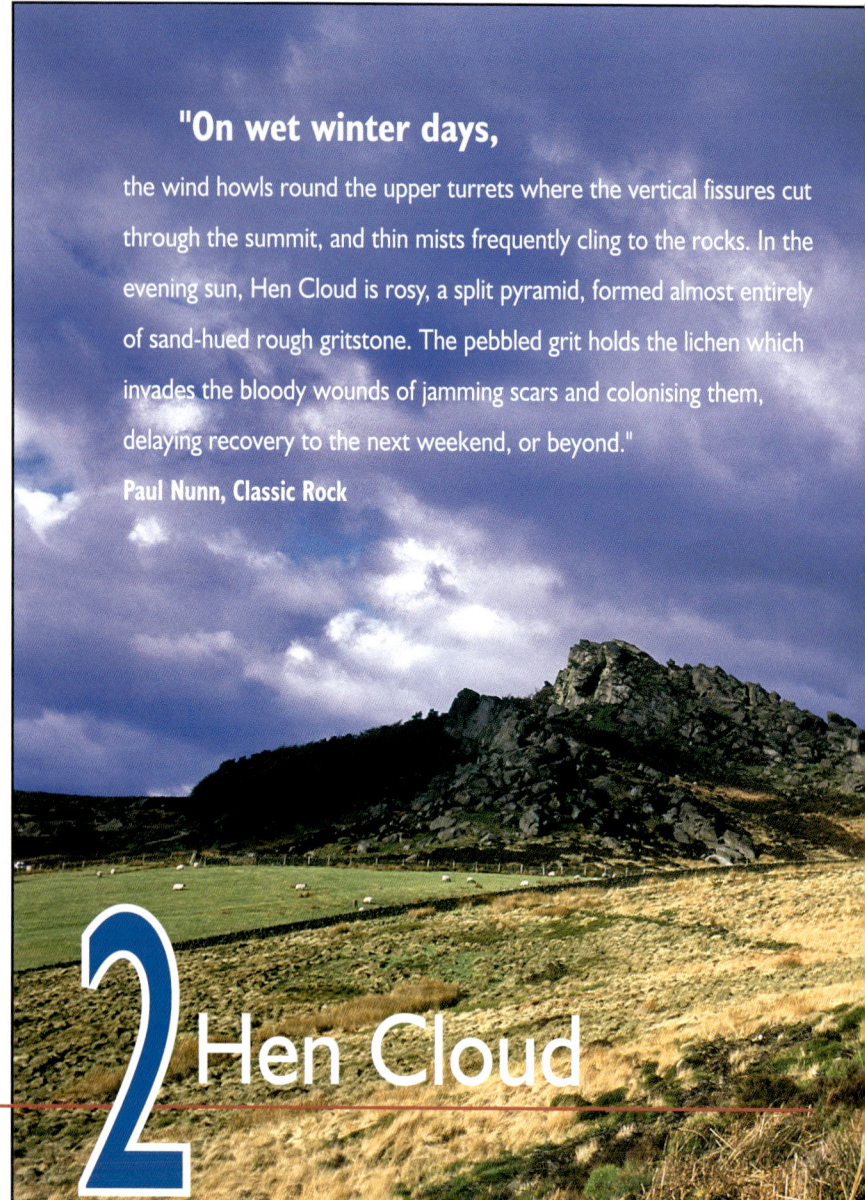

"**On wet winter days,**
the wind howls round the upper turrets where the vertical fissures cut through the summit, and thin mists frequently cling to the rocks. In the evening sun, Hen Cloud is rosy, a split pyramid, formed almost entirely of sand-hued rough gritstone. The pebbled grit holds the lichen which invades the bloody wounds of jamming scars and colonising them, delaying recovery to the next weekend, or beyond."
Paul Nunn, Classic Rock

2 Hen Cloud

Nic Sellers on Starlight and Storm, V6 (page 167). Photo: Adam Long.

Staffordshire Grit

Hen Cloud

by Niall Grimes

O.S. Ref. SK008617 — Altitude: 400m a.s.l.

The massive gritstone fortress of Hen Cloud is without doubt one of the most noble and majestic crags in the whole of the Peak District. Proudly guarding the summit of a steep hillside, its impending walls rise abruptly from the escarpment, and to those unused to the crag, project the forbidding impression of a grim fortification. On closer acquaintance, the crag will indeed be found to be steep; however, it is far from impregnable. Get to grips with the climbs here and you will tend to find good holds and generally sound protection, making them welcoming, while still retaining a formidable level of challenge.

Challenge and reward come in equal measures, of course, and the satisfaction gained from an ascent of one of Hen Cloud's fine routes is not to be matched anywhere on grit. The climbs here have traditionally been considered hard for their grade. This may well be true if one arrives at the crag unfit; the steepness then can seem unforgiving. However, for the climber with a bit of get up and go, the climbs will be found to be peerless challenges. Fierce but honest, bold without being dangerous. And in many ways, once a climber has climbed a route of their grade on Hen Cloud, they can fairly claim themselves to be a master of that grade.

Conditions & aspect

With its elevation and aspect, Hen Cloud is a superb crag to visit when the sun shines and, especially on summer evenings, is a great place to watch the sun set. In colder, and especially windy weather its exposed position can be keenly felt and sometimes, in the wetter months, parts of the crag become green. However, this often appears much worse than it actually is, and the crag has an unfair reputation for being lichenous. Black Wall does take a lot of drainage and can be very slow to dry after prolonged rain. It faces generally west and south-west, with plenty of south faces getting early sun, and for most of the day. Main faces come into the sun early afternoon, and remain in it until sunset.

The climbing

Superb, with 170 routes. Generally long, steep cracks and faces. High quality, but a limited number of easy routes. Mid and higher grades are very well served with some of the best routes in the area.

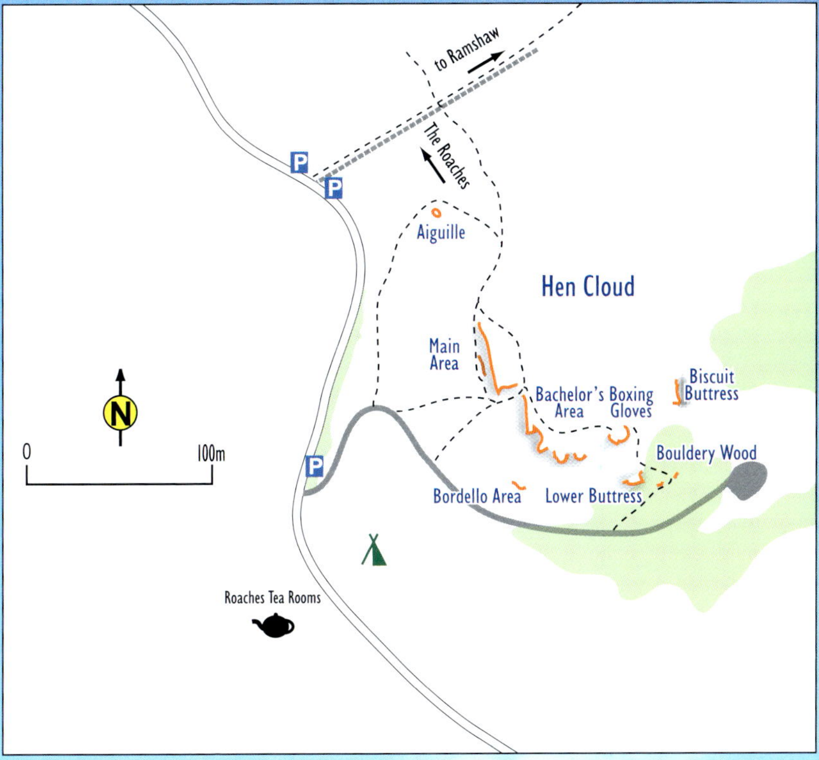

Hen Cloud Intro

Staffordshire Grit

On Hen Cloud can be found the pick of the climbing.

It is as shapely and defined a summit as any 3,000ft sgurr in the western highlands. We will tackle the most prominent of this handsome set of teeth as a first trial of what the Staffordshire sgurr can offer in the way of problems. It is not a considerable climb – quite the reverse – yet not too easy. Let us call it a tussle with gloves on. For if, as is likely, the stony giant knocks you backwards, there is a thick pad of heather to fall back on, with deep cushions of peat below.
EA Baker

Parking & approach

Parking is available in the lay-bys on the road below the crag, but beware the restrictions on parking on the verges, which are periodically ruthlessly enforced. From the gate on the road, walk along the unmetalled lane that runs under the crag. A track leads to the Central Area from the first bend, or a little further on, a larger one runs up to the middle of the crag. Both are steep warm ups (5–10 minutes). For the Bordello area, the Bottom Buttresses, the Lower Buttress and Biscuit Buttress areas, follow the unmetalled lane below the crag. The Bordello area comprises a group of small crags about 50m up from the track and 100m before the woods. For the others, walk as far as the cattle grid in the woods, where a track leads up left to the first rocks almost immediately. Finally, a track leads across from the right end of the Roaches (10 minutes), giving handy access to The Aiguille and the left side of the crag.

Access

The whole crag is in Open Access and currently owned by the Peak National Park. In recent years Peregrine Falcons have taken a liking to the Black Wall area and have reared young successfully thanks to climbers' co-operation. These are the first Peregrines in this area for close to 100 years. Notices will be placed on site to advice climbers and marking out any restricted area. This will normally be in force from early March to mid-June. This information will be updated onto the BMC RAD site also.

Dave Noddings on High Tensile Crack, HVS 5b (page 171). Photo: David Simmonite.

The Aiguille

The first climbs lie on an attractive pinnacle close to the road, and slightly left of the main crag. The lines are in that murky area between routes and highball boulder problems. They are probably best enjoyed with pads and a spotter. Whichever way you care to climb them, they are magnificent.

1 Starlight Left V4 (6b)
Superb moves lead up the narrow face, using both arêtes, to the break. Step right to join Starlight and Storm, or jump off.

2 Starlight and Storm V6 (6c)
An exquisite micro-route. Boulder up the right side of the arête to the break, from where further inventive climbing gains the summit: *see photo on page 163*.

3 Simon's Slab V7 (6c)
Scratch desperately up the centre of the slab past the pocket.

4 The Aiguillette S 4b ★   1913–27
6m The right arête, via a well-protected but gung-ho high step near the top. At this grade step off the boulder to start. Starting from the ground gives a few more excellent moves at about 5c.

Jon Read, one of the main driving forces behind new routing at Hen Cloud in recent years, seen here picking off another of the crags last problems: Mandatory, E5 6a (opposite page). Photo: Justin Critchlow.

The Pinnacles

The first area of crag proper is characterised by a distinctive row of pinnacles. The rock on some of the areas can be sometimes a bit scratchy and the routes a little shorter than on the main sections, but they are great routes nonetheless.

The first rock of any consequence is a flat clean wall known as **Zoom Wall**. This contains three problems, the left and right sides being 4c and the centre being 5a (all V0-).

5 Nutted by Reality E1 6b ★   1978
7m The rippled wall 10m right, directly up its centre. Few will manage the start first go (V4), but every effort needs to be made to flash the easier, but rounded and unprotected, finish. This is where the nutting may occur.

A poor route, **Slipstreams** (HVS 5a, 1979), climbs the twin cracks on the right of the dirty wall 8m right. Other lines are possible. **Little Pinnacle Climb** (HVD, 1968–73) is the corner-line to the right.

The next routes all begin off a grass ledge starting a few metres above the path.

6 November Cracks HS 4b   1927
12m Climb the cracks on the front face to the ledge, then the corner crack behind. Good stuff!

7 Bulwark E1 5a ★   1957
12m Exposed situations combined with thoughtful protection and some rather soft and sandy holds make for a memorable lead. Start on the right wall of the tower, and tiptoe out to the arête, whereupon a tricky move gains a scratchy ledge. Delicate climbing now leads up to an awkward finish on good flutes.

8 Slowhand E1 5 ★★   1978
11m Bulwark's smarter brother which follows the scoop just right. From the recess near the gully, pull out left and move up to a deep flake crack. The blind flake above is used to gain the airy summit.

*The awkward descent to the right (**Chockstone Chimney**, M, 1947–51).*

9 Mindbridge E7 6c   1984
11m The steep right wall of the gully features an inverted coffin-shaped shadow, the substance of this climb. Boulder up the wall to a break, and possible protection, and a chance to wish your friends goodbye. From here, the way ahead is dark and lonely…

Hen Cloud The Pinnacles

10 Master of Reality E6 6c ★★★ 1983
11m A contender for the best E6 in the county; a stunning route with consistently fine climbing, it is based on the unique dinosaur's spine of grit running up the front of the second pinnacle. Work up the lower wall on positive features and marginal pro. At the break, place good medium nuts and cams, take a deep breath, and let rip with everything you've got, aiming for the next break. Inspirational.

11 Master of Puppets E6 6b ★ 2003
11m The arête to the right by reachy moves above a nasty back-breaking block.

*The notch (called **The Notch**) between the second and third towers can be gained by a crack (4c), or a ramp to the right (5b).*

12 Chicken E1 5b ★★ 1960s
12m A really good route with plenty of variety. Follow the steep crack that cleaves the buttress to a break. Swing right to a ledge, then back left up an unnerving scoop to the top. Two variations exist: **Pullet** (E1 5b, 1978), climbing the lower right arête, and **Chicken Direct** (E4 6b, 1981), which climbs the left arête above the first crack, but these both lack the charm of the original.

13 Piston Groove VS 5a 1957–68
11m A technical start allows major fun to be had in the tight V-groove.

14 Man oh Man E4 6a ★ 1999
9m Climb the crack in the wall right of the groove. Good climbing in restricted situations.

15 Mandatory E5 6a ★ 2007
9m Climb the left-bounding edge of the buttress until beneath the hanging crack of Man oh Man. Place gear and head directly over the bulge and into Mandrake; finish up this grittily: *see photo opposite.*

16 The Mandrake E5 6a ★ 1979
10m From Victory (and a runner level with the overlap), make a powerful hand-traverse leftwards to the brittle flake on the arête and finish boldly up this.

17 Mandrill E5 6b 2000
10m Knuckle down to the wall on the right, pulling over the overlap at the good hold on The Mandrake to a very thin crack (small wires and micro-cams), then direct to the top.

18 Victory VS 4c 1957–68
9m The crack to the right; nice climbing. The thin crack just right is **Short 'n Sharp** (E1 5c, 1978).

Staffordshire Grit

19 Green Corner HS 4b   1957–68
8m The corner is green. And usually slimy too.

20 Blood Blisters E5 6b   1981
9m A gnarly overly-hard route which gains the upper arête of the wall. Boulder up the wall below the crack to small pro. Go left to the arête and scratch frantically to a biodegradable finish. High in the grade. **Blood Blisters Direct** is a V3 (6b) problem up the lower arête.

21 Electric Chair E2 5c ★★   1978
9m The line of least resistance. Climb the right edge of the wall to a ledge, then traverse left to a crack and the first protection. From here, good moves lead up and right into a final scoop. Bold.

22 Bad Joke E4 5c ★   1979
8m *I say, I say, I say…* from the ledge on Electric Chair, continue up the wall via long and satisfying cranks. Totally unprotected, but the moves are obvious and never nasty. Low in the grade.

23 Gallows E2 5b ★   1978
8m Bold and tricky. Climb the hanging arête on its left to a disappointing break. Swing quickly right and gain the summit using a pocket. The route can be climbed all the way on the right, slightly easier, or continued on the left to the top at E4 5c: **The Trap Door Finish** (1990s).

24 Sand Castles E4 5c   2007
7m Step off the boulder in the gully and head centrally up one of Hen Cloud's few slabs.

25 Recess Chimney VD   1957–68
7m Climb the chimney, then either exit to the top.

26 Black Eyed Dog E6 6b ★   1987
8m The rounded arête right of the chimney, gained from the ledge, leads with greater and greater difficulty to a rounded finish. Unprotected.

27 The Sorcerer E3 6a ★   1978
8m The wicked crack on the front has a bouldery start, then a continually technical and rounded battle all the way to the top. A good climb.

Hen Cloud

Hen Cloud Black Wall

28 High Tensile Crack HVS 5b ★   1962
8m The little corner crack just right has a strenuous start on stiff technical hand jams, but soon relents: *photo on page 166*.

29 Justin Time E5 6b ★   2006
8m One of the Hen Cloud LGPs. The hanging crack is gained by slappy bouldering from a height which you wouldn't want to roll from.

Black Wall

The obvious flat black wall at the lower level is home to a number of fingery crack climbs. The rock here is of a different nature to the rock elsewhere, with slightly lower friction. Unfortunately it seeps badly, but when dry, the routes offer excellent climbing.

30 Buster the Cat HVS 5b   1979
8m The slim crack and groove.

31 Pug VS 4c   1968–73
8m The main crack at the left gains a hanging garden.

32 A Flabby Crack E6 6c ★★   1992
10m A line of hopeless seams and nothing finger-pockets is followed to a desperate final move. Well protected, but almost F7b+.

33 The Stone Loach E5 6b ★★   1981
10m A very good climb combining a powerful and technical first half with something altogether different in the second. Cracks lead upwards with difficulty and good protection, to the wide break. Now the fun begins. The prehistoric gash above your head is longer than it looks.

34 Myxi E6 6c ★   2008
10m Climb the wall between Anthrax and Stone Loach with a fingery crux a long way above any protection. Kill a rabbit on the way down.

35 Anthrax E4 6a ★★   1975
20m A varied battle up two very different sizes of crack. The thin bit; a bouldery start leads to nice holds and protection. The crack above is steep and tough to the very end. Now the thick bit; at the break, banish all thoughts of sandwiches, and stomach-traverse left and climb the tough upper gash of The Stone Loach.

36 The Lum HVS 4c   1957–68
10m A despicable skirmish up the unaccommodating chimney line.

37 Scrumptious E4 6b ★   2004
10m The arête right of The Lum is a technical delight.

38 Bantam Crack VS 4c ★   1957–68
10m Fine jamming up the varied hand crack. Less pleasant when the top is dirty, although a prior inspection and cleaning is easy. The bouldery arête a couple of metres right gives a fine problem: **Alan Whicker**, V3 (6a).

Brown and Whillans day out

Undoubtedly the greatest partnership on British rock, these two dominated new route activity from the late 1940s right into the late 50s. Their legacy is some of the best lines anywhere, mostly around the VS to E1 range. Anyone who feels they are competent at these standards may wish to try their luck repeating all their routes in a day.

They are, starting at **Ramshaw:** Don's Crack, Prostration, Brown's Crack, The Crank, Masochism, Great Zawn; Ramshaw Crack
Hen Cloud: Bachelor's Climb (**left-hand finish**), Bachelor's Left-Hand, Hen Cloud Eliminate, Second's Retreat, Slimline, Reunion Crack, Delstree, Main Crack, En Rappel.
Roaches: Choka, Rhodren, The Bulger, The Mincer, Matinee, Valkyrie Direct, Crack of Gloom, Dorothy's Dilemma, Teck Crack, Ackit, Lightning Crack, **Slippery Jim**, The Sloth, Saul's Crack, Aqua.

As an idea of how tough this challenge is, it has been dubbed:

"The Staffordshire Nose"

Laybacking joy for the Bazooka-bicepped VS leader, Reunion Crack bears all the hallmarks of the Rock and Ice Club (opposite page). Photo: David Simmonite.

Delstree Area

The crag now starts to reach its characteristic form, with big, strenuous cracklines on sound rock. Steepness gives a continually challenging feel to the routes, although they also tend to be well-protected, and superb.

39 **Chockstone Crack** M   1947–51
11m A deep and meaningful experience up the rocky cleft. The grassy rampline just to its left is an awkward access route from the top.

40 **The Better End** E3 6a ★★   1962
11m At the left end of the terrace, a forceful crack climbs a leaning wall. Ascend said crack to a slopey ledge. With protection placed, set sail on the butch leaning layback – somewhat alarming – which leads to the surface. Excellent. The tempting scoop to the left is unclimbed.

41 **The Raid** E4 6a ★   1978
13m A good route with a bouldery start and a fine headwall. Climb the angular scoop in the arête (with the spotter well lashed down) until a pull left gains a crack and a ledge. Small wires protect the cracked upper wall, although the confident will find this straightforward.

42 **En Rappel** HVS 4c ★★   1927
12m A couple of exposed mantels lead into a rampline. Follow this to a good ledge. From here, pull out left onto the crest of the crag, and over onto the heather above. The original finish traversed right from the good ledge to gain a wide finishing crack (known as **Blizzard Buttress**). Less direct, but providing more adventure.

43 **Caesarian** E4 6b ★★★   1978
12m The centre of the steep wall is brilliant; top of the range, in every sense, with just about every move being 5c or more. Boulder up past vertical flakes to reach slanting breaks and good gear. An almighty move from here gains the next break, and a still tricky finishing crack. One of the big 3 E4s on the crag.

172 Hen Cloud

Hen Cloud Delstree Area

44 Catharsis E7 7a ★★ 2006
12m Boulder up the shallow flake to the long break. Somehow cover the next 2 metres of blank rock before placing large cams and heading up and left on tinies to join Caesarian at the top: *see photo page 31*.

45 Main Crack VS 5a ★★ 1957–61
12m Men have disappeared for days in this fissure. Some have never returned. The big crack is mean to start, but then relents with fine jamming. However, dimensions once again turn nasty near the top, and knees may be called for. A must for the hairy trousered adventurer. Following the diagonal cracks leftwards is **Pointless but Pumpy**, E1 5b (2002).

46 Delstree HVS 5a ★★★ 1957–61
20m The superbly positioned corner perched on the front of the face is a real gritstone classic. Start under an awkward overhang. Negotiate this, surprisingly gymnastic, then move delicately left to the base of the shallow corner. Jamming ecstasy follows to a balding finish. 5a every magnificent step of the way.

47 Levitation E5 6a ★ 1979
20m The steep arête. From the foot of Reunion Crack, climb a thin crack, then the wall above, heading for the arête. A difficult crux high above the runners makes this hard for the grade, so beware.

48 Reunion Crack VS 5a ★★ 1957–61
20m The overhanging corner/flake is impending and strenuous; however, the gear is plentiful, and the holds are as friendly as can be. It is gained by surmounting the overhang as for Delstree, then following the ramp rightwards to the base of the corner. A brisk layback follows: *see photo opposite*.

49 The Pinch E1 5c 1978
20m From a long way up the easy gully (**Slab Way**, M), climb the arête of the black tower to the left. The last move (crux) is pointlessly easy for the tall, and easily impossible for the short. The grade is meaningless.

50 Fat Old Sun E3 5a, 6a ★ 1974
A traverse of the buttress gives constant exposure and covers much fine rock.
1. 11m Climb the Bitter End to the ledge, then traverse right to the scoop of En Rappel.
2. 26m Step down, then stretch along the rounded break, passing the base of Caesarian's crack, to a hiding place in Main Crack. Move up, then forcefully tackle the disappearing undercut to a less good hiding place in Delstree. Step up again before airy moves gain the big jug on Levitation, leading to the top.

Jon Read demonstrating what may or may not be the best way of doing Borstal Breakout, E4 6a, 6b (opposite page) which, along with Caesarian and Chameleon, is one of the crag's great E4 ticks. Photo: Niall Grimes.

Hen Cloud Central Area

Central Area

The biggest section of rock on Hen Cloud is the complex fortress of the Central Area. Numerous corners and ledges break this section up, although the climbing in between the ledges tends to be forceful. The main features of the area are the dominating corner system taken by Central Climb, and The Terrace, a lush grass covered ledge, bisecting this climb at half height. The rock, apart from some sections towards the left, is good and clean, although some of the more classic climbs on the right are now a little polished. **Descent** for these climbs is down the path to the right.

51 Qantas E1 5b   1978
8m Climb the thin groove on the left of the wall to a good nut, then swing right to the next little groove to finish. Sweet.

52 Press On Regardless E2 5b   1978
10m From the break on Qantas, traverse right to the arête, gaining an amount of exposure as you go. A tricky move up the left side of the arête leads to steadily easing climbing. Bold.

53 The Ape E1 5b   1962
11m Climb the wide crack till it is possible to monkey rightwards along a horizontal break, then finish.

54 The Monkey in your Soul E3 5c 1978
15m Climb the thin, steep, well-protected crack in the centre of the wall to its termination. From here, traverse right to the poor finish of Broken Arrow.

55 Broken Arrow E1 5b   1978
11m Climb hollow flakes at the right of the wall until difficulty and unpleasantness force one round right. Pull left again onto the face to finish.

56 Roof Climb VS 4b, 3b ★ ★   1947–51
A route that takes an easy line amid some imposing territory.
1. 20m The square-cut corner is followed, first on the right, then the left, where some back and footing leads to The Terrace.
2. 10m Climb the easy gully right of the arête, or much better, do Final Crack (Route 60).

57 The Long and the Short E1 5b, 5b ★   1960s
A technical first pitch is followed by a frantic thrash on the second.
1. 15m The elegant groove is bridged romantically to The Terrace. This pitch alone gives a quality HVS.
2. 10m Casting all thoughts of elegance adrift, submit to the wide crack bounding the steep wall. Escape right onto the face at half-height, and finish up an open groove.

58 Anaconda E4 6a, 6b ★   1976
Generally good climbing, but spoiled by the odd scruffy interlude.
1. 15m Climb the tight right-angled groove, very reasonably, to a green overhang. Pull strenuously round left to gain gear and good holds, and move up to a flake. An apocalyptic top-out now follows.
2. 10m On the steep wall above The Terrace, stand on a ledge, and make a desperate move to a poor finger-jam. Traverse more easily left to a black flake to finish.

59 Borstal Breakout E4 6a, 6b ★ ★ ★   1978
The sublime first pitch features meaty bouldering in safe situations. **Photo opposite**.
1. 23m Attack the steep hand-jamming crack above the grassy ledge, and climb this to a little roof. Above, the crack peters out. Move up and execute a superb and very testing sequence on big open holds to gain salvation.
2. 10m Start as for Anaconda, but continue direct to easy ground. An unbalanced pitch.

60 Final Crack HS 4b ★ ★   1947–51
10m Magnificent jamming on perfect rock. Starting on The Terrace (gained from Roof Route or Central Climb), take the obvious crack right of the flat wall with the final bulge providing the crux.

61 Central Climb Direct
VS 5a, 4b, 4a ★ ★   1947–51
A series of variations on the original.
1. 8m The sinuous fissure below the fine arête is a classic example of the gritstone udge.
2. 11m Climb the middle pitch of the parent route, or the exposed flakes to the right.
3. 11m The noble groove just to the left is followed to the summit.

Staffordshire Grit

176 Hen Cloud

Hen Cloud Central Area

The towering architecture of Hen Cloud's central area dominates climbers embarking on the crag's oldest and most venerable classic, Central Climb, HS 4c (opposite page). Photo: Niall Grimes.

Hen Cloud Central Area

62 B4XS E7 6b ★★★   1986
10m Crikey! An all-out lead of the highest order up the dominating rounded arête. Thin, smeary and serious, only the luckiest of leaders will miss the crippling ledge in the event of a fall. Begin on the first ledge of Central Climb, gain the arête, and follow it, using holds and flutings on the right side.

63 Hens Dropping E1 6a   2002
8m A filler-in pitch. Climb the black flake right of Central Climb Direct to a wide break. Stand up here with some difficulty and continue direct.

64 Standing Tall E2 4c, 5b   1979
A mopping-up exercise with some nice climbing, starting at an obvious square niche.
1. 15m Pull out of the niche directly and climb the bulging rounded rib above to a ledge. Continue up, right of the corner, on positive flakes.
2. 16m A bold rambling pitch. From 3m up the corner, hand-traverse the ramp right to Encouragement and so to the ledge. Move up and left on good, but spaced, holds before stepping back right and exiting carefully past a loose block.

65 Central Climb HS 4c, 4b, 4a ★★★   1909
A route with a superb line and flawless historical pedigree, although the lower sections are beginning to age. The belays are all magnificent. Start at the well-worn shallow corner just to the right. *See photo opposite*.
1. 10m Climb the cantankerous crack to a ledge.
2. 11m An awkward corner (excellent thread) leads to a second ledge. Thrill seekers can avoid this by a bold 4b traverse right to the ledge on positive finger-holds. Steep cracks above lead to The Terrace.
3. 11m Go directly up the well-used cracks above, or veer rightwards at half-height (slightly easier). Prudent climbers will carry either a headtorch or a chauffeur: *see photo opposite*.

66 Encouragement E1 5b, 5b ★★★   1960s
A beautiful and balanced climb, with a thoughtful first pitch, and a steep second pitch where the less time spent thinking the better.
1. 15m Gain the square-cut hanging groove. Follow this with sustained bridging and a cunning swing left near the top to a handsome belay ledge.
2. 15m The crack above succumbs to a satisfying series of hand and finger jams. This pitch is steep and testing, but protection is perfect. Finish up the ridge.

67 Jean the Bean E5 6b ★   1997
15m A fine bold climb up the short unprotected arête to the right of Encouragement's first pitch. Very high in the grade.

68 K2 S 4a, 4b ★★   1927
30m A great expedition, demanding on the arms.
1. 12m The next major corner leads steeply to a ledge.
2. 18m Above the stance, follow the steep Y-shaped crack. This is more technical than any obscure Himalayan namesake, and more slippy. Above, an easier groove leads to the summit ridge.

69 7 of 9 VS 5a   2002
30m From the base of the K2 corner, climb a steep crack to the rib. Continue steeply up the left side of the rib then follow a short crack to rejoin K2.

70 The Arête HVD 4a ★★★   pre-1913
30m Follow the exposed stepped ridge all the way to the summit of the mountain, with a exposed but positive step at half height for the crux. Better than anything in the Alps: *see photo overleaf*.

This crack repulsed a good number of pioneers

before being climbed by John Laycock in 1909. Unfortunately his second, AR Thompson, was unable to follow it as 'he was handicapped by a congenital disability that made all climbing a matter of heroic endeavour'! Laycock continued but became benighted and was rescued several hours later by a sturdy chauffeur. He later confessed: 'Not everyone has been benighted on gritstone and, though one ought to be ashamed of a want of prudence, the episode is delightful to me in retrospect; gritstone has its romance no less than granite.'

Paul Nunn on Central Climb

When Manchester's Rucksack Club visited Hen Cloud in the years before the First World War they accounted for some of the crag's first climbs. These antiquities would go on, a century later, to be Hen Cloud's easy classics, none more so than The Arête, HVD. Even today, with its unusual length, distant protection and fantastic exposure, it is still a memorable lead that cannot be taken for granted (previous page). Photo: Jon Read.

Hen Cloud Ampitheatre Walls

Amphitheatre Walls

Right of The Arête, the walls and routes taper up to the central path. All the climbs benefit from morning sunshine. The first of these lies on the left wall of the big gully.

71 Arête Wall VS 5a ★   1957–68
18m The first steep crack on the gully wall is strenuous going on perfect jams. From a block move right and go up. A poor man's Crack of Gloom.

72 Easy Come VS 4c   1978
12m A thin crack 4m right again is steep and stiff. Finish diagonally rightwards via a slab onto The Arête.

73 Easy Gully M   1913–27
35m The moderately easy gully.

74 Songs of Praise E2 5c   1971
12m Undercut and layback the wild flake on the upper wall of the gully. A very awkward move is needed to escape right to easy ground and finish.

75 Loose Fingers E2 5c   1980
9m The crack just downhill is consistently awkward and often dirty.

76 Prayers, Poems and Promises
E1 5b ★   1978
11m Just right again, gain a ledge on the arête. Using a hole on the arête and the crack to the left (small pro useful), climb up the rib to a rightwards exit and an easy finish.

77 Modern HS 4b ★ ★   1947–51
18m A super climb that heaves its way up the chunky flakeline on the front of the face. While steep, generous holds give the climb a friendly aspect. From a stance, climb the tough right-hand of two steep cracks on the vertical wall.

A fingery boulder problem climbs the clean wall above the ledge on the front of the buttress, V2 (6a). This was originally the start of **Flexure Line**, which carried on up the buttress (1981).

78 Ancient HVD 4a ★   1947–51
18m A good climb with a fine finish. Gain the niche on the front of the buttress, then pull out left and follow a line just left of the arête to a ledge and possible belay. Follow the steep, left-hand crack-line above.

79 Even Smaller Buttress HVS 5a   1985
6m A delightful solo which ascends the steep arête on sidepulls. Like this? You'll love Solid Geometry.

Staffordshire Grit

80 Small Buttress HVS 5a ★ 1979
6m Monkey up the front of the little buttress. Even smaller than Even Smaller Buttress. The arête on the little buttress just right is **Andrei's Route** (HVS 5a, 2002), but is artificial.

81 Bitching HVS 5a ★ 1978
7m The crack in the left wall of Bow Buttress. The crux is the start but the rest has a certain urgency.

82 The Driven Bow E7 6c ★★ 2002
8m A thrilling sequence, a long, long way above the safety net. Climb the short crack, and fiddle in some pro at its apex. From here, fingery cranking leads upwards past an alarming slap and a desperate pull onto the top.

83 Bow Buttress HVD 4a ★★ 1924
8m A little climb, but strenuous. Climb the rising right-trending line, which intersects the arête, as far as the wide crack. Move up this then finish up left under the capstone.

84 Solid Geometry E1 5b ★★ 1980
8m The fine arête followed direct all the way. Exciting but positive, and difficulties are short-lived.

Bachelor's Area

To the right of the descent path lies one of the finest walls on gritstone. The bulging wedge-shaped wall is home to many strong lines, and many required the strengths of the Brown/Whillans and Allen/Bancroft teams to subdue them. In many ways, it is the routes on this wall that give Hen Cloud its reputation, a reputation based on hard-fought struggles of the highest quality up steep, soaring crack-lines. It is worth noting that above some of the climbs belays are hard to find and you may have to go back a ways.

85 Right Ramp V0 (5a)
The rising ramp at the left of the wall.

86 Left Vein V2 (5c)
The left-hand vein system is quite tricky.

87 Right Vein V2 (6a)
The right-hand system is trickier again.

88 Stokesline E2 6b 1977
6m A problem start leads to the slightly easier crack; highball V4.

Hen Cloud Bachelor's Area

89 This Poison E3 6b   1981
6m Boulder up the wall between the cracks using a pebble: highball V5.

90 Slimline E1 5b   1957–61
9m The crack to the right, with most of the activity centred around the widest section: highball V1.

91 Peter and the Wolf E6 6b ★   1990
10m Classy bouldering at an uncomfortable height. Using a good pocket, gain the half-height break. From here, good pinching and undercutting brings better holds to hand, and a sprint to the top. Protection only arrives after the climbing has eased off.

92 Fast Piping E4 6b ★   1981
11m A stiff wall climb with hard moves leading away from good gear. Gain the short crack, then make desperate moves up and left to get established in the next crack. Uneasy moves then gain the brittle flake. The upper crack is followed with well-protected relief.

93 Hedgehog Crack VS 4b ★★   1947–51
11m The obvious steep crack, with superb jamming leading to a slightly wide finish.

94 Comedian E3 6a ★★★   1976
12m A superb route with tough, technical moves. Climb the crack till stiff moves lead right to a horizontal break. Nibble back left to the crack, which is followed on helpful jams to an entertaining groove through the final bulge. Large cams useful.

95 Frayed Nerve E5 6a ★   1981
12m Good delicate climbing with an entertaining fall potential. Climb the steep groove left of the big crack, then some chunky horizontals, to a deep break. Place some large cams here, and commit to the less steep wall above, exiting via the little rounded groove. Sporty.

96 Second's Retreat HVS 4c ★   1952
15m The steep V-groove heaves and bulges, and provides good climbers with a thrilling series of deep, wide challenges. Again, lots of big cams can ease the passage, and the growth in the crack is not the problem it would appear.

97 Second's Advance HVS 5a ★   1962
15m Climb a thin crack and the narrow groove above to a jug below a steepening. Above this, a grossly overhanging hand-crack leads beefily to a slabby ledge below a scoop. Traverse left to the chimney crack to finish (the direct finish, following the scoop above, is a nasty, poorly protected E2).

98 Corinthian E3 5c ★★★   1976
17m A fine steep crack climb, where the holds and protection are never quite as good as they would appear. Climb to the base of a faint bulging crack containing a rusty peg. From here, grapple up the rounded, pumpy crack. Testing, but still the easiest of Bancroft and Allen's 'C' routes.

99 Hen Cloud Eliminate HVS 5b ★★★ 1957–61
18m One of the best routes of this grade in the Peak. The discontinuous cracks give gruelling jamming, but the finish, struggling into the groove where the rock lies back, gives the crux. Prudent mountaineers will carry no fewer than two large cams for this section: altogether now, 'I bet Joe Brown didn't have them'.

100 Cool Fool E6 6b ★   1981
20m The steep arête features hard insecure climbing in a thoroughly terrifying situation. Begin up a shallow groove until a ledge, where protection can be placed behind a boulder. Go left, and climb the bold arête, until a crack on the right (Rib Crack) is reached with great relief, and gear. Move left again and continue to a rounded top.

101 Rib Chimney S 4b ★★   pre-1913
20m This soaring and confident line gives one of the best chimney outings in the Peak, with a particularly technical bridging section in the middle. **Rib Crack** (VS 5a, 1962), is the enjoyable crack in the upper left wall.

102 Caricature E5 6a ★★★   1976
22m John Allen's western masterpiece, one of the best E5s on grit, taking a tortuous and sustained line up big wall. From a ledge on Rib Chimney, place a high runner, and make a difficult traverse right, using small holes for the hands, to the front face. Gear. Tough moves lead into a scoop, followed by continually demanding moves right to the very top.

Staffordshire Grit

103 Chiaroscuro E6 6b ★ 1985
24m An eliminate line seeking out some fine areas of rock. From the top of the first crack of Bachelor's Left-Hand, undercut left and balance up the rib as far as Caricature. This section alone would make a very good direct start to Caricature, at E6 6a. Move right, place a runner in the Bachelor crack, and gibber up the bulging slab, trending slightly left.

104 Bachelor's Left-Hand HVS 5b ★★★ 1957–61
25m A majestic climb, continually steep and challenging, and as good as anything on grit. It takes a sweeping line up the right side of the wall, starting from below a prominent crack. Gain this crack with difficulty. At its terminus, make a powerful swing right to a horizontal flake crack then move up to the rounded ramp above. From here, the major crack to the right is taken, which, while still steep, is less taxing than what has gone before: *see photo on page 186*.

105 Parallel Lines E6 6c ★ 1985
25m The smooth wall to the right is taken, using a ridiculous series of hopeless non-holds, up and into a shallow groove and a respite: side-runners used.

106 Bachelor's Climb VS 4c ★★★ 1947
27m A carnival of jamming up the butch crack leads to a possible stance on The Pulpit. Traverse left and finish up Bachelor's Left-Hand. The poorer, easier original version escaped up Great Chimney from The Pulpit.

107 Space Probe E4 6a, 6a ★★ 1979
1. 12m Step right to the arête, and follow this till a committing reach gains a break. Go round right, and balance up to the ledge.
2. 8m The **Helter Skelter Finish**. A single tricky move up the arête above gains good holds leading left to an easy finishing groove.

Hen Cloud

Hen Cloud Bachelor's Area

108 Night Prowler E6 6a ★★ 2005
18m From the ledge of Space Probe head straight up the dominant lonely arête with committing moves from the word go. Said, by some, to be scarier than a night out in Biddulph.

109 Great Chimney HVD 4a ★★★ 1913
18m An excellent climb of the old type. Any combination of the corner cracks can be used although starting in the left one and transferring to the right at Pulpit height is the most obvious: *see photo page 189*.

110 Rainbow Crack VS 4c ★★ 1947–51
18m The confident flake crack on the wall right of Great Chimney. Gain a ledge at half-height by either of the two starts. Both are strenuous and slightly awkward, although the superb jamming of the upper half makes it all worthwhile.

111 Arêtenophobia E6 6b ★ 1996
16m The arête left of Chameleon. Traverse right to place a runner in the flake at the overhang, then back left to climb the bold arête.

112 Chameleon E4 6a ★★★ 1977
12m The handsome line on the steep wall is everything E4 should be. Climb to the overhang, then make an exacting traverse left to a deep flake in the roof. Determined pulls from here gain the upper flake, which still needs a bit of huff and puff. Magnificent.

113 Sauria E5 6a ★ 1986
10m The right arête. Runners are quite low and the climbing higher up is sustained and slappy.

114 Left Twin Crack HS 4b ★ 1957–68
9m The left of the, er, twin cracks. Short-lived, but fine laybacking or jamming after a problem start.

115 Right Twin Crack VS 4c 1957–68
9m The right crack has a spectacular finish.

116 Flour Wall E2 6b 2002
8m Boulder desperately up the wall left of the arête to the crack. The finish, to the left of the crack, is harder than it looks.

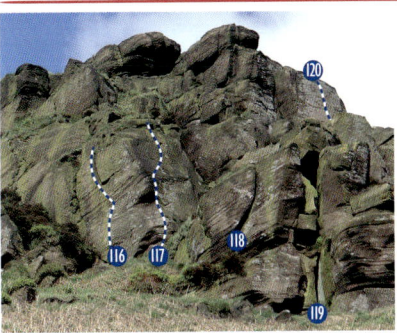

117 Dead Banana Slab HVS 5c 2002
7m Start below the arête and boulder up to gain the obvious good hold on its right above the bulge. Step right, and ascend the slab via pockets.

Below and 15m to the right, a small buttress emerges with an obvious chimney.

118 Just Thirteen VS 4c ★ 1995
5m Layback and jam the frisky flake up and left from the chimney. Fun.

119 Footpath Chimney HS 4c pre-1913
28m Climb the chimney with an awkward bulge. Scramble over blocks and finish up an arête.

Above here the crag recesses back and up for 20m.

120 Desperado E4 5c 1993
8m Climb the steep clean slab and wall at the back of the recess.

Hen Cloud HVS

Hen Cloud has been traditionally seen as being stiffly graded, and this nowhere more than in the HVS grade. Routes are steep, and need a fight to get up. Because of this, upgrading has been suggested. On the other hand, maybe they are just hard for the grade – 'proper HVS'. Whatever your opinion, the three big classics, and subject of most debate, **Delstree**, the **Eliminate** and **Bachelor's**, have been left as HVS. However, if you are successful on them, you are probably ready for most E1s.

Andi Turner punching it out on the blockbusting upper flake of Bachelor's Left-Hand (page 184), one of the crag's top three HVSs, and one of the best on grit. Photo: Mike Hutton.

Hen Cloud Thompson's Buttress

Below and right of the last route is a small slab with two problems on it. The left arête is V0– (4c) and the wall just right is V0 (5b). Opposite these problems is a grossly overhanging arête. This feature has been investigated by some of the strongest climbers in the area, and maybe top-roped once. However, it remains without doubt Hen Cloud's 'Last Great Problem'. The upper right arête of this block contains **Wavelength** (E1 5c, 1990). The easier-angled slab on the top gives a nice HD (best approached via one of the next routes).

Thompson's Buttress

About 20m further on, the path drops down a little just before the next set of rocks.

121 Thompson's Buttress Route One
S 4a ★   pre-1913

15m The first corner crack is climbed, then the steep fissure above and right. Good moves, if a little broken. The wide chimney to the left of the buttress, followed by the crack in the sidewall above, is **Thompson Twins**, HS 4b (trad).

122 Thompson's Buttress Route Two
HVD 4a   pre-1913

15m Just right, a set of giant stairs is climbed to the ledge. Climb the wide crack above.

123 Tree Chimney HS 4b   pre-1913
15m The obvious chimney, passing a steepening on the right. **Tunnel Vision** (HVS 5a, 1979), climbs the face to the right, somewhat artificially.

124 Touched V2 (5c)
5m Up around the corner on Thompson's Buttress and facing the Inaccessible Pinnacle is a short wall splattered with rugosities, climb the centre of this.

The Inaccessible Pinnacle

Right again, across a broad grassy gully, is a rounded buttress with a little pillar laid against its front face. **Descent** is slightly tricky. Either reverse the short back face (a 5a ascent), awkward, or go down the slab and make a little leap across the chasm.

125 Cold Sweat E1 5b ★   1979
8m Nice climbing up the wall left of the arête, trending towards the arête to finish. Bold.

126 Pinnacle Face VS 4b ★   1947–51
12m Climb up the slabby crack formed by the little pillar to its summit. Step left, and follow the absorbing slab on little ripples, with protection finally arriving just below the top. A more recent route, **Face Value** (HVS 5a, 1978), having started up the front of the pillar, climbs the slabby wall just right of Pinnacle Face.

127 Pinnacle Rib HVS 5a ★   1957–68
11m Brilliant obscure movements, the essence of gritstone. Gain the top of the pillar by its right-hand crack. From here, all sorts of moves are needed to scurry up and right, then on to the summit. **Delusion** (HS 4b, 1979), is a poor route up the V-groove to the right, escaping right at midway.

Staffordshire Grit

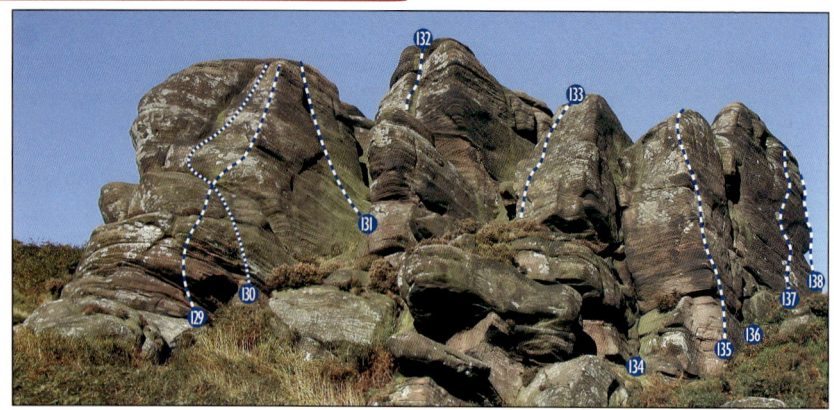

The Boxing Gloves

Forty-five metres to the right is a triple buttress of boxing glove type formations.

128 Shoe Shine Shuffle HVS 5b   1979
8m A strenuous crack on the left wall of the first glove. Swing right onto a projection and scuffle to the top.

129 Triumph of the Good City HVS 5a   1979
11m Juggy bouldering over the roof of a small cave leads to a ledge. Continue up the arête above.

130 Diagonal Route VD   1957–68
12m The dog-legged crack gained from the right.

131 Jellyfish E4 5c   1979
8m The unprotected rampline on the fluorescent wall, gained from the boulder in the gully. A more direct start is 6a, while **Flourescent Squid**, V4 (6b), is a scary but artificial line direct to the top of the ramp.

132 Pete's Back Side HVS 5a ★   1979
7m Very peculiar moves are needed to ascend the runnel above the ledge on the next boxing glove.

133 Central Tower VD   1968–73
8m The slabby face just to the right. Unprotected.

134 The Nutcracker S 4a   pre-1913
8m An historic struggle up the crack to the right.

135 Heart of Gold E2 5c ★★   1976
10m The arête is a little gem, well worth seeking out. Climb directly to a useful hole. Wobble into a standing position in this, then proceed thoughtfully to the top. Sustained and varied.

136 The Deceiver VS 4c   pre-1913
8m The short, but fierce, crack just to the right of the arête.

137 Touch E4 6c ★★   1985
7m A ferocious boulder problem, V7, leads up the wall to an unhelpful break, where desperate measures are called for.

138 Scrabble E3 6a ★   1993
7m The arête right of Touch has tricky climbing at an uncomfortable height.

Hen Cloud was once the site of a private zoo

when animals were moved from London and Chester for their safety during WW2. The animals eventually escaped, and began breeding in the area. Bennett's wallabies were once common, as was a roaming yak. The yak was last seen heading for Buxton! On top of Hen Cloud are some old metal pegs – the remnants of a large aviary where the zoo's birds were kept.

An excellent climb of the old type. Claire Aspinall deep in Great Chimney. HVD (page 185), one of the strongest and most compelling lines on the entire crag, and that's saying something. Photo: Mike Hutton.

Staffordshire Grit

The Lower Buttress

Fifty metres in front of The Boxing Gloves, and at a lower level, another little row of outcrops is located at the upper edge of the woods. The area is clearly visible from the drive below, and can most conveniently be approached from below (turn uphill at the cattle grid).

At the left end of the buttresses is a gully bridged by a large leaning block. Some 15m below is a prominent Scots pine. The first route takes the slabby arête that forms the right wall of the gully.

139 Boysen's Arête E2 6a ★   1990s
7m The perfect little bouldery arête, above a nasty drop.

140 The Young Pretender E8 6c ★   1998
6m The attractive boulder problem arête, thrusting like the bow of a ship, just to the right. Although short, its difficulty is of the highest order and the landing is not very good.

To the right, separated from each other and their neighbouring buttresses by a series of broad gullies, are two arêtes.

141 Hal's Ridge VD   1962
11m A slightly disappointing climb up the fine ridge.

142 Short Man's Misery HVS 5a   1976
9m The more substantial steep arête, followed on its left-hand side, has some fine open moves. Oddly, with its long reaches, the climbing favours the tall.

143 Crispin's Crack HVS 5a ★   1962
11m A very good test of jamming skills. Climb the short hand crack left of the oak tree, until a ferocious move gains a little slab. Finish up the sweet scoop.

144 Duck Soup HVS 4c ★   1978
9m Open climbing; easy moves but with little protection. Start right of the oak tree, and follow a sharp ramp to join, and finish up, Crispin's Crack.

Some 10m right of Duck Soup some greener blocks nestle closer to the trees. The first substantial one has a chimney and a slim arête on its left (**Boboon**, VD, 2002). Just right, the small overhang and bulge above give **Mark of Zorro** (VS 5a, 2002). The arête just to the left is VS 5a. Around the corner, the right face has a serpentine crack springing from a horizontal break at 3m and a triangular flake to its right.

145 Mick's Metaphor E1 5c   1990s
9m The sinuous crack starting off a block on the right is short but technical. The frictionless little wall above the ledge provides an excellent comedy top-out (6a).

The wider crack to the right is **V0–** (4c), finishing at the dirty slab. A leftwards traverse from its base, is **V2** (5c). A good project would be to pull left from Mick's Metaphor onto the bulging arête and finish via flakes. However, a very horny tree awaits to do you some damage if you were to fall off this the wrong way. On the buttress just right, **Probably Boysen's Arête** is the beautiful cracked arête, with bold 6a/b climbing.

Hen Cloud The Lower Buttress

The Bordello Area

Back down at a low level, this is the next area encountered on walking along the track. The first (once quarried) buttress has a silver birch to its left and a big flat boulder below.

146 Bordello E3 5c ★   2003
10m Starting at a drilled thread, climb the arête to a good foothold. Trend left (hidden hold), passing a short crack to finish. Unprotected and harder than it looks.

147 Border Skirmish E1 5b   2003
10m Starting on a ledge below a scoop to the right of Bordello, hand-traverse a slanting borehole rightwards. Step onto a ledge on the right arête of the buttress, and climb the face past a sloping ledge.

A larger buttress is 20m right, split by a wide crack.

148 Sedition and Alchemy E3 6a   2003
12m Based on the arête to the left of the wide crack. A groove leads to a good ledge on the right (crucial small nut). Step left and up to reach breaks (crux – harder for shorties), and continue up the arête on good holds.

149 Fire Down Below VS 4c   2003
12m The unforgiving wide crack can be jammed or laybacked but needs big cams at this grade.

Trouble at t'Mill (HS 4b, 2003), is right of the wide crack. Start at a steep little arête (V2 on its right side) to gain a big ledge. Climb grooves and ledges above. Escapable. **Appocaliss** V3 (6b), is the isolated arête some 10m further right.

The Bottom Buttresses

The first of these lies directly below Mick's Metaphor.

150 Mad Lines E1 5b   1997
5m The prominently pocketed, rounded left arête, climbed direct, is reachy, balancy, much harder than it looks… and unprotected.

The name **Hen Cloud** has several possible sources. One was Hern's Cloud. Hern the Hunter was the ancient god of The Chase, and this was his domain. Hern was horned like a stag, reminiscent of the peak's double horns.

The alternative is that it comes from the ancient Briton word for 'boundary', as the peak was once the boundary between different realms.

Cloud is also thought to come from the old English word for 'high up'.

Staffordshire Grit

The Advanced Beginner

The routes on Hen Cloud and Ramshaw err towards a higher general standard of climbing, but there are still some fine easier classics worth seeking out. The following routes are good climbs for beginners to tackle, but generally require a bit more competence than beginners' routes on the Roaches.

Hen Cloud

- **Central Climb** 3 pitches, each of which offers challenge, particularly the second which gives a tough struggle;
- **K2** a fine open climb with very interesting, but well-protected, technical moves;
- **The Arête** airy and scenic, with sketchy protection (where it counts) lending it a serious feel particularly in less than perfect conditions;
- **Modern** tucked away but surprisingly challenging on close acquaintance;
- **Rib Chimney** a poor name for a fine feature which is architecturally interesting and offers crack climbing with a serious feel;
- **Great Chimney** very good, particularly if the left-hand finish is taken;
- **Thompson's Buttress, Route One** for a few moves this generates a big climb feel, if you enjoy this and Great Chimney add Route 1 on Ben Nevis's Carn Dearg to your sports plan.

Ramshaw

- **Phallic Crack** mixing it at an easy standard in apparently big country;
- **Boomerang** also has a big feel, particularly in overcoming the initial moves, but succumbs easily, though elegantly, thereafter;
- **Magic Roundabout** delicate slab work. Good conditions are essential, but then it is a delight.

151 Spacepube S 1997
5m The ramp to the right is also poorly protected.

152 Pluto's Ring E1 5c 1991
5m The right arête with committing reaches to and from the unforgiving rounded break.

The second Bottom Buttress is a few metres round to the right. On its left is an bulge split by a thin crack.

153 Bewhiskered Behemoth E2 5c ★ 2003
11m Climb up to the bulge and apply yourself to the crack to a gruelling jam-cum-mantelshelf finish.

154 Sanitarium E5 6a 2003
9m Starting at the impressive, wide crack on the right, scamper up to the ledge and place protection before moving right and tackling the fearsome gritty bulge above. A side-runner in the flake of the following route seems sensible. A **direct start** up the lower wall to the ledge is V7 (6c).

155 Jetez le Pantalon E2 5b 1990
9m Climb direct to the prominent flake/spike just right and thence to the top.

Various problems exist on the scattered boulders hereabouts. About 50m along and right from the Bottom Buttress, above the trees and within sight of the Heart of Gold area of the upper crags, is a narrow buttress with a chimney on the left. **Last View** (HS 4a, 1979), is the small face left of the chimney, while down and right is a clean little ramp. This is **The Weirdy** (S 4a, 1968-73). The wall to the right is HS 4a.

Biscuit Buttress

A further 50 metres on is the last of the rocks. By now, the rock has deteriorated quite a bit, but it is still a fine spot for those looking for solitude.

The climbs include **High Energy Plan** (HVS 5a, 1979) which climbs over the first roof encountered; **Shortbread** (HVS 5a, 1969), climbing a groove 3m to the right and finishing to the left; **Shortcake** (E1 5b, 1976), a rightward finish to the previous route; **Gingerbread** (HS 4a, 1976), the face to the right; **Ginger Biscuit** (VS 4b, 1976), the arête right again. The chimney left of Gingerbread is HVD 4a.

Hen Cloud First Ascents

1909	**Central Climb**	John Laycock, AR Thompson *A direct finish was added in 1927. An eventful and historic first ascent.*
pre-1913	**The Arête, Rib Chimney, Footpath Chimney, Thompson's Buttress Routes, Tree Chimney, The Nutcracker, The Deceiver**	*The latter two routes were known as Hall Cracks 'A' and 'B' respectively. 'Exceedingly destructive to the climber's well-cut tweeds.' All recorded in the Rucksack Club Journal in 1913, the first guide to Hen Cloud.*
1913	**Great Chimney**	Siegfried Herford, Stanley Jeffcoat *A powerful team. Herford went on to add, in 1914, Scafell's Central Buttress, one of the country's most celebrated climbs.*
1924	**Bow Buttress**	
1913–27	**The Aiguillette, Easy Gully**	
1927	**November Cracks, K2, En Rappel**	Arthur Burns *En Rappel was known as Blizzard Buttress until an ascent by Joe Brown.*
1947	**Bachelor's Climb**	
1947–51	**Hedgehog Crack, Rainbow Crack, Chockstone Crack, Chockstone Chimney, Roof Climb, Central Climb Direct, Final Crack, Modern, Ancient, Pinnacle Face**	*'Hedgehog Crack is beset with thorny problems, all of which can be solved if the hands can be persuaded to stay jammed.'* **1951 guidebook.**
1952 May	**Bachelor's Climb** (Left-hand finish), **Second's Retreat**	Joe Brown and party *The first addition by one of Hen Cloud's, and everywhere else's, major figures.*
1957	**Bulwark**	Clive Shaw *Marked the formation of the North Staffordshire Mountaineering Club.*
1957–61	**Main Crack, Delstree, Reunion Crack, Slimline, Hen Cloud Eliminate**	Joe Brown
1957–61	**Bachelor's Left-Hand**	Don Whillans
early-1960s	**Encouragement, The Long and the Short, Chicken**	Tony Nicholls
1962	**Second's Advance, Hal's Ridge, Crispin's Crack, Rib Crack**	Bob Hassall
1962	**High Tensile Crack**	Colin Foord
1962	**The Ape**	Pete Ruddle
1962	**The Better End** (1 pt.)	Dave Salt *Originally named The Bitter End. Climbed free in 1975 by John Allen and Steve Bancroft, and renamed from a spelling mistake in Crags Magazine.*
1957–68	**Piston Groove, Victory, Green Corner, The Lum, Bantam Crack, Arête Wall, Left Twin Crack, Right Twin Crack, Pinnacle Rib, Diagonal Route, Recess Chimney**	*All of these routes appeared uncredited in the 1968 guidebook.*
1969 May	**Shortbread**	John Yates
1971 Apr	**Songs of Praise**	John Yates
1968–73	**Little Pinnacle Climb, The Notch, Pug, Central Tower, The Weirdy**	
1974 Aug 18	**Fat Old Sun** (1 pt.)	John Allen, Steve Bancroft (AL) *Climbed free in 1978 by Steve Bancroft and Dave Humphries (AL).*
1975 Jul 27	**Anthrax**	Steve Bancroft, John Allen (AL)
1976 Feb 26	**Comedian**	Steve Bancroft, John Allen *The first of the really great routes to be added by the Sheffield raiders. Started on the right where Frayed Nerve now starts. The described start was climbed by Dave Jones in 1980.*
1976 Jun 20	**Heart of Gold, Short Man's Misery, Shortcake, Gingerbread, Ginger Biscuit**	Nick Colton, Con Carey, Jim Campbell, (various leads), John Tout
1976	**Corinthian**	Steve Bancroft, John Allen
1976	**Caricature**	John Allen, Steve Bancroft *'Allen stepped over the threshold of the possible to produce Caricature, after several airborne retreats.'*
1976	**Anaconda**	John Gosling
1977 Jul 16	**Chameleon**	Steve Bancroft, Nicky Stokes, Al Manson
1977	**Stokesline**	Mark Stokes
1978 Apr 2	**Slowhand**	Dave Jones, Roger Bennion, Gary Gibson
1978 Apr 2	**Electric Chair, Nutted by Reality, Pullet, Gallows**	Jim Moran, Simon Horrox, (various leads), Geoff Milburn, Dave Jones, Roger Bennion
1978 Apr 2	**Face Value**	Gary Gibson (solo)
1978 Apr 5	**Short 'n' Sharp**	Dave Jones, Ian 'Hots' Johnson, Gary Gibson *Climbed by Simon*

Staffordshire Grit

Horrox as the cheekily named Apology, knowing that Jones had failed to lead it previously. However Horrox did not know that Jones had returned three days earlier to lead it.

1978 Apr 16 **Easy Come** Al Evans, Geoff Milburn

1978 Apr 17 **Borstal Breakout** Jim Moran, Al Evans, Simon Horrox *A day off work was needed as the route had been cleaned but not completed on the Sunday. Top-roped first by Simon Horrox on April 4. It was erroneously assumed for some time that Jim Moran et al had completed both pitches. The second pitch was actually climbed by Dave Jones with a nut for aid in 1978. The route in its described form remained unclimbed until after the production of the 1981 guidebook which had described a free ascent! It had certainly been led clean by 1983 but who actually made the first complete free ascent will probably remain a bone of contention.*

1978 Apr **The Monkey in Your Soul, Prayers, Poems and Promises** Al Simpson, with John Holt or Dave Jones

1978 Apr **Duck Soup** Al Evans

1978 May 17 **Bitching** Gary Gibson, Kons Nowak

1978 May 17 **The Pinch, Broken Arrow** John Holt, Dave Jones, (various leads)

1978 May **The Raid, The Sorcerer** Jim Moran, Al Evans

1978 May **Qantas, Press on Regardless, Zoom Wall** Dave Jones, Al Simpson

1978 Jun **Caesarian** Martin Berzins, Bob Berzins *This was with a deviation to the left, avoiding the main difficulties. Climbed direct by Jonny Woodward in September 1980.*

1979 Feb 25 **Space Probe** Jonny Woodward, Ian Maisey *The second pitch, Helter Skelter, had been climbed in 1977 by Steve Bancroft and Al Manson.*

1979 May 29 **The Mandrake** Jonny Woodward *'I placed runners in Victory, level with the overhang, but these are probably unnecessary since when a hold broke off from the flake I hit the deck despite the runners.' Possibly unrepeated until an ascent from Jon Read in 2003.*

1979 **Cold Sweat, High Energy Plan, Jellyfish, Bad Joke, Small Buttress, Triumph of the Good City, Last View** Gary Gibson, solo, or with Phil Gibson or Ian Barker

1979 Jun 10 **Shoe Shine Shuffle** Phil Gibson, Gary Gibson

1979 Jul **Levitation** Phil Burke *Climbed with very high side runners, which were eliminated by Simon Nadin in 2001.*

1979 **Slipstreams, Buster the Cat, Standing Tall, Tunnel Vision, Delusion, Pete's Back-Side** Dave Jones *All climbed during guidebook work.*

1980 Sep 14 **Loose Fingers** Gary Gibson (solo)

1980 Jun **Solid Geometry** Dave Jones (solo)

1981 Jun 28 **Blood Blisters** Gary Gibson

1981 Jul **Fast Piping, Flexure Line, This Poison** Gary Gibson, with Jon Walker or solo *The upper crack of Fast Piping had been climbed previously as a variation to Hedgehog Crack.*

1981 Aug **Chicken Direct, Cool Fool, The Stone Loach, Frayed Nerve** Gary Gibson *A good month! The lower arête of Cool Fool had been climbed as Charisma by Nick Postlethwaite in 1980. James Pearson probably did the second ascent in 2003, without the runner in the lower boulder. On The Stone Loach, a long sling was clipped into a wire in the pod to protect the crux moves which had been practised extensively on an abseil rope.*

1983 Sep 22 **Master of Reality** Simon Nadin *The lower front face was climbed a few days later.*

1984 Sep 26 **Mindbridge** Simon Nadin (solo) *Protection exists, but Nadin decided to solo the line to provide the concentration necessary for success. Unrepeated.*

1985 Apr 18 **Chiaroscuro, Even Smaller Buttress** Gary Gibson *Chiaroscuro is an undergraded dark horse at E5 6a originally. Finally repeated by Jon Read in 2006.*

1985 Jul 31 **Touch** Simon Nadin

1985 Aug 3 **Parallel Lines** Simon Nadin *While attempting to eliminate side-runners in the 1990s, Dan Honeyman fell and smashed up a wrist. Unrepeated?*

1986 Jun 6 **B4XS** Simon Nadin *Second, third and fourth ascents all came in one day from Seb Grieve, Jean Minh Trihn-Thieu and Dave Jones, 1996.*

1986 Oct 10 **Sauria** Martin Boysen *Unrepeated?*

1987 May 6 **Black Eyed Dog** Andy Popp *Misnamed as Dog Eye Rib in the previous edition. Climbed on-sight by Sam Whittaker in 1996.*

1990 Mar 16 **Peter and the Wolf** Andy Popp

1990 Mar 16 **Wavelength** Graham Cole, John Hattersley

1990 **Jetez le Pantalon** Colin Cheetham, John Perry, Rob Barnett

Hen Cloud First Ascents

1991	**Pluto's Ring**	Justin Critchlow
1992 Feb 25	**A Flabby Crack**	Neil Travers
1993	**Scrabble**	Justin Critchlow
1993	**Desperado**	Mark Katz
1995	**Just Thirteen**	Mark Katz

1996 Feb **Arêtenophobia** Seb Grieve Needing the extra impetus to succeed on the bold lead, Grieve had no option but to don one of his wife's dresses for the ascent. The underwear was his own. Grieve recalls climbing the arête on the steep and featureless left side. However, Neil Bentley recalls that "…He climbed it on the right, I'm sure, I was there. Seb never remembers that sort of stuff." Second ascent followed immediately by 'Aussie' Dave Jones.

1997 **Jean the Bean, Mad Lines, Spacepube** Justin Critchlow

1998 Jan **The Young Pretender** Mark Katz Unrepeated?

1999 **Man oh Man** Simon Nadin

1990s **Boysen's Arête, Probably Boysen's Arête, Mick's Metaphor** Martin Boysen Claimed by Boysen long after the event, considering them insignificant at the time. Variously reclimbed and reclaimed over the years.

1990s **Trap Door Finish** Richard Pickford

2000 **Mandrill** Andy Cave, Martin Veale, Rab Carrington, Martin Boysen, Tom Leppert

2002 **Hens Dropping, Pointless but Pumpy** Niall Grimes, Richard Harland

2002 **Mark of Zorro, Boboon** Andi Turner

2002 Feb **Dead Banana Slab** John Cox **Andrei's Route** Andrei Kosenko **Flour Wall** Andrei Kosenko, Bob Smith

2002 Sep 13 **7 of 9** Graham Cole and Alison Trinder Originally started further right.

2002 Oct 19 **The Driven Bow** Jon Read, John Wilson

2003 **Master of Puppets** Mark Sharratt, Andi Turner

2003 Mar 12 **Sanitarium** Mark Sharratt, Martin Dearden

2003 Mar 13 **Bewhiskered Behemoth** John Perry, Andi Turner

2003 Jun 22 **Trouble at t'Mill, Bordello, Sedition and Alchemy, Border Skirmish** John H Bull (solo) The first route climbed after a week marked by redundancies at work. On Sedition and Alchemy, a sling was clipped into the crucial runner during a solo ascent.

2003 Jul 5 **Fire Down Below** Jon Read, Dave Garnett and John H Bull

2004 Apr **Scrumptious** Jon Read, Debs Read Named after their cat.

2005 Nov 29 **Night Prowler** Mark Sharratt, Andi Turner

2006 Oct 30 **Justin Time** Jon Read, Andi Turner, Mark Sharratt

2006 Nov 4 **Catharsis** Andi Turner, unseconded

2007 Apr 22 **Sand Castles** Jon Read

2007 Sep 11 **Mandatory** Jon Read, Justin Critchlow, Andi Turner

2008 Feb 14 **Myxi** Andi Turner, very unseconded

Hen Cloud Bouldering First Ascents

Alan Whicker Jon Read, 2005
Appocaliss Justin Critchlow
Blood Blisters Direct Start Justin Critchlow, 1994
Flourescent Squid Col Allot, 2006
Simon's Slab Simon Nadin, 2000
Starlight and Storm John Allen, Martin Veale, 1986

One of the best lines at Ramshaw and a joy to climb, Boomerang, VD (page 215) is certainly a route you will come back to time and time again. Photo: David Simmonite.

3 Ramshaw Rocks

Ramshaw Rocks

by Richard Patterson

O.S. Ref. SK019622   Altitude: 410m a.s.l.

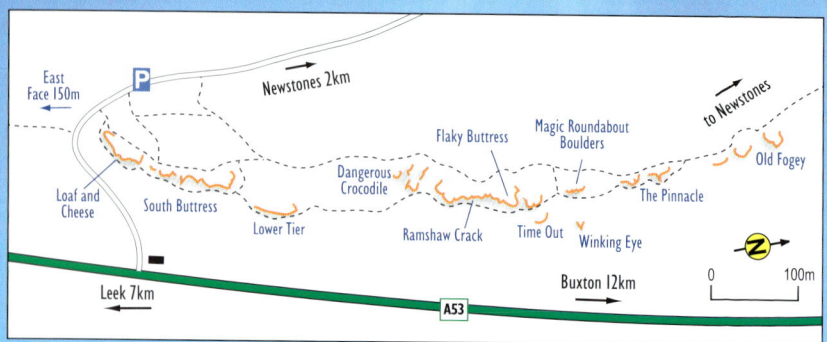

Ramshaw Rocks, though forming part of the triumvirate of larger gritstone crags in this area, has a character and atmosphere all its own. As its name suggests, it is more a series of buttresses than a continuous edge in the classic gritstone style. Viewed from the road below, the rocks present a Gothic nightmare: vast jutting fins and prows of rock, mainly overhanging, split by many wide, steep cracks and fissures. The plane of the rocks, combined with the brutal weathering, has accentuated the roughness of the larger grained grit, leaving a coarse, pebbly and, in places, less compact skin. This fragile surface has led many to be wary on first acquaintance and, in truth, it does seem strange to those used to the finer grit of the Eastern Edges. At Ramshaw, perseverance has its reward and, in general, the grain adds to the adventurous feel rather than detracts from the climbing – however, this statement may seem less convincing the further one is from protection! Testpieces abound, but equally there is scope for the beginner to hone their movements on more moderately angled grit.

The climbs at Ramshaw favour those with technique (the cracks), confidence (the slabs), and sheer bloody-mindedness (the weird offwidths). Even more than at most gritstone crags, the effort expended and satisfaction gained are certainly at odds with the length of the routes. These attributes, combined with Ramshaw's odd aesthetics and its relative unpopularity, provide a gritstone experience which a climber of any grade is unlikely to forget, whether later basking in the glow of success, or ruefully licking their (often bloody) wounds.

Ramshaw Rocks Access

The routes at Ramshaw

reflect the various stages of its development well. The fifties and early sixties left behind both classic easier cracks and strange wide fissures, whilst the late sixties and early seventies saw the addition of more open friction climbs. As both rubber and protection advanced, at the turn of the eighties, more audacious climbs became possible, limiting the more recent additions to the more improbable and outrageous walls and arêtes.

Conditions & aspect

East facing, Ramshaw is undoubtedly at its best on a sunny morning, and an alpine start on a fine summer's day will reveal a truly delightful aspect denied to the lazy. Sitting proudly atop the ridge, the crag unsurprisingly catches the wind. On the credit side this means that the main buttress fronts will dry quickly in most circumstances, and the crag can provide a welcome escape from the heat on warm summer afternoons. This exposure can, however, make for an (extremely) cold day out in winter. Plenty of sun until the afternoon. There is also some rock facing south remaining in the sun for most of the day.

Routes

Superb. Over 150 routes of all grades. Lots of pebbly slabs, steep walls and ferocious cracks.

Bouldering

Very good. Over 40 problems. Lots of pebbly slabs and arêtes and brutal slappy test-pieces.

Parking & approach

See map. Parking on the A53 is not recommended as it is a fast, busy road.

Access

The crag is on Open Access land owned by the PDNPA. N.B. Do not climb on the Winking Eye section which has been vandalized in the past. The BMC has agreed no climbing on this unique gritstone formation in order to preserve it in its present state.

The first climbing is found on a lone pinnacle south of the lane, about a 150m hike through the heather. There are several routes, making it worth a visit for the dedicated. **East Face** *(M, pre-1973) climbs the very small slab facing the lane, while* **After Eight** *(S, 1979) takes the short wall just left of the south-east arête to finish up the arête. A line just left is a nice V2 (5c).* **Southern Crack** *(S 4b, pre-1973) is a better route, taking the obvious wide fissure in the centre of the south face to finish on the crenellated top. Other routes and some boulder problems have been claimed here, but their stature is slight and they are best left to be periodically rediscovered by the adventurous.*

"Arrive there on a warm summer evening, fighting fit and determined, preferably with a few preliminary bouts under your belt, crash the jams in, move quickly, and the climbs submit.

"Arrive on a bad day, and it is a different story; the rock will maul you and you will retire, bloodied, to lick your wounds."

Martin Boysen

Midge and Cleg

Dangerous Crocodile

Lower Tier

CRACK School

Richie Patterson

My personal opinion is that the modern climber is somewhat under-skilled in the area of crack climbing, so in a spirit of generosity(?) I have set a task which when completed will (maybe) enable even the indoor addict to face that prime stopper of gritstone climbing – the crack.

Within the text I have selected a tick list of Ramshaw's best crack climbs that should enable any climber that completes them to hold their head high and proud in any pub in the land. Hopefully this mastery will lead them to espouse the virtues of the bloodied hand, (fist, elbow, and knee?) and to continue to pass on the grand gritstone tradition, which Johnny Dawes so presciently called

"THE best forgotten art"

The CRACKER'S Dozen

1. **Phallic Crack HVD** Spectacular climbing on a big buttress.
2. **Great Scene Baby S** Short and stiff to hone the technique.
3. **Tricouni Crack HS** Not quite hard as nails.
4. **The Crank VS** Now you're really learning. A Joe Brown crack. A jammer's milestone.
5. **Green Crack HVS** An awkward change of angle.
6. **Great Zawn HVS** Wide, ballsy and committing.
7. **Brown's Crack E1** Very short, but just plain hard.
8. **Foord's Folly E2** Thin hand technique can but help.
9. **Imposition E2** Another difficult change of angle.
10. **The Undertaker E3** Short lived but perplexing.
11. **Ramshaw Crack E4** Hands to fists to arm-bar.
12. **National Acrobat E6** The path to true mastery.
13. **Melvin Bragg V8** New for 2009! Off-fists, off-feet, off your rocker. You better be. The hardest crack in Staffordshire.

Andi Turner giving his all to Melvin Bragg, V8 (page 202). Photo: David Simmonite

Ramshaw Rocks Loaf and Cheese

Loaf and Cheese Area

The main edge starts 35m east of the lane at a flat-topped block – the Loaf and Cheese. The first route climbs the left side of the steep front face.

1 Assembled Techniques E4 6a ★   1986
8m A good climb that tackles the front face of the Loaf and Cheese via some awkward climbing. Move up to a hand-jam slot and either go straight up onto the ledge then right onto the Cheese, or right to the scooped hole and a committing rightward finish.

2 Loaf and Cheese HVS 5a ★   pre-1973
11m Difficult but thankfully short-lived moves up the rather crumbly crack lead to a ledge. A further ledge is gained by a mantel, and from here the pinnacle can be climbed at the front or the back to give a pleasant finish.

3 Dream Fighter E3 6a   1984
8m A worrying finish on a less than sympathetic surface gives this route its character. Gain the crack, followed by a committing pull onto the slab above.

4 Green Crack HVS 5b ★   1972
8m Despite appearances, a superb route epitomising the Ramshaw experience in miniature. Climb the green groove into the wide crack, where difficulties force a welcome, but almost certainly ungracious exit onto the slab above. Crack School no. 5.

5 National Acrobat E6 6c ★ ★ ★   1978
11m The short non-crack on the left of the buttress was at one time the cutting edge of crack desperation; it isn't much easier today. The crux section, getting established in the hanging groove, is one of the meanest sequences on grit. Crack School no. 12.

6 Traveller in Time E3 5c ★ ★ ★   1977
11m A less difficult but equally fine climb. Climb the steep groove until a stretch left gains a smaller flake and small gear. Shuffle left and mantel up then address the slabby scoop directly. Low in the grade with a Friend 5, high in the grade without.

7 Body Pop E4 6b ★ ★   1984
11m More commitment required! From the top of the groove, the right arête is gained adventurously. Luckily, as height is gained, the climbing eases enough to keep you moving in the right direction.

8 Wall and Groove S 4a   pre-1973
9m Starting from beneath the prow (or direct), move up to gain the chimney. Better than it looks.

9 The Arête S   pre-1973
9m Climb the arête on tongue-like flakes.

10 Louie Groove E1 5b ★   1968
8m The square-cut groove is easy at the bottom but more intimidating as height is gained, and has seen a few wobblers. Sneaky gear for those who look.

Staffordshire Grit

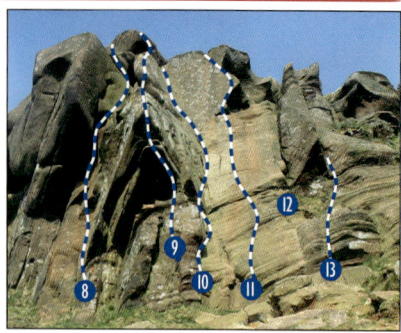

11   Leeds Slab   HS 4a   1980
8m Ascend the centre of the cutaway on 'chippers' to finish up the notched rib.

12   Leeds Crack   D   pre-1973
6m The short crack gives introductory jamming. The short blunt arête to the right is a pleasant HVS 5b.

13   Honest Jonny   D   1976
5m The short little groove just right of the rib.

Fifteen metres right and higher is a blunt-nosed pinnacle.

14   The Undertaker   E3 6a ★   1973
6m A mini National Acrobat, and like that route, only a fierce approach (or a very long reach) aids progress as the crack in the front of the pinnacle turns unhelpful a frustrating distance below the next good holds. Crack School no. 10.

15   Pink Flake   VI (5b)
The obvious booming flake. The rounded green topout will feel worrying, and a spotter on the ledge is most useful. ⊝

16   Mantel   V0 (4c)
Squirm onto the ledge to the right.

17   The Letter T   V3 (6a)
Use the rounded flake just right to gain the rounded top.

18   Melvin Bragg   V8 (6c)   1973–81
The wind tunnel above The Undertaker is split by a nasty crack which holds a classic roof struggle. Climb the crack from the back with every conceivable jamming technique (avoiding the footledge at this grade). Mooted to be harder than Ray's Roof. Crack School no. 13. **Photo on page 200.**

Ten metres right of The Undertaker is a double buttress.

19   Overdrive   E3 5c   1977
7m Something of a gripper, climbing the left of two triangular roofs. Using good but creaky holds, gain the lip of the roof and mantel boldly up to finish on a selection of gritty slopers. The two cracks underneath this have also been climbed as **Twin Cracks** (Diff, pre-1973), and **Double Chin** (VD, 1973–81), both of which finish up the wider groove above.

20   Prowler   VS 4c   1973–81
6m Take the very friable roof to the right at its widest point and finish up the secondary prow.

The Crank Area

This is the series of jutting buttresses starting across to the right. These give many striking climbs. On the left wall of the first buttress, facing Overdrive, are a couple of scritty problems.

21   Steeper   V0+ (5a)
The gritty groove on the left. ⊝ The even grittier slipway / ramp to the right is **Equilibria**, VI (5b).

22   The Great Zawn   HVS 5a ★★   1950–65
8m The wide crack in the deep V-slot just screams to be climbed! Initially wide and tricky, a good hold at mid-height provides welcome relief; then it gets tough again. Crack School no. 6.

Ramshaw Rocks Crank Area

23 Broken Groove D ★   pre-1973
8m The striking feature provides a good, easy route with a big feel. The arête just right, **Broken Groove Arête** (D, pre-1973), is also worthwhile.

24 Gully Arête E1 5c   1986
6m The arête, climbed strictly on the right, is harder than it looks. The upper arête is easier: highball V1.

25 Wellingtons VD ★   pre-1973
8m The wide crack to the right invites a 'get-stuck-in' approach. Big boots may help. Good fun.

26 Masochism HVS 5b ★★   1950–65
9m Aptly named. The disconcertingly steep hand-to-fist crack leads with venom to a large ledge. The second bulge is less savage but with 'chockstone et al' it still maintains interest to the end. Good fun and obviously undergraded but what the hell.

27 T'rival Traverse E3 6a ★   1987
6m A delicate and tenuous climb. From the ledge, follow the holdless ramp to the sanctuary of a small flake, then make a scary high step to reach the break. Finish direct. Gear is put in the break up and right at this grade: how far along determines how scared you get. **Rock Trivia** (E2 6c, 1987) climbs through the right side of the traverse.

28 Trivial Traverse HVS 5a   1977
6m Traverse the sidewall using the horizontal break. Can be finished either by going up when a large foothold is reached or by carrying on to the arête, which is pleasantly ascended on flutings.

29 Sneeze E1 5b ★★   1979
8m The incipient crack is gained from the left and, though protectable, seems best savoured without the encumbrance of a rope. A fine climb.

30 The Crank VS 5a ★★   1950–65
8m Some real Joe Brown jamming, and delightful with it. Climb the crack on sinkers until a step right forces a bit of thought and leads to a wider finish. Crack School no. 4.

31 Ultimate Sculpture E8 7a ★   1994
8m "7b, top end, deffo!" The incredible blank arête provides the sternest challenge at Ramshaw. Climb it using faith, friction, and immense talent. Very minimalist!

"The Traveller

on the once-important coach road from Buxton sees glowering above him, on Ramshaw Edge, a grotesque succession of ghoulish faces, bovine and porcine heads, and half finished monsters springing from the parent rock. And beyond, where Hen Cloud extends its array of pinnacles, he sees still more impossible shapes set in stone, outlines that only the camera may prove less than vertical or only slightly overhanging, but to the eye appear like curving horns, their points overweighted with threatening tons of rock."

EA Baker
Moors, Crags and Caves of the High Peak

Staffordshire Grit

South Buttress

The next buttress is the most substantial on the whole edge. It is particularly good for its easier routes, which cover impressive terrain at a moderate standard.

32 Chockstone Chimney VD   pre-1973
8m The chimney quickly gives in after a short spar with the obvious chockstone. ◐

33 Maximum Hype E4 5c   1987
10m A bold route tackling the left wall of the buttress. From the top of the chimney, gain a short blind flake and move up and slightly left with difficulty to gain a more centrally placed good hold. Another good hold follows as well as some protection and an easier finish back out to the arête. Gritty.

34 Waiting for the Lions E3 5c ★   2009
14m A butch start allows you to reach the biggest single hold in the UK. Monkey along this (pull-ups optional) and mantel into it. From here, careful footwork and a hidden sidepull will get you into the upper reaches of Tally Not.

35 Gumshoe E2 5c ★★★   1977
14m One of the best routes at Ramshaw, with a disconcertingly obscure crux. Start up the shallow green groove to arrange some rather disappointing protection. Move up left to better holds and a more reasonable finish. A bold indirect finish, **Wine Gums** (E4 6a, 1985), makes a difficult stretch up and right after the crux to gain reasonable but gritty holds. Finish direct or slightly right.

36 Tally Not HVS 5c ★   1972
14m Follow the lower corner up and right. Make a difficult move out left to the second corner, which still needs all your attention for a couple of moves until the climbing eases. Cleaner than it looks, and harder, although it has been climbed by a squirrel. A direct start, entering the lower, left-hand groove steeply from below, is a burly E3 6a.

37 Battle of the Bulge VS 4b ★   pre-1973
9m A superb little crack climb. Not half as tricky as the name implies.

Ramshaw Rocks South Buttress

38 The Cannon VS 4c ★ pre-1973
13m Make a difficult start up the friable flakes to gain a short shallow crack, and use this to gain the main groove above. Alternatively, and just as logically, climb the wall left of the short crack at HS 4b before moving right to the same point. Above, pass the 'cannon', and step right to a direct finish.

39 Torture E4 5c 1981
12m A poor route crossing the low roof. The initial unprotected moves, to gain the break over the lip, are relatively easy, but involve pulling on a very loose flake. Why not cycle down the A53 blindfold? It will be a more fun way to go.

40 Whilly's Whopper VS 4c ★ 1979
12m From Phallic Crack, either step in above the low roof or, better and harder (5a) pull in steeply from below to gain a short hanging groove. Finish direct via a grapple with the, shall we say, prominent feature?

41 Phallic Crack HVD ★★ pre-1973
12m Wide at the bottom, thrutchy at the top, with fine climbing in between. Follow the crack, wrestling the large knob on the way, to finish up the obvious groove. Very good sport. Crack School no. 1.

42 Alcatraz HVS 5b ★★ 1968
12m A fine climbing following the stepped crack. Initial tricky moves lead to a wider crack, which is followed more reasonably. Though a little green at the start this route gives good climbing.

43 Juan Cur E5 6a 1991
12m Follow the wall and arête right of Alcatraz as far as possible, until a step left can be made to join the final 3m of that route. A tied-off piece of wood was used in the 'handrail' to protect the first ascent. 1" × 2" × 12" if you really want to know!

44 The Untouchable E1 5b ★★ 1968
11m Just right of the arête, a finely positioned crack-line snakes up the buttress edge. Gained from the right, the thinner lower section of the route is hardest; the wider upper section, once gained, is testing but with more solid climbing.

45 Corner Crack S 4a pre-1973
8m The crack to the right is short but sweet.

46 The Rippler HVS 5b ★ pre-1973
8m The route to the right provides intricate and fingery climbing. Starting round to the right of the previous route, use ripples to reach a better rail at mid-height. Finish slightly right on very good edges. Bold. A direct start can be made at a fragile 6a coming in from nearer the left arête. **Cold Wind** (E2 5c, 1984) follows the right arête.

Below and right is a small face.

47 Midge V3 (6a)
The twin cracks present some decidedly old-school troublems. ⊖

48 Cleg V0– (5a)
The hanging groove on the right.

Staffordshire Grit

The Lower Tier

Approximately 50m down and right, is a short but very steep buttress, a mini crag in its own right, and home to a number of superb routes and some classic all-weather bouldering.

49 Crab Walk Direct V2 (5c)
A steep crack from a low start. ◐ **Sensible Shoes** VI (5b) crosses the roof left of the hanging crack.

50 Smoothment Traverse V4 (6b)
A despicable problem that moves right from the crack, under the overhang, and with the aid of undercut slots and blobs, gains flakes at the right end of the roof before moving up. Crossing the overhang directly from the cuppy undercut is a reachy V2 (5c): **Overlap**.

51 Sketching Wildly E6 6c ★   1994
11m The tiered roofs provide a stiff battle. Climb to the first roof, place poor cams, and make difficult moves rightwards to better gear and more hard moves over the final roof.

52 Crab Walk S 4a ★   pre-1973
20m A good long climb covering interesting terrain. Start near the centre of the buttress and climb up left via good holds to gain a ramp line which is followed leftwards to finish up a short crack.

53 Brown's Crack E1 5c ★★   1950–65
14m A gem from the old master. Gain some giant holds below the obvious crack, breathe deep, then fight, fist and furkle your way up the unhelpful crack. Short and just plain hard. Crack School no. 7. An eliminate, **Outflanked** (E1 5c, trad) climbs the short green groove left of the crack with one hard move.

54 Prostration HVS 5a ★★   1950–65
14m A good climb. Follow the short crack to the roof, somehow gain the ledge, realise you're stuck, struggle upright (crux), and scuttle up the secondary crack. Not to be taken lying down!

55 Rock Climbing in Britain V7 (6c)
A desperate traverse. From a sitting start, slap up the rising lip, past a rounded hold, along the very sloping shelf and finish as for Collywood; hard.

56 Roll Off V2 (5c)
Gain the evil sloping shelf and rock leftwards onto the ledge. A low start to this, climbing sharp crimps on the overhang below, is **Tit Grip**, V10 (7a). However, it has suffered from hold breakage, and may not be repeated in its present state.

57 Cake V2 (6a)
From the good cup hold on the lip, pull up to flakes above to get established into Don's Crack.

Ramshaw Rocks Lower Tier

58 Collywood V5 (6b)
Another hard traverse. From a sitting start, with hands in the low jam crack, slap left along the lip, past a good cup hold and up to a a pinch on the lip above. Swing powerfully up and left into the groove above. ⊙

59 Colly Wobble E4 6b ★★   1987
11m The short wall, marked by four holes, the remnants of an old plaque (which said "*No climbing on these rocks*"), provides an unusual and technical outing. Gain the holes and make a long stretch for the ledge above. Luckily a half-sized Tri-cam in one of the holes makes it all a little more amenable.

60 Don's Crack HVS 5b ★★   1950–65
11m Notably difficult for the pint-sized climber, the steep crack provides another test of crack technique. Follow the initial crack to a hole (birds' nest *de rigueur*); from here, a long reach or some funky jamming provides access to the upper crack, which eases towards the top.

61 Hem Line V5 (6b)
The traditional girdle of the buttress mooches across, left to right with feet a couple of metres off the ground never encountering much difficulty until beyond Don's Crack. The action starts here. Slap rightwards on slopers then pull up as for Tierdrop then follow the gutter to finish as for Last Drop.

62 Tierdrop V6 (6b)
Although its original stature has been diminished by the use of pads, this is as fine a highball as can be found anywhere. Reach the blobby pinches in the roof, either direct or from the right, both crimpy. Using determination, finger strength and burl, get to a chipped runnel on the lip. From here, crimps two feet away tantalise... but can you commit? **Sam's Left Hand** is a slightly harder variant, reaching left from the runnel to a sloping slot leading to the top.

A superb sit start bumps up the difficulty of the original version significantly. Start with left hand in the good flake sidepull and right in the crack (long arms useful) and slap up to gain the pockets and crimps of the original. This will now feel more exhausting than ever – V7 (6b).

63 Tier's End V1 (5b)
From the finger jugs below the groove just right, pull steeply up into the groove above. ⊙ Starting this up Tierdrop Sit Start gives a good burly V6.

64 Last Drop V1 (5c)
Starting a metre right, pull up steeply using the chipped gutter.

65 Abdomen HS 4a   1968–73
34m A funny girdle of the Lower Tier. Using gut instinct follow the central break under the roof, gained from grassy ledges at the left-hand end, to finish above Colly Wobble.

Staffordshire Grit

Dangerous Crocodile Bouldering

Back up on the main edge, and about 100m past South Buttress, is a broad open area with a scattering of boulders. The right-hand of the larger, twin buttresses in the midst of this contains Dangerous Crocodile Snogging. The boulders around this contain a very good circuit.

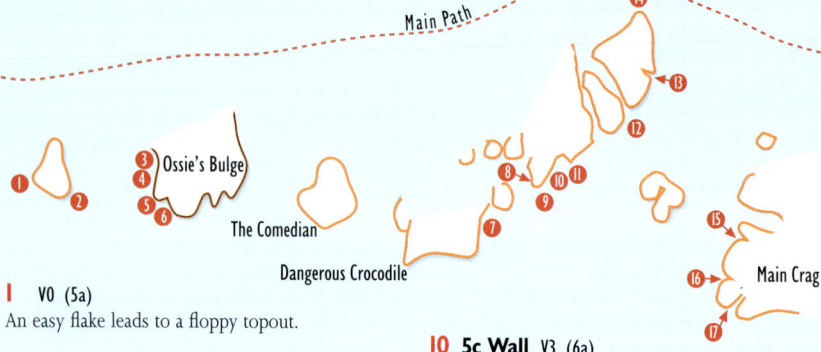

1 V0 (5a)
An easy flake leads to a floppy topout.

2 Little Prow V6 (6b)
Start on the shelf and climb the rounded arête.

3 The Scoop V1 (5c)
Swing up into the scoop and mantel gloriously onto the summit. ○

4 The Lurch V4 (6b)
Lurch for slopers and power directly upwards on treacherous holds.

5 Ossie's Bulge V3 (6a)
From a good slot, mantel upwards then scamper left to finish. ○ So good, in fact, you'll want to do it again. This time, go straight up at V4 (6b).

6 Ram Air V8 (6c)
A modern classic with a sustained rounded sequence up the arête. Hard for the grade, and be careful with that landing. *See photo opposite.*

7 Elastic Wall V6 (6b)
Lurch upwards from the crimpy sidepull.

8 Arête on Left V1 (5c)

9 Arête on Right V1 (5c) ○

10 5c Wall V3 (6a)
The crimpy little wall, on crimps.

11 Baby Groove V0– (4a)

12 Mansize V9 (7a)
Starting in a bit of a pit, swing up to gain a very broad pinch for the right hand and crank to the top. A great Font-style problem if clean – it often isn't.

13 Hanging Crack V0 (5a)
Delightfully brutal, m'boy.

14 Classic Mantel V1 (5c)
A tricky mantel at the point of the block. ○

15 Johnny's Groove V8² (6c)
The groovy seam is entered by dynamic high-speed double bridging techniques (see Best Forgotten Art). Far out.

16 Crocodile Slot V1 (5b)
An exacting struggle up the wide slot, requiring full body awareness. ○

17 Right Slot V2 (5b)
More 'bouldering' Ramshaw style, up the tall offwidth near the arête.

Jon Fullwood grapples with Ram Air, V8 (opposite page), one of John Welford's handful of classy additions to Ramshaw. Photo: Adam Long.

Staffordshire Grit

In a way, I find belaying more terrifying than leading. I remember Seb Grieve doing the first ascent of Clippety Clop. He'd top-roped it alright, but when he went to solo it, he just started shouting at himself. It was mad.

"I am Jerry Moffatt. I am Jerry Moffatt. I'm on top-rope..."

constantly. Then on the crux, he took his feet off and screamed "Nooooooo...", and I just thought, this is it. He's off. But it was all part of the plan.

Andy Popp

Oh no! Julian Lines about to lose all points of contact while attempting the second ascent of Clippety Clop (E7 6c). Photo: Paul Higginson.

Ramshaw Rocks   Dangerous Crocodile

On the left-hand of the two buttresses among the boulders is:

66 The Comedian   VS   pre-1973
9m Climb the front face to below the roof and three possible exits. Left is 4a, straight up is an exciting 5b, and right is a 4c crawl, to finish one metre right of the arête. The undercut rib and hanging scoop left of this is **Paul's Rib** (E5 6c, 1994).

67 Camelian Crack   VD ★   pre-1973
6m The crack on the next buttress is short and sweet. The slab left of the crack is 5b.

68 Dangerous Crocodile Snogging
E7 6c ★★★   1986
12m The next square buttress has a remarkable flying fin on its left-hand side; this route picks its way delicately across the sidewall covering some unlikely ground. From below the left arête, steeply gain the wide break, and the rounded hold above, at the base of the arête. From here, struggle into a standing position on the left of the arête. Make one (hard) move up and stretch left for an elusive small flake in the middle of the wall. Matching here allows a breather (though no way out) while the final moves up are uneasily insecure. Easy for 6c.

More a cayman's kiss than the real thing, **Blockbuster** (E5 6b, 2001) is a shorter (though reachy), more direct Crocodile but with some difficult climbing nonetheless. Place gear high in Camelian Crack and move up and right to the flake of Crocodile, to finish grimly as above.

69 Clippety Clop, Clippety Clop, Clippety Clop   E7 6c ★★★   1991
12m One of the great lines on grit: the immaculate and ludicrous arête bypassed by Dangerous Crocodile is taken in its entirety. Start as for Crocodile, then rock onto the ramp on the right of the arête. Grapple and stretch to good holds on the arête, and ride this to a layback finish. A Friend 6 in the break has reduced the grade from its original E8: *see photo opposite*.

70 Elastic Limit   E3 6b ★   1974
9m The crack in the centre of the buttress seems a lot nearer than it actually is. A difficult and dangerous stretch from below occasionally sees success; if so, swing up and right to gain a ledge then finish direct. Spotters strongly recommended.

The Main Edge page 201

Just to start you off with a tussle, here's a couple of problems to test your will, one a scary green highball, the other a lesson in Ramshaw scrittle.

| 1 | **Pink Flake** | (15) |
| 2 | **Steeper** | (21) |

Drop down over the ridge and follow the path, shuddering past Masochism, and below the Crank buttress to...

| 3 | **Chockstone Chimney** | (32) |

Make sure you have your excuses ready, because this could be embarrassing.

| 4 | **Midge** | (47) |

Filthy, frustrating and high. But really good!

| 5 | **Crab Walk Direct** | (49) |

A frustrating crackline which should by all accounts be much easier than it feels.

| 6 | **Collywood** | (58) |
| 7 | **Tier's End** | (63) |

A narrow track leads across the moorland from here. Follow this until it curves up right into a shallow heathery valley directly up to the hanging fin of Clipperty Clop, Clipperty Clop.

Dangerous Crocodile Boulders page 208

| 8 | **The Scoop** | (3) |

Thank goodness it's not at the top of a route.

| 9 | **Ossie's Bulge** | (5) |
| 10 | **Arête on Right** | (9) |

Right foot, or left foot?

| 11 | **Classic Mantel** | (14) |

Taken with a run up.

| 12 | **Crocodile Slot** | (16) |

If you jam this then you're just showing off, rightly.

Loaf and Cheese
1
2
South Buttress
3
4
Lower Tier
5 6 7

The Main Edge page 217

Skirt around the buttress keeping your left hand on the rock until you are led into a tunnel, go up through this and continue straight on through the fissures until you re-emerge. Traverse directly across the slabs until faced with a wavy wall centred with a handsome hanging crack.

| 13 | **Little Nasty** | (86) |

Fill the landing with camera cases and duvet jackets and get involved in the perfect Ramshaw crack.

14 Head directly down the hill to the right of the finger. When you can't see any more rocks in front of you turn around and you'll see The Big Slab: climb it anyway you wish, the left side being easiest although the only decision really needed is 'run or slide?' (4c-5b)

Further along the track a herd of boulders can be seen up on the ridge, sitting looking out to Morridge. These rocks contain Ramshaw's highest concentration of excellent problems and simply should not be missed:

| 15 | **Magic Roundabout Super Direct** | (106) |

A technical delight, but it gets high.

| 16 | **Magic Arête** | (111) |

Ramshaw Rasher

Say hello to my little friend! You are about to get the Ramshaw experience, with all that that entails. Only when you can walk on rice paper without making a mark should you embark on the scrittly slabs. Only when you can take the pebble from the master's hand will you be ready for the steep walls. Only when you can pick up the hot coals without burning your arms will you be ready for the wide cracks. This circuits drips character from every orifice and will give you a great insight into one of the county's madder crags. Enjoy 21 oddities from V0 to V5, burly, technical and tough all the way.

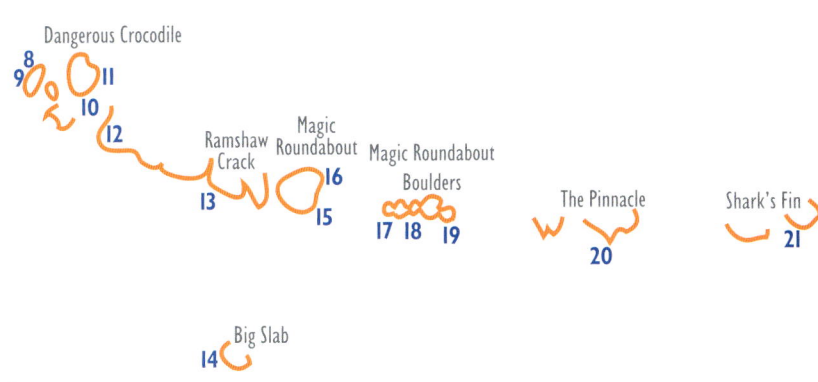

Magic Roundabout Boulders page 221

17 The Rammer (5)
If you haven't done it, you haven't lived.

18 The Pinches (7)
One of the best problems on Staffordshire Gritstone, it's a shame it's not on a route.

19 Cracked Arête (10)
Hop on and go. To do the start without a bounce or a stack of pads will certainly impress the Staffordshire elders, not that they'd let you know.

The Main Edge page 222
Carry on to the bulging shards of The Pinnacle

20 Press Direct (126)
Have a go at Foord's Folly if this is easy.

Follow the top path until over the summit of Ramshaw and head down towards the frog, below which is:

21 Shark's Fin (137)
Here is it, the moment you've been waiting for, go on, be like Johnny.

Staffordshire Grit

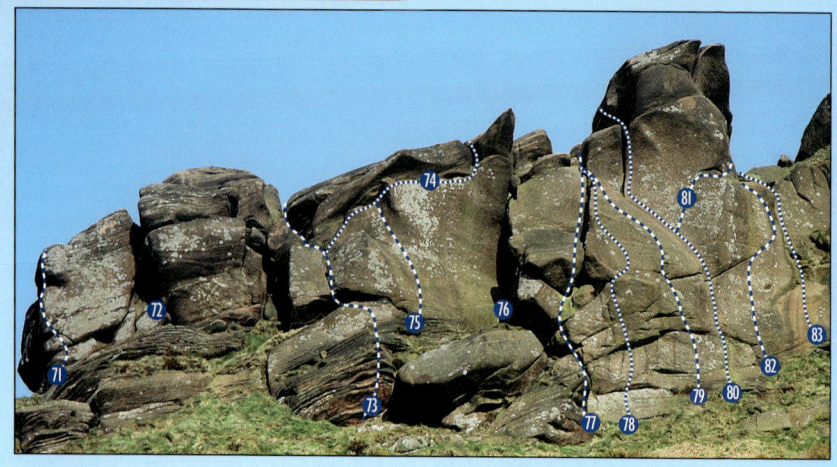

Boomerang Buttress

Having stopped for a quick breath, the blasting buttresses begin anew, just dripping with rough pebbly quality. The first set leads to the fine Boomerang Buttress, home of the great VD.

71 Creep, Leap, Creep, Creep E4 6b   2001
6m The blunt arête climbed on its right-hand side with gear at two-thirds height. Apparently can be done dynamically from the break.

72 Wriggler HS 4b   pre-1973
6m Severely wide but very short lived. Fun, despite everything.

73 Arête and Crack VD   pre-1973
13m Climb the short blunt arête left of the cave and follow the crack above to a wide exit left.

74 Handrail E2 5c ★★   1977
12m As the crack of the previous route peters out step up and place gear in the prow on the right, then boldly swing round the arête to follow the obvious traverse line. With feet and mind pedalling simultaneously carry on fearlessly to an exit up the wider crack. Very good but high in the grade.

75 Handrail Direct E4 6a ★   1984
9m Go up the easy groove to stand below a blank scoop. Climb this on smears and pebbles to join the original before the swing right. Okay as long as you don't fall. The vague green streak to the right is **Cedez le Passage** (E6 6b, 2000), which joins the previous climb when holds run out. Utterly pointless and totally terrifying.

Ramshaw Rocks Boomerang Buttress

76 Assegai VS 5a ★ pre-1973
11m Uncomfortable on the sharp end! The knobbly, sharp, gritty corner is harder than it looks, especially moving onto the slab.

77 Bowrosin VS 4c ★ 1969
12m A good, though broken, route. Climb the slab to where a step across leads to a crack, which is followed with a hard move as the angle changes.

78 English Towns E3 5c ★ 1979
12m Takes the impressive shield of rock. Go direct up the steep wall left of centre to a break where a scary mantel up and right leads to a more positive stance. Follow the easier angled slab to the top. The grade is for an ascent without side runners in Bowrosin. Good.

79 Spanish Fly E2 5c 1992
12m A counter to English Towns. The wall left of Boomerang is climbed to the wide break. Move left until a mantel from here allows the slabby nose to be climbed.

80 Boomerang VD ★★★ pre-1973
12m The wide crack is a great gritstone feature, and makes for a superb and well-protected climb. Finish left or via a short steep crack on the skyline (better but harder). A great first lead, although it feels exposed at the top: *see photo on page 196*.

81 Wick Slip E5 6b 1987
12m A dream come true for the pebble cognoscenti. Having rounded the first bulge of Boomerang, place some gear up and left. A quick move on pebbles soon gains the good slot in the arête. Place a good cam and step out right to finish.

82 Monty E4 6b 1990s
12m The slab below is followed on pebbles to a horizontal crack and some gear. Traverse right and finish up the blunt arête. At this grade a step is made into The Watercourse for contemplation before the arête is climbed.

83 The Watercourse VS 4b 1969
15m The wide groove/scoop has a tricky start. Follow this to a second groove and traverse left to finish up a cracked nose. **Up Your Slip** (E2 6a, 2001) is an extended problem over the short roof right of the finish of The Watercourse.

84 Dan's Dare VS 4c 1969
9m Up and right is a green and awkward flaky groove just right of a short chimney. Climb this.

Arthur Scargill's Hairpiece is Missing, (5b, 1984) is a better name than a route and follows the right-hand side of the small prow to the right. The prow direct would also be a good problem.

85 Gully Wall HVS 5a pre-1973
9m Starting from a pedestal right of Dan's Dare, follow a short groove up to a wide crack then a small ledge, with a tricky move to leave this and gain the wide break.

I'll huff and I'll puff and I'll blow your house down! Richie Patterson digging for victory on the crag's proudest fissure, Ramshaw Crack, E4 6a (opposite page). Photo: David Simmonite.

Ramshaw Rocks Ramshaw Buttress

Ramshaw Buttress

The big buttress is the epitome of Ramshaw. As well as looking as mean as hell it provides, amongst others, two of the most stunning routes on grit, albeit with distinctly different characters.

86 Little Nasty E1 5b, 5a ★   1968–73
14m The crack is pretty grim for 3m but then relents to give pleasant climbing to a ledge and belay. ◉ From here the thin groove in the middle of the top of the side wall of the buttress is aimed for, to provide a reasonable finish.

87 Electric Savage E4 5c, 6a   1978
14m Nasty piece of work. After the initial moves of Little Nasty, a thin traverse right out of the crack gains a crack leading to the large ledge (belay). From here, climb the 'roof-like' crack on the left edge of the buttress. This pitch has bamboozled many leaders, so beware.

88 Ramshaw Crack E4 6a ★★★   1964
7m The strangely beguiling and ridiculously steep crack moves from hand to fist to arm-bar width all within twenty feet. Climb it. One of grit's great cracks and still an intimidating lead even after all these years. Crack School no. 11. *See photo opposite.*

The thin crack and arête right of Ramshaw Crack have been top-roped at F8c.

89 Four Purists VS 5a ★   pre-1973
7m Back at the lower level, this is the next obvious crack right of Electric Savage. Steeper, wider and more difficult than it first appears, the short crack to the ledge is very worthwhile. Can be finished up the second pitch of Little Nasty.

90 Never Never Land E7 6b ★★★   1986
12m The sublimely subtle wall to the right succumbs to a more contemplative approach. Follow and place high gear in Four Purists, then make difficult moves to leave this and hook the obvious flake in the middle of the wall. Tinker here for poor gear and without getting lost (boys) follow the line of small crimps and scoops direct to a mother of a finish. Easier if you don't panic!

91 Green Corner S 4a   pre-1973
6m Climb the slabby groove 5m right until it steepens to require more pull to get up the short crack.

The main path heads down from here but right of the gully the crag continues up past several very short cracks known as the Zig-Zag cracks, giving some good sport in the 3c to 4c range. Past these is a mini-ledge, and a much more impressive buttress bounded on its right by a wide crack.

As the screaming, biting wind howls in the dying dregs of a bleak December afternoon, the near-hypothermic spotters, the will to live long gone, even the dogs, their faces frozen into masks of canine agony. The team looks on, hands frozen in the pockets of thin jeans, their pale visages revealing the horror that they know deep inside. That Gus probably has a few more goes in him before they can go home. Force Nine, E4 6c (page 221). Photo: Jon Read.

Ramshaw Rocks Imposition Area

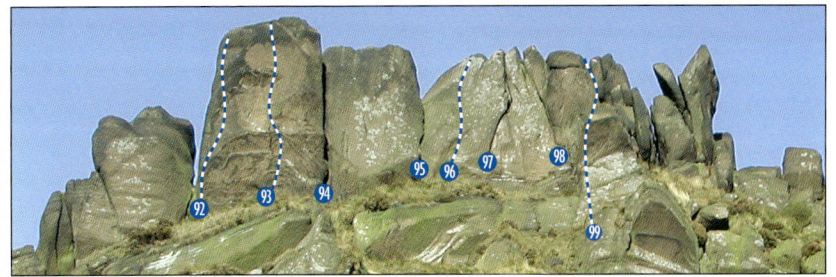

Imposition Area

A nice little parade of cracks, some tough, some not.

92 Rollercoaster E6 6c ★   1990
10m Climb directly up the blunt arête to gain protection in the horizontal break on the right. Finish desperately up the horrendously slanting break, to an equally sloping top out. Hard and scary.

93 Boom Bip E7 6c ★★   2002
8m An audacious route which crosses rather than climbs some very unlikely territory. Climb directly up to the centre of the large overhang, to the large jugs and gear. From here, screw your courage to the sticking place and attempt the full-body dyno direct to the top of the crag. Must be seen to be believed!

94 Imposition E2 5c ★★   pre-1973
8m The crack on the right always seems just too wide and provides a difficult exercise. Very good. Crack School no. 9.

95 Iron Horse Crack D   pre-1973
6m The tiny jamming crack next right.

96 Scooped Surprise E3 6a   1984
6m A two move wonder, which uses pebbles and the short blind crack just right of Iron Horse Crack to pull into the shallow scoop. Finish direct. Bold.

97 Tricouni Crack HS 4a ★   pre-1973
6m The next crack is a pleasant exercise for fat fingers or thin hands. Crack School no. 3.

98 Rubber Crack VS 4c ★   1973
6m To the right again is a short crack and corner.

99 Darkness S 4a   pre-1973
9m Lengthened by starting up the slab below Rubber Crack, this route takes the curved crack on the right to a ledge, then immediately up the first crack encountered.

Below here is a block with a small roof, bounded by small grooves on either side, giving two Diffs, **Army Route** *and* **Dusk** *(pre-1973).* **Scout In Situ** *(5a, 1987) pulls round the roof of the small prow and another,* **Antlers Hall** *(5b, 1994) climbs the sharp arête up and right of Dusk.*

Flaky Buttress

Thirty metres to the right is a tall, jagged buttress containing some dramatic raspers. **Flakey Gully** (M pre-1973) is just left of Flakey Wall

100 Flaky Wall Direct VS 4b ★   pre-1973
14m A good solid climb. Just to the left of the prow is a green streak which is followed on good holds to reach a ledge. Step left then go straight up past some large spikes into a groove that certainly maintains interest to an airy perch.

101 Flaky Wall Indirect VS 4c ★   pre-1973
16m Follow the Direct to the ledge, move up and right via some flakes and move round the corner. The finish up the front face is the most difficult section. The **Super Direct** (E1 5b ★ 1996) joins the top of this by climbing the left side of the steep arête.

102 Cracked Gully D   pre-1973
14m The wide blocky groove to the right is a good introductory route. The arête to the right has been claimed as **Cracked Arête** (VD, pre-1973).

Staffordshire Grit

103 **Arête Wall** D   pre-1973
9m Take the V-shaped groove for 4m then finish up a slightly steeper flaky crack.

104 **Crystal Tipps** E1 5c ★   1976
7m Climb the wall about 1m right of the left arête making a committing move to gain the obvious layback flake and grass above. Good fun: highball V2.

105 **The Ultra Direct** E2 6b ★   1984
7m About 3m in from the arête is a jug at head height. Using this and the thin seam above, make a hard mantel to get established on the slab. Finish direct and still with interest. Neat! Highball V5.

106 **Magic Roundabout Super Direct**
     E1 5c ★   1975
7m The next flake in the bulge, about 1.5m right, is climbed to gain the slab above. Carry on to finish between the normal route and The Delectable Deviation. Hard at the start and committing at the top. Highball V2.

107 **Magic Roundabout Direct** HVS 4c ★ pre-1973
7m Take the final shallow groove, crux, to the break. Trend right and aim for the luminous slot directly above the start of Magic Roundabout.

108 **Magic Roundabout** S 4a ★   pre-1973
7m A fine delicate route. Start at the small broken niche on the right of the buttress. Follow the lowest break to finish at a black flake.

109 **The Delectable Deviation** HVS 4c   pre-1973
9m Start 2m to the right and walk along the higher break. Somehow not as good as the others.

110 **Perched Flake** D   pre-1973
9m The short flake and blunt rib above.

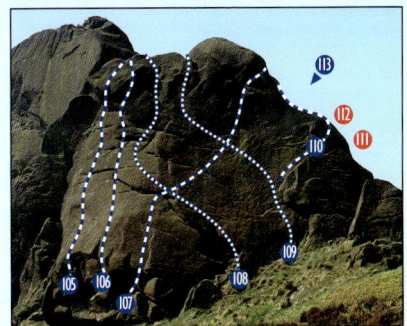

111 Magic Arête V2 (5c)
The sweet arête on its right. ⓒ

112 Be Calmed V6 (6b)
The scoop right of Magic Arête is gained from the left or right and entered via a desperate mantel.

113 Force Nine E4 6c ★★   1985
9m Good bouldering at an even better height. To the right, the pebbly wall/scoop is climbed with difficulty, aiming for a thin flake at 4m. A gnarly move here should gain a standing position and the top: *photo on page 218.*

Hidden below Magic Roundabout is a small outcrop.

114 Port Crack S 4a   pre-1973
8m Start by bridging from below or from the slab on the left. Good stuff.

115 Time Out E2 5c ★★   1979
9m The central crack. Moving right to a subsidiary upper crack provides the crux.

116 Starboard Crack E1 5b ★   pre-1973
9m Vile but fun: the right-hand crack is like jamming porcupines.

Magic Roundabout Boulders

A brilliant and often tough mandible of blocks lies to the right. The finger just left is V0– (4a).

1 Jamless V1 (5c)
The perfect hand crack fortunately demands no jamming.

2 Arête on Left V6 (6b)
The mantel to the left is V2 (6a), and a harder one left again is V5 (6b).

3 Project
The holdless arête, climbed on its right side, is a tough proposition.

4 Epilogue V5 (6b)
Reachy, and with a desperate top-out.

5 The Rammer V0– (4b)
One of the Peak's better chimney problems. Squirm up the constricted fissure, using heads, shoulders, knees and toes. A real undresser. ⓒ

6 Monologue V9 (6c)
The right arête of The Rammer is minging hard.

7 The Pinches V4 (6a)
Climb the features on the overhanging arête. ⓒ

8 Practice Chimney V0– (4a)
A much friendlier chimney.

9 Dialogue V8 (6c)
Crucify your way up the front of the block using a good deal of power. A modern classic.

10 Cracked Arête V1 (5c) ⓒ

Staffordshire Grit

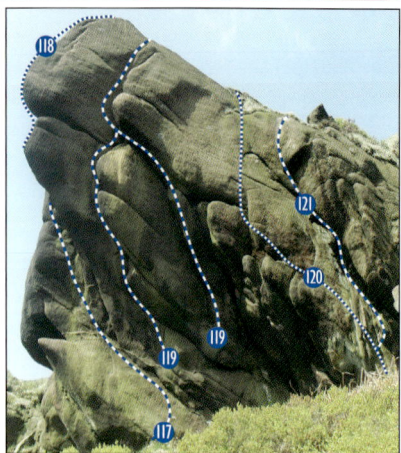

Roman Nose Buttress

This is home to more steep Ramshaw challenges.

117 **Big Richard** VS 4c ★   pre-1973
10m The first routes start under a prominent spike at 3m. Gain the spike – either direct, strenuous, or via the ramp to the right, technical. The chimney above is most difficult to enter; exit to a ledge and finish up the wall/groove on the right.

118 **The Proboscid** E1 5b   1980
10m Do the start of Big Richard, then layback the exposed and serious nose above.

119 **The Crippler** HVS 5a ★★★   1969
10m Starting further right again is another route to inspire. Climb from the back until forced left, and make difficult moves to gain a groove. Getting stood at the top of this is also entertaining, from where a slabby finish can be made. *See photo on page 224.* A more direct approach can be made though a bulge to join the original; 5b. A good problem, **Wheel of Misfortune** (E2 6a, 2002), can be had up the hanging prow just right, avoiding the block on the right.

120 **Escape** HVS 5b   1977
8m As height is gained the difficulties increase on the wall to the left of the large chimney. Very green but still fun.

121 **Mantrap** HVD 4a   pre-1973
8m The chimney itself yields to less of a struggle than first appears.

The Pinnacle

Another pointed outcrop lies across the wide gully. It rocks.

122 **Great Scene Baby** S 4b ★   pre-1973
10m The smart crack to the left is gained from 2m up the groove. Climb the crack on good jams onto a slab and finish over a small neb. Crack School no. 2. A direct start is a painful 5b. A direct finish is 5a.

123 **Groovy Baby** HS 4b   pre-1973
10m Guess where this goes? Not as good as its name; short and green.

124 **Pile Driver** VS 4c ★   pre-1973
17m A good route with an exposed finish. From the groove, join the crack on the right, which is climbed to its end. A step right leaves one below the final crack.

125 **The Press** E1 5b ★★   1971
15m Another belter, which is solid at the grade. Where Pile Driver goes up, continue right along the obvious break until a beefy pull can be made into the steep crack. This is followed round the arête to an easier finish: *see photo on page 3.*

This area also has some superb, powerful bouldering to offer, a lot of which stays dry in light rain.

126 **Press Direct** V4 (6b)
Climb twin seams dynamically to join the crack. ◎ The obvious bum start to this problem goes at a mighty V7 (6b).

127 **Lust Left-Hand** V7 (6c)
Follow the crimpy handrail rightwards and into the niche on the right.

128 **Night of Lust Start** V5 (6b)
The first moves, into the niche, make a superb crimpy problem. Starting from the low flat jug beefs the difficulties up to V6 (6b).

Ramshaw Rocks The Pinnacle

129 Runnel Entry V5 (6b)
From the low, flat hold, head up and enter the shallow water runnel directly above.

A super highball problem would be to climb directly up the bulging arête to the point where Night of Lust meets The Press.

130 Night of Lust E4 6b ★   1984
14m A desperate start leads to easier climbing above. Make a series of thin pulls to gain a niche and some gear. Grope over a bulge, then pull up and left to join The Press. Gaining the route from the gully is an exposed E3 5c.

131 Curfew HVS 5b ★   pre-1973
12m Very Ramshaw. Another burly pull off the ground is the main feature of the steep corner crack. The rest is merely pleasant.

132 Foord's Folly E2 6a ★★★   1968–73
10m Valiantly attempt to climb the exasperating crack without wrecking digits. If successful, move out to an easier finish up the thin hand crack above. For those carrying and placing gear it's probably E2, for those soloing, a bold E1. The fact remains it's hard 6a for both. Crack School no. 8.

133 The Swinger HVS 5a   1972
13m Takes the right edge of the buttress with a difficult start on a couple of sloping ramps. From the ledge continue up the arête above. A rather contrived girdle, **Screwy Driver** (VS 4c, 1968–73) crosses the prow at two-thirds height starting from the gully left of Great Scene Baby and finishing right of The Swinger.

Up and behind this section the rocks are smaller, greener and very broken although there may be a little scope for exploration. Fifty metres to the right is an undercut nose with a short wall above and to the left which features an obvious crack at its left end.

Martin Kocsis emerging shattered and bruised from a heavyweight session on the lower flakes onto the featherweight finish of The Crippler, HVS 5a (page 222). Photo: Mike Hutton.

Ramshaw Rocks Last Rocks

135 California Screamin' V8 (6c)
A brilliant boulder problem over the bulge and arête just right, with hard slappy moves to gain the upper ridge. The top feels high.

136 The Brag VS 5a pre-1973
9m The short groove to the right has a difficult start to much easier climbing. Finish up a little prow.

137 Shark's Fin V0 (5a)
A classic. Up on the ridge, is a short very steep wall/roof. Climb the obvious flake under the roof. ⊙ A **double dyno** from the base to the top is V5 (see Stone Monkey), and the lip traverse is V1. And it bears repeating, beware the giant frog!

Thirty metres further on is a more substantial buttress.

138 Rash Challenge E1 5b ★ 1976
8m A very exciting little number. The main roof is gained from the right or left slab and tackled boldly from slightly left of centre to gain a groove. The groove to the left is **Early Retirement** (D, pre-1973).

139 Honking Bank Worker E2 5c 1984
8m The arête is climbed to where the wall steepens and bold moves on smaller crimps commence.

140 Extended Credit HVS 4c 1973
9m The flakes to the right are climbed to a short finishing groove. A little loose and overgrown.

The next buttress is 20m right

141 Caramta S 4a pre-1973
12m The short jamming crack through twin noses.

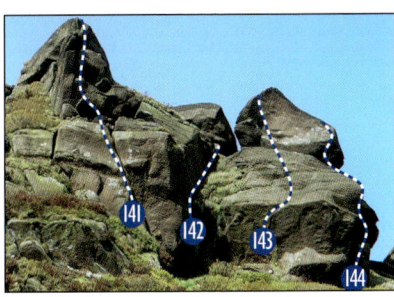

Last Rocks

Dotted along the last remnants of the Ramshaw ridge are a cho-cho of small buttresses. These are seldom visited, but contain enough routes with their own charm to be worth a visit.

134 Slow Hand Clap E2 5c 1979
8m The wall 2m right of the crack seems ok until the last move. **Modesty Crack** (VD, pre-1973) climbs the crack left of the nose to finish right over blocks.

142 The Prism HVD 4a pre-1973
9m Sort of good in a desperately bad way. Bridge up the corner on the right. Finish left or right.

143 Approaching Dark E1 5c 1984
9m The flake and overhang to the right are tricky but shouldn't keep you all day.

144 Lechery VS 4c pre-1973
9m A short but fun route taking the arête to the right on big holds. Finish over the second prow.

Staffordshire Grit

Forty metres right is a pair of buttresses:

145 Ceiling Zero HVS 4c   1980
6m Start direct or from the left and cross the main roof at its widest point.

146 Pocket Wall VS 4b   pre-1973
6m From the right-hand end of the shelf, good holds ease a stiff start into the short hanging groove. Move right and climb up via a couple of substantial pockets. The flake crack just right is V0 (5a).

Below and right is a buttress containing a large overhang. **Curver** *(HVD, pre-1973) climbs under the overhang following the slab from left to right, to finish up a flake. Poor. Fifteen metres to the right is another substantial buttress but this time containing a couple of the best routes at Ramshaw.*

147 Old Fogey E3 5c ★★★   1977
12m An absorbing lead. Starting a little way up the gully, move right on reasonable holds to a standing position on a mini 'horn' on the arête. Boldly climb to a break and finish direct on better holds.

148 The Fogey Prow V9 (7a)
A brutal desperate with a great line. From a sit start and a good hold, climb the sharp prow.

149 Old Fogey Direct E5 6b ★★   1980
15m A superb and much fallen-off route. Climb the lower wall on pebbles to reach better holds. Swing left to join the original at the arête. Luckily the ground below is fairly soft.

150 King Harold VD ★   pre-1973
9m The wide chimney to the right is much better than a poke in the eye.

151 Little Giraffe Man HS 4a ★   1968–73
12m A worthwhile route which takes the arête right of the chimney to where an exciting step across leads on to the main buttress. Move left and finish up the thin crack.

The Lady Stone

This is a small outcrop lying a couple of hundred metres beyond the end of Ramshaw and lie in private land. The owner has refused all reasonable requests for access for climbing. Again the routes are included for completeness. On the left of the buttress is a small slab which goes at 4a, and a short overgrown chimney to its right can also be climbed at Diff. Gaining the arête from the chimney is **Farmhouse Arête** (HS pre-1973). For **Childhood's End** (HVS 5a, 1978), take the overhang 2m right of the arête, step up left then go rightwards through the overhangs to a final slab. **Ladies' Route** (S, pre-1973), takes the wide fissure in the centre of the buttress. **Evil Crack** (HVS 5a 1973) is the best route on the buttress. From below the obvious crack climb to a hole then make difficult moves up and left to gain the sloping tongue and enter the wide crack, which gets easier quite quickly. Strenuous.

Ramshaw Rocks First Ascents

1950–65	**Brown's Crack, Don's Crack, Prostration, The Great Zawn, Masochism, The Crank** Joe Brown, Don Whillans	
1964 Sep	**Ramshaw Crack** Joe Brown Some aid used. Climbed free by Gabe Regan in 1976.	
1968 Oct 9	**Louie Groove** John Yates, Colin Foord **The Untouchable** Colin Foord, John Yates	
1968 Oct 16	**Alcatraz** Dave Salt	
1969 Jan 15	**The Watercourse, Dan's Dare** Pete Ruddle	
1969 Jan 16	**Bowrosin** Barry Marsden	
1969 Feb 5	**The Crippler** John Yates	
1971 Oct	**The Press** Bob Hassall	
1972 Aug	**Tally Not** (1 pt.) Bob Hassall, Norman Hoskins Climbed free by Martin Boysen later in the same year.	
1972 Oct 9	**Green Crack** Pete Harrop	
1972	**The Swinger** Martin Boysen	
1973 Jul 7	**The Undertaker** (1 pt.) Dave Salt, Barry Marsden Climbed free by Jonny Woodward in 1976.	
1973 Jul 8	**Rubber Crack, Evil Crack, Extended Credit** Steve Dale, Dave Salt, various leads	
1968–73	**Screwy Driver** Bob Hassall	
1968–73	**Foord's Folly** (2 pts.) Colin Foord See note overleaf. FFA by John Allen in 1973.	
1968–73	**Little Nasty** Dave Salt Only the finish was climbed. The first crack had obviously been done before, probably by Joe Brown. **Abdomen, Little Giraffe Man** John Yates, Julian Yewdall	
pre-1973	**East Face, Southern Crack, Loaf and Cheese, Wall and Groove, The Arête, Leeds Crack, Twin Cracks, Broken Groove, Broken Groove Arête, Wellingtons, Battle of the Bulge, The Cannon, Phallic Crack, Corner Crack, The Rippler, Crab Walk, The Comedian, Camelian Crack, Wriggler, Arête and Crack, Assegai, Boomerang, Gully Wall, Four Purists, Green Corner, Imposition, Iron Horse Crack, Tricouni Crack, Darkness, Army Route, Dusk, Flake Gully, Flaky Wall Direct, Flaky Wall Indirect, Cracked Gully, Cracked Arête, Arête Wall, Magic Roundabout Direct, Magic Roundabout, Delectable Deviation, Perched Flake, Port Crack, Starboard Crack, Owl'ole, Middle Route, The Shoulder, South Cheek, North Cheek, Collar Bone, The Veil, Big Richard, Mantrap, Great Scene Baby, Groovy Baby, Pile Driver, Curfew, Modesty Crack, The Brag, Shark's Fin, Early Retirement, Caramta, The Prism, Lechery, Pocket Wall, Curver, King Harold, Farmhouse Arête, Ladies' Route, Chockstone Chimney** These routes marked the publication of the 1973 guidebook which was the first to attempt to describe all of the routes on Ramshaw Rocks. Many of these had almost certainly been climbed before in the past, yet all were named, and some were climbed for the first time, by the North Staffs. M.C. who did as many routes as possible in one frantic weekend.	
1974 Autumn	**Elastic Limit** Andrew Woodward (solo) Gained from the right. The direct start added by Nick Longland in 1977.	
1975 Oct	**Magic Roundabout Super-Direct** Jonny Woodward (solo)	
1976 Spring	**Honest Jonny** Jonny Woodward (solo)	
1976 Apr 10	**Crystal Tipps** Andrew Woodward (solo)	
1976 Aug	**Rash Challenge** Jonny Woodward (solo) Counter-claimed as Overdraught by Martin Boysen in August 1977.	
1977 Jun 2	**Traveller in Time** Andrew Woodward, Jonny Woodward. Counter-claimed by Martin Boysen as Jumbo in July 1977. The debate still runs over this one and at the time was a big bone of contention between the two.	
1977	**Gumshoe, Trivial Traverse, Overdrive, Handrail, Escape, Old Fogey** Martin Boysen	
1978	**Childhood's End, National Acrobat, Electric Savage** Jonny Woodward National Acrobat is still one of the hardest cracks on grit. Climbed by Sean Myles and Johnny Dawes on the same day in 1996, possibly the first repeats after 18 years. First ground-up ascent by Patch Hammond, 2001. Only the top pitch of Electric Savage was climbed. The first pitch added by Nick Longland in 1979.	

Staffordshire Grit

1978 Apr	**After Eight**	Nick Longland (solo)
1979 Jun 3	**English Towns, Time Out**	Gary Gibson, Ian Barker
1979 Jun 28	**The Sneeze**	Nick Longland, Dave Jones
1979 Aug	**Slow Hand Clap**	Gary Gibson (solo)
1979 Aug	**Whilly's Whopper**	Dave Jones, Gary Gibson, Nick Longland
1980 Apr 10	**Ceiling Zero**	Gary Gibson, Derek Beetlestone
1980 May 9	**Old Fogey Direct**	Jonny Woodward (solo)
1980 May	**The Proboscid, Leeds Slab**	Nick Longland
1981 Aug 10	**Torture**	Gary Gibson (solo)
1973–81	**Double Chin, Prowler**	
1984 Mar 21	**Handrail Direct, Scooped Surprise**	Simon Nadin The former with a hanging rope.
1984 May	**The Honking Bank Worker, Arthur Scargill's Hairpiece is Missing**	Allen Williams (solo)
1984	**Approaching Dark, Dream Fighter, Cold Wind**	Richard Davies (solo)
1984	**Body Pop, Night of Lust, The Ultra Direct**	John Allen, Mark Stokes The first ascent of the latter is something of a bone of contention. Certainly it may have been climbed before by either Allen Williams or Richard Davies.
1985	**Force Nine**	Simon Nadin
1985	**Wine Gums**	Nick Dixon
1986 May 7	**Dangerous Crocodile Snogging**	Simon Nadin (solo) Originally finished more directly up the slab on pebbles whereas subsequent ascensionists have gone slightly left. As yet, the route has no known ground-up ascents.
1986 May 26	**Never Never Land**	Simon Nadin, Richard Davies.
1986	**Assembled Techniques, Gully Arête**	Richard Davies Right-hand version to the former added by Richie Patterson in 1999 but possibly done before.
1987 Apr 16	**T'rival Traverse**	Graham Hoey, John Allen, Martin Veale
1987 Apr 16	**Rock Trivia, Maximum Hype**	John Allen, Graham Hoey, Martin Veale
1987 Jul 16	**Scout In Situ**	Pete Oxley
1987 Aug 6	**Wick Slip**	Nick Dixon, Andy Popp
1987 Sep 28	**Colly Wobble**	Simon Nadin, John Perry Apparently originally called 'Take Me To Cleveland'.
1990	**Rollercoaster**	Simon Nadin Unrepeated?
1991 Oct	**Clippety Clop Clippety Clop Clippety Clop, Juan Cur**	Seb Grieve Clippety Clop was a significant addition as it claimed one of the most outrageous lines on grit as well as introducing Seb Grieve to an unsuspecting public. As yet, the route has no known ground-up ascents. Climbed by Seb wearing his trademark jeans for better friction for a 'knee mantel' finish. Famously fallen off by Julian Lines on a repeat attempt who gained a break for his troubles. 'On a rope it all seemed easy but on solo it's always more gripping. I was so stretched I couldn't tell if my hands were on the holds, and then….' Since he had also previously fallen off but walked away from Dangerous Crocodiles Snogging, it has to be said one out of two ain't bad. Juan Cur named after the bounder who nicked Seb's gear from the belay while he was top-roping the route!
1992	**Spanish Fly**	unknown
1994 Apr	**Ultimate Sculpture, Antlers Hall**	Justin Critchlow Ultimate Sculpture is probably unrepeated.
1994 May	**Sketching Wildly**	Rob Mirfin Probably unrepeated.
1994	**Paul's Rib**	Paul Higginson
1996 Aug	**Flaky Wall Super-Direct**	Paul Harrison, Nick Jowett
1990s	**Monty**	Mark Cluer
2000 Sep 23	**Cedez La Passage**	Nik Jennings
2001	**Blockbuster**	Andi Turner
2001	**Up Your Slip**	unknown
2001 May	**Creep, Leap, Creep, Creep**	Nick Dixon, Andi Turner Ramshaw became a very popular venue in 2001, as it was one of the few crags to be opened during a Foot and Mouth crisis that swept the British countryside that year. This line may also have been climbed previously by Rob Mirfin.
2002 April	**Wheel of Misfortune**	Mark Sharratt
2002 Sep	**Boom Bip**	Tom Briggs Boom Bip was generously donated and belayed by Neil Bentley, the route's original suitor, after an injury in late 2001 precluded an ascent. This is a thoroughly modern effort with possibly the longest dyno on any route. Tom took the fall on his first go and due to the amount of slack needed to complete the move finished only 4 feet off the ground! Possibly unrepeated.
2009	**Waiting for the Lions**	Martin Kocsis

Ramshaw Rocks First Ascents

Ramshaw Rocks Bouldering First Ascents

Be Calmed Graham Hoey, 1986
California Screamin' Tom Briggs, 2002
Cleg Nick Longland, 1979
Epilogue, Monologue, Dialogue Andi Turner, 2001
Fogey Prow John Welford
Hem Line Nick Longland, 1978
Johnny's Groove Johnny Dawes
Mansize John Welford

Melvin Bragg Pete Whittaker, Tom Randall, 2009
Midge, Press Direct Martin Boysen, 1977
Ram Air John Welford, 2000
Sam's Left Hand Sam Whitaker, 2003
Sensible Shoes Dave Jones, 1980
Tier Drop Nick Longland, 1980
Tier's End Nick Longland, 1979
Tit Grip Paul Higginson, 1990s

Foord's Folly - A history

In the mid 1960s at least four pegs, relics from earlier times, were resident in the grit edges. One in the overhang of what is now "Hanging Around" (U. Tier) soon disappeared; another in rock climbed by "Torture" (Ramshaw) lasted longer, while a third is still usually clipped by supremely trusting leaders on "Corinthian" (Hen Cloud). The fourth was also on Ramshaw, sprouting from the top of a striking crack.

At the time, climbing was a "games option" at Leek High School, but these lessons were out of the ordinary due to an exceptional group of pupils; notable among them being Peter Harrop, Barry Marsden, Harry Scurfield and in particular, John Yates. Steven and Brian Dale also came on the scene when Westwood High School joined in. Enthusiasm, shared by Dave Salt and myself, was extraordinarily high and among the wealth of climbing done in school time, (including a good number of new routes), the first ascents of Death Knell (1970) and Up the Swanee (1971) were accomplished with "Sir" holding the rope.

One fairly manky day, while cowering under the overhangs of Ramshaw, John and I decided to have a look at the peg high up in the crack. I did the leading giving a masterclass in the gentlemanly art of "nuts for aid". Some time later I compiled the manuscript for the first comprehensive guide to the rocks and to amuse Dave Salt, (Editor), at the relevant point I pencilled in "THE BIG FRIG. VS. A ½ ". When the book was published there was much mirth (at my expense) created by Dave's name change attached to a description of the route - which by then had been done in somewhat better style, (2 pts aid), probably by John Yates. In 1973 John Allen did things properly to establish a classic which bears my name although I was never able to do it "clean"; even though intensively coached on one occasion by an elite selection of the "Altrincham All-Stars". A "Folly" maybe - but with a lucky outcome!

Colin Foord 2009

The delicate moves into the scoop on Incognito, VS 4c, on the fabulous Baldstone (page 242).
Photo: Mike Hutton

Newstones
to Back Forest

including **Baldstones**, **Gib Torr**, **Wolf Edge** and **The Hanging Stone**

4

With revulsion and despite, it saw within its own perspective the dawning twilights of the dark idea's insufficiency: bound and determined reflections of itself spewing forth from shaggy-fired but otherwise styll-bald stones that had freed themselves from a previous star only to systematize themselves around – or even worse, behind – Lucifer instead.

Oughtist

Newstones and Baldstones

by John H Bull

These broken edges present a continuum of scale that encompasses minor problems and substantial routes in almost equal measure. Newstones gives superb bouldering with good landings, as well as climbs that receive fewer roped ascents than they deserve. The rock is very rough Staffordshire grit, which for the most part is sound and clean. In many places unique veins or dykes of dark, tough rock protrude from the parent gritstone, providing positive holds ranging in size from tiny edges to boilerplate jugs. These contrast with the many rasping holds of the granular bedrock that abrade fingertips at an alarming rate.

The rocks at Baldstones are slightly grander in scale, the main buttresses offering substantial and strong lines as well as subtler bouldering charms with a serenely remote feel. The rock here is generally fine-grained and relatively forgiving to human skin. A few fragile flakes and sandy surfaces can be encountered' especially after wet weather.

Newstones to Back Forest   Newstones

Conditions & aspect
Two clusters of outcrops on a faint moorland ridge running north from Ramshaw Rocks towards Gib Torr. They are fairly exposed and quick drying. East-facing, they get early morning sun, although this goes off Baldstones by the late morning, and off Newstones by early afternoon. Nevertheless, evening sun can be found at both crags.

Approaches
Park at the road junction and follow the track past Corner Cottage to Newstones (1–2 minutes). Please have some consideration for the occupants of the cottage, who are very sympathetic to, and tolerant of, climbers. Let's keep it that way. For Baldstones, continue to where a gate and stile lead onto open moorland. Follow the path north for a few hundred metres until Baldstones Pinnacle comes into view. 5–10 minutes.

Access
Newstones is on Open Access land partly owned by the P.D.N.P.A. and partly in private ownership. You are requested not to climb on the small outcrops to the east towards the main road. The whole area is an SSSI.

Baldstones and Gib Torr are in the ownership of the Staffordshire Wildlife Trust who are currently (2008 – 2015) regenerating the area from the hideous coniferous tax-haven to mixed woodland and moorland in order to conserve and encourage diverse flora and fauna. Please adhere to any access advice on site from time to time during regeneration. Do not cross from Gib Torr to Baldstones, or vice-versa, directly. The area is an extremely sensitive conservation location. A public footpath leads from the south end of Baldstones by 'Pants on Fire' to meet the tarmac lane.

Another golden Staffordshire evening. Tom Randall and Peter Whittaker. Photo: Nick Smith.

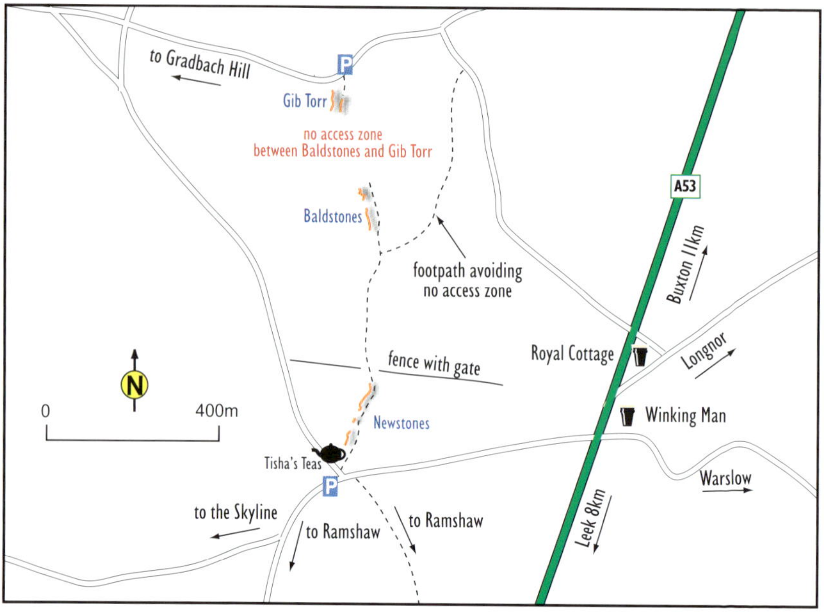

Staffordshire Grit

Newstones

O.S. Ref. SK018638   Altitude: 420m a.s.l.

Charlie's Overhang

1 S&M V7 (6c)
From the flake jug, move up to gain the vertical flake-crack and a desperate direct finish. The left-hand finish is V6, and the sit-start from the flat slot down right adds a grade to both.

2 Leather Joy Boys V8 (6c)
Gain the all-evil all-sloping diagonal break and scorch across to the right arête: **photo page 239**.

3 Little Traverse V2 (5c)
From the jug below S&M, traverse nice blobs right to their conclusion.

4 Charlie's Overhang V3 (5c)
The main overhang direct. Many are called but few are chosen. E2 in old money. **C**

5 Newstones Chimney VD   pre-1973
6m Either of two short cracks leads to the upper chimney, which is climbed insecurely.

234 Newstones to Back Forest

Newstones to Back Forest Newstones

6 Moonshine El 5b   pre-1981
6m The bulging wall to the right has number of problem starts (around V1) and a steep, bold finish. Highball V2, a mini-Charlie's.

7 Praying Mantel HVS 5a   pre-1981
6m Negotiate the prow on the right, then pay homage to the vague depression via a tantalising stretch. The sit start, slapping up both sides of the low prow, is V4 (6b) and a low traverse of this wall is V2 (5c).

"Gritstone is to be found in abundance in Yorkshire, Derbyshire and Staffordshire. I have purposefully not mentioned gritstone before, since it requires a special technique of its own. There are many climbers who are brilliant on gritstone, yet cannot do anything on ordinary rock. Severe though many of them are, gritstone climbs are not a very important part of real climbing. So I advise you to leave them alone."

Colin Kirkus, Let's Go Climbing.

8 Wraparound Arête V5 (6b)
The undercut bulging arête just right. The small buttress 5m right has some problems at around V1.

Top Block

There are many problems and variations, all with low starts that may one day bank out with accumulations of shed epidermis.

9 Square-Cut Face V2 (6a)
Follow the end face on big holds. **☉**

10 Arête on Left V1 (5c)

11 Wall Past Mono V3 (6a)
Only a touch harder without the mono.

12 Varicose V3 (6a)
The wriggling vein is a lovely feature. **☉**

13 Grinding Sloper V3 (6a)

14 Easy Slab V0- (4c)

15 Uppermost Traverse
This can be done right to left at various levels with various finishes, from V3 to V5. The wall right of the crack is V0– (3b), but gives a good V0 if done no-handed. The right arête is V0 (5b) if the obvious sidepull is used, lovely V1 (5c) sloper action without.

Staffordshire Grit

16 Left Twin Arête V0– (4a)
The left of 2 arêtes just below.

17 Right Twin Arête V0– (4c)

18 Flake Slab VI (5b)
The delicate slab. ⊙ A sit-start is **V4 (6a)**.

Hazel Barn Buttress

The next main buttress has a distinctive rippled left wall.

19 Ripple V3 (6a)
A fingery classic, finger-traversing the unique wafers: *see photo opposite*. ⊙

20 Martin's Traverse VI (5b)
The lower break leads to the right-hand arête, often meting out comical corporal punishment to knave technicians and optimistic smearers. Avoid ignominy by going straight up the wall from a couple of moves along, V2 (5c).

21 Crack and Arête V3 (6a)
The overhang crack leads to an ungainly rightwards exit onto the slab. The excrescent slab itself is **Short Wall** VI (5b), and after this is **Short Chimney** (D).

22 Hazel Barrow Crack HS 4b ★ pre-1973
6m The first main crack-line leads from the toe of the buttress to a protectable exit.

23 Hazel Barn S ★ pre-1973
8m The excellent crack and groove just to the right lead to a reachy finish. A line just right is V0 (5a).

24 Hazel Traverse V3 (6a)
Go right on jugs and slopes to finish up Hammy. ⊙

25 Hazel Groove V3 (6a)
Plenty of holds, just using them's the problem. ⊙

26 Nutmeg VS 4c pre-1981
8m Grind up huge juggy flanges to the upper prow, which is climbed on its left for the full experience.

27 Nutmeg Groove V2 (5c)
The slight groove in the face is excellent.

28 Hammy V2 (6a)
From a sitting start, climb the stepped overhang and arête above.

29 Mister Coconut V3 (6a)
The rounded, undercut shelf just right of Hammy, is depressingly hard.

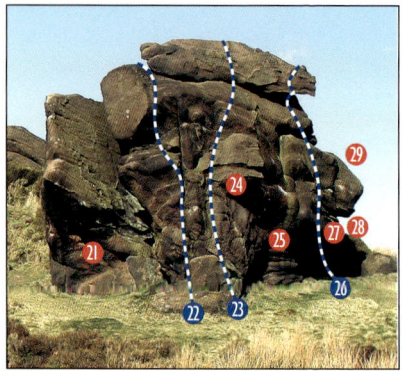

Fingery cranking on unique holds makes Ripple (V3) a memorable Newstones classic (opposite page). Luisa Giles concentrating hard. Photo: Niall Grimes.

Staffordshire Grit

Rhynose Buttress

The next buttress has a cow and a calf both offering their own distinct pleasures.

30 Scratch Crack V0 (5b)
The steep crack on the left wall. A sit-start is V4 (6b). The wall to the left can be climbed with an eliminate approach at V2 (6a).

31 Scratch Arête V5 (6b)
Slap out to and up the arête from a sit start.

32 Itchy Groove V4 (6a)
Gain the slim groove direct. Technical.

33 Itchy Fingers V2 (6a)
The appealing slabby arête gained from the right.

34 Bridget V0 (5a)
The short slab in the recess.

Rhynose Buttress

35 Drain the Main Vein E1 5b ★   2002
8m Roll up your sleeves, start at the back of the gully and progress rightwards along the skyline dykes. At the last rugosity make a bold mantelshelf. Strangely appealing, despite being escapable upwards at almost any point.

36 Puffed Up E3 6b ★   1986
8m Slightly left of centre of the wall is a poor undercut at about 4m. Make use of this to finish direct: makes for a brilliant highball V7.

37 Ponsified E4 6a   1989
8m From 3m up Rhynose, climb the bulge on the left to gain a prominent vein in the headwall. Finish up this.

38 Rhynose VS 4b ★   pre-1973
8m Gain and climb the atmospheric groove to the right. Bridge airily left, or finish more easily and logically rightwards (HS).

39 Hippo HD   pre-1973
8m A shallow groove to the right leads to the upper face, which is climbed direct.

40 Rosehip S 4b   pre-1981
8m Climb curious projections over the bulge, and the slab above just left of some stacked boulders. **The Witch** (D, 1951–73) is the line formed where the stacked boulders meet the crag, while **Candy Man** (S 4a, 1951–73) takes the easiest line up the stacked boulders to the right.

Andi Turner feeling the painful pleasure of Leather Joy Boys, V8 (page 234). Photo: David Simmonite.

Staffordshire Grit

Sly Buttress

The biggest buttress at Newstones.

41 Trepidation E4 6a ★ 1975
9m An impressive line taking the steep wall above the gully. Climb cracks to a sloping break and cam protection. Reach up a short groove, and climb the headwall trending first left then right to a bold finish at the apex of the face.

42 Stallone Arête V6 (6b)

43 Sly Traverse V2 (5c)
A left to right traverse. V6 (6b) if you keep your feet off the slabby ramp. ☉

44 Sly Stallone V3 (6a)
The dyno for the lip is a bunch of fun. ☉

45 The Snake HS 4b pre-1973
12m An entertaining route that rates an equally worthwhile Difficult if started from the gully. Gain the ledge above the steep wall, and wriggle leftwards until easier climbing gains a ledge. Go up and right to a higher ledge, and a wide finishing crack.

46 The Fox E1 5c pre-1973
9m Give chase to the sly chockstone in the left-hand crack, unless sabotaged by the offwidth start.

47 The Vixen HVS 5b ★ pre-1973
9m The right-hand crack gives short, sharp jamming with good protection.

48 The Sly Mantelshelf HVS 5a ★ pre-1973
9m Hand-traverse in from the left end of the vein and mantelshelf at its centre. Finish up the weakness in the slab above: highball V1.

49 Valley of Ultravixens E3 5c 1989
9m Step left and tread delicately up the slab.

50 Sly Superdirect V2 (HVS 5c)
Gain the parent route direct using the smaller vein.

Top Block

Charlie's Overhang   Twin Arêtes   Hazel Barn

Newstones to Back Forest Newstones

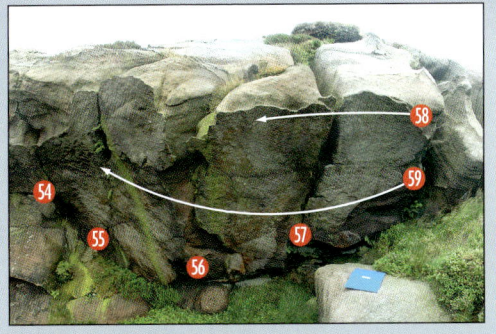

51 Captain Quark V6 (6b)
9m Just right, use small crimps and a pocket to move up for the main vein. Continue, if the mood takes you.

52 Sly Direct V2 (HVS 5b)
The right-hand entry to the vein leads to the same mantel. ⓖ

53 Sly Corner VS 4c ★ pre-1973
9m Around to the right is a small, often damp wall. From this, grope leftwards around the arête, and foot-traverse along the vein to finish as for The Sly Mantelshelf.

Stegosaurus Bouldering
Around the back is some distinctive armour plating with good steep, if short, problems. The problems are graded for sit starts where possible.

54 Tiny Crack V0– (4a)

55 Left Crack V0 (5a)

56 Tyrannosaurus Hex V1 (5b) ⓖ
Layback the flakes on the left of the crack from sitting.

57 Prehistoric Offwidth V0– (4b)

58 Soup Dragon V0+ (5a)
Traverse the top plates to finish above Tiny Crack.

59 The Clanger V2 (5b)
The lower traverse is juggy but still burly. ⓖ

Twenty metres right is a clam-like boulder.

60 Yo Clam V0 (5a)
Start way round on the left arête. Traverse right, past some veins and flakes, then drop down onto the wriggling vein. Hand traverse this right and mantel back onto it. Walk all the way left to finish above where you started. ⓖ

61 Clammy Hands V0 (5a)
From the wriggle, gain and climb the crack.

> "I remember doing that sort of thing when we were kids. We never used to call it bouldering though, we just used to call it farting about."
>
> Ian Dacre, grown-up non-climber, on witnessing his mates' weekend activities

to Baldstones 400m →

Scratch Buttress   Rhynose   Sly Buttress

Baldstones

O.S. Ref. SK019644   Altitude: 405m a.s.l.

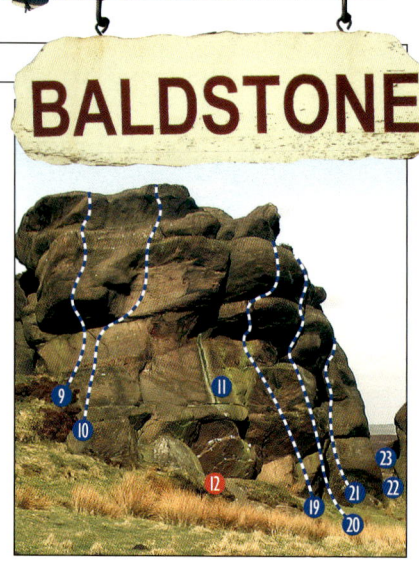

Baldstones Pinnacle

The Pinnacle is composed of superb sculpted gritstone topped with huge fluted jugs. It provides a concentrated selection of high quality routes in the VS-E2 range, with the slight drawback that its tapered shape imposes common finishes on several climbs.

Descent: Either rap from an iron stake on the summit, reverse Perambulator Parade, or downclimb the back of the pinnacle and jump off.

1   Perambulator Parade   VD ★   pre-1951
11m Climb the short leftwards-slanting ramp starting at the ruined wall, then move right to the summit by the easiest route ◐.

2   Pants on Fire   HVS 4c ★   2001
15m A spiralling ascent of the Pinnacle, starting up Perambulator Parade. Gain the break in the hanging slab and traverse it to join the arête. Step up, gain the higher break on the front face and traverse this to join Baldstones Arête.

3   Incognito   VS 4c ★   pre-1981
9m The hanging slab via a pocket, finishing up a leftwards-slanting groove: *see photo on page 230*.

4   Baldstones Face   VS 4b ★   pre-1973
11m A ramp leads rightwards from the ruined wall to a blunt arête. Climb the arête on its right-hand side, past flutings to finish.

5   Original Route   E2 5c ★★★   1960s
9m A route full of surprises, one of the finest in the area. An overhanging groove (V2) leads to a short crack and the lonely upper slab.

6   Baldstones Arête   HVS 4c ★★   pre-1973
11m Starting below the stepped overhangs a few metres right, yard up juggy flakes to a resting ledge and cam placements. Gain and climb the right arête in a superb position.

Newstones to Back Forest Baldstones

Mongolian Throat Singing (E1 5b, 2001) follows the bouldery arête to the left then a minor variation on the upper section, taking the slab on pockets.

7 Prelude to XB E4 5c   1992
10m Start directly up the nose under the overhang on the corner of the buttress. Climb the right-hand side of the overhang, aiming for the ledge on the arête above. Pull onto this and finish up the arête.

The rock to the right is taken by **Burning Pete**, V8 (6c). Go up to thin break (with right hand just above the little round pocket) then use a poor intermediate to rock to better holds.

8 Tasmanian Tendencies E2 5b ★   1995
10m Around the arête is a grassy bay. From the top of the easy crack in the corner, hand traverse the break leftwards using the scoop for footholds, aiming for the arête. Delicate and bold.

Gold Rush Buttress

Ten metres to the right is the face that holding some stern and sometimes green challenges.

9 National Hysteria E5 6b   1997
10m Climb the easy slab to a horizontal break, where RPs can be arranged. Climb the steep wall left of the scoop direct by several hard moves.

10 Gold Rush E4 5c   1976
10m Pad easily up to the hanging scoop. Step right into the scoop and aim for the break above, which is capped by a tiny finishing crack. A bold and impressive line but unfortunately rather sandy.

11 Goldsitch Crack HVS 4c   pre-1973
12m Above the bouldering area is a proud, unmistakable crackline (★ ★), or a repulsive suppurating orifice (•) – you choose. Gain it via an undercut start and a green slab, and squirm up the cleft to scatological fulfilment. Rubber gloves optional; psychiatric help mandatory: *see photo on page 250*.

12 Baldy V3 (6a)
Start low on crimps (feet only on curving ramp) and climb the flake and holds above to the ledge. ⊖

13 Baldstones Dyno V3 (6b)
Dyno to the the lip then gain the ledge above. ⊖

14 Throwball V7 (6c)
From the positive crimps, lunge for the flatty and continue to a sharp crimp and the top. **Muzzle**, V8 (6c) is the low traverse into this problem.

15 Baldstones Low V8 (6c)
A desperate variation on the original traverse that avoids all the larger slopers, to finish up Baldy.

16 Baldstones Traverse V7 (6b)
A very sloping and difficult traverse going right to left along the finger-rail to finish as for Baldy.

17 Easy Exit V3 (6a)
A cheaper variation follows the traverse left then escapes up to the good flake and the ledge. ⊖

18 Crank Cuffin V9 (7a)
Go from a low hold on the top of a mini-arête via a gaston, a sandy flake and a pop.

It's over thirty years old, but Ray's Roof (E7 6c, opposite page) is still a renowned devastator, still with less than ten ascents. Here, Pete Whittaker prepares to go deep. Photo: Nick Smith.

Newstones to Back Forest   Baldstones

19 Riding the Gravy Train E6 6c   1997
11m The bulging territory to the right of Goldsitch Crack. Climb directly to an incipient crack in the roof below a deep horizontal break. Gain the break, traverse right for a few moves, step up to a crimp and RP, then finish via a sloping crux.

20 Blackbank Crack HS 4b   pre-1973
12m A few metres right of the bouldering traverse is a short layback crack. Muscle steeply up this (flakes slightly left are also climbable) to gain the wide ledge. Step left to a finish up a wide crack.

21 Forking Chimney D ★   pre-1951
9m The chimney provides temporary relief for homesick cavers.

To the right is a green buttress that remains luminous even in the height of summer.

22 Bareleg Wall VS 4c   1977
8m Climb the groove 3m right of the chimney and then balance rightwards along a break to the curving finishing crack.

23 Morridge Top HVS 4c   1977
9m Climb the colonised green wall up its centre. Probably best to wait for hard winter conditions and the inevitable development of dry lichening.

Ray's Buttress

The buttress just right, with its lustful crack.

24 Minipin Crack HVD 4a   pre-1973
6m The short dog-leg crack has a wide finish.

25 Last Banana Before Sunset V2 (HVS 5c)
The wall 2m to the right, past a tiny curved ledge to finish right of the pinnacle.

26 All-Stars' Wall HVS 5a ★   1970s
6m From the toe of the buttress, climb a rib, then use a small pocket to attain the higher break and the top.

27 Ray's Roof E7 6c ★ ★ ★   1977
8m Gain and climb the impressive roof-crack, using a variety of limb jams and counterintuitive postures. An significant testpiece that has seen only a handful of ascents since 1977, when it was graded definitive 5.11c. However, this is not a route where mere numbers will give you any idea of what to expect: *see photo opposite*.

28 Johnny's Indirect Rear Entry
E5 6b   c.1990
6m The break in the wall to the right, gained from the right, and followed leftwards. Enigmatically compared by its creators to a three-dimensional slug trail.

29 Indirect Arête V7 (6c)
The arête on its left-hand side.

30 Indirect Arête Right V2 (5c)
The arête is much easier on its right. ●

It's enough to bring a smile to your face :-) Rachael Denks on one of the best V0s in Staffordshire, The Elephant's Ear. Photo: David Simmonite.

Newstones to Back Forest Baldstones

Elephant's Boulder
The buttress to the right has some brilliant bouldering.

31 Ganderhole Crack V1 (5a)
The wide crack. The featured wall to the left will never go! Never! Not ever!

32 Fielder's Indirect V1 (5b)
Move right around the rib to climb the wall on pockets.

33 Fielder's Corner V4 (6a)
A technical and satisfying classic above a thoughtful landing.. The groove above a perplexing start. Not Justin's favourite problem, okay! G

34 Fielder's Wall V8 (7a)
The face to the right via a large pocket and a pebble that's no longer there.

35 Elephant's Eye V4 (6b)
Cool stuff. From the ear to the right, reach left to the lower pocket and make a burly lock-off to the juggier higher pocket. G V1 if you move left to the higher pocket instead of the lower.

36 Elephant's Ear V0 (5a)
The gorgeous layback flake is as good as it gets: *see photo opposite*. G **Elephant's Ear Sit-Start** is a classy arm-busting low start: V5 (6b).

37 Clever Skin Left-Hand V9 (7a)
The classic arête to the right can be climbed on its left side at a much higher grade.

38 Clever Skin V7 (6c)
The baffling arête on the right is a good test of grit technique. Good conditions help.

Just right is a little bun of rock. To the left of this, a groove and arête, from a sit-start, is V1 (5b). Manteling the left side of the bun, just to the right, is V3 (6a). **The Wart** gains this from the non-pocket below at a grade of V7 (6c). Manteling at the bun to the right is V3 (6a).

A further 15m right a jutting prow forms the uncanny **Gurning Bulldog**. *To its left is an easy slab and crack.*

33 Lucid Reams E2 6a   2001
6m Climb the easy slab for 2m, then step right onto the short wall. Intense moves past mauling hand-jams lead to a rounded finish. Further right, **Pyeclough** (VS 4b, pre-1973) climbs the steep gash slightly to the right of the neck of the buttress.

Next is a slabby face bounded on its right by an easy slanting rampline. **Heathylee** (HS 4b, pre-1973), *climbs the faint groove to the left of the easy rampline. At the break move left to a ledge, or finish direct. Alternatively take the easy rampline trending right* (HD).

Fifty metres further on is the last buttress. **End Game** (VS 4b, pre-1981) *is an arbitrary route that climbs the wall and prow at its highest point.*

Double Overhang Bouldering
To the right of this, tiered roofs marks out some bouldering. This is slightly limited, but its overhanging nature makes it a good option in rain. A juggy flake on the left, which is traversed left to easy ground, is V0 (4b). To the right, there is a large flake in the top roof. Gain this by using a pocket and sidepull flake, **Below the Flake**, V2 (5c). A sit-start using the mono is V3 (6a). The roof may or may not have been crossed using this flake. **Overhanging Crack** is a significant jamming test, crossing the bulge from a sit-start, V2 (6a). **Short Crack** is on the right, V0– (4c). Traversing between the cracks is V2 (5c), while continuing the traverse between the roofs as far as the juggy flake is V3 (6a).

Do not go any further!
Gib Torr is prominent across the wooded valley of Black Brook, although access from Baldstones is not permitted, as the area between the two is a highly protected SSSI. Please respect this situation.

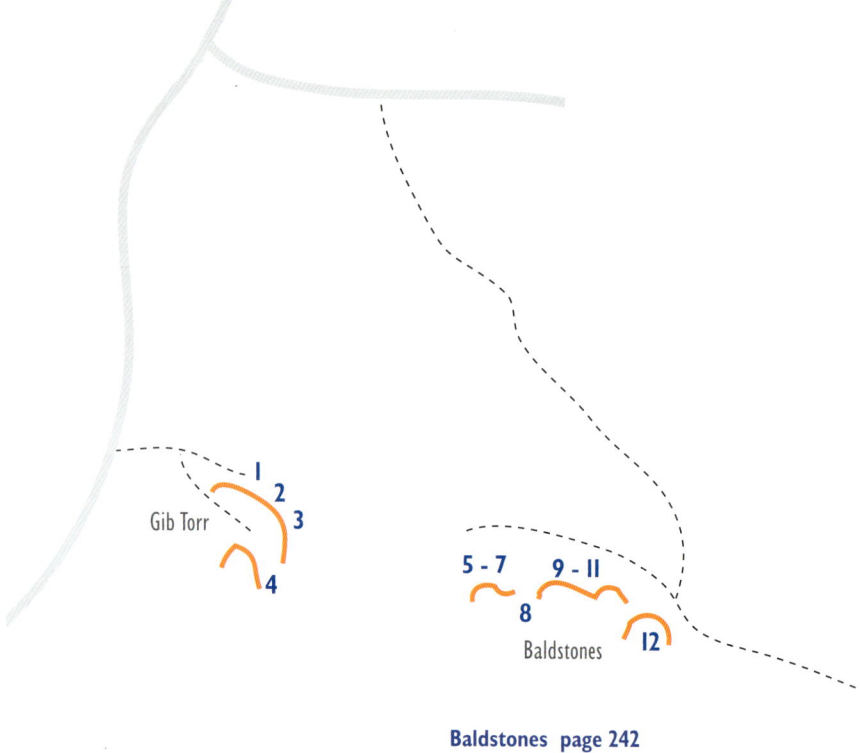

Baldstones page 242

Now you're warmed up, either take the footpath across the moor to Baldstones (do not go direct: see map on pag 234 or drive round to the Newstones parking and make the ten minute approach to the Elephant boulder. Treats await!

5	Elephant's Ear	(36)
6	Elephant's Eye	(35)
7	Fielder's Corner	(33)
8	Indirect Arête Right	(30)
9	Easy Exit	(17)
10	Baldstones Dyno	(13)
11	Baldy	(12)
12	Perambulator Parade	(1)

This is actually a VDiff route, although it is well within your capabilities, and it would be a shame not to get the summit tick. If you're feeling confident, Incognito makes a slightly more challenging problem.

Gib Torr page 251

The circuit starts with a quick visit to this quiet roadside craglet.

1	Little Traverse	(18)
2	Gobble	(11)
3	Gibbon Take	(8)
4	Gib Torrture	(21)

Royal Blue Circuit

The interrupted ridge opposite the Royal Cottage pub has always been a favourite with boulderers. Here's a journey that takes in some of the best, some of the most interesting and some of the least known problems hereabouts. Be prepared for a good range of difficulty, from V0 to V4, which will mean that you might find some problems too easy, and you might find some too hard. That's life. There's a few highballs along the way and it's up to you whether you fancy a bit of spice.

Newstones page 232

The short lovely walk betwixt the two 'Stones brings you to Sly Buttress. The first problems are to the right, on the back of the rock.

13	Yo Clam	(60)
14	The Clanger	(59)
15	Tyrannosaurus Hex	(56)
16	Sly Direct	(52)
17	Sly Stallone	(44)
18	Sly Traverse	(43)

From here, continue past Scratch Buttress. This has a bunch of great problems but due to erosion, no one has been singled out. Do one that takes your fancy.

19	Hazel Traverse	(24)
20	Hazel Groove	(25)
21	The Ripple	(19)
22	Flake Slab	(18)
23	Varicose	(12)
24	Square-Cut Face	(9)

Now that you've got some great climbing under your belt, confident and climbing well, it's time for the best and boldest problem on the tour, a local treasure. Grit your teeth, check your spotters and go!

25 Charlie's Overhang (4)

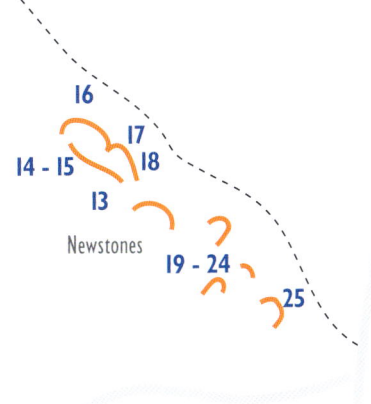

The important thing is that you're enjoying yourself. Paul Harrison, near the top but with at least ten minutes still to go, on Goldsitch Crack, HVS 4c (page 243). Photo: David Simmonite.

Gib Torr

by Sam Whittaker

O.S. Ref. SK018648 — Altitude: 420m a.s.l.

A small crag with a big personality, a kind of baby Almscliff, containing lots of quality bouldering and a small but significant body of routes. The setting is very friendly, currently sat near a pine forest, yet with a very open aspect, and gives good views across the Baldstones–Newstones ridge-back. A very good little crag.

Conditions & aspect

The crag is very clean, apart from a couple of the routes on the lower buttress. It gets good shelter from winds, and is more sheltered from rain than most crags. It faces east, and gets early morning sun, making it good for cold mornings or hot afternoons.

Routes & bouldering

Sixteen routes, tending to be quite vicious despite a friendly appearance. Best around HVS. About 25 problems, usually bulging sloping action, but with one superb arête and one of Staffordshire's best highballs.

Parking & approach

See map on page 234. Park by the gate. See it now? Approach in seconds.

Access

Don't walk from here to Baldstones as the area in-between is an SSSI.

Lower Tier

This is the lower of two tiers.

1 The Fin V5 (6b)
A bold scratchy classic up the front of the jutting prow. A great sit-start off pockets is V7 (6b). The crack on the left wall is **Left Fin, V2 (5c).** This is good but has more trouble with heather than Paul McCartney ever had.

2 The Fink V7 (6c)
A tough fingery problem up the left side of the steep wall. Scary.

3 5c Wall V2 (5c)
The easier wall just right is bold.

4 Gibbering Left V4 (6b)
From the sloping finger-hold, exit left.

5 Gibbering Right V5 (6b)
Starts the same, but makes a harder exit up and right. The **Gibbering Lip**, V8 (6c), continues draping right along the hanging lip to pull up above a good hold.

Staffordshire Grit

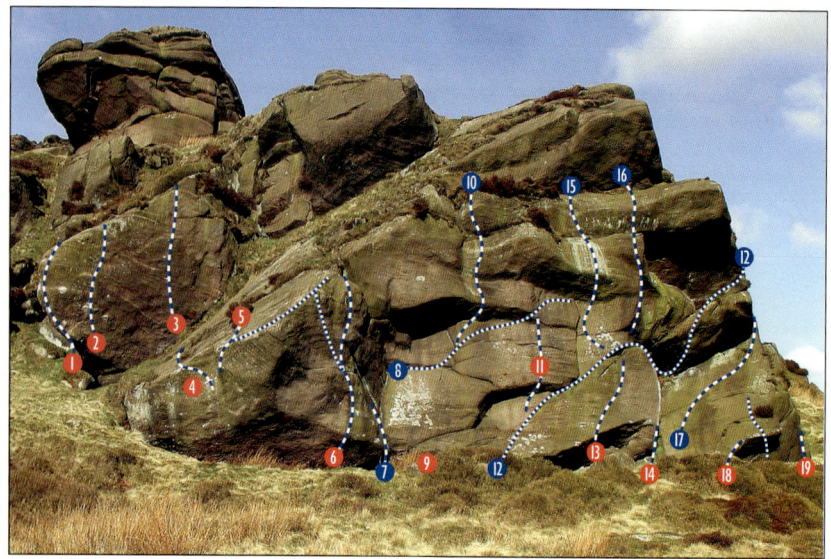

6 Gibby Haines V4 (6a)
From pockets and a sloper, go up to gain the top of the crack. **Staying Alive** V8 (6c), comes from the sidepull pocket way under the overhang, making very fingery moves to gain the original. Fans of space travel may enjoy trying **Maurice Gib**, a dyno from the good flat hold on the original to a flat jug about 6 miles up and left. Somewhere in the V10 range. Linking this to the sit-start will be a superb challenge.

7 Gibber Crack HS 4b   pre-1973
6m The twisting crack leads to a grovelling exit.

8 Gibbon Take HVS 5b ★   1977
15m From Gibber Crack, traverse the sandwiched slab. Good delicate moves. Protection may do more harm than good, a bouldering mat being more use. The route originally joined The Gibe, although boulderers may prefer to come back down that route: highball V1. **G**

9 Porridge Wall V3 (6a)
Start in the very low jug, and yank up to gain the round pocket. Not that nice. The ledge to the left gives a good mantel, V1 (5b), avoiding the crack.

10 Porridge at Morridge Top E5 6b ★   1980s
9m A bold technical climb that usually requires a brushing beforehand. Easily gain round holds under the second overlap. From here, a short but trying sequence leads up the scoop to salvation.

11 Gobble V0+ (5a)
A nice highball leading to the thin flake under the high roof. Reverse The Gibe to escape. **G**

12 The Gibe HVS 4c ★★   1974
9m A Gogarth classic. Go up the flake to the pedestal. Drop down then go steeply up to a big jug (can be reached more easily direct up the groove below). From here, catcrawl right along the sloping gangway and finish round the arête. A fairly serious adventure. The crack above the catcrawl is reported to have been climbed but no-one has, so far, confessed.

13 Martin's Problem V5 (6b)
Start low on a big hold and snatch up and right on a series of rounded crimps.

14 Stall Arête V6 (6c)
The beautiful hanging arête is a supreme test of gritstone technique, requiring power, balance and a

Newstones to Back Forest   Gib Torr

load of stickiness. **Stall Sit-Start** V9 (6c) is just as classic, and requires a bit more of all of the above, especially the power bit. And don't dare use the slab on the right.

15 Stall   E5 6c   1989
8m 'Very grisly and esoteric,' according to the first ascensionist. Having done the problem start, move up and left under the bulge and, with what gear you can muster, tackle the 6c bulge above.

16 Montezuma's Revenge   E5 5c ★   1979
9m A good, albeit absolutely terrifying, climb that would require a clean. From the pedestal (last possible gear), climb up and left through the overlaps on round holds to the ledge. A sobering proposition.

17 Gibble Gabble Slab   VD   pre-1973
8m The slab and wide crack.

18 Little Traverse   V2 (5c)
Traverse the lip. ◉ The mantel through the middle of this is V4 (6b).

19 Gary's 5c   V3 (6a)
Set back and to the right of this section is a triangular green wall. This problem takes the cracked arête. A V0 (5a) problem is possible to the left.

20 Seams Green   V4 (6a)
The mossy wall to the right is climbed on poor holds.

Mike Hutton on Extended Torrture, V4 (next page) Photo: Martin Kocsis.

Staffordshire Grit

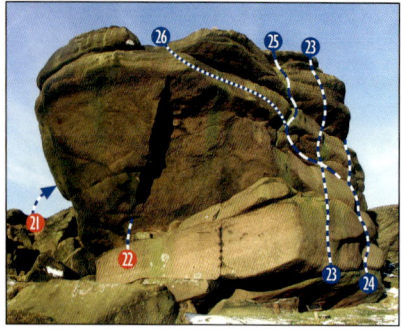

Gibbon Buttress

This is the prominent 'boulder' above the Lower Tier.

21 Gib Torrture V2 (5c)
Gain the short crack on the left wall, and climb it as quickly as possible. ➲ Or continue along the break, **Extended Torrture**, to go up the crack nearer the arête, V4 (6a): *see photo on previous page*.

22 Gibbering Wreck V8 (6c)
A Tierdrop for the new millenium. Great flakes lead to the lip, where a small pocket awaits. Use this with a degree of committment to lunge for the break. One of the best highballs anywhere, although its original grade of E6 6c may well feel warranted if no pads are used.

23 Gibe Turkey HVS 5b   1992
6m Lunge for the ledge then pull up and over the overhang direct.

24 Gibling Corner S 4a   pre-1973
6m Up the little corner then finish off right, or direct at 4b.

25 Gibbon Wall HS 4b ★   pre-1973
8m A nice route that tackles the steep well-protected bulge on chunky jams.

26 Gibeonite Girdle HVS 5b   pre-1973
12m A meaty route that continues past Gibbon Wall to attack (or be attacked by) the horizontal crack to its steep conclusion.

The Upper Tier

This lies just to the right.

27 Gibraltar S 4b   pre-1973
8m The awkward corner and crack to a wide exit.

28 The Ensign HVS 5a   pre-1973
8m The bulging finger-crack.

29 Gib E2 6b   1970s
9m Desperate bouldering (although there's a trick, apparently) leads to a flake. From here the climbing eases off to the top.

30 The Gibbet HVS 5a   pre-1973
9m From Giblet Crack, make a delicate diagonal up the wall leftwards to finish at the arête.

31 Giblet Crack VS 4c ★   pre-1973
9m Follow the wide crack then make a surprising traverse left to the arête to finish.

Rock-climbing has the advantage

over many other motions in that it has no rules save respect. The rock just seduces you, first by its look, then by its touch and then its moves, finally becoming a warm glow. Each special route for me has a glow almost as reminiscent in extent as a feeling you have for a lover when you shut your eyes and feel what is left when you cannot see them.
Johnny Dawes

Gradbach Hill

by Paul Smith and Robert Lavin

O.S. Ref. SK001653 | Altitude: 390m a.s.l.

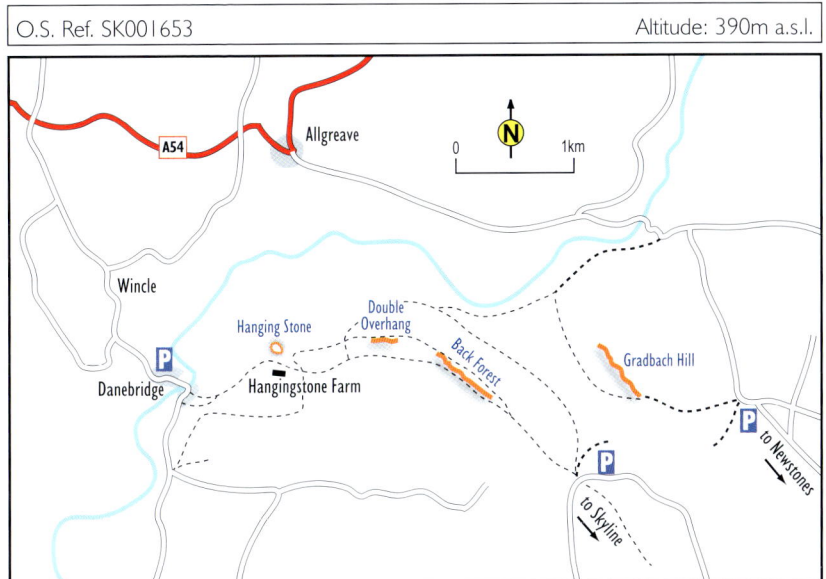

For seekers of isolation, good rock and beautiful views, the small collection of buttresses known as Gradbach Hill is a truly delightful venue. It is a silent and personal crag, which seems incongruous with its relatively short approach and the multitudes of climbers not far away. The sunny aspect makes it a very pleasant place to visit.

Conditions & aspect
The crag gets lots of sun and no seepage. It is clean and suitable for year round climbing. It faces south-west and gets sun from late morning to sunset.

Routes & bouldering
25 routes. Easily enough to merit a visit. Mostly up to HVS with one brilliant E4. A superb venue for the more moderate boulderers with good problems on good features and generally friendly landings.

Parking & approach
Park sensibly at the junction. Follow the rough track slightly uphill, and over a stile. Where the path goes downhill, follow the crest rightwards, along a very rough sheep track, directly to the rocks. 15 minutes.

Access
The PDNPA places a high value on the peace and quiet of this area, so does the wildlife, and so should you. No large groups, as this will jeopardise access.

The climbs are described from left to right. The two most obvious features on the crag are The Pinnacle, the tallest tower at the left side, and The Yawning Stone, a 5m high boulder above the crag, 200m to the right.

Staffordshire Grit

Cynic's Buttress

The first routes lie on a buttress 120m left of The Pinnacle.

1 Fat Old Nick VD 1980
9m Climb a crack on the left of an overhang, then move right and go up the front slab. **Al's Abdominal Start** takes the overhang direct at E1 5a.

2 For Tim D 1980
9m The wide central crack. **Whose Line is it Anyway?** (HVS 5a, 2000) climbs the buttress immediately right on small pockets and edges.

3 Old Son HVD 1980
8m Climb the corner-crack and arête above, right of the central crack.

The Pinnacle Area

The best feature in the valley is the tall pinnacle 120m right, home to a bold Staffordshire test-piece. To its left is a smaller buttress with two wings.

4 Pot Black E2 6a 1986
9m Climb the wall just right of the left arête to a ledge. From the ledge, climb the left arête passing an obvious snapped flake by some technical moves.

5 The Billiard Table HS 4b ★ pre-1973
9m A fine, tall climb. From the lowest point of the buttress, climb a crack to a bulge. Go over this awkwardly to the ledge and exit up the corner-crack.

6 The Cue VD pre-1973
6m The crack on the right side of the buttress passing the right edge of the ledge. Thrutchy. Climbing the wall just left of the crack is **The Chalk** (HVS 5a, 1980).

7 The Hour Glass E3 6b 1997
5m The undercut sidewall to the right is climbed, desperately, above a bad landing.

The Phantom pinnacle lies just to the right. The short back side is Diff and the side just to the left is a good VD.

8 Cleft Route VD pre-1973
12m The very traditional crack on the left wall. Follow this past a large moving chockstone and move round to finish up the easy back route. The steeper crack to the right is **Green Crack**, which traverses into Cleft Route to finish (HS 4b, pre-1973). **X Marks the Spot** (E1 5b, trad/1997), is the thin groove / crackline on the left side of Phantom Pinnacle.

9 The Phantom E4 5c ★★ 1971
15m A superb and spooky route, a classic Staffordshire head-game. Go up a crack then step left onto a small ledge. Climb the vague rib above, past a ghost of a bolt to a big ledge. Go over the top bulge by a thin crack, or climb direct to the summit from the ledge: *see photo opposite*.

Just round to the right lie a few boulder problems. **Cave Crack** V3 (6a) jams the finger crack over the cave, without recourse to the slab behind. Starting at the back adds a bit more spice. **Little Rib** V1 (5a) climbs

Mark Sharratt on The Phantom, E4 5c, one of Staffordshire's more obscure hard classics, well worth seeking out by the adventurous (opposite page). Photo: Jon Read.

Staffordshire Grit

onto and up the little hanging ridge, above a bad landing. **The Hanging Arête** V0 (4c) is the lovely bold arête above, aided by a flat hold and some flakes. **The wall** left of the arête is V0– (4b). **Thin Crack** (HVS 6a, trad) is the thin bouldery crack topped by a small roof, 10m right of The Pinnacle. **The Overhang** (HVS 5a, trad) is a short overhang in the bracken another 15m to the right, while **Pip** (HVS 5c, 1997) is the wall just right of this, using a pebble.

10 Little Arête S 4a ★   1980
6m A short but pleasant climb up the arête 60m right. Skirt the overhang to the left. Climbing it on its right side is a really nice, reachy, HS 4c jug fest.

Eighty metres right the rocks re-emerge from the hillside. Before these rocks, a boulder built into the wall below gives several problems. On the face facing The Phantom, the left arête is V0 (4a), and the wall to the right is V0 (5a), or 4b using the right arête.

The Gape Area

About 100 right are two punchy outcrops above the ridge and a fine, steep buttress below. The leftmost of the upper outcrops contains some nice problems:

11 Tip-Toe Arête V0 (5a)
The delicate left arête on its left side.

12 Front Crack V0+ (VS 5a)
Superb. Climb the steep crack on the front of the block. This could also be led, as it is a little high. The crack just right of the arête is also steep, but more awkward, V0+ (5b).

On the edge below, the next route begins behind a tree.

13 Oak Tree Crack VD   pre-1973
6m On the edge, below and right, the crack behind the tree leads to an easier finish. **French Connection** (E1 5c, 1985) climbs the slab just right, then over the bulge continue direct.

Newstones to Back Forest — Gradbach Hill

14 John's Arête HVS 5a ★★   1980
9m Climb the arête right of the oak, then go directly up the slab. Pleasant climbing, but right at the top of the grade.

15 Sleepwalker HS 4b   1969
9m Climb the crack to a double overhang. Traverse strenuously left on creaking flakes, then trend rightwards up the delicate slab.

16 Barbiturate HS 4b ★   1969
7m Gain the handsome hand-sized corner-crack and climb it direct. The little hanging arête, climbed on its left, is **Morpheus** (E2 6b, 1997).

17 Anniversaire E2 5c ★   1985
8m Climb directly through the overhang immediately left of Chockstone Crack. Technical. The overgrown crack to the left was once **Marsden's Crack** (VS 4c, 1969).

18 Chockstone Crack S 4b ★   1969
8m The prominent crack. A big jug eases the passage of the overhang.

19 The Gape HVS 5a ★★   1980
8m Good climbing in fine situations. Start up the arête, but move left and climb the front face on good features and superb rock. Bold and reachy, being more 5b for the short: *see photo overleaf.*

20 Sense of Doubt E2 5c ★★   1980
8m Nicely exposed climbing up the main arête of the pinnacle. Follow the blunt arête closely with a hard move above the horizontal crack.

21 Spragbach E3 6b ★   2009
8m A massive reach is useful to cover the right wall of the buttress, past a pocket.

The Phantom Bolt

The classic of the crag once sported a bolt which, over the years, became the subject of wildly creative speculation. A "mysterious Boy Scout" mentioned in an earlier guide was probably not involved, but instead, mediums now speculate that the "gremlin with the gizmo" might have been a paranormal being of ghostly quality. It seems probable therefore that the origin of the "iron demon" might only ever be known to the Keeper of the Pearly Gates or the Doorman of a Fiery Furnace.

Colin Foord was the first mortal to give The Phantom an earthly reality. He used the bolt for aid, having first hung a short sling on it as he had heard that it had been placed too high to be reached on the day of the supernatural deed. John Yates subsequently made a spirited ascent without pre-placing the sling, and in 1977 Jonny Woodward upped the spook factor by using the bolt for protection only. Ian Dunn removed the ferrous impurity prior to his wizard achievement in 1986.

The Yawning Stone

The bulging perched block to the right has a superb concentration of good problems. Some of these feel high, but the landings are generally on your side.

22 The Bitch V0− (4b)
The short wall on the left of the tapering sidewall leads to a sloping mantel.

23 Slim Groove V0+ (5a)
The shallow groove to the right is climbed delicately on sloping finger-holds.

24 Mishmash V0− (4a)
The arête is climbed on its left side above a bad landing, finishing on good jugs on the front face.

Staffordshire Grit

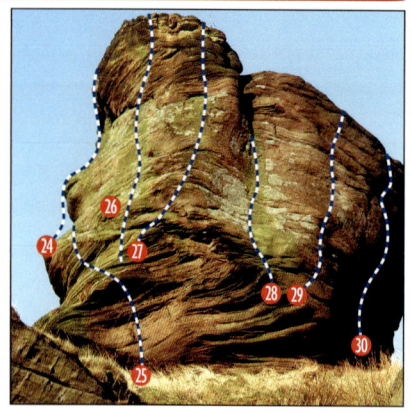

25 **Woody** V1 (5c)
Below the front face is a cave. Starting low on a pinch, trend left and make a gruesome mantel over the lip. Strenuous.

26 **The Yawn** V0+ (5a)
Classic. Pull straight over the centre of the roof using some short cracks and continue on superb holds to the top. Always juggy, but strenuous. A fingery low start is possible.

27 **The Bishop** V1 (5b)
Start for The Yawn but ape right to the arête and surmount it on rounded holds. A great problem. Starting low on small crimps is V2 (5c), but less pleasant.

28 **The Green Streak** V7 (6c)
Gain the green streak direct on unhelpful holds.

29 **Brown Wall** V4 (6b)
The fingery wall just right, passing a hole.

30 **Chunky** V1 (5b)
Great holds lead up the leaning wall to a sketchy top-out.

The last climbs lie on twin slabs 100m to the right. On the left-hand slab the right edge and left side are 4a and 4c respectively, and **Feed the Enemy** *(HS 4b, 1978) is the blunt arête of the right-hand slab (currently overgrown).*

Martin Kocsis storming The Gape, HVS 5b (previous page). Distant runners, fine moves, great rock and a remote setting all come together to give a fine buzz. Photo: Mike Hutton.

Outlying Crags in the Gradbach Area

by Dave Bishop

Ludchurch

O.S. Ref. SJ987656

This remarkable ravine, steeped in history (and vegetation), is on the north-eastern slopes of Back Forest Ridge. Receiving practically no sunshine, its side-walls are cloaked in vegetation and most of the rock remains wet and greasy except after a drought. Ludchurch thus affords a rare environment for thirsty plants suffering photophobia and as such is thought to be of greater significance to the botanist and ecologist than to the climber. Although a few routes have been unearthed on the north wall in the past, such as Subterranean Sidewalk and Dead Man's Creek, they should remain as historical epitaphs to the climbers who no longer come here.
Climbers are requested not to climb here.

Castle Cliff Rocks

O.S. Ref. SJ985658

There is a group of shattered pinnacles near Ludchurch which offers a few minor problems unworthy of climbers' attention, but makes a nice picnic spot.

Gibbons Cliff

O.S. Ref. SJ971664

One kilometre downstream from Allgreave Bridge, Clough Brook winds through a short length of wooded valley with very steep sides. There are a number of outcrops here which are in the main overwhelmed by vegetation. The two cleanest buttresses are situated on the west bank directly above the ruins of an old mill. The old mill provides marginally more attractive problems than these rocks.

The Ballstone

O.S. Ref. SK013658

This is a gigantic perched boulder in the grounds of Green Gutter Stake Farm. Whilst it may offer bouldering, the farmer is understandably unwilling to allow climbing since it lies in his back yard!
Climbers are requested not to climb here.

Flash Bottom Rocks

O.S. Ref. SK018657

The name may have Freudian attractions for you; resist them. In the past some climbing has taken place here and the crag is now in Open Access land the ownership of which has yet to be determined. In 1999, before the advent of Open Access, the BMC agreed a no climbing restriction for this site in order to protect climbing elsewhere under threat. This restriction can no longer apply. However, the area is vital for the long-term survival of some endangered species and you are requested to keep noise and disturbance to a minimum.

Wolf Edge

by John H Bull

O.S. Ref. SK021674 | Altitude: 450m a.s.l.

...Magnesium, proverbs and sobs,
Howling the pack in formation appears...

Wolfpack, Syd Barrett

Wolf Edge is situated high on the Staffordshire moorland, and is effectively the first gritstone outcrop to emerge from the ridge that Axe Edge Moor throws off to the south, gradually leading to Ramshaw Rocks. It is host to a multitude of excellent easy and mid-grade problems. The Edge forms the northern boundary of a small valley that drains into the river Dane. It overlooks the sheep pastures and tumbledown stone walls that form the farming hinterland of Flash, a tiny village that claims to be the highest in Britain. A faint air of abandonment permeates the area, perched as it is on the very edge of habitability.

Wolf Edge has somehow escaped documentation in previous editions of Staffordshire Gritstone or any other guide to Peak climbing, presumably due to a combination of its diminutive stature and its invisibility from the A53 Buxton-Leek road. However, the bouldering deserves recognition, and this introductory description hopes to rescue the Edge from unjust obscurity.

Conditions & aspect

This modest edge is the county's highest and, as such, is exposed to the worst of the elements. However, it is sunny of aspect, very pleasant, fast-drying. At the time of writing, the neglected rocks feel gritty and slightly friable, but regular traffic will do much to improve matters. The edge faces south-east.

Routes & bouldering

This is basically a bouldering crag, with about 30 problems, mainly in low to mid grades. On the whole the landings are friendly.

Parking & approach

From Flash, a road leads uphill past the New Inn pub. At the edge of the village (very limited parking), walk up a rough lane that leads past the last house on the right, over a brow from which the edge is soon visible. Where the lane forks, take the left branch for the Warren and Fin areas, and the right branch for the Quarry area. 10 minutes.

Access

All of Wolf Edge is now Open Access apart from the obvious pasture below The Warren. Yes it's daft. The BMC will be trying to resolve this nonsense in the review of C.R.O.W. 2000 due about 2010. In the meantime if asked to leave do so and let the BMC know.

Bouldering Areas are described from left to right. To aid description, the most obvious problems are detailed, being split into 3 areas. The first area is approached from the right from the lane that crosses the edge, and is thus described.

Newstones to Back Forest Wolf Edge

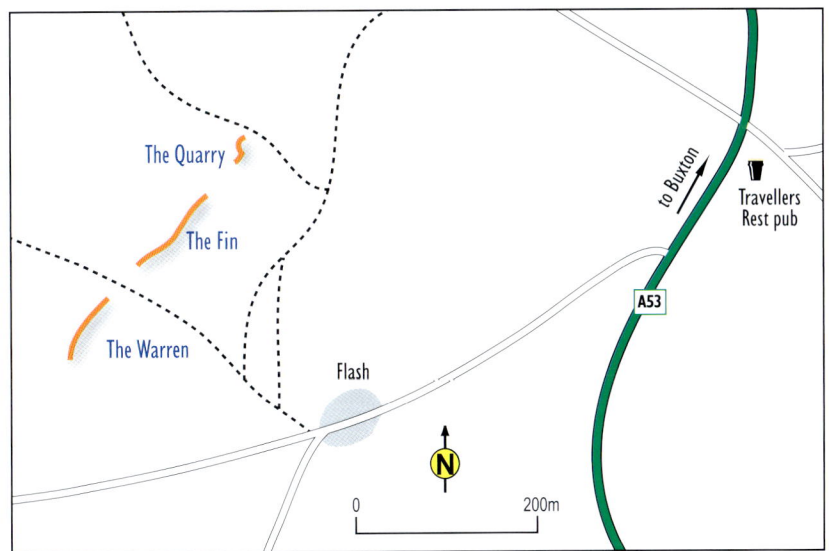

The Warren

This is the lowest part of the edge to the left of the lane. Approaching from the right, the first obvious feature is a tower-like buttress with a rounded arête on its right (unclimbed) and a stone-built fold at its foot on the left. Further left is a small **sharp arête** VI (5b); to its left, a **dyno** face problem, V4 (6a). Directly downhill is a boulder with a superb triangular south face: **hand-traverse** left to right from a sitting start to gain the top, **V2 (5c)**; or climb the face past **creases** finishing left, V4 (6b). Up on the main edge, over the wall to the left is a **fine slab**, VI (5a) with an easy **right arête** V0– (4c). To the left is a small bay– traverse into the bay on breaks and move up the crack to give **Hairy Hat Man**, a superb V3 (5c). Just downhill is a boulder with a scooped face above a rabbit hole, **Warren Piece**, V0 (5b).

The Fin

This area lies to the right of the lane. Just right of the lane is a small **flying arête** that at present is in need of cleaning, followed by several **easier arêtes** V0–. **The Fin** (VS 4b ★; V0) climbs the arête on its left. On the **left wall** of the arête is a cleaned face problem, **This is My Church** V5 (6b). On its right wall is a distinctive **ear-shaped flake** (HS, 4b; V0–). Right again, set back is a **steep arête** VI (5a) with a harder sit-start. To the right is a square promontory whose **left arête** VI (5b), **face** V4 (6a), and **right arête** V2 (5c) are excellent. Slightly further right is a **prow** giving a superb V2 (6a) sit-start. Isolated 20m to the right are the distinctive **Twin Arêtes**: left of the first arête is a **mantelshelf** VI (5c); the left arête is small, strange and dirty (**Gollum,** V4 6b). The arêtes are separated by a **deep jam** crack (V0– 4b); the **right-hand face** (sit-start) is VI (5b); a **low traverse** is VI (5b). A further 30m to the right is the fine **Ramp Boulder: left arête** V4 (6b); **right arête** from the left V2 (6a), **face** VI (5c), **ramp** V0– (4b), and **face** (no holds on the ramp) V2 (5c).

The Quarry

130m to the right of the Ramp Boulder is this square-cut bay. The problems include the **left arête** VI (5b sit-start), **crack** V0– (4a), **face** VI (5c), and to the right of the corner several face and arête problems (V0–V1).

Further documentation of this and other local 'wild' bouldering in the area can be found in the High Over Buxton bouldering guide, available from local climbing shops.

The Hanging Stone and Back Forest

by Paul Smith

The Back Forest crags are a collection of short buttresses widely scattered along the natural continuation of the Roaches ridge that runs from Roach End to Danebridge. The main crag is by far the most extensive and forms a delightful spot for family picnics or an evening's soloing. The aspect is pleasant, the views fine, the rock sound and clean, the routes, almost without exception, friendly and worthwhile. The routes on the Rostrum and on the western outcrop are slightly more dramatic and exposed, whilst those on the Hanging Stone are impressive and imposing.

Conditions & aspect

The main crag is fairly sheltered and can be a pleasant sun-trap in winter. The Hanging Stone can be windy. All the crags dry quickly and are all-year venues. They face south-west to south, and get afternoon and evening sun.

The climbing

About 50 short routes, mostly in the VD to HVS range. Many soloable by the competent, with the occasional sterner challenge. Excellent easier bouldering, currently with pleasant grassy landings. Considerate use of bouldering mats will reduce erosion and would be greatly appreciated by regulars.

Parking & approach

See the map on page 255. For the main crag and Western Outcrop, the best approach is from Roach End. Cross the wall to the north of the limited parking area, by the narrow stile, and follow the path along the ridge, initially alongside a wall. Either continue along the ridge to the top of the crag, or take the left fork where it dips down to the left, over a further stile, before reaching a rushy hollow where the main crag is visible. About 15 minutes. The Western Outcrop lies about 600m farther along the ridge.

Whilst the Hanging Stone can also be approached along the ridge (in 10 more minutes), by far the best approach is from Danebridge (OS ref. SJ965652). From the bridge, follow a wide track upstream on the Staffordshire side for 50m. Cross the fence on the right via a stile and follow another path up through the wooded valley, then cross the field to Hanging Stone Farm. Pass between the farm buildings and continue on up the hillside to reach the block (15 minutes). Do not park on the track below the Hanging Stone.

Access

Hanging Stone: The crag is in private ownership and the owner has refused all reasonable requests for access. He is an occasional visitor and you will be asked to leave. There is a concession footpath to the crag.

Back Forest: All of this land is in Open Access and is a SSSI and currently in the ownership of the PDNPA. Group use (such as groups under instruction or large parties of climbers) is discouraged. This is sensible not just for wildlife reasons but also because the top belays are sparse and can be friable.

Beneath this rock,

August 1st 1874, lies buried, **BURKE**, a noble mastiff, black and tan, faithful as a woman, braver than a man, a gun and a ramble, his heart's desire, with the friend of his life, the Swythamley squire.

Commemoration on the Hanging Stone.

Laurie Carefoot on Bollard Edge, VS 4b (page 269). Back Forest is one of the golden crags for lower grade climbers looking to pack in a good bunch of routes, with quick leads and friendly solos, in a relaxed and beautiful setting. Photo: Mike Hutton.

Staffordshire Grit

The Hanging Stone

O.S. Ref. SJ974654   Altitude: 320m a.s.l.

The impressive hanging block has two plaques on it; the left one commemorates the heart-warming devotion of a dead dog and the other is a memorial to a notable member of the Brocklehurst family.

1 Left-Hand Crack VS 5a   pre-1973
8m The corner right of the steps leads to a break. Struggle with the crack through the overhang above to gain the top. Amusing.

2 The Bridge of Sighs E3 5c ★★   1977
12m Difficult climbing up the arête (crux) leads to the uppermost break. Compose yourself and then hand-traverse out across the lip, before rocking over and climbing the final groove to the top.

3 Hanging Stone Crack HVS 5b ★★   pre-1973
11m A great muscular and airy struggle. Climb the shallow groove on small holds, one metal, to gain an upper crack, which is followed by tricky jamming, and/or holds out to the right.

4 Right Bow E1 5b   1977
8m Climb the bulging right wall of the buttress to gain a high flake and finish up it strenuously.

The buttress can be girdled from left to right at three points. **The Low Girdle** is Severe, **The Drifter's Escape**, VS 4c, uses the central break and **The High Girdle**, HS 4a, crawls along the uppermost break.

Back Forest

The Back Forest crags are now strung along the ridge.

The Western Outcrop

O.S. Ref. SJ981655   Altitude: 355m a.s.l.

The first of the Back Forest crags is a double overhung buttress high on the ridge, 700m past the Hanging Stone, and 600m west from the main Back Forest crag.

1 Burnham Crack VS 4c   1971
9m The steep green corner left of Double Overhang.

2 Double Overhang E1 5b ★   1971
11m A spectacular and not over-protected route taking the fine overhangs directly. The first is tackled centrally via a long stretch for a super-jug on the lip. Use similar tactics to overcome the second, but slightly to the right.

3 Mr Creosote HVS 5b   1991
11m Climb the hanging right-hand arête of the buttress.

4 The Gaping Void VD   1971
11m Starting on the left side of the buttress, traverse right with an exposed move across Burnham Crack and sneak between the overhangs to finish right.

Fifty metres after this buttress lies a small isolated crag containing **Suspended Sentence** *(VS 5a, 1974), which climbs the crack through the overhang.*

Stephen Coughlan in the bathing evening light, enjoying a pummel up Mustard, S 4b (page 270).
Photo: David Simmonite.

Staffordshire Grit

The Rostrum

O.S. Ref. SJ986653   Altitude: 365m a.s.l.

The main section lies 600m further along. Before this, an outcrop sits on the crest of the ridge, with a smaller outcrop sat to its right.

5   The Rostrum   VS 4b   ★   pre-1973
7m Pull up the very steep wall on good holds until an ungainly exit can be made leftwards onto the great shelf itself. Finish easily above.

6   John's Route   HVS 5a   1979
7m The bulging wall 3m right of the Rostrum taken direct.

7   Bumper Cars   VS 4c   2003
7m The pumpy, bulging wall to the right of the holly is climbed direct. **Ruth's Septic Trench** (D, 1999) takes the obvious and often unpleasant chimney on the right side of the outcrop.

8   Pinnacle Buttress   VS 5a   2001
6m Climb the pinnacle direct.

To the right of the main outcrop is a small buttress; **Racer's Rock** (S 4b, pre-1981).

The Main Crag

O.S. Ref. SJ987652   Altitude: 360m a.s.l.

This lies almost 100m along the ridge. The first rock met is Holly Tree Buttress. The first route is the short **Green Crack** (HVD 4a, pre-1973), bounding the left side of the buttress. Good fun can be had by wearing **Action Trousers** (VS 4b, 2002), which stride right from the start of Green Crack, along the main, lower, break and round the arête. Finish up Holly Tree Niche left or right.

9   Twin Thin   VS 4c   pre-1973
8m The eponymous vertical cracks 1m right. Finish up the vague groove.

10   Eye of Japetus   HVS 5a   ★ ★   1974
9m Climb a thin crack left of the arête. Make a mighty lunge to gain the break (or pull elegantly over the nose just right). Finish direct via a faint flake. Satisfying.

11   Holly Tree Niche Left Route
HS 4a   ★   pre-1931
9m The main arête of the buttress on its right side. At the first bulge move left and make awkward moves up the left-hand side of the nose.

12   Holly Tree Niche Right Route
D 4a   pre-1931
6m Attain the niche and finish up the corner. The holly is no more, making tweeds redundant. **Blow Hard** (S 4a, pre-1981) is the flaky crack right of the niche. The wall just right again is S.

13   The Keeper   HVS 5a   1975
6m Gain the middle of the steep left-hand wall of the next buttress by an awkward pull, and then pass a ledge to finish up the right arête. **Back Forest Gâteau** (E2 6a, 1994) is a desperate, though artificial, problem through the undercut arête to the right.

14   Portcullis Crack   S 4a   ★ ★   pre-1973
6m Take the steep, technical crack, complete with chockstone, on the front of the buttress. Pass the overhang and finish leftwards to the arête. Excellent.

Newstones to Back Forest Back Forest

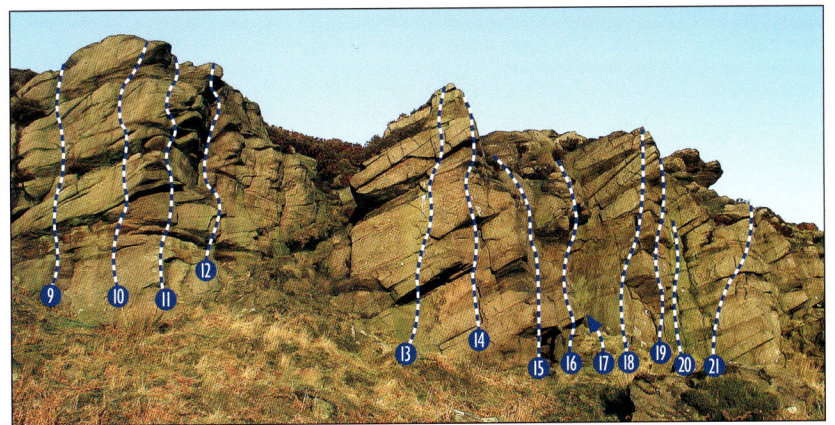

15 Keep Face S 4a pre-1931
6m Gain a ledge on the right and use an L-shaped crack to move up and left to a mantelshelf finish.

16 The Saucer Direct VS 4c pre-1981
6m Past the chasm is a little capped slab. From the right of the slab, climb to the overhang and move right to pass it. A right-hand start is 4c. **The Saucer** (VD, pre-1931) climbs the slab, then moves left around the corner to finish via a crack.

17 Capstone Chimney HS 4b pre-1931
6m A traditional exercise, up the wide chimney, passing outside the chockstone. **Wrestle Crack** (VS 4b, pre-1931) attacks the horrendous-looking crack, using hidden holds, 1m to the left. Hard for its time.

18 Bollard Edge VS 4b ★★ pre-1931
8m A must-do; well-protected, steep and committing. From the foot of the buttress skirt the overhang to the left by a crack to reach the top of the bollard. Try not to think what it's attached to, and press on just left of the spectacular arête to gain the top: *see photo on page 265*.

19 Toe Rail HVS 5a ★★ 1979
8m Excellent. The impressive steep face taken more or less directly on bumper holds and protection. For a consistent route at this grade, step in from slightly right to start. Even better is the **Direct Start**; a big reach and staunch pull using thin flake crack overcomes the initial bulge for a classic HVS 5c: *see photo on page 270.*

20 Pseudo Crack HVD 4a ★ pre-1931
8m The groove and crack exiting right at the top, or better, finishing left via an airy traverse all the way to the arête: HS 4a.

21 Bastion Corner VD pre-1931
7m On the face just right, follow holds rightwards to finish up the vague arête. **Bastion Face** (D, pre-1931) gains the same point directly via a break and a black flake. A small rounded buttress to the right has a poor Severe arête; **Filler In**.

To the north,
Manchester's great glow heralded a vast complexity, while in the same direction but closer by, the homelier presence of Macclesfield could be guessed at. Turning south a myriad of roads, hamlets, villages and towns inexplicably coalesced into the Potteries from where we had come that evening. Alongside the illuminated roads lay the lanes and paths, the canals, rivers and streams, unseen but still felt.

Andy Popp
At the End of an Evening's Climbing in Staffordshire.

Staffordshire Grit

Broken Nose Buttress

lies 10m to the right.

22 Green Shaker S ★   pre-1973
8m On the front of the buttress, gain a ledge. Step left onto the side-wall and a small flake, then move rightwards to the top. **A Fist Full of Freshers** (HS 3c, 2000) goes up the wall to the left, past a black hold to an interesting finish.

23 Central Route HS 4b ★   pre-1931
8m From the ledge, follow the ridge to the second overhang and turn this awkwardly to the right.

24 Not So Central Route S 4a ★   pre-1981
8m Move right below the initial overhang of Central Route and finish direct.

25 Thin Crack HS 4b ★   pre-1973
8m Follow the inviting thin crack, after stepping in from the right. Starting direct is a finger-licking 5b.

The corner is **Hanging Stone Crack**, M. *The next climbs are on the steep wall to the right.*

26 Requiem for Tired Fingers
HVS 5b ★   1974
6m Nip up the left side of the wall by a thin pull to reach better holds before finishing slightly right. Not quite as foreboding as the name suggests, but don't blow the top.

27 Grasper VS 5a ★   pre-1973
7m Tackle the centre of the wall to a tough finish up the cracks.

28 Mustard S 4b ★   pre-1931
5m Start just left of the arête. Make some thin pulls to get established and then climb easily to finish at the top of the arête: *see photo on page 267.*

Stephen Coughlan leading Toe Rail, HVS 5a (page 269). Photo: David Simmonite.

Newstones to Back Forest Back Forest

29 Rocking Stone Ridge HD 4a pre-1931
7m Climb the front of the buttress, after an awkward start and finishing near the top of the left arête. The right edge of the buttress is **Weathered Corner, D,** coming in from the right. The direct start to the left arête is a gut-busting 5c mantel, best savoured as the finishing move of the low traverse of the break, **V3** (5c).

The final section of the crag offers some shorter routes, whose stature makes them more appropriately seen as tall boulder problems.

30 Harrop's Pride V0– (4c)
Strenuously climb the undercut wall and then the arête. **Simple View,** 5a, starts up the thin crack just left, but is rather dirty and indistinct thereafter.

31 Dog-Leg Crack VD (3c)

32 Armstrain V1 (5c)
The attractive undercut face on good breaks, starting on the left.

33 Dog-Leg Corner VD (4a)

34 Problem Arête V2 (6a)
Climb the arête on its right-hand side. On its left is V0 (5b).

Solitude and natural beauty
are common traits to all the crags in this chapter. While it would be good to see them get more deserved attention, above all, we must respect these areas, and allow them to continue to flourish without the heavy hand of man. Please do all you can to minimise your impact here. Go in small teams, or alone; keep the noise down; stick to the paths, remove any traces of your visit. By doing so, these special areas will remain special for a long time to come.

35 Paul's Wall V4 (6b)
The excellent slabby wall, crossing the roof directly.

36 Contract Worker V0 (4c)
Climb the obvious thin recessed crack topped by an overhang. Finish excitingly by pulling directly over at the highest point. A mini-classic. The final blunt arête is taken by **Unseen Face** (4b). The final arête is 5b.

Staffordshire Grit

Newstones to Back Forest First Ascents

pre-1931	**Rocking Stone Ridge, Central Route, Bastion Face, Bastion Corner, Pseudo Crack, Mustard, Bollard Edge, Capstone Chimney, Wrestle Crack, The Saucer, Keep Face, Holly Tree Niche Right Route, Holly Tree Niche Left Route** *All appeared in the Rucksack Club Journal of 1931.*		**The Rostrum, Left-Hand Crack, Hanging Stone Crack, Low Girdle, High Girdle, Oak Tree Crack, Cleft Route, Billiard table, The Cue** *All appeared for the first time in the 1973 Staffordshire Gritstone guidebook.* *Paul Nunn's selective guide,* **Rock Climbing in the Peak District (1975)** *gave different names: Overhanging Crack and Ferox, respectively.*
pre-1951	**Perambulator Parade, Forking Chimney** (originally known as Y-chimney)	1974 May	**The Gibe, Requiem for Tired Fingers, Suspended Sentence** Tony Barley
1969	**Marsden's Crack, Chockstone Crack, Barbiturate, Sleep Walker** Barry Marsden.	1974	**Eye of Japetus** Jonny Woodward, Andrew Woodward
1960s	**Original Route** Martin Boysen	1975 Jul	**The Keeper** Tony Barley
1971	**The Phantom** (1 pt. aid) Colin Foord *Climbed free by Jonny Woodward in 1977 with the bolt for protection and without by Ian Dunn and Claudie Dunn in 1986.*	1975 Nov 2	**Trepidation** Jim Campbell, Con Carey
		1976 Jun 19	**Gold Rush** Jim Campbell, Nick Colton
		1977 Jul	**Ray's Roof** Ray Jardine, Clive Jones *In the late 1970s, the man who invented Friends was at the height of his powers, and still took 4 days to climb the route. In 1977 he also climbed the Phoenix, Yosemite's first 5.13.*
1971	**Burnham Crack, The Gaping Void, Double Overhang** (1 pt.) Dave Salt, Colin Foord *The aid on Double Overhang was a nut on the initial roof. Climbed free by Tony Barley and Robin Brown in May 1974.*		
		1977	**Bridge of Sighs** Dave Jones, John Gilbert
pre-1973	**Baldstones Arête, The Ensign, The Gibbet** North Staffordshire Mountaineering Club members	1977	**Right Bow, Morridge Top, Bareleg Wall, Gibbon Take** Jonny Woodward (solo) *Bareleg Wall apparently climbed in 1975 as Let Out.*
pre-1973	**Newstones Chimney, Hazel Barrow Crack, Hazel Barn, Rhynose, Hippo, The Witch, Candy Man, The Snake, The Fox, The Vixen, The Sly Mantelshelf, Sly Corner, Baldstones Face, Goldsitch Crack*, Blackbank Crack*, Minipin Crack, Ganderhole Crack, The Brund (later known as Elephant's Ear), Pyeclough, Heathylee, Gibble Gabble Slab, Gibber Crack, Gib Sail, Giblet Crack, Gibraltar, Gibling Corner, Gibbon Wall, Gibeonite Girdle, Contract Worker, Dog-Leg Corner, Dog-Leg Crack, Harrop's Pride, Grasper, Thin Crack, Green Shaker, Portcullis Crack, Twin Thin, Green Crack (Gradbach), Green Crack (Back Forest),**	1978 May	**Feed the Enemy** Gary Gibson
		1979	**Toe Rail** John Holt
		1979	**John's Route** Gary Gibson
		1979	**Montezuma's Revenge** Nick Longland
		1970s	**All-Stars' Wall, Gib** Martin Boysen.
		1980	**The Gape, Sense of Doubt, John's Arête, Little Arête, The Chalk, Old Son, For Tim, Fat Old Nick** Nick Longland, John Holt
		pre-1981	**Moonshine, Praying Mantel, Nutmeg, Rosehip, Incognito, End Game, Problem Arête, Armstrain, Simple View, Not so Central Route, The Saucer Direct, Blow Hard, Racer's Rock, The Drifter's**

Newstones to Back Forest First Ascents

	Escape Appeared for the first time in the 1981 guidebook.	
early '80s	**Porridge at Morridge Top** Martin Boysen Named by Paul Mitchell who believed he had done the first ascent in 1984.	
1985	**French Connection, Anniversaire** Ian Dunn, Claudie Dunn.	
1986	**Puffed Up** Martin Boysen Named by John Allen from an ascent in 1989. The actual first ascent was unearthed from Boysen's memory in 2003 when he happened upon Neil Pearsons attempting what he believed was to be the first ascent. Pearsons was hanging off a cam when "along shambles an old man. 'Ah, someone trying my new route,' he says. 'I never did write that up. It's about 5c.' This was after a few days effort, thinking it would be English 7a." On The Edge	
1986	**Pot Black** Ian Dunn	
1989 Jun/Jul	**Valley of Ultravixens, Ponsified** John Allen	
1989	**Stall** Johnny Dawes The start climbed by Martin Boysen in the early '80s.	
c.1990	**Johnny's Indirect Rear Entry** Jonny Woodward, Johnny Dawes Both on-sight solo 'in caravan'.	
1991	**Mr Creosote** Roger Nichols	
1992 May 23	**Prelude to XB** Richard Pickford, Rob Weston.	
1992	**Gibe Turkey** Geoff Hornby, Mark Turnbull	
1994	**Back Forest Gâteau** Rob Mirfin	
1995	**Tasmanian Tendencies** Richard Taylor Also claimed as Onychophagia by John H Bull.	
1997	**Riding the Gravy Train, National Hysteria** Sean Myles Gear placed on the lead. The latter route climbed on the day of Princess Diana's funeral.	
1997	**The Hour Glass, Morpheus, Pip** Mark Katz	
1999	**Ruth's Septic Trench** Ruth Creamer	
2000	**Fist Full of Freshers, Whose Line is it Anyway** Paul Smith, Rob Lavin	
2001 July	**Pants on Fire, Gallstones, Lucid Reams, Mongolian Throat Singing** John H Bull, the latter with Kieran McCusker.	
2001	**Pinnacle Buttress** Paul Smith	
2002	**Drain the Main Vein** Justin Critchlow, Mark Sharratt (both led)	
2002	**Action Trousers** John H Bull	
2003	**Bumper Cars** Becca Ward, Paul Smith, Sam Clarke	
2009	**Spragback** Andi Turner	

Newstones to Back Forest Bouldering First Ascents

Captain Quark Jon Barton, Rupert Davies, 9th November 2003

Charlie's Overhang Tony Barley, 1974

Clever Skin Martin Boysen, early 1980s and called Elephant's Trunk. Claimed as Clever Skin by Johnny Dawes in 1989, the latter name having stuck.

Fielder's Wall Johnny Dawes, March 27, 1989.

The Fin John Allen, 1984. Although possibly Martin Boysen, early '80s. Sit-start by John Welford, 1990s.

Gibbering Left Tom Leppert, 1986.

Gibbering Wreck Previously a top-rope problem, probably the work of Jerry Moffatt, it was soloed and named by Sam Whittaker in 1998. It turned out to have been soloed by Andy Brown in 1994, with the name Gib Torr Roof.

Last Banana Before Sunset Chris King, 1989.

Leather Joy Boys Mark Stokes, 1984.

Martin's Traverse Martin Boysen.

Maurice Gib Pat Rainbird, October 2003. A long term project of local Andi Turner. Pat double-dynoed his way to glory under Turner's nose after making the mistake of trying the problem when out with a strong team.

Paul's Wall Paul Smith, 2002.

Stall Martin Boysen, early 1980s. Named by Johnny Dawes.

Churnet champion Stuart Brooks on Blue Nunn, V5, Well Hidden Buttress (page 296). Photo: Brooks collection.

The Churnet 5

A fairytale land of deep, wooded, crag-rimmed dales containing babbling brooks and rivers, towered over by castles and halls. A land so Tolkienesque that one expects Bilbo Baggins to skip round the corner singing merrily, heading a happy band of pixies, elves and gnomes, ready to sweep you along on one of their adventures.

Simon Alsop, On The Edge

The Upper Churnet Valley

including Sharpcliffe Rocks, Belmont Hall Crags, Harston Rocks, Oldridge Pinnacle and Garston Rocks by Gary Gibson

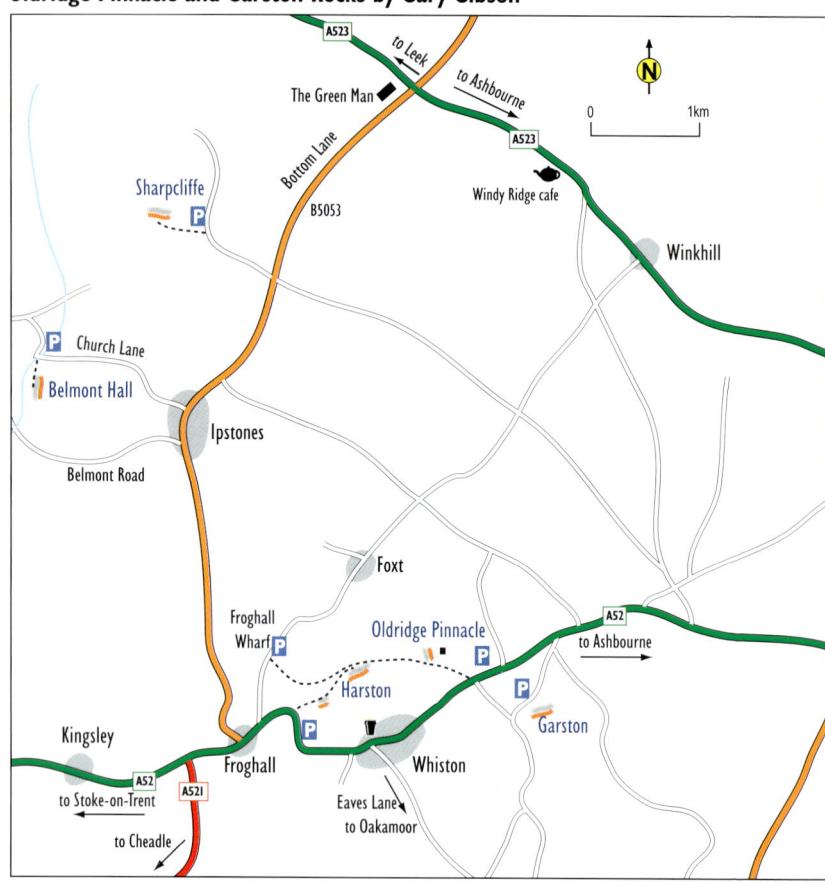

The five main crags of the Upper Churnet, packed into a small geographical area around the pretty village of Ipstones, all manage to have vastly different characters, and as such, give entirely different climbing experiences.

Sharpcliffe is probably the most individual, with its terrific pebble cornice and big experiences out of all proportion to its height; Belmont Hall has its sweet, easy-to-enjoy cracks and walls; the mythical Harston Rock is here too, a perched obelisk with a small number of the best routes in the area – a must-visit crag. And if you are having an 'obelisk' day out, it's a short hop to Oldridge Pinnacle with its merry band of bold routes/exciting highballs; finally, the gentler Garston Rock, with its herd of climbs in the lower orders. All good stuff, essential experiences for the adventurer.

The Upper Churnet Sharpcliffe Rocks

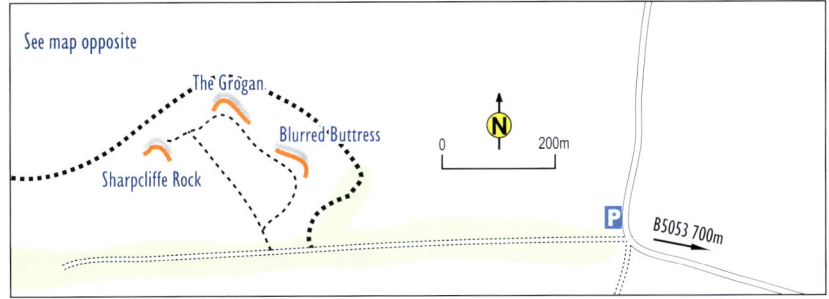

Sharpcliffe Rocks

O.S. Ref. SK015521 Altitude: 320m a.s.l.

Even for the Churnet Valley this is an eccentric crag. Nicknamed Pebblesville by its original explorers, it is a series of buttresses, some little ones of good gritstone, and one big one made from a readymix of good sandstone and bunter pebbles. The little ones offer good bouldering, while the big one offers some of the most memorable climbing in the area. Ironically, its weakness is its strength, and the sometimes harrowing nature of the climbing makes the routes memorable out of all proportion to their length.

Conditions & aspect

The crag faces generally north with the front face getting early morning sunshine, and the main right wall getting it in the afternoon. Seepage is not a problem. Climbing is possible year round though some of the bouldering gets green in winter.

Routes & bouldering

All routes areworthwhile. Better for extremes. Tend to be bold. Good easier bouldering (25 problems) on interesting rock, as well as one futuristic highball.

Parking & approach

Park at a sharp right-hand bend. A metalled road continues straight on here into the grounds of Sharpcliffe Hall itself. Take this for 400m, then break out right over a gate into some rough open ground. 10 minutes.

Access

The rocks lie in the grounds of Sharpcliffe Hall. The owners do not allow climbing but allow clay-pigeon shooting and quad biking. This land was originally scheduled to be Open Access under CROW 2000 but was lost on an appeal to which the BMC did not get invited. We will be attempting to rectify this bewildering decision under the CRoW Review due in about 2010.

For the bouldering, turn right off the main path soon after you have crossed the gate. The first problems lie on the far side of the rhododendron ridge. The talented may wish to note a 5m block on the crest of the ridge. This has a beautiful, sharp and gruesomely overhanging arête on it, and a perfect jug at its base. Anyone? Just below is a large block with a through cave at its base, known as the Straw Boulders.

1 Peep Show V0 (4c)
The left-hand crack and flake on the front face of the block.

2 Cabana V1 (5b)
Superb. The bulging right-hand flake gives a sterner test.

Blurred Buttress

This is the next set of boulders, 40m further on.

3 Pebblesville V0+ (5b)
To the left of the initial crack lies this excellent problem, pulling over the bulge into a scoop. A problem just left is also possible. **Hush Puppy** V0– (4a) is the awkward wide crack to the right, and **Hot Dog** V0– (4b) is the next slanting groove.

Staffordshire Grit

4 Johnson'sville V1 (5b)
Small knobs and dinks lead up the wall to the right. Gets harder ascent by ascent!

5 Bowcock's Chimney V0– (4a)
A classic Leek name: they had something on their mind? The chimney to the right.

6 Cannabis Arm V4 (6a)
Technical moves up the overhanging arête to the right.

7 Puffed Wheat V1 (5b)
The centre of the wall to the right. The attractive right arête, on its right, is unclimbed.

The Grogan

This is heavily sculpted, flat wall, 80m along the broad ridge. It lies on the right just before some small boulders on the top.

8 Gorgonzola V0 (5a)
Good moves up incipient cracks lead to the left side of the tower. The awkward crack to the left is V0 (5a).

9 Mr Grogan V1 (HVS 5b)
The wall taken at its centre via pockets, pebbles and rugosities. Superb climbing.

10 Charlie Farley V0 (HVS 4c)
Getting even better. The shallow groove in the right-hand side of the buttress. Pockets, pebbles and buckets. An eliminate is possible between this problem and the arête, V1 (5b). The bulging arête direct would also be possible.

11 Rusks And Rye V2 (5b)
The atrocious, bulging crack on the front face of the buttress. Try it without tape.

Many possibilities lie among the jumbled rocks in the next 30m. After that distance, and around the corner, is a 6m wall with a clean tall arête.

12 Genetix V1 (5b)
The crack in the sidewall of the buttress.

13 Bond It V3 (5c)
The handsome arête itself is exciting, due to its height.

14 Blu-Tac V2 (5c)
The left-hand side of the front face.

Stickfast V0+ (5b) is the centre of the wall. **Raven** V0– (4a) is just to the right and just left of the arête. **Spirella** V0– (4a) waltzes along the obvious break from right to left. **Meninges** (M, 1973) is a slab on the right.

Sharpcliffe Rock

The main rock now lies 100m across the broad grassy area, or is reached directly from the gate by following the main path. Grab a rope, some runners and a tube of glue! The rock is bounded on its left by a deep chimney (**Marsden's Eliminate**, M, 1973). To its left is a little prow. Following the niche through this is **Underhung Chimney** (S 4a, 1973), while climbing the right arête is a pleasant HS (**Konsolation Prize**, 1980). Next lies the main crag, with its bulging pebble infested overhangs. A difficult new route would be possible up the steep pocketed wall right of the chimney. The first route is based on the very steep front face of the rock.

15 Knossos E5 5c ★★★   1979
18m An impressive and uncompromising challenge taking the front face head-on. Prepare yourself for limited protection and variable stability of holds. Climb up to a vague break and swing left along it before climbing the pink, pebble-dashed wall to reach a wide crack round the left arête – good large nuts. Exit frantically right and upwards on the nose of the wall. A more difficult start at 6a leads directly to the wide crack.

16 Krushna E4 6a ★   1980
16m Another fraught experience aiming for the prominent roof crack on the right-hand side of the front face. Climb the pink-coloured wall 5m to the right of Knossos to reach a break and then gain the impressive wide crack above. This provides a mean, hand-crushing finale.

The Upper Churnet Sharpcliffe Rock

21 Kudos VS 5a   1979
8m This route starts on the highest platform. Climb a depression on the right side of the wall. A bold eliminate, **Krakatoa** (E3 5c, 1979) climbs the slab to the left, keeping left of easy ground.

22 Special K HVS 4c ★★   1973
18m Technically reasonable climbing giving access to some fine situations. From the platform on the right-hand side of the rock, step down to the left and follow a break across the wall to reach flutings leading to the top.

The main mass of Sharpcliffe Rock is bounded on the right by a pleasant undercut buttress. **Golden Sovereign** V0– (4a), is the wall to the left of the obvious undercut arête. **Doubloon** V0 (5a), the undercut arête. **Pieces of Eight** V0– (4a), the slab to the right. All 1973. A number of other problems are available in this area although by this time the owner may well have thown you off!

17 Kenyatta E4 5c ★   1980
15m Less friable and more amenable than the last route, though more scary, up the vague right-hand arête of the front face. Climb the wall 2m to the right passing a break and awkward bulge to reach flutings. These lead more easily to the top.

18 Kaleidoscope E1 5a ★★   1973
16m Another Churnet classic well worth seeking out if visiting the area. Climb from the end of the little platform up and right directly up, over the bulge, and into the narrow square cut groove to finish direct. Moves are reasonable and gear exists. It remains, however, an E1 experience.

19 Killjoy E2 5b ★★   1979
14m Climb the wall just to the left of a diagonal crack, to gain a break. Continue slightly leftwards via a scoop to the top.

20 Kobold E3 5c ★   1979
14m Climb the obvious diagonal crack to reach the break. Continue directly to the top via a series of small pockets.

Staffordshire Grit

Belmont Hall Crags

O.S. Ref. SK007504 Altitude: 190m a.s.l.

These are a pair of steep compact buttresses in a beautiful wooded setting, along a tranquil and picturesque little hillside. The rock is sound, and the cleaner routes are good quality.

Conditions & aspect
The crag can be somewhat green in parts after bad weather although a couple of dry days and a quick going over with a soft brush should return routes to a good state. Easily worth the effort. Faces north-west and gets little sun. A good cool summer venue.

Routes & bouldering
Twenty three routes on vertical rock. Some good easier cracks but also some dirty ones. The harder routes tend to be better and cleaner, with technical climbing and some runouts.

Parking & approach
From Ipstones, follow Church Lane for about 1 mile, past some sharp bends, to park at the bottom of a hill by a stream. Follow the pleasant track for 250m and the buttresses are on the hillside on the left. Five easy minutes. See map on page 276.

Left-Hand Buttress

The first buttress provides the best routes on the crag. The harder routes are certainly well worth seeking out and classics of their type.

1   Life In The Left Lane E3 5c   1986
14m Pull over the initial overlaps and continue up the rib and over the third bulge with poor protection back on the ledge below.

2   Life in the Wrong Lane E1 5b   1979
14m Pull over the overlaps onto the rib as for the last route. Step right and climb the left-hand groove finishing leftwards.

3   The Clown E3 6a ★★   1971/75
15m A fine steep little route with technical climbing and small fiddly protection. Three metres right again a finger-hold over the lip enables access to the wall above via a mighty heave and rockover. Continue via the slabby wall to gain the central groove above. Finish directly: *see photo on page 282*.

4   The Jester E5 6a ★   1979
15m A superb wall pitch giving sustained and varied climbing. Climb the roof just to the left of the chimney, an easier entry than The Clown. The bold

The Upper Churnet Belmont Hall

face and arête above lead into the steepening crack in the upper face. This gives a fitting finale.

5 Kneewrecker Chimney HVS 4c ★★   1962
15m The powerful central crack of the buttress is a classic of its type. Climb the narrowing cleft between the buttocks of the crag and battle with the holly tree towards its top.

6 Face E5 6b ★★   1986
15m Superb. The immaculate clean wall to the right leads boldly to a break and peg runner in the wall above. Difficult moves past this lead onto a flake and a bold finale on the magnificent upper wall.

7 The Joker E3 6a ★   1971/75
15m Another steep and well-protected line. From 6m up the slanting groove, swing up and left into the base of a steeper groove. Climb this with difficulty at first to an easier and exposed finish.

8 Deadwood Groove HVS 4c   1962
11m The slanting groove is tricky at its finish. Sparsely protected. A difficult problem on the short wall to the right provides **Allen's Fingers** V4 (6a).

9 Deadwood Crack VS 4c   1962
11m The obvious crack right again. Bypassing the rotten tree leads to a rotten finish.

10 Crimes of Passion E4 6a   1982
11m A technically testing pitch up the vague rampline to the right. From the obvious hole finish directly up the slab. Bold and dirty.

Right-Hand Buttress

Situated 100m downstream and clearly identified by its central cave. This gives a number of very worthwhile pitches although the first few routes are in a poor state due to an overgrowth of heather and lichen. The rest of the routes here are generally cleaner.

The first routes are situated on the left-hand wall of the buttress. The filthy crack and bulge above a cave at the left-hand side of the buttress give **Sale's Bulge** (VD, 1962). The wide crack to the right of this is **Twisting Crack** (D, 1962). Just to the right a shallow groove, thin crack and nose give **No Pegs Please, We're British** (HVS 4c, 1989), and the crack right again is **Hassall's Crack** (VD, 1962).

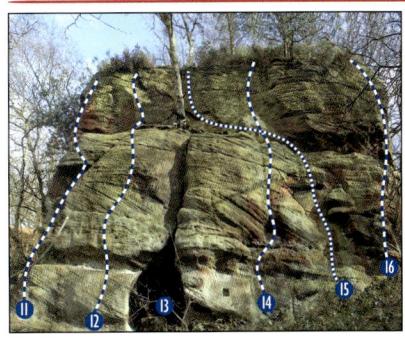

11 Cave Rib VS 4b   1962
12m The prominent rib finishing right around the overhang.

12 Flake Escape E2 5c   1989
8m The wall via an obvious flake. Reachy.

13 Cave Crack VS 4b ★   1962
11m From the cave, bridge out and struggle up the prominent crackline to a difficult exit onto the ledge. The finish necessitates a bizarre manoeuvre involving the tree.

14 Distant Runners E3 5c ★   1989
11m A good pitch. The thin crackline to the right gives access to the ledge. The finishing groove no longer contains a peg runner and is sometimes dirty.

15 Flake Traverse HS   1962
15m A flake 3m to the right leads to a ledge. Traverse left and finish via Cave Crack.

16 Wigglette HVS 5a   1962
11m The blunt arête to the right. Climbed on its left-hand side to a break from where a bulge and slab lead to the top.

17 In Days of Hold E2 6b   1989
6m The short right-hand arête of the flat face to the right has a desperate start but soon eases.

Richard Fielding on The Clown E3 6a (page 280), one of the many fine extremes that make Belmont Hall Crags worth the effort. Photo: David Simmonite.

Flintmill Buttress, Consallforge

OS Ref: SK 004484: This is a large crag bristling with overhangs and cloaked in masses of vegetation from glorious moss beds to large hanging vines. The routes now resemble their original state before they were gardened and whilst an impressive venue, the cliff will require major excavations before its routes can be reascended. The best approach is from the A52, Stoke to Ashbourne road. A small lane runs between Kingsley and Kingsley Moor, through the villages of Hollins, Hazles and Hazles Cross. Between the latter two a public footpath runs down to Consallforge and is well marked. At the left-hand end of the crag, a disjointed groove merges into an overhanging and very vegetated chimney. This is the **Constant Rrumble** (HVS, 1970). **Grumbling Wall** (VS, 1977) lies to its left. Two aid routes tackle the overhangs to the right. **Miller's Melody** (A2, pre-1971) is the smaller overhang whilst **Death Wish** (A3, 1974) is the big roof. Nine metres right again are twin grooves. **Full Frontal** (HVS, 1971) follows the right-hand groove, with a point of aid along the way; **Indecent Exposure** (HVS, 1977) is a more direct version with even more aid; **Manifesto** (HVS, 1970) struggles past the tree to the right; **Peeping Tom** (HVS, 1978) is the line to the right; **Nosey Parker** (E1, 1971) climbs a crack 5m to the right, 2 pegs for aid; 5m right again, **The Missus** (VS, 1971) is based on the slab and chimney; **Spearhead** is the last line taking the buttress right of the gully.

Price's Cave Crag

OS Ref: SK 002493: From the Black Lion Inn at Consallforge, follow the Devil's Staircase, which leads towards Belmont Hall. Part way up these steps a prominent arête is visible: Here Be Dragons (E2 5c, 1990) starts from a block on the right; climb the arête mainly on its steeper right-hand side. An in-situ thread in a pocket above an overlap provides the only worthwhile protection although a low siderunner was used to safeguard the initial moves.

Wetley Rocks

OS Ref: SK 967495: These lie on the northern side of the Stone to Leek road. Whilst they have been climbed on over the years, they offer little for the accomplished climber. A good ridge is available at the Difficult standard to the left of the service station.

Are you a Staffordshire Obscurist?

One of the great features of Staffordshire climbing is how the blatantly classic and popular can live so close to the delightfully obscure. Venues tucked away in woods or farmland, little pinnacles or bold secret buttresses. All are worth visiting and offer rewards not found on the more popular patches. Here is a selection of routes to get you started on your obscure journey. If these leave you with the taste then turn to page 362 for the next step up.

- **Crabbie's Crack** VS 4c, The Clouds
  Okay, maybe not that obscure, but one of the better HVSs in Staffordshire
- **Honky Tonk** HS 4c, Far Skyline
  Obscurity amidst the madding crowd.
- **Goldsitch Crack** HVS 4c, Baldstones
  This will raise a few eyebrows when they ask where you got those scabs.
- **The Gibe** HVS 4c, Gib Torr
  A bold route to bring you to your knees.
- **The Gape** HVS 5b, Gradbach Hill
  A remote gem with a bit of a local reputation as a sandbag.
- **Double Overhang** E1 5b, Back Forest
  Not one overhang, but two! Double the fun in a remote moorland setting.
- **Crispin's Crack** HVS 5a, Hen Cloud
  Good rock and good climbing on a lovely out-of-the-way buttress.
- **Rash Challenge** E1 5b, Ramshaw
  A part of Ramshaw that few ever reach.
- **Period Drama** 5a, The Cube
  One for the boulderers giving a fresh view of the Roaches.
- **Cave Crack** VS 4b, Belmont Hall
  The more obscure of Belmont's central cracks, and that's saying something.
- **Toast Rack** HVS 4c, Lord's Buttress
  Smear yourself in butter and learn to jam.
- **Ina's Chimney** S Ina's Rock
  A real journey into the bowels of a hidden gem of a crag.

Good luck!

The Churnet Valley Crags

Andi Turner with all guns blazing on Pair O' Genes, E7 6c, Harston Rock (page 287). Photo: Jon Read.

Harston Rocks

O.S. Ref. SK035478 Altitude: 210m a.s.l.

by Stuart Millis and Gary Gibson

Harston Rock is the Upper Churnet's *pièce de résistance*, offering a handful of very fine routes on good rock with an imposing position above a beautiful and heavily wooded valley floor. The open nature lends itself to cleanliness not seen on the neighbouring buttresses, and its inspiring steepness has caused it to be home to the area's two hardest climbs. The small bluffs littered along the rim of the valley are currently in a very poor state and are best ignored.

Conditions & aspect

Harston Rock is north-facing, with an east and west flank and gets little sun. It is relatively clean (although you still might want to pack your brush) and gets little seepage, even in winter.

Routes & bouldering

Eleven routes on the main rock offer great climbs from HVS to E7.

Parking & approach

Park in the small lay-by on the outskirts of Whiston. Walk back down the hill to the sharp bend and follow a farm track to its end at a farmhouse. 50m beyond the farm the path crosses the ridge and the first buttress is 30m above up the ridge line. The rest of the buttresses are strung along the ridge from here. Best to ignore all these and continue along the main track to Harston Rock, 400m further on, where it can be seen 30m up on the right. Approach: 10–15 minutes. An alternative approach is from the large public car park at Froghall Wharf and follow the Staffordshire Moorlands Walk until the crag looms high above on the hillside, maybe 2 mins longer, if you're not distracted by ice creams.

Devil's Rock

An obvious bulging nose protrudes through the trees and offers a tapering wall to its left. **The Nose** (HVS 5b, 1970) is the broad groove on the front of the nose to an awkward finish. The overgrown slab to the right once gave Introduction (**VD**, 1952). For **The Cheek** (VS 5a, 1970), climb the tricky wall just left of the arête and finish more easily. Originally this was gained via a traverse in from The Nose. **Devil's Crack** (S, 1952) is a crack in the tapering wall. **Rugosity** (S 4a, 1952) is just to the left, while **Footpath** (VD, 1952), is the chippings left again. **Alternative Ulster** (4b, 1978) is the last line. **Saunter** (S, 1952) traversed the rock. Gib Buttress lies 40m left. It is now overgrown, and once contained **Wave** (D), **Ripple** (VD), **Crest** (VD), **Breaks** (**VD**) and **Backwash** (VD). All 1952. The buttress below is Biscay Buttress. This is now overgrown and once held: **Emerald Groove** (VD, 1952), **As You Like It** (M, 1952), **Flake Wall** (HS, 1951), **Original Route** (VS, 1951), **The Web** (HS, 1952), **Black Widow** (E3 5c, 1970s), **Emerald Wall** (VD, 1952), and **Corner Traverse** (D, 1952). Just left is Pinnacle Buttress. It is overgrown. It

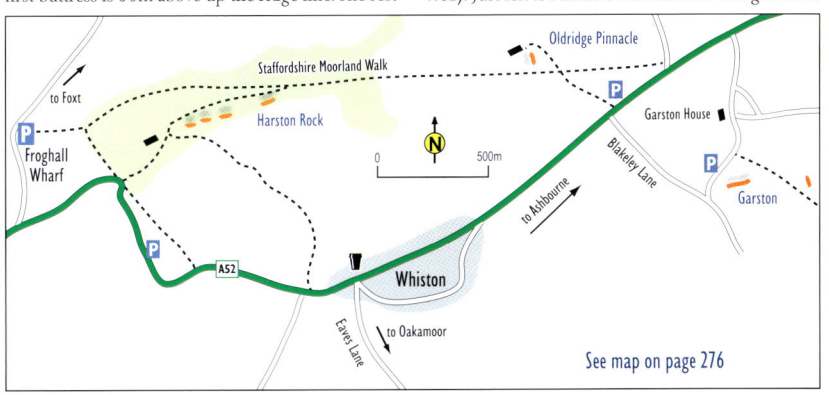

Staffordshire Grit

once held: **Moore's Crack** (D, 1952), **The Sting** (E1 5a, 1970s), **Titan's Wall** (E2 5a, 1952), **Ostentation** (E2 5a, 1970), **Fandango** (HS, 1952), **Magenta Corner** (HS, 1951), **Glyph** (S, 1952) and **Rotondas** (S, 1952). In the land to the left are three isolated buttresses, with a single route on each. They are **Oak Spur** (D, 1952), **Moss Rose** (VD, 1952), and **Frequency** (S, 1952). They are of little interest and the land is very overgrown. Cave Buttress comes next, 40m away. It once held: **Vereker's Venture** (VS 5a, 1952), **Taming of the Shrew** (HVS 5c, 1978), **Much Ado About Nothing** (E3 6a, 1975), **The Cave Crack** (S, 1951), **Palsy Wall** (E2 5c, 1970s), **Palpitation** (HVD, 1952) and **Shelf Route** (HVD, 1952). Thity metres left again is Technician's Wall. It once held: **The Technician** (5a, 1978) climbs the right-hand wall; **Tiptoe** (HVD, 1952), **Diagonal Crack** (D, 1952), **Clam** (5b, 1952), **Limpet** (4a, 1952) and **Megalomania** (5b, 1978).

Harston Rock

Follow the main track from the farm, hopefully passing below all the dirty buttresses above until, after about 400m, the main rock is seen above (200m from Technician's Wall). The rock is sound and despite its wooded setting, is generally not badly effected by any lichens. The overlaps at the back of the pinnacle lead to the summit and also provide the easiest means of descent (Mod).

1 Hatscheck's Groove HVS 5a ★ 1952
14m The broken crack on the left of the left sidewall leads to a large ledge. The shallow groove above gives a difficult and airy finish.

2 Old King Cole E6 6b ★ 1990
16m A superb, tough route, featuring steep and powerful climbing up the centre of the clean north wall of the obelisk. The thin discontinuous crack in the steep tower is gained via a long reach and followed with fine moves to its end. The final wall provides a fitting climax. A notable historic route as the first ascent was done on-sight.

3 The Impending Doom E4 5c ★ 1970
18m A fine steep pitch up the flakes in the left-hand side of the arête leads to a difficult rounded finish. Protection is barely adequate.

4 One Chromosome's Missing
E7 6b ★ ★ ★ 1984
18m A gritstone gem to rival any in the Peak District, and one of the first routes of its grade in the country. The right-hand side of the left arête of the front face offers absorbing technical climbing in a serious position. A cunning Rock 3 may or may not protect the upper section.

5 The Boysen-Carrington Route
E6 6b ★ 1990s
20m A high-quality eliminate, combining sections of two adjacent desperates to find a more reasonable way up the wall. Climb the arête of One Chromosome to the break. Traverse right to the Weetabix thread on Pair O' Genes to finish up this.

6 Pair O' Genes E7 6c ★ ★ 1999
18m Superb, technical and bold climbing up the

The Upper Churnet Harston Rocks

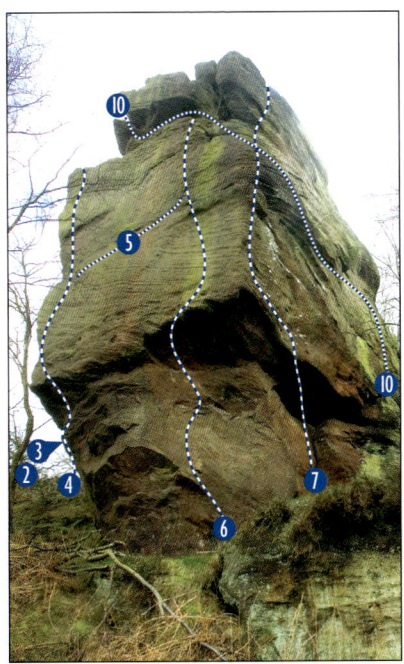
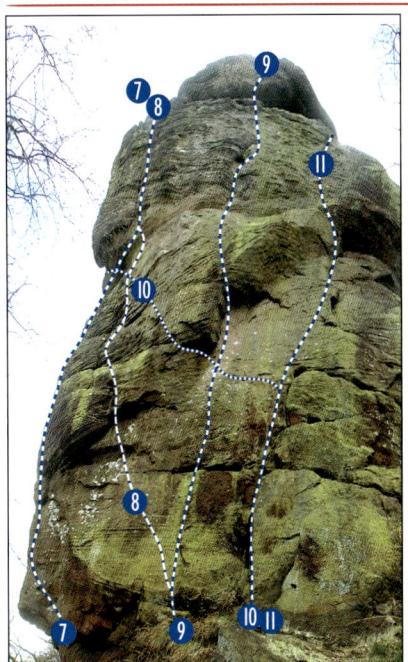

centre of the face. Start 3m left of DNA. Climb to the overhang and make desperate moves through it to gain the steep slab above. Continue precariously to gain the horizontal break and the sanctuary of an in-situ thread runner. Finish directly: *see photo on page 284*.

7 DNA E4 6a ★★ 1977
18m A classic of the late 1970s and a typical sandbag of its time. Fine, scary climbing via the right arête of the front face. Gain the undercut scoop in the prow by a series of awkward moves. Leave the scoop on the left using a horizontal break, then make technical moves up the rib to the next break: protection, though available, does not inspire confidence. Finish via the steepening wall of Melancholy Man.

8 Melancholy Man E2 5c ★ 1978
14m Starting just left of Via Trita, traverse left across a small slab. Pull onto the hanging slab above and climb it to a break. Step right to finish via the steepening wall.

9 EMS E1 5c 1990
18m Climb the wall just to the right continuing through an overlap to a small ledge. The steep wall above, via a flake, provides the crux.

10 The Helix HVS 5a ★★★ 1952
22m An excellent and very delicate outing, something of an expedition for gritstone, spiralling around the pinnacle. From a point 3m up Via Trita, traverse left to an overlap. Continue leftwards to a small ledge and then climb a slab to gain a horizontal break. Follow this leftwards across the exposed front face to finish up a groove above the far arête: *see photo overleaf*.

11 Via Trita E1 5b ★ 1952
14m Climb the crack in the right-hand side of the face and make a tricky mantelshelf to gain a ledge, bold. The upper wall gives delightful climbing on a series of ripples.

Leon Zablocki getting his gurn on on one of the great mid-grade classics of the Churnet, The Helix, HVS 5a, Harston Rock (previous page). Photo: Alex Ekins.

Garston Rocks

O.S. Ref. SK051476 Altitude: 270m a.s.l.

This is a pleasant crag composed of good quality sandstone with weathered features and holds. Although green and with the odd friable section, the crag has very good easier routes with the odd problem thrown in for good measure. A large bouldering mat will be very useful to get most out of a visit. The prows face north with walls getting the sun early or late. To approach, turn left off Blakeley Lane to limited parking below the crag. **See map on page 285.**

Access
Please ask for permission to climb here off the farmer, Mr Keeling, who lives in Garston House.

1 Tequila Sunrise E1 5b ★   1978
6m The prominent knife-edge arête, starting awkwardly on the right. The bouldery wall to the right is **White Widow** (V3 (6a)). The cleft is Diff.

2 Runaway E2 5c   1978
6m The difficult bulging left-hand wall of the gully.

3 Feet of Strength HS 5a   1952
8m The wide crack on the left. A dirty struggle.

4 The Arête HVD ★   1952
12m A good route taking the prominent arête with a huge thread runner at half-height. Start left, and continue past the thread to a chipped finish. Classic stuff.

5 Hole and Corner Crack S 4a ★   1952
10m The crack to the left with a cave at half-height. The wall and scoop to the right can be climbed at HVS 5a (**Technocrat**, 1978).

6 Don Quixote E2 6a ★   1978
10m A super little problem. A porthole to the left enables a scoop to be gained, followed all too briefly by a wall.

7 Skull Crack HS 4b ★★   1952
11m Another real taking the twisting cracks.

8 The Chute S 4b   1952
8m The pleasant corner. Moving right from the corner to pass a break to gain the top via a vague rib is **Tricky Woo** (HVS 5a, 1978). The left arête of the corner is **Pillow of Wind** (HVS 4c, 1978).

9 One Knight Stand HVS 5c   1978
5m Climb directly up the centre of the next wall. The start is delicate for all but giants.

10 The Bishop's Move HS 4a ★   1952
8m Move up just to the left and follow the slanting crack rightwards to finish left of the arête. Excellent.

11 All the King's Horses HS 4b ★   1978
18m Even this cliff gets the girdle-traverse! From the arête of The Bishop's Move continue down, across Tricky Woo and on into Hole and Corner Crack. Finish just to the right of this.

At the back of the bay is a good bouldering wall. The following routes are on the left-hand wall of the bay. **Larva Wall** (S 4a, 1952) is a slab and overhang on the right extremity of the buttress. **The Stadium** (HVS 5b, 1978) features thin moves over a bulge to the left, leading onto an easier slab. **Left Arête** (VS 4c, 1952) has an awkward start leading onto the obvious feature.

12 Cave Wall S 4a ★   1952
8m Climb up to the obvious cave on the left wall. Exit onto the wall above and left and use thin cracks to gain a finishing bulge.

13 Rainbow Recess S 4a   1952
8m Gain a ledge 2m to the left, then step right and up to finish leftwards.

14 Triack VS 4c   1952
7m A series of cracks on the left extremity of the buttress. Awkward to start.

The track running east leads past a cottage and after 150m a gate on the left leads down to a mainly hidden area of good boulders. The largest arête is **The Last Post,** V1 5b.

Staffordshire Grit

Oldridge Pinnacle

O.S. Ref. SK043480 Altitude: 250m a.s.l.

A gritstone obelisk standing amidst lush open fields. There are no easy routes here and the hardest are esoteric classics of their type. These tough extremes, however, will give well-spotted and well-padded boulderers a handful of superb highballs, all above a perfect landing. You are certainly going to be on your own here save for a watchful eye from the residents of the local farm.

Conditions & aspect
The north-facing side is very green and uninviting. The south gets lots of sun, and is where the better climbing is. Sheltered, and climbable all year.

Parking & approach
Take a left turn a half a mile after passing through Whiston. This track leads to a farm tucked in alongside the pinnacle. Ask the farmer for permission to climb as a matter of courtesy. A path leads from here to Harston Rock, a few hundred metres away. **See map on page 285**

Access
As The White Stripes said, I've said it once before but it bears repeating: **PLEASE ASK THE FARMER'S PERMISSION** before climbing here.

1   The South-West Crack   VS 4c   1952
8m The awkward fissure lying to the left of the drystone wall on the west face. Tweeds optional.

2   Boats for Hire   E4 6a ★   1984
7m The left-hand arête of the overhanging south face gives a route with a split personality. The initial crack proves very, very steep. Traverse left above the dry-stone wall to finish delicately via the bulging slab. Highball V5 for the first half.

3   The Fatalist's Canoe   E4 6a ★★   1986
7m From the flake just right, climb upwards and leftwards. Finish just left of the next route. Highball V4.

290 The Churnet Valley Crags

A great venue for some esoteric highballing. Sam Whittaker on The Gateless Gate. V4. Photo: Adam Long.

4   The Gateless Gate E3 6a ★★   1978
7m The central line on the face is strenuous and frustrating. Starting at a crack and hole, move up and slightly left to a tough well-protected finish. Highball V4: *see photo above*

5   Qui Vive E3 6a ★★   1978
7m The right-hand arête leads, via a series of rockovers, to a thread runner and obligatory rounded finish, crux. Highball V4.

7   South-East Crack HS 4b ★★   1952
8m A lovely sustained route with a summit tick. The wide corner-crack provides the easiest route on the pinnacle and the best means of descent.

The square-cut arête directly to the right is **Ivanhoe** (HVS 5b, 1978). **Nom De Guerre** (E1 5b, 1978) is the thin crack just to the right of the arête. **The North Face** (VS 4c ★ 1952) gains the top of the boulder below in the centre of the face. Finish by climbing the thin crack above. Good but dirty. **Tour De Force** (E1 5b, 1978) is the very green north face just to the left of Battle Royal. Move up and then right to a hidden hole on the arête. Use this to gain a shelf and finish up the wall above. **Battle Royal** itself (E3 5c, 1978) is the arête facing the farm with the crux leaving the small groove.

The Churnet Valley Crags

Staffordshire Grit

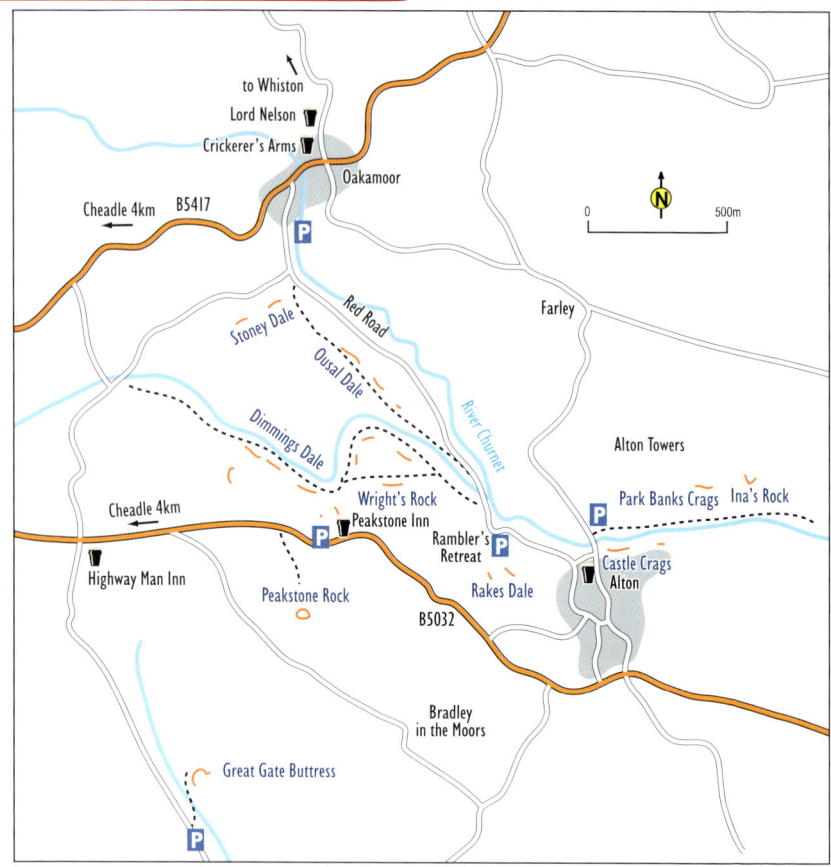

The Lower Churnet Valley

This is a collection of crags lying roughly along the banks of the River Churnet between the picturesque villages of Oakamoor and Alton, and all within screaming distance of the mighty Alton Towers. The crags vary greatly in height, quality and character, from the towering ferocity of Ina's Rock, with powerful climbs of up to E8 calling for the boldest of leads, to small sit down boulder problems on Cottage Rocks; from the crumbling horror of Castle Crag to the secluded calm of Ousal Crag. The settings are pretty and varied, being amongst pastoral farmland, wooded hillsides, or rhododendron-jewelled river-banks. Whilst not to everyone's taste, the Lower Churnet has tremendous variety for climbers in search of adventure. The Rambler's Retreat serves great food including chips, cake and coffee, and is ideally situated at the bottom of Dimmings Dale. For the thirsty, pubs are available in Alton, Oakamoor, and The Peakstone Inn.

Mark Sharratt about to launch up the crucial top section of Sole Survivor, E5 6b (page 299), one of the harder classics of the Lower Churnet. Photo: Ian Parnell.

Leah Crane eyeing up a fierce eliminate on Cottage Rocks (page 304). Photo: Paul Philips.

The Lower Churnet Dimmings Dale

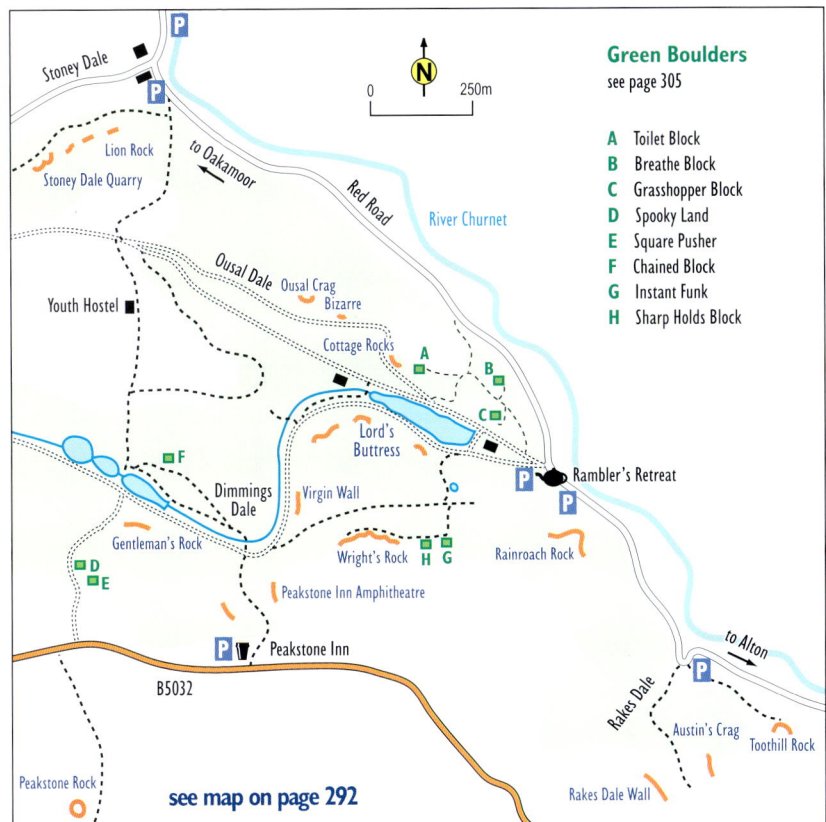

Green Boulders
see page 305

A Toilet Block
B Breathe Block
C Grasshopper Block
D Spooky Land
E Square Pusher
F Chained Block
G Instant Funk
H Sharp Holds Block

The Dimmings Dale Area

The numerous crags and cragettes secreted along the beautiful wooded and watered Dimmings Dale area is one of the more popular destinations in the Churnet area. In recent years boulderers have made the circuit there popular – Wright's Rock, Virgin Wall, Gentleman's Rock, Cottage Rocks and Ousal Crag are a firm favourite with plenty of finger and arm busting problems at all grades, as well as a great supply of traverses. These areas are popular in poorer weather as the low-lying crags get less rain than the Peak District, and most of them stay dry in the rain anyway.

The area is also good for leading, albeit better in the Extreme grades. Lord's Buttress, Peakstone Inn Amphitheatre, Wright's Rock and Ousal Crag all have fine routes, the odd one tending towards the esoterrific – a worthy experience.

The Rambler's Retreat sets everything off nicely, cake-hounds, chip-chompers and tea-guzzlers alike will all find their Mecca there.

The crags are all described in as logical an order as possible, although if logical orders are your kind of thing, then perhaps you'd be betterer off climbing somewhere else.

The Churnet Valley Crags

Staffordshire Grit

Stoney Dale

O.S. Ref. SK048439   Altitude: 175m a.s.l.

A little string of crags and craglets, not far from the road, gives a fine and contrasting train of experiences for boulderers and routers alike. Thirty five routes, with the harder ones generally being better. Some good boulder problems on a vertical wall. The main quarry is good vertical sandstone, with climbing on small holds or fine arêtes. Lion Rock is natural overhanging fare.

Conditions & aspect
Crags face north-east, and are not very sunny. All the routes that are climbable come into condition quite quickly. A soft brush is useful on some routes beforehand.

Parking & approach
Park at the large car-park at the old station, which is on the south side of Oakamoor. Walk down the road for 200m to the Red Road. Follow this for 100m, then veer uphill on a little track just before the brick wall (built by prisoners from Moor Court in the late 1800s). Go right after 30m and follow a footpath to the quarry, comprising 2 right angled vertical walls,

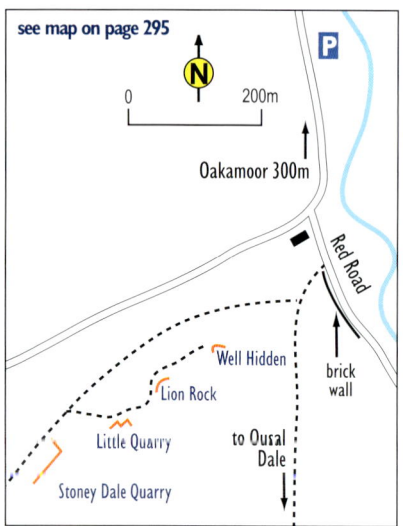

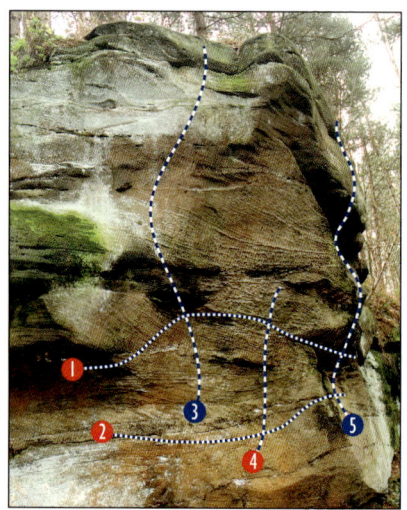

300m away. The other venues are in the woods above the path, but are most easily referenced from the quarry. Approach 10-15 minutes.

Well-Hidden Buttress

The first buttress is hardest to see. The rock is very good. It lies on the same level as Lion Rock, about 80m away to its left.

1   Peace Traverse   V2 (5c)
Cross the wall on good holds.

2   Miss You Already   V7 (6b)
Traverse the lowest break on small crimps.

3   The High Priest   E4 6a ★   1988
9m The steep wall on the left exiting via a short groove. The first ascent was protected by a specially prepared nut in a slot at two-thirds height.

4   Blue Nunn   V5 (6b)
Climb the steep crimpy wall from a sit start: *see photo on page 274.*

5   Monk's Blues   E3 5c ★   1988
9m Climb the gently leaning wall to gain the ledge and surmount the final overlap using a small sapling.

The Lower Churnet Stoney Dale

Lion Rock

A very impressive buttress. To get there, go through The Little Quarry, then exit left down a slight path leading to the crag, 50m away.

6 Rocking Stone Crack VS 4c ★   1972
10m The obvious layback crack to the left. Pleasant. The blunt rib to the left is **Rocket to 'em** (HVS 5c, 2002), while a dirty corner left again gives **Descant** (HS 4a, 1972). **Canticle** (VS 4c, 1979) takes the steep arête to the left. The mossy unprotected wall to its right is **Ex-Lion Tamer** (HVS 5a, 1990).

7 The Pride E6 6b ★ ★ ★   1988
18m A brilliant pitch of upside-down spacewalking. Climb the flake to the left-hand side of the roof, then make an intimidating series of moves rightwards to, and along, the lip and up the headwall to the top. The route was led on the first ascent but the only runner would be desperate to find and place on-sight. Most recent ascents have soloed/ bouldered the route.

8 Hand Jive E6 6a ★   1979
18m A spectacular and bold route with creaking flakes and little by way of worthwhile protection. Reach and follow the flake across the overhang to the right-hand side of the lip. Fingery pulls and a slap lead to a short groove on the left and the top.

On the right-hand side dirty twin cracks provide **Evensong** (VD, 1972). Diagonally leftwards and up via a slab left of this is **Psalm** (S, 1972). **Magnificat** (S, 1972) is the overhanging crack bounding the nose on its right-hand side.

The Little Quarry

On returning back down the track from Stoney Dale Quarry, after 25m, a vague track leads off to the right. This leads after 100m into a small quarry.

9 The Whirling Pit V0 (5b)
The wall left again is **Lisa Lust**, V0– (4b).

10 Short Ride V0 (5b)
The fine little arête.

11 Roger Melly V0– (4c)

12 Billy the Fish V0– (4b)

13 Crumble in the Jungle V6 (6b)
Start hanging the break and climb the wall on pockets.

14 Fat Slags V3 (6a)
Going left at the top is V5 (6b).

15 Don't be Strangers V6 (6b)
A left to right traverse finishing up Lawnmower Man.

16 Layered Cake V3 (6a)
Start hanging the break and trend left to the pocket.

17 Credit Crunch V3 (6a)
Start hanging the break.

18 Lawnmower Man V3 (6b)
The right-hand arête.

Staffordshire Grit

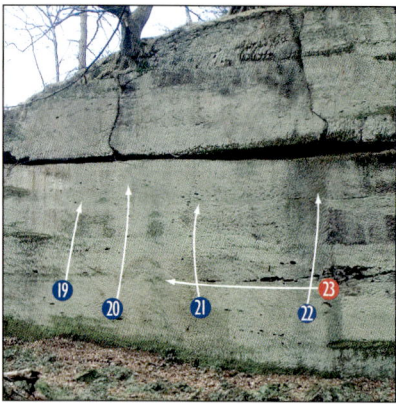

Stoney Dale Quarry

The main event, the quarry to the right, has a bunch of esoteric vertical boulder problems and a selection of routes, from poor to excellent, including one classic.

The routes are described from left to right, starting at the left of the long wall. **Chiropodist's Nightmare** (HS 4a, 1989) is the left arête gained from the right. Moving diagonally rightwards from the arête to gain a ledge is a filthy HVS 5a (**Klangerman**, 1990). **Maid Marion** (E1 5c, 1979) is the wall to the right, starting from the letterbox. Dirty.

19 Gain Entry to Your Soul E3 6b ★   1990s
9m The superb little wall yields with a difficult start. Highball V4 (6b) to the break.

20 Robin Hood E3 6b ★   1979
9m Gain the bow-shaped crack in the wall below the big tree with difficulty. This gives an easier finish. Highball V3 (6b) to the break.

21 Cad Cam Warrior E3 6a ★   1990
9m E5 if you don't have a size 6 cam! Starting at a deep slot a few metres right, sustained climbing leads up the wall with trying moves to stand in the break. Step right to reach a good hold, then move up and left to finish. Highball V4 (6b) to the break.

22 Friar Muck E1 6b ★   1979
9m Start below a prominent crack. Difficult moves up the very vague rib gain a break. Finish up the crack. Highball V4 (6b) to the break. Another problem, in a similarly technical vein, climbs the wall 1m left; V3 (6a).

23 Heavenly Action V6 (6b)
The traverse of the wall, leftwards from the mossy ledge, has a particularly fingery crux. Continue left to finish left of Gain Entry to Your Soul.

The next routes are on the right of the main mucky corner.

24 Cave Crack E1 5b   1980
12m Dirty holds in the mossy groove to the left gain a cave. The difficult and dirty crack above leads to a sandy finish. **Long Lankin** (E1 5b, 1980) starts up this route, then gains and climbs the repulsive crack to the left. The direct start is also repulsive.

25 Doina Da J'al E4 6a ★   1979
9m One of the better routes in the quarry, but still requires cleaning. The arête is taken initially on its right-hand side to the break. Finish boldly on its left-hand side. Taking the arête on its left side is **The Brazilian** (E4 5c, 1987), while climbing it all the way on the right is...

26 Your Own Undoing E4 6a ★   2002
9m A thrilling variation on the last route is to climb the arête on its right side all the way. A very enjoyable route, although bold, despite a runner just below half-height.

27 Longstop E2 5c   1983
10m The corner to the right is currently in a filthy condition. **Little Nikki** (E1 5c, 1980) is the prominent crack 4m right, with easy climbing to an impasse at a peg runner. Once the sandy shelf is gained finish leftwards. Two routes existed to the right, but are now in a state of disrepair: **My Mother is a Rhinoceros** (E3 6a, 1990) is the wall 2m right, and **General Accident** (E1 5a, 1989) is the vaguely scooped wall 6m left of the arête.

28 Dance of the Flies E2 5c   1979
18m Once a local classic, now dirty. The wall 1m left of the arête, when clean, gives good edgey climbing. A poor peg protects.

29 Sole Survivor E5 6b ★★★   2002
18m The Master's Edge of Staffordshire. The eye-catching arête taken on its right-hand side. Initially desperate moves gain a good hold, peg (this can be avoided on the left). Superb laybacking gains a good edge, peg, and the final, crux moves to gain good holds and the top. For the tall, the peg on the left can just about be reached: *see picture on page 293.*

The bay to the right is bounded by two blank, unclimbed corners. The right-hand dirty crack in-between is **Pegger's Original** (A2, pre-1970).

Cotton Bank Crag: O.S. Ref. SK058463 A moss-enveloped boulder lurking in a dark wood on a steep bramble-choked slope. Currently unclimbable. Beneath the upholstery lies what would be quite an impressive slab but unfortunately cleaning would be a Herculean and, probably, ecologically unsound operation. It is no longer described here. See **www.thebmc.co.uk/guides** for details.

Staffordshire Grit

Wright's Rock   page 310
Wright's Rock may seem a bit steep to start on, but you may as well get used to it — things ain't gonna get any easier. To get there, take the left fork on the main track from the Rambler's and follow this to the start of the first pool. At this point a well worn track angles off on the left leading up through trees, over a stile, past a pool to a fenced-in track. Go left along this to a gate and waddle up to the Out There block, turn right past the Sharp Holds block to arrive at the Niche area of Wright's.

| 1 **Hob Traverse** | (44) |
| 2 **Nose Section** | (C) |

Continue up Alternative Start for the full tick.

| 3 **Thorns Section** | (A) |
| 4 **Niche Traverse** | (7) |

Gentleman's Rock   page 308
Head back down to the fenced-in track below the field and turn left, following the fences then over a stile and down through the trees to the main riverside path at a sharpish bend just by some wooden steps and a footbridge. Note the point you join this as it is useful when you come to locate Virgin Wall. Continue left, upstream on the main path. After about 70m there is a bench on your left beside a small track running left uphill. Ignore that — for future reference, that track leads off up to the Peakstone Inn Amphitheatre — and carry on the main path. After a couple of hundred metres there is a series of small dams and pools on the right. Halfway along the first pool, and about 60m before a forestry track leads off left (towards Spooky Land), the overhanging wall of Gentleman's Rock sits about 25m up and left. Go thither.

| 5 **Low Traverse** | (11) |

Try linking this into Jill the Traverse for the full V6 tick.

Virgin Wall   page 308
Return to the main path again (the Chained Block boulder sits in the hillside directly opposite at this point), turn right and double back on yourself, following the path downstream. Eventually you will arrive again at the sharpish bend near the wooden steps where you came down from Wright's. From the bend continue for about 50m and find a vague track up into the trees on the right. There is not much of a path direct to Virgin Wall, so follow this one which leads to the end of a line of rocks. If you contour left along these rocks, through the rhodedendron, you arrive at Virgin Wall. Fondling some of the holds on this wall provides more frottage than Cottage.

| 6 **Virgin Wall Traverse** | (1) |

Cottage Rocks   page 304
Tired yet? Don't worry. You're halfway there. Back down again to the main path and turn right and follow the path downstream for another hundred metres or so as it curves rightward. At the apex of the curve is a bench with a wooden bridge below. Drop down to the bridge, but do not cross it. Instead follow a muddy track rightwards, parallel with the main path above, as it runs down along a wall then turns left to cross a little bridge at the head of the lowest pool. (For future reference, if you were to contour the hillside from Virgin Wall, past lots of lo-kwal rock, then Lord's Buttress is directly above you at this point.) Having crossed the little bridge you join another large path. Turn right and follow this along the poolside until, halfway along, a forestry road cuts off on the left. (The small path that runs into the hillside in front of you leads to the Toilet Block area.) Taking the forestry road uphill, follow this until Cottage Rocks comes into view just before a right-hand bend.

7 **Pine Wall**	(17)
8 **Orange Crush**	(10)
9 **Glory Hole**	(14)
10 **Cottage Slab**	(6)

Ousal Crag   page 302
Wasn't that fun! Rejoin the forestry road, switching right then back left. This passes the bulging black lump of Lone Buttress then the overhanging wall of Bizarre. A hundred metres later, a knee-high wall sits on the right of the track. Step up on a tree stump and cross the wall and dally up to Ousal Crag.

| 11 **Booze** | (3) |
| 12 **Ousal High** | (7) |

Good news. You're done. Now retreat to the Ramblers where you can dip your fingers in a bowl of cold water and have some well-earned cakes.

A Churnet Ramble

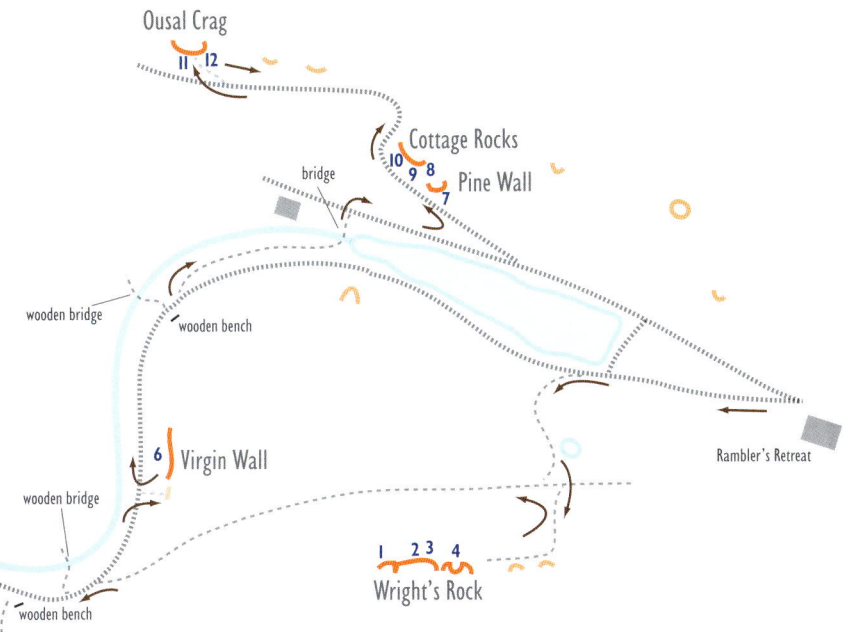

Geology really was having a laugh when it made the Churnet Valley. The dark delights of this dastardly dale have discmbobulated dilettantes and dabblers alike for years now, always keeping an air of mystery for all but dutiful devotees. Well, now's your chance to become intimate with the cherished secrets of Dimmings Dale and Ousal Dale. Here is a circuit that will take you on a tour of the finest the valleys have to offer. You may notice that there are not as many problems as on the book's other circuits. Don't fret. You will not be short changed. The problems are physical, steep and fingery and feature a good number of traverses, often quite long ones, which are among the best traverses on Staffordshire. The circuit also points out other crags that may be of interest in future visits to help you to get the measure of the place. As such it is an ideal itinerary to follow for the first-time visitor. The problems vary in difficulty from V2 to V5. But don't worry if this isn't your grade range – most crags will have easier substitutions; all, most certainly, have harder. Set aside a whole day for the tour, and perhaps consider a belay session in the Ramblers befor visiting Cottage Rocks.

Staffordshire Grit

Ousal Dale

O.S. Ref. SK055436 Altitude: 165m a.s.l.

This is the right-hand tributary of Dimmings Dale and offers a number of smaller buttresses, giving a few routes and lots of very good bouldering. To reach the dale follow the right-hand path from the Rambler's Retreat. Branch off right up a track from halfway along the first pool: see map on page 295.

Ousal Crag

The path takes a sharp right by Cottage Rocks and about 250m after the sharp left-hander, having passed two small buttresses along the way, Ousal Crag is seen in the trees on the right, about 30m from the path. The up-problems are quite good here, but the two traverses are mega-classics.

1 Ooze V1 (5c)
Start low and pull over to the higher break.

2 Sneezy V3 (6b)
From a sitter, pull on and slap for the big fat sloper then head slightly leftwards to reach upper traverse.

3 Booze V0 (5a)
Climb the juggy hanging nose to the upper holds.
◐ A grim sitter off two polished crimps is V2 (6a).

4 Little Rib V0 (5a)

5 Uzi Lover V0– (5a)
Start low and climb the blunt arête. A variation starts the same but climbs rightwards on pockets: **V1 (5c)**.

6 Ousal Low V6 (6b)
A classic crossing the crag in either, or both directions. It can be started on the sloping shelf at the extreme right, or the blunt arête just left:
see photo opposite.

Norman Gilman on Ousal Low, V6 (opposite page). Photo: Mike Hutton.

7 Ousal High V3 (5c)
The upper traverse has bigger holds, and is every bit as classic. ⊙ The obvious circuit is linking the high and low traverses at their ends and doing laps. The low has a hands-off rest, which feels a bit like cheating. However, this can be missed out by coming down Little Rib.

Solo Chimney (S 4a, pre-1970) is the good chimney on the left side of the face and **Thum** (VD, 1979) the wall and crack through the bushes to the left. **Impacted Bowel** (VS 4c, 4b ★, 1978) is a good high-level girdle of the crag starting high on the left.

8 The Tantrum E4 5c   2003
11m Climb the blunt prow directly and top out using a diagonal flake crack as for Moto Perpetuo.

9 Moto Perpetuo E2 5c   1979
12m From Little Rib, move up the scoop to gain the wide break. Move a couple of metres leftwards along this to a rightwards slanting finishing crack

10 Prowler E5 5c   2002
12m Nutters Ahoy! From Uzi Lover take a direct line through the prow above. Good moves but utilising a creaky flake of suspect strength.

About 100m back towards the Rambler's Retreat is a 3m high overhanging buttress right by the path that you passed on your way up.

11 Bizarre V9 (6c)
From a sit start, hands on the flake, climb the steep wall past crimps. Be as gentle with it as possible.

Lone Buttress

Continue along the main track, Rambler's-ward, for another 50m. This next buttress lies on the uphill side of the track. On the left-hand side is a fine steep wall. **Lone Wall** (E1 5b, 1979) takes the right-hand side of the wall past a thin crack. **Even Lonelier** (E1 5c, 1979) starts from a ledge 1m to the left. Traverse right to a ledge below an overhang. Cross this with great difficulty, near the arête, using a ripple.

Staffordshire Grit

Cottage Rocks

A lovely little venue with perfect landings. While it gets the sun, the trees afford a lot of shade. Problems are a combination of steep fingery yarding on positive holds, or delicate slabby walls. It is at the bend on the main track, 140m from the pools. See map on page 295.

1 Adam's Arête V8 (6c)
From a sit start, slap left and up the arête on crimps.

2 Short Wall V0+ (5b)
Climb to the right-hand end of the wide break, then follow it left to finish up the arête.

3 Billy Bunter V0+ (5b)
Climb the wall, passing a large pebble.

4 Crusty V0− (4b)
Climb the dotty crack to the top.

5 Sid the Sexist V1 (5b)
Climb the wall past a pebbly pock and ledge.

6 Cottage Slab V1 (5b)
Go up the wall just right to gain a high hole. ☉

7 Green Wall V4 (6a)
Tricky moves past the bulging right side of the wall, using a sloping finger-ramp for the right hand.

8 Sapling Bugle V4 (6b)
From the low jug, climb directly to the tree (finger-ramp for left hand).

9 Tufa V2 (5c)
Pinch up the good feature on the arête.

10 Orange Crush V2 (5c)
Good pocket-pulling leads to the top break. ☉

11 Pocket Wall V0+ (5b)
A great problem up the centre of the steep wall. A good sit-start is V4 (6b).

12 The Wafer V2 (5c)
Ascend the steep wall direct from the little fin as far as the big break. A stiff sit-start is V3 (6a).

13 Strenuosity V0− (4c)
A wide voyage up the mean crackline. At the top, moving left to swing along the upper break is V1 (5b).

14 Glory Hole V3 (6a)
From the crack, traverse left to a good hold then drop down to follow more good holds to the arête. Continue in this line (feet on sandy ledge) to finish up Tufa. ☉

15 Cottaging V6 (6b)
A long traverse from the wide crack, along the lower break then along the same line to finish up Short Wall.

The Lower Churnet Ousal Dale

Pine Buttress

Three more good problems lie on a bulging right-facing wall on an outcrop 10m right. (The wall just left is Diff.)

16 Left Pine V5 (6b)
Start sitting at the back of the recess. From a small crimp, crank upwards on edges to reach a rounded feature at half-height.

17 Pine Wall V3 (6a)
Just right, start sitting with hand in a hole. Move left and up through a groovy feature to get established in a flake crack higher up. Retreat from here. **G**

18 Right Pine V4 (6b)
From the same start, move up and right to eventually gain the top of the thin crack at the top of the rock. Bail out from here.

About 25 meters up and right is a hidden bay containing the beautiful arête of Push.

19 Push V4 (6b)
from a sitter on left, slap up arête to a big finish.

The last buttress in the dale lies just below. **Footpath Chimney** (D 4a★, pre-1970) is a lovely route tackling the overlaps and flake in the centre of the buttress; **No Veranda** (VS, 1991) is the overgrown wall just left.

Green Boulders

In recent years the extensive scattering of blocks throughout the valley have been developed by Churnet Valley Champions to give many more problems than the original circuits. Stuart Brooks and Rob Mirfin have been responsible for the majority of exploration and development here.

However, these problems often lie on buttresses composed of significantly more delicate rock than the original routes, and will never manage the amount of traffic without suffering. Others are on rock that is naturally dirtier than the classics, or are significantly slower to dry. Because of this they are not given full treatment here, with only location descriptions being given and a note of the main lines. Feel free to go and explore. Full details of these problems are available for download at: **www.thebmc.co.uk/guides.**

A - Toilet Block: A very clean boulder with good rock although it can be very hard to find in summer when the ferns are high (as can the oher two). In the bay which contains the right hand fork up to Cottage Rocks is a path which doubles back on itself. Take this into the hillside and wind up to the ridge. Turn left and follow the fence of a field until you see the block. The up-lines are between V0 and V2.

B - Breathe Block: As for the Toilet approach, and gain the ridge (and vague track). Follow ridge path towards the car park. Keep a look out for a random track which veers off leftwards. If you stomp across the woodland for about 20m left of this track you will come to a series of outcrops. Walk to the bottom of these and the block is situated on the furthest wall north-westwards. The main arête from a sitter is **Footprints**, V3, and the wall 2m right, passing the sloper, is **Breathe**, V6.

C - Grasshopper Block: Carry on the same ridge path. About 20m before the ridge starts to descend the block and be located on the right. You have to fight your way through bracken drop down a small slope and contour right wards which should bring you underneath it. The central up-line is **Grasshopper**, V2 and the up-line to the right is **Duck Billed Platypus**, V6.

Never get out of the boat! Rob Clifton treading delicate on one of the Lower Churnet's great wall climbs, Top Brick, E2 5c (opposite page). Lord's Buttress offers some of the most exciting leads in the valley, with a great sense of exposure and an almost tower experience. Photo: David Simmonite.

The Lower Churnet Dimmings Dale

Dimmings Dale

O.S. Ref. SK062432 to SK045436
Altitude: 125 - 175m a.s.l.

A beautiful dale of woods and waterfalls running away from the Rambler's Retreat. Amid much overgrown rock there are three buttresses of significant worth. Lord's Buttress offers a handful of excellent routes on good quality sandstone making them worth carrying a rope for. The Long Wall and Gentleman's Rock have become the domain of the boulderer and offer many good problems, most especially of the horizontal nature. See map pn page 295.

On the left side, before Lord's Buttress, two overgrown crags lie in the trees: Fisherman's Buttress and Smelting Mill Buttress. The routes on these are no longer described. See www.thebmc.co.uk/guides for details.

Lord's Buttress

The most imposing crag in this dale. It has big tall routes on vertical rock which is sometimes a bit fragile. It is obscured by trees in summer. It lies directly above a small footbridge at the head of the first pool, near Earl's Rock cottage. Strike up the bank opposite the bridge and there it is, recognisable by its tall tower and central crack.

At the left-hand side of the crag is a small wall with some good problems on perfect pockets. To the right lies a gully with a protruding nose to the right again. **Slippery Caramel** (E3 5c, 1979) climbs the gully then the right wall of the tower via a couple of cracks.

1 Overlord E3 6a ★★   1992
20m Great, varied crack climbing in a fine situation. Climb the short hand-crack on the front of the buttress to a ledge and possible belay (4c). The fine thin crack above the ledge gives sustained interest with good protection to a sapling. Traverse right to finish up the arête.

2 Lord's Arête E4 6a ★   1979
18m Tricky climbing in an exposed setting. Climb the groove just to the right of the main arête of the buttress to a ledge (or if this is dirty, climb the gully). Continue up the wall with difficulty, sling runner. to gain a break, peg. Swing back left onto the arête and finish up this.

3 Top Brick E2 5c ★★   1979
15m A Churnet classic, with good wall climbing. From the foot of the chimney around to the right, move out left onto the face, thread runner, and pull up to the cave (peg on left). From the cave, climb steeply to a wide break, then finish up the wall above: *see photo opposite*.

4 Toast Rack HVS 4c ★   1979
18m A good traversing line with an exposed crux. From high up the chimney, cross the left wall on good holds to reach the front face. Traverse delicately across the slab to a ledge and walk off to the left. Originally started up Toast Rack.

5 Mental Traveller E1 5b   1983
9m The right arête of the chimney (**Lord's Chimney**, VD, 1979) is climbed using a fragile fin and several fragile pockets.

6 Travelling Light E2 5b ★   2002
9m The centre of the front face provides a stern test of nerve with steep climbing on varied and unusual holds. Very worthwhile.

7 Travelling Bag E4 5c   2002
9m The even bolder right arête of the wall gained via the undercut prow below.

Nine metres to the right of the chimney is a dirty corner. **Reverse Charge** (VS 4b) follows a break leftwards from the corner and climbs the arête via a flake. Step left and finish direct. Thirty metres to the right lies the next small buttress. This contains **Rhody Crack** (VD), climbing via two prows. Another 150m on lies the notably Pebble Buttress. The slab and crack on its right-hand side is **Grott** (D) – bet you can't wait. All 1979.

Staffordshire Grit

Virgin Wall (Long Wall)

This flat wall has several overgrown (no longer described) routes and one of the best traverses in the valley on beautiful pocketed holds. To locate it, find the sharp right-hand bend in the main track, about 300m from Earl's Rock cottage. It has a wooden staircase leading down to a wooden footbridge. Staying on the main track return towards the Ramblers for 50m then follow a vague path up the hill to the dwindling right extremity of a band of rocks. Countour the base of these leftwards for about 40m to a lovely flat vertical wall.

1   Virgin Wall Traverse   V4 (6a)
Usually done from the large tree on the right-hand side of the crag at a low-level and finishing at the first step up on the left-hand side of the crag. ⊕ The traverse can be extended at both ends. Leftwards and slightly upward via pebbles and crimps is V6 (6b). Beginning the traverse 8m right of the tree and moving leftwards to gain the original traverse is V8 (6c).

Gentleman's Rock

Continuing along the drive and around a right-hand bend leads to the lower of another series of pools and waterfalls. This buttress lies to the left of the first waterfall. It is a small steep crag with a long traverse, and some powerful up problems. Bits tend to be damp in muggy weather, while other sections will stay dry in a downpour. In the centre there is a sacrificial altar: see map page 295.

1   Jack the Traverse   E5 6a ★   1978
30m A physical and very worrying traverse of the upper break from a boulder on the left to Gentleman John. Possible to be seen as a boulder problem, although the altar may demand a sacrifice.

2   Jill the Traverse   V4 (6a)
The lower traverse from the shelf on the left to the central crack with a balancey fingery crux.

3   Moon Jumper   V5 (6b)
At the left-hand end of traverse move up the vague arête from low-level jugs to a sloper and pocket to gain jugs above. This gives an older established problem – **Hey Diddle Diddle** V4 (6b). From the good jugs gain a thin flake and move up and right to finish on the Electrofly rail.

4   Electrofly   V6 (6b)
From 4m right of the arête, use a rounded green finger-pocket to gain high jugs (an established V5 to here). Ape a metre left from the jugs, then rock up to finish matched on the rail above.

5   Martin's Mono Problem   V7 (6c)
Use an undercut to gain a mono and pop to a pocket.

6   Fifty Pence Problem   V8 (6c)
From just left of the altar, use a coin-shaped pebble to gain a good pocket up and left.

7   Humpty Dumpty   V7 (6c)
The groove via pebbles.

The Lower Churnet Dimmings Dale

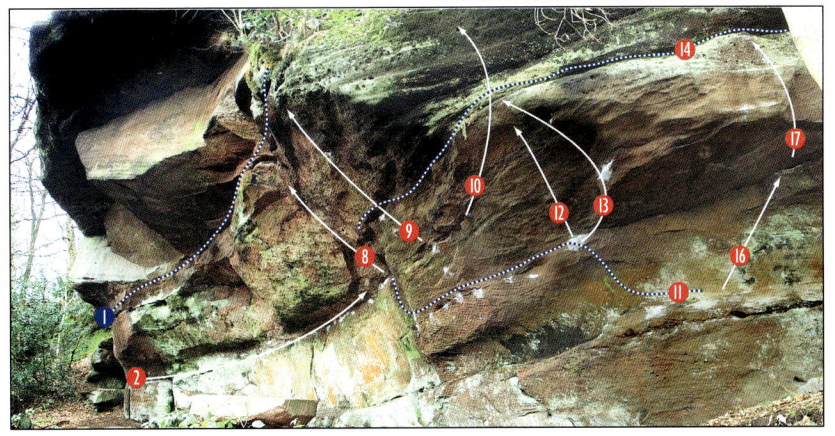

8 Gentleman John V4 (6a)
The savage finger crack.

9 High Speed Imp Act V6 (6b)
A superb problem up the leaning wall yields to power, a long reach and a slap to the finishing jug.

10 Clover Field V5 (6b)
From a standing start, with hands in the letterbox, move to the ledge then up the oft-dirty wall to the top.

11 Low Traverse V4 (6b)
Starting on the very low shelf, traverse up and left to the jugs on Gentleman John. ✪ Reversing this into Lockit to the Pockit is V6.

12 Pegasus V8 (6c)
An enormous dyno from the starting holds of The Nose to the break far above. Far out.

13 The Nose V5 (6b)
Start as for the Low Traverse, move up then crank steeply rightwards to finish over the bulging nose.

14 Mindbenderjelly V6 (6b)
A right to left traverse starting on a break right of the nose problem. Can be dirty.

15 The Mega Traverse V7 (6b)
Do Jill the Traverse, drop down the flake, reverse Low Traverse and continue to finish up The Nose.

16 Lockit to the Pockit V3 (6b)
A good move from the flat ledge to the deep pocket above.

17 Limp Lizard V8 (6c)
The bulge from the pocket using a sloper and the short groove. Very reachy.

D - Spooky Land: Follow the path beyond Gentleman's as it curves left uphill into the woods. As it levels out, you can see a buttress on the left. **Spooky Arête** takes the arête left of the V-cleft (V3) and **Flowtation** takes the wall to its right (V4). Both sit starts.

E - Square Pusher: A small steep wall hidden in the trees to the left. The central line is **Squarepusher**, V4, from a standing start.

F - The Chained Block: This lies on the hillside facing Gentleman's Rock, on the other side of the river. Strike up the hillside for about 60m directly across from Gentleman's. This has a wonderful collection of sloper problems from V4 to V8. It can take a little time to dry out due to the vegetation on the top of the block. For more details, see **www.thebmc.co.uk/guides.**

Hermit's Rock lies in the trees on the opposite side of the dale near Earl's Rock cottage. Further down the dale is the tall Rainroach Rock. Now overgrown, the routes are no longer described. For more details, see **www.thebmc.co.uk/guides.**

Staffordshire Grit

Wright's Rock Area

O.S. Ref. SK057429 Altitude: 175m a.s.l.

The rock and climbing, and specifically, the bouldering, is the best the Churnet has to offer. Steep powerful up-problems, many over large roofs, as well as brilliant traversing. It has the ambience of many of the more open crags of the area, and the views of the surrounding countryside, including Alton Towers, are superb.

Conditions & aspect
Wright's Rock stands proudly overlooking farmland on the southern rim of Dimmings Dale. Its aspect is very open. It faces north and gets virtually no sun. The crag dries quickly and can be climbed on most of the year round. Avoid the crag after spells of wet or humid weather, the latter enticing clouds of midges. It stays dry in the rain. Good in hot summers.

Parking & approach
See map on page 295. From the Rambler's Retreat, follow the track up the left-hand side of the Dale. At the foot of the first pool a path runs up the hillside on the left of a shallow valley to meet a track beside a wooden fence. Use the gate to the left to enter the field and wander to the crag ahead. 10 minutes.

Access
Some changes and development of late, such as the new fence. So far access is tolerated, but keep an eye out for any changes.

Left-Hand Outcrops

Before the main event, there are various outcrops on the same level, to the left. The first, **Painter's Rock**, is 300m left in the trees. Currently unclimbable, it once contained **Recess Corner** (VD), **Working Hunter (HVS 5b)**, **Rabbit Stew** (E3 5c), **Bright Eyes** (E2 5c), **Glossy Finish** (VS 4c) and **Undercoat** (HVS 5b). All 1979.

G - Instant Funk: A low, undercut, overhanging wall directly above the gate you came through. **Instant Funk, V8,** is a right to left traverse to gain thin ledge above the portholes. See **www.thebmc.co.uk/guides.**

H - Sharp Holds Block: 10m right, before the main rock, is a flat wall, bulging at the left and tapering at the right. **Wright's Giza, V7,** follows pebbles and crimps through the right side of the half-height slot; the shorter wall to the right is **Keith Sharp Holds, V8,** using a teeth-like crimp. See **www.thebmc.co.uk/guides.**

Wright's Rock

A short distance to the right the main crag begins. The first rock encountered is centred around a small cave. This contains both routes and bouldering. The routes have become somewhat neglected and would require a clean.

The climbs are described from left to right starting at the prominent cave. **Stonemason's Route** (S, 1959–63) is the wall left of the cave. The next three climbs are on the bulging walls right of the cave. **Cherry Rare** (E5 6b, 1990) pulls through the right-hand side of the cave to a break. Worrying moves using a flake then gain the ledge above. **The Clumsy Too** (E5 6a, 1990) moves straight up from the break on Cherry Rare to continue using a huge pebble and poor undercut. **Never Never** (E4 6a, 1990) climbs the right arête of the cave to a break. Step left and gain the short crack. **Puppet Life** (E2 5c, 1990) goes from 3m right of the cave over the bulge and traverses right and up past a peg runner to gain a rounded break. Move left and up to finish at a tree.

The Lower Churnet Wright's Rock

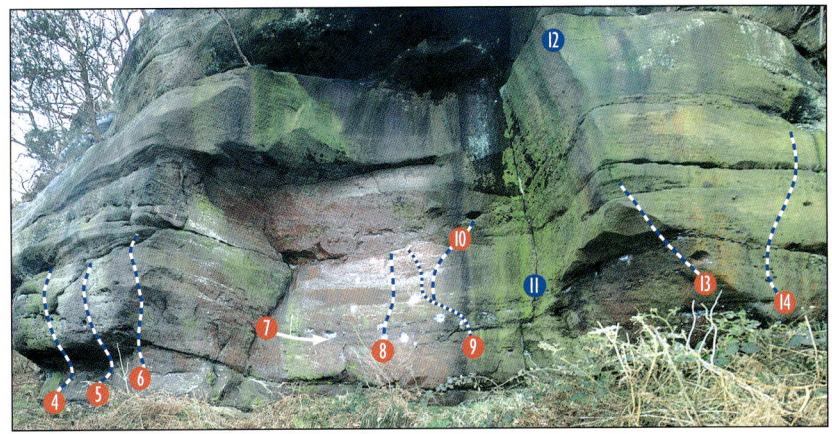

1 Wright's Unconquerable V6 (6b)
Climb the roof crack from a thread hold at the back: morpho.

2 Crumble Roof V3 (6b)
Start at chest-height holds and climb directly out A line linking start of this to the finish of the Unconquerable is **Dave's Traverse**, V3 (6a).

3 Cave Overhang V2 (5c)
From the right-hand end of the cave, reach up for crusty jugs and climb the bulge.

4 Jug Wall V3 (6b)
Climb to the break on big crack features.

5 Threapwood Bulge V2 (6a)
From a low flat hold gain a pebbly sidepull pocket and use this to gain the break above.

6 Threapwood Arête V3 (6a)
Climb the steep arête on packets and pobbles.

7 Niche Traverse V4 (6b)
Good in either direction, and twice as good if done both ways. ⊙ Continue on to Problem 13 at V6 (6b).

8 Rocket Ride V5 (6b)
Move up to gain a prominent gaston-crimp with the right hand (good quartz pebble for the left) and use this to lock out for the jug ledge above

9 Davros V6 (6b)
An eliminate on the last problem. From a sitting start (hand in pocket down and right) move up to the sidepull-crimp, this time with the left hand. Use this to fall for the Rocket Ride ledge. V5 from standing.

10 Albatross V6 (6b)
An eliminate... on an eliminate... such is today's world. Follow Davros to the sidepull and make a massive reach for the pocket on Sauron. V5 from standing. An eliminate on an eliminate on an eliminate avoids the sidepull altogether at a morpho V8.

11 Sauron HVS 5b ★   1970
9m A super little route up the right-hand corner of the square niche. Climbing to the pocket gives a V0+ problem.

12 Sauroff E2 5b ★   1979
9m The green and rounded arête to the right of the corner, with the occasionally rounded hold. A fine solo.

13 Sauroff Sit Start V3 (6a)
The low start. An eliminate rocks up and right using the frictionless pebble: **Iron Pebble**, V3 (6b).

14 Sculptor's Wall V0− (4a)
The wall to the right on chippers.

The deep crack is **Central Crack** (D, 1959–63).

Staffordshire Grit

The Main Crag

The main face lies just right. It is famous for its bouldering, but also has some fine routes.

15 Thorns E4 5c ★   1979
12m An impressive route with some friable holds. From the ledge, climb the thin flakes just right of the tree. The bulge and wide crack relent above. Avoiding use of the tree may prove problematic.

16 The Leading Firemen E2 5b ★   1988
11m From the the recess on Thorns, move right and up, via a rounded crack, to the break below the capping roof. Traverse this rightwards to an exit on the slabs above. A gripper.

17 Simple Simon E4 6c ★   1992
9m The classic problem was originally topped out, with a few pushy moves up the wall to join the final section of Fireman.

18 Pie Hard E6 6c ★   2009
9m A scary and very high highball. An independant start 1m left of Fingers gains the break above. Swerve left and continue up the blank wall to reach the Fireman break: highball V8.

19 Fingers in Every Pie E6 6c ★★   1988
9m Desperate bouldering up the bulging nose (Fingers Start) gains a peg in the break below the flake. Make hard moves to get established on the flake – very much the crux – then an easier finish.

20 Alternative Three E6 6c †   1979
12m An air of mystery hangs over this Woodward offering, originally graded E4 6a. A top rope ascent deemed it harder than Fingers. Gain and use the flake to reach the lip (Alternative Start). Moving left and then up to the Fingers flake proves even more difficult.

21 The Warp E5 6c ★   2007
12m From Alternative Three stretch up and right to a distant undercut pocket. Use this to gain the bald headwall and finish with a series of pulls on various conglomerates and tufts. The crux may be protected by a size 4 nut but its holding power depends on the strength of the woodlice.

22 Wright's Traverse V8 (6c)
Maximum boom! The superb traverse is sustained and fingery, giving one of the best hard traverses anywhere. Usually done from Thorns Start to finishing up Last Wrights.

You won't get up anything at Wright's without a bit of hurly burly. Dave Norton giving it the old heave ho on Fingers Start, V6, one of the many brutally steep testpieces hereabouts (page 314). Photo: Dave Parry.

Staffordshire Grit

23 Thorns Start V0– (5a)
Groove round the bulge to get hands on the break then pull onto the ledge above.

24 Blazes V2 (5c)
Climb directly to the roof and cross this to jugs.

25 Fireman Indirect V5 (6b)
From the jugs on the last problem, swing rightwards to gain the base of the curving finger-ramp.

26 Sam Sam Tan V8 (6c)
A harder variation on Simple Simon. Move up from the jug to the crimp rail above (as for Simple Simon) then use holds in the groove to the left to slap desperately for the bottom of the Fireman ramp. Using the groove holds alone is a project, as is the attractive flakeline 2m left.

27 Simple Simon V8 (6c)
A desperate brute of a thing, with all the odds stacked against you. From the good jug on the lip, launch directly upwards to gain the ramp.

28 Wrong's Traverse V8 (6b)
Start at a flake and traverse rightwards below Wright's Traverse using crimps, pockets and undercuts to finish past a crucial mono. Linking this into a reverse of the original traverse is reputedly F8a, while capping it off with Simple Simon is F8a+.

29 Simple Simon Indirect V6 (6b)
A really good problem. From a sitter, with hands on flake crimps under the roof, use pockets and slots to slap for main holds on Wrights's Traverse then bear leftwards to attain starting hold of Simple Simon.

30 Thumbs V9 (6c)
A burly problem, even for Wright's. From the good holds under the roof, reach round to a two-finger pocket. Use this and an edge to force left into Simple Simon. Finish up this.

31 Fingers Start V6 (6b)
A highball line following the vague nose. From the big holds under the hanging rib, yard up and left to another jug then use the positive crimps to access the hanging groove. Two finishes are possible: a big span with the right hand to the break or deviate left to crimps and on to the main horizontal break: *see photo on page 313.*

32 Johnny Utah V7 (6c)
From the start of the next problem, undercut out left to reach the Fingers crack with the left hand then do the right-hand finish of that problem.

33 Alternative Start V3 (6a)
Use good holds to cross the first roof to a good hold below the big roof (V1 to here). Using a flake in its underside, gain the break above. V5 from a sit start.

314 **The Churnet Valley Crags**

The Lower Churnet Wright's Rock

34 Tyler V7 (6c)
An eliminate problem that avoids the Alternative jugs. From a sit start down and right, use pockets to reach the holds on the traverse and then use the sidepull flakes above and crimps to gain the break. Using the Alternative roof flake for the left and an undercut for the right, reach the break up and right.

35 Point Break V8 (6c)
A big line giving a brilliant extension to an older problem. From the traverse, use an undercut pocket to get established on the square flake above. This gives an established problem, **The Undercut**, V6 (6b). From here, use a left hand undercut to beast onwards and get established in the break over the roof.

36 War Child VII (7a)
Another little classic grows up. Start low and use diagonal crimps to reach slopes below the roof. Share here for **The Old Sloper Problem**, V6 (6b). For War Child, move left and use an undercut in the roof to make all-out moves across the roof to the break above. Wild stuff.

37 Bhodi V7 (6c)
Another extension to The Old Sloper Problem moves right and makes a long reach to the upper break.

38 Little Groove VI (5c)
The narrow groove.

39 Last Wrights V2 (6a)
From a low start, climb the bulge on good holds. Finishing as for Bhodi gives a great big problem at V5 (6b).

Traverse Variations

For those still not replete with ballbusting highballs, a few of the individual sections of the classic traverse give some great problems in their own right.

A Thorns Section VI (5b)
Starting in a low pocket. traverse leftwards to gain and finish up Thorns Start. ◐

B Fireman Section V4 (6b)
Starting from the same pocket as Thorns Section, traverse right to gain the porthole. At this grade you need to be strict about not standing on the flat rocky ledges. The rule is that if you could balance a sausage on it, you cant use it.

C Nose Section V2 (6a)
A very steep and juggy passage. From the big porthole, traverse the good holds, with a huge span to cross the blank section. Continue to the first moves of Alternative Start as far as the flat hold under the big roof. Continue to the upper break for a V4 tick. ◐

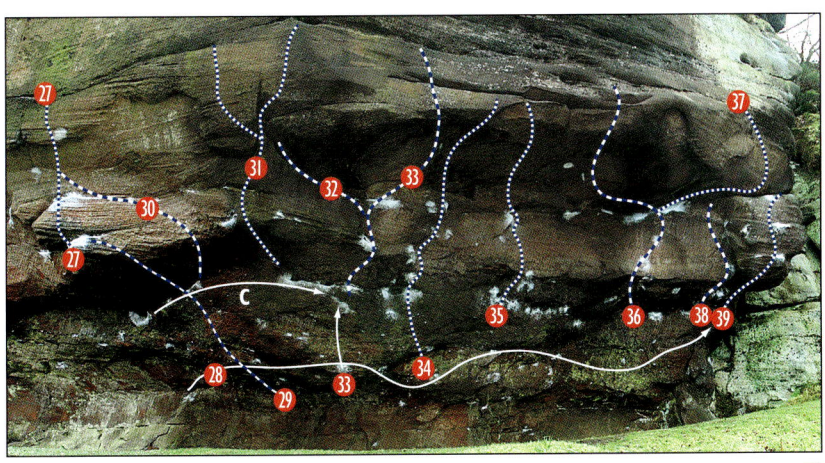

The Churnet Valley Crags

Staffordshire Grit

Right's Rock

The little wall just past the chimney (**Tunnel Chimney** D, 1959–63), has a few final problems and routes.

40 The Crack V6 (6b)
The rounded venture on the left side, from a sit start to a rounded top: *see photo opposite*. An eliminate, not using the crack, is V8 (6c).

41 Calyx V8 (6b)
The bulge from a sit start.

42 The Hob V0– (4c)
The line of least resistance. Continuing up the wall above gives a VS 4c of the same name (1970).

43 Hob Knob V4 (6b)
An eliminate on the last problem following the arete. Avoid stepping left until the top is reached.

44 Hob Traverse V1 (5b)
The generous traverse of the break. ☉

Further to the right and above an old ricketty fence lies the upper tier. **Tiger's Wall** (VS 4b, 1970), climbs the highest part of the wall and **Ugly Puss** (VS 4b, 1970), the flake to its left. **Motorbike** V7 (6b) is a hideous little problem down below Tiger Wall. Pad the boulder below

Do the Wright thing

Over the last few years Wright's Rock has really been discovered by the bouldering masses. This is great, but anyone who has regularly been visiting the crag, indeed any of the crags on the area, will have noticed evidence of this increased popularity. Amazingly the rock itself has stood up really well, but holds have become a chalk-caked mess. What can you do? Well, obviously only use as much chalk as you need, and brush it off when you're finished. Also, if you are the last visitor of the day and you have some water left, use this and your toothbrush to scrub up a few of the holds. Try to avoid ugly chalk ticks – donkey marks – if you can. Make sure you tidy up when you're finished, taking away finger tape, orange peel or any other leftovers you find, not just your own. Be extremely sensitive about where you go to the toilet. We have lost other bouldering crags through shitting in our own nest. Be nice to the people you meet, climbers and non-climbers. The owners live in a house nearby and currently allow climbing. Isn't that nice of them. Access to these places is not to be taken for granted and showing respect for others' property is one of the best ways of showing that we, as climbers, can be trusted. Be a good ninja.

John Nightingale on The Crack, V6 (opposite page). Photo: Paul Philips.

Peakstone Inn Amphitheatre

O.S. Ref. SK055428 Altitude: 160m a.s.l.

This is a collection of crags lying on each side of a deepening wooded vale leading into Dimmings Dale. The rock, like on many local crags, varies in quality: crags on the left-hand, shadier side, are generally poor and unattractive. Those on the right-hand side offer a handful of good harder routes, and are a pleasant place to be when the sun shines.

Conditions & aspect
The left-hand crags don't get much sun, so tend to be dank. The right, north-west facing side, gets afternoon sun, and combined with its more open aspect, has some perfectly clean rock.

Parking & approach
Park in the Peakstone Inn car park (the owners don't seem to mind especially if you buy a pint afterwards). From here, a series of steps lead down the hillside where a small track leads to Dimmings Dale – of course this point can be gained from the Rambler's Retreat. The crags are either side of the small track. Approach, under 5 minutes.

Left-Hand Side of the Amphitheatre

From the pub car park, follow the steps until a bridge is reached. From here the first of several buttresses will be seen through the undergrowth up and to the left.

These are now overgrown and once contained: **Northern Lights** (S, 1978), **Dancing Bear** (E1 4b, 5b, 1978), **Scoop Wall** (HVS 5a, 1971), **Chockstone Crack** (S, pre-1951), **Rock Around The Chock** (HS,1990), **Right Wall** (HVS 5a, 1971), **BJM** (VS 4b, 1971) and **Scout Wall** (VS 4c, 1971).

Right-Hand Side of the Amphitheatre

From the far side of the bridge at the foot of the steps, strike diagonally rightwards across the bank to reach a small group of crags, visible on the crest of the hill. It can also be gained by making a 300m traverse on feint paths from Wright's Rock.

The right-hand part of this has an overlap at 5m and offers a number of short problems including a good fingery traverse V4 (6a). Towards its left side a thin crack splits the roof, **Supermac** V5 (6b), 1988, mat essential. To the left, the rock becomes a lot more attractive. **One Dunne** (HVD, pre-1951) is the pleasant arête at the left-hand of the overlap to chips.

1 All Day and All of the Night
E4 6b ★   1988
9m Superb fingery climbing on steep clean rock. From 5m left of the large block to the left, tackle the centre of the leaning wall with a hard start, past a rounded break to the top. Two thread runners protect.

2 Suckin' Pebbles E5 6b ★   1990
9m Another fierce and technical climb, thankfully well protected by in-situ runners. The thin crack and leaning arête to the left gives a series of fingery moves. Two pegs and one thread runner.

3 Pocket Hercules E3 5c ★   1990
7m Steep positive moves in an exciting setting. From atop the block to the left move up via a pocket to a break. Swing merrily right along this to finish via the vague arête on distant holds.

4 Ripples E1 5a ★   1990
6m Continue directly up the wall above the start of Pocket Hercules and finish rightwards via an 'ear' on a short prow.

5 Dead Tree Slab VD   pre-1951
9m The dirty slab at the left-hand end of the wall. **Dead Tree Crack** (VD, pre-1951) is the overgrown crack to the left with a finish via the arête.

The Lower Churnet > Castle Crag

Churnet Valley: The Lost World

Illustration: Duncan Bourne.

Rakes Dale

O.S. Ref. SK063424   Altitude: 150m a.s.l.

This is the wide and fairly open dale with two crags. Can be slow to dry. Park on the horseshoe bend on The Red Road, 500m from Alton. A path marked Toothill Wood goes steeply uphill. Don't take this – unless you want to go to Toothill Rock – which you don't – unless you are a weirdo – which you probably are – in which case you probably should become a guidebook fieldworker. Marginally less weird people should instead take the road just right of this, leading to Rakes Dale House. After 150m, a path on the left leads past a barn into an open grassy dale. The crags lie on the flanks of this dale. Approach 5 minutes.

Austin's Crag

Lying on the left side of the upper part of the dale, just before the wooden building. It dries relatively quickly but gets little sunshine. Starting 5m from the left, **Dust Storm** (E1 5b, 1979) gains a flake, traverses 3m left then climbs a bulge and crack above. Dirty. **Castles of Sand** (E3 5c, 1991), climbs the wall 4m to the right of and elderberry shrub to the right. **Sandbagger** (HVS 5a, 1979) takes the tree-lined crack to the right. **Austin's Chimney** (M, 1979) is obvious by name on the right. **Desert Rat** (HVS 5a, 1979) is a hanging corner in the right wall. **White Mouse** (VD, 1979) starts on the front face and traverses into the chimney. All 1979.

Rakes Dale Wall

A fine wall, steep and featureless, and covered in pebbles sitting high on the right side of the dale. The climbs here are generally very bold. It can stay wet during the winter period and gets little sunshine unless you arrive early in the morning. One criticism of the climbs could be their 'saminess', although you are unlikely to be doing them all. Unique Churnet. It lies directly above the barn at the lower end of the dale. There is an overgrown flake at the left side. Routes start from here. The first route, **Legosaurus Rex** (E4 5c, 1991) is the now-overgrown wall 20m right of the flake. **Duplo Magic** (E4 6a, 1991), is the wall 3m right with a very vegetated exit.

1   The Plastics Factory   E5 6b   1991
12m A fine little route. Starting 5m right of Duplo Magic, climb up to the bulge, runner! Lunge around this and stand up somewhat precariously. Finish more easily.

Photo: Paul Philips.

Above: The Peakstone Inn is a fine stopping off place in the Churnet with easy access to the Dimmings Dale crags. Here, Steve Clark attends a lively meeting of guidebook fieldworkers as they attempt to agree on whether to use 'V' grades or Font grades for the bouldering scale. Photo: Nigel Edley.

2   Raiders of the Lost Bark E5 6b   1991
12m Start just to the right of a recess 5m to the right, small arrow. After a technical start on pebbles the climbing above eases significantly.

3   Stickle Brick Wall E6 6b   1991
12m Start 4m to the right. Move up to gain a series of poor slots and pebbles leading leftwards via a slight bulge. Continue leftwards to finish at a tree.

6   Legoland E5 6a ★   1989
12m Unusual climbing with just sufficient protection. At the far right-hand side of the wall a peculiar brown 'lump' adorns the face. Start 15m to the left of the lump. Climb the bulge and slab to reach a break. Step right to a hole and make hard moves to reach a tiny tree that aids a worrying exit. **Rakes Dale Chimney** (HVS 5a, 1979) is to the right.

Toothill Rock O.S. Ref. SK068425 The rock commands an impressive position overlooking the valley, although the climbing is terrible with copious amounts of vegetation. It is best regarded as a superior vantage point for Alton Tower's fireworks or as a picnic site. The routes here are no longer described. For details see www.thebmc.co.uk/guides.

The Churnet Valley Crags

Staffordshire Grit

Peakstone Rock

O.S. Ref. SK052422 Altitude: 185m a.s.l.

This is a peculiar group of rocks and buttresses forming a small ridge with a pinnacle halfway along, situated on the south side of a shallow hollow on Alton Common. Interest is concentrated on the south face. The climbing is mainly on pebbles, generally fairly solid, and gives unique and fingery climbing. The crag dries quickly, and is ideal for an evening visit. It gets sun in afternoon and evening. The climbs, in the main, are probably best enjoyed as highball boulder problems, i.e. with a mat and spotter. Landings are generally very good.

Parking & approach

The crag is difficult to locate on your first visit. Park in the Peakstone Inn car park (the owners don't seem to mind, especially if you buy a pint afterwards). Walk along the road for 300m (towards Cheadle), then follow a farm track, past a bungalow to a farm at the end. The cliff is across the field below to the right some 400m away. Permission at the local farm should be requested and this has always been granted. Since a public footpath passes the cliff, it would be very difficult not to. Climbs are described left to right, starting on the wall left of the central corner-crack (Afrodizzycrack). Approach: 10 minutes.

1 My Arse E4 6a ★   1990s
13m A big route on a little crag. The left-hand side of the buttress leads to the front face of the pinnacle. Start at the blunt arête and left of an elder tree. A steep start leads to increasingly worrying moves trending rightwards to a welcome breather below the overhung pinnacle. Attack the right-hand edge to an alarming sandy finish.

2 Time's Arrow E4 6a   1979
9m The scoop 3m left of the corner moving left to a break below a roof. Step left and pull over the bulge using a jug and finish up the slab. Hard.

3 Afrodizzycrack HVS 5a   1971
8m The dirty corner proves awkward.

4 Five Thousand Volts E1 5c ★   1979
7m Worthwhile. Starting 3m right of the corner, climb direct with difficulty. (V2). The sharp wall to the right can be climbed at V3 (6a), jumping off on easy ground.

5 Plebble E1 5c   1971
8m On the front face, climb the obvious scoops into the fat crack: V2 to the break. The overhanging arête itself can be climbed at V4 (6a).

6 Dimetrodon E3 6a   1979
8m The shallow groove left of the bush leads to a break. Step left and climb the face using small holds. V2 to the break, but award yourself V8 if you break through the thorny cornice. A crack once lived under the gorse to the right (**Peakstone Crack**, VS, 1971).

7 Stumblehead HVS 5a   1971
8m A gorsey journey. From the obvious wall, climb the face moving leftwards. Stepping right at half-height and following a hairline crack to the top can make an alternative finish: E1 5b.

8 Back Side V0− (HS 4b)   1959–63
This route gains the summit of the pinnacle. Climb the short side on large holds to an awkward finish. To descend, either reverse the route or abseil from a lone tree.

Great Gate Buttress

O.S. Ref. SK046410 Altitude: 180m a.s.l.

A drastically steep buttress containing a handful of sickening challenges. However while the sight is impressive the rock is a bit disappointing and loose which adds a layer of seriousness to a crag that simply doesn't need it

Conditions & aspect
Walls face north and west. The north wall is a little greener, and takes a while to dry. The west wall gets some late afternoon and evening sun.

Routes & bouldering
Only 5 routes, but you are unlikely to run out of things to do. All steep and long, physical and serious due to hollow rock. No bouldering.

Parking & approach
On the B5032, go south at Threapwood (by The Highwayman Pub, the ultimate rock venue). Pass 2 farms on the left, and park at a recessed gate 400m after the second (Lightoaks Farm). This gate is by some pools, and 1.3 miles from The Highwayman, and a friendly pony lives in the field. Go over the gate and at 20m, where the track bends, head diagonally left then direct up to some crags. Contour their base leftwards for 200m to the main crag. Approach 5 minutes.

Access
The ownership of these crags is unknown and best left undiscovered. Please keep a low profile, and if asked to leave, then do so politely.

1 Moov Over E7 6c   1990s
18m Some of the hardest climbing in the area in the most exposed situation in Staffordshire. Gain the obvious left-facing flake from the left, then the break running across the buttress. Traverse right on this until below a peg runner in the next break. Difficult moves above this lead to two pegs below the final bulge. Move gingerly rightwards to pull over.

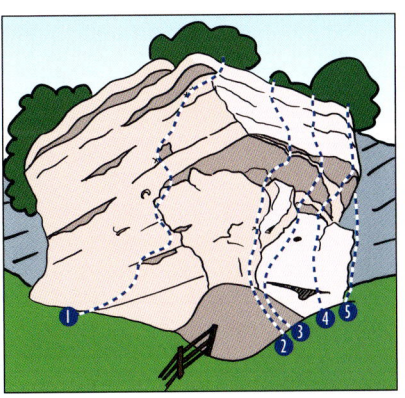

2 Pull the Udder One E6 6b   1990s
12m Begin on the front face 5m right of the fence and just left of a right-facing flake. A difficult start past a peg runner leads to sustained climbing directly up the wall. Continue direct through the overlap above. Small cams protect.

3 Black and White E5 5c   1990s
12m Climb the right-facing flake and swing up and left to the break. Ease through the overlap on a dinner-plate hold and with poor protection.

4 Curd be Cheese E6 6a   1990s
12m Climbs through the heavily-holed bulge to the right again finishing by a stern pull over from the hanging arête. Limited protection.

5 John's Route E3 6a   1990s
11m Climb between the breaks on the right-hand side of the crag starting via a short arête. Well-protected.

Staffordshire Grit

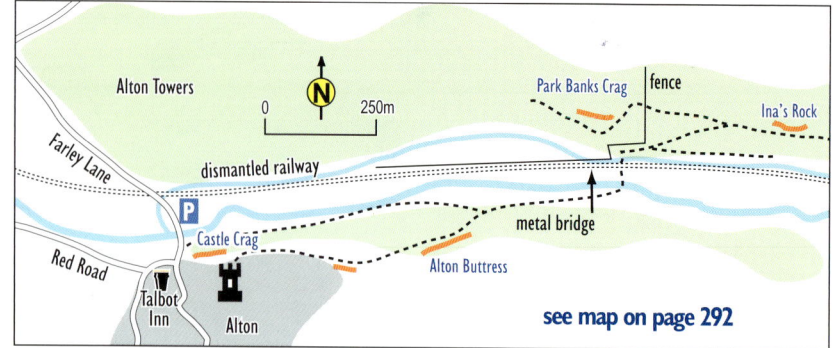

see map on page 292

Castle Crag

O.S. Ref. SK073425   Altitude: 120m a.s.l.

This lies directly below the walls of the old castle in Alton. A strange cliff, its construction and character is dominated by the infamous bunter pebbles. The rock on the right-hand side of the walls is more compact sandstone whilst in its centre it has a paler complexion. Most routes are in a poor and overgrown state.

The rock quality varies from okay to poor, mainly depending on pebble soundness. Crag faces north and gets little sun. Park in the village. Access paths, like the cliff, are a bit overgrown, so make the best of what there is. The climbs are described from right to left beginning at an old metal pipe running down a corner at the right-hand side of the walls. **Daedalus** (VS 4a, 1970), is the pleasant, open and bold arête. **Minos** (VS 4c, 1970) is the crack-line to the left. **Minotaur** (VS 4c, 1970), is the twisting crack left again past a thread runner. Move right into a chimney complete with tree to finish. **Theseus** (HVS 5b, 1970), takes the wall 7m to the left, step right and go up via a vague crack-line to a ledge. Continue up a crack via its retaining groove to the top. Thirty metres left is a wide, left-facing crack. **Icarus** (E1 5b, 1971). On the left of the bay is a through cave. **Zeus** (E2 5c, 1971) bridges up the right side of the cave then the overhanging crack above. **Pasiphae** (VS 4c, 1970) goes right from the tree, to then go a long and very random way left. The opposite side of the through cave around to the left gives the start of **The Gallows** (E1 5b, 1970), the vertical cracks above the cave. **The Labyrinth** (HVS 5a, 1970) is the traverse of the buttress. At the far end of the wall, just before a series of slabs, is a short wall. **Death Mask** (VS 4c, 2002) is a small nose and wall via a break gains a twisted tree.

Two hundred metres beyond Castle Cliff is another buttress containing two overgrown routes: **The Prodigal** (E1 5c, 1971) and **The Graduate** (VS 4a, 1971).

Four hundred metres left again is **Alton Cliff**. This is best approached by a track coming down from the castle which meets the valley track under the buttress. Routes are described this time from left to right. In the centre of the cliff is a prominent roof. **The Molegrip Kid** (HVS 5c, 1990) climbs the wall to the left of the overhang to continue directly up the slab. **Rig A Dig Dig** (E2 5c, 1971) is dirty. From a short groove at the left end of the buttress, traverse right beneath the overhang to an easier finish via a crack. **Restless Natives** (E1 5c, 1990) is the undercut rib to the right with a peg runner. The top bulge requires a strategically placed tree root to exit. **The Brothers** (E1 5b, 1971) is the pebble-dashed arête to the right. The steep wall to the right contains an obvious crack. **To Live Again** (E3 5c, 1978) is an undercut arête left of the crack. **Transit Crack** (S, 1971) is the crack itself. **Down To The Elbows** (E3 6a, 1978) is the vicious overhanging offwidth crack to the right of the gully. **Pull Johnny** (E1 5b, 1978) is a pleasant route up the crack 9m to the right. Step right at its top and finish at a tree.

The Lower Churnet Park Bank Crags

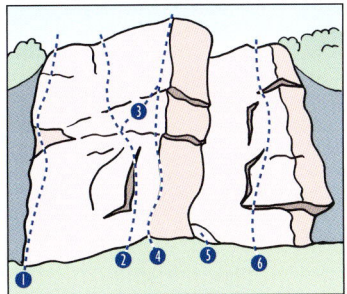
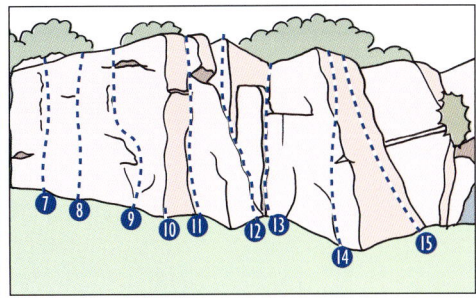

Park Bank Crags

O.S. Ref. SK085429 Altitude: 145m a.s.l.

This fine crag was once one of the major crags in the area. Now, as it is within the grounds of the famous amusement park, multiple layers of barbed wire, surveillance cameras, machine-gun nests, minefields and the Alton Towers Republican Army mean that you are very unlikely to ever access this crag. As access is so unlikeley scant details are given here. For full descriptions, see www.thebmc.co.uk/guides. To approach, follow the Ina's Rock directions. Go through the kissing gate, as for those directions, and along the fence to where the Ina's path strikes up and right. At this point go directly up the hill along the fence. There was traditionally a hole in the fence which allowed access. This is no longer true. The crags lie along the walkway which leads to Ina's Rock. Pass the main crags along the walkway. 100m beyond the left-hand buttress is a smaller buttress contains: **Tre Cime** (VS 4b, 1971), **Per Rectum** (VS 4b, 1971), **Extractum** (HVS 5b, 1971), **Mark** (S, 1971), **Stark** (VD, 1971), **Stephen** (VS 4a, 1971), **Dark Star** (E3 5c, 1975). Back on the main rock The Overhang (E1 5b 1976) is the overhang on the left end of the crag.

1 Time Flies By E4 5c   1986

2 Patient Weaver E6 6a ★★   1978

3 The Humble Potter E5 6a ★★   1989

4 Miss Understood E6 6a ★★   1989

5 Brad's Chimney S ★★   pre-1951

6 Open All Hours E4 6a   1989

The buttress to the right of this provides **Honest John** (E1 5a, 1971), Fifty metres right is **Four Horsemen** (E2 5c, 1977), **Uchimata** (D) and **Blunder** (D, 1959–63).

7 Grounded E5 6b ★★   1989

8 No Future E6 6b ★   1988

9 Anthem for a Doomed Youth E4 5c   1975

10 You'll Always Reap What You Sow
    E5 6a ★   1988

11 The Renaissance VS 4c ★★   1970

12 Left Twin Crack S 3c   1959–63

13 Right Twin Crack S 4a ★   1959–63

14 Chilton's Superdirect VS 4b   1959–63

15 Defiance VS 4a ★★   1959–63

16 Fast and Bulbous E2 5b   1984

Besides these routes the crag also contains: **The Height Below** (E1 5c, 1977), 12a **Alien Wall** (HVS 5b, 1970), 12b **Aliens** (E3 6b, 1988), 15a **Hopeless Holly** (E1 5c, 1977), 15b **Hollybush Hell** (S, 1959-63). 50m right, the first buttress contains **Coelred's Crack** (HVS 5c, pre-1951), which is the obvious crack through a roof.

Careful! The Churnet will do this to you. Mark Sharratt having to dig deep on Inaccessible, E5 6a (opposite page). In recent years this has been acknowledged as one of the best hard wall climbs in the Churnet with mad but well protected climbing on bunters and bubbles. Photo: David Simmonite.

Ina's Rock

O.S. Ref. SK082628   Altitude: 145m a.s.l.

One of the great crags of the Churnet. Interesting rock, varied routes and stars across the grades. The newly-added desperates join a host of 70's classics to bring this crag truly into the modern limelight. What a great place.

Conditions & aspect
The crag faces south-west getting sun in the afternoon and evening, is very sheltered and dries very quickly. It is great for year-round climbing, although nettles can be a problem in summer.

Routes and bouldering
The climbs are on tall vertical walls, giving bold faces and arêtes, and some steep, stiff cracks. Routes of all grades are on offer, but a good Extreme leader will find more here than the lower grade climber.

Parking & approach
See map on previous pages. Park just across the north side of the River Churnet and follow the railway track for 1km until a kissing gate is located on the left-hand side of the track, 100m after a metal bridge. Go through this to be confronted with the huge fence protecting Alton Towers from the outside world. Turn right and follow a track for 100m. By a brown metal box, angle upwards on a path. This meets the walkway (leading leftwards to Park Banks Crags) on the level above. Follow this rightwards for 150m to the rock: 25 minutes.

The first routes are quite minor and overgrown. They are **Rawhide** (S, 1970), a chimney near the left, **Gladiator** (VS 4b, 1970), a crack to the right, **Donor** (S, 1971), a scoop and corner to the right, and **Amazing Grace** (VS 4c, 1971), a chimney right again. However, the next batch of routes are probably the best pitches worth carrying a rope for in the Lower Churnet Valley.

1 Ina's Chimney   S 4a ★   pre-1951
18m A confident line providing a deep journey into the bowels of the earth, in the recess left of the strange pillar.

2 Little Maia   E5 6a   2007
15m Start just right of the strange pillar up the rib and into the crack. Place some runners here and head out right up the pockety wall to reach the break near to the arête.

3 Cornelius   E8 6c ★ ★ ★   2008
8m Hard and very high bouldering, with a truncated tree trunk positioned below to potentially punish plummeting aspirants. From beneath the stepped roof climb up and rightwards, avoiding the steepest rock, until it is possible to move left to a resting hold on the lip. Make a big move up to the faint ripple above and shuffle leftward to join the arête then gain the ledge. Now well established as a super-highball V9. *See photo overleaf.*

4 Thumbelina   E6 6b ★ ★ ★   2007
8m Safe but scary. Make steep moves on the lower section of wall, then frightening long stretches on flat edges to gain the ledge and a scary mantel. A pre-dangled rope or a slither down Atlas awaits. Opinions vary on the grade, thought by some to be highball V6, due to the nature of the climbing and flat landing. Either way it remains superb.

A link-up of the hard start of Cornelius into the big stretches of the upper section of Thumbelina has been climbed – **Cornelina** (E7 6c, 2009).

5 Inaccessible   E5 6a ★ ★ ★   1990s
20m Brilliant rock and good gear make this a classic of the cliff. Climb Atlas to the half-height break. Move left and with bomber nuts, pull through the bulge at a short crack to a knobbly break (smallish cams). Continue directly up the wall via breaks and numerous knobbles, to the final bulge (it may be worth cleaning leaves from the top-out jug first): *see photo opposite.*

6 Atlas   E2 5c ★ ★   1970
15m A good chunky classic, although this crack is a more helpful size. In the centre of the crag is an amphitheatre, centred by a deep cave. Exit the cave (awkward) and follow the crack. The bulge from the mid-height ledge provides a fabulous crux. **Big Mike and the Deadlift of Doom** (E3 6a, 1990s) is an alternative start up the hanging rib left of the cave

Yikes! Ben Bransby making the crux stretch on the recent Churnet super route, Cornelius (page 327). This, along with Thumbelina next door, was the subject of much debate over whether these were routes or boulder problems. If you don't mind fifteen foot falls with your back onto a tree stump, V9 is appropriate. Otherwise the original grade of E8 might be closer to the mark. Photo: Adam Long.

The Lower Churnet Ina's Rock

7 Jacquimo V8 (6c)
A problem that comes out of the right hand side of the cave. Start on the obvious letterbox slot (feet on the rock not the stones) and make long moves to the lip. Contort left and launch upwards to the break. Starting at the lip is about V6.

8 Inasense V6 (6b)
Just left of the start of Ground Support take unhelpful limestone-like holds and hump your way through the bulge to the ledge.

9 Ground Support E1 5b ★★   1970
15m Another excellent pitch. Follow the thin crack just right of the cave. The wide crack above gives fine climbing and positions.

10 Whispering Myth E3 6a   1979
20m From 3m up Ground Support, traverse right to reach a vague leftwards line. This gives initial hard and quite scary moves to reach a bolt from where moves right gain a ledge (possible stance). Finish up the thin crack to the left of a wider crack on the right (Tactical Weapon).

11 Lethal Weapon E5 6a ★   1989
15m Fine, technical and bold. From the plaque below the arête to the right, climb the perfectly formed arête and tiny right-facing groove to a rounded ledge. Escape here or tackle the face above moving leftwards to finish up the upper arête.

12 Tactical Weapon E1 5b ★   1970
15m Climb the crack and rugosities to the right pleasantly to the ledge. Finish via the crack above.

13 Ina City Riot E4 6b ★   1990
9m Superb bold moves on the right-hand side of the arête to the right: highball V5.

14 Inaquality V5 (6b)
The vague rib right of Ina City Riot is climbed by a little pop above a growing drop

The dirty groove around the corner gives **Initiation Groove** (VS 4b, 1970). A girdle traverse of the crag has been done from left to right taking stances as and when required – **Crud on the Tracks** (E1 5b, 1978). Forty-five metres to the right an isolated buttress gives: **Bloody Crack** (VS 4b, 1970). The lower crack to the ledge – escape right to avoid the upper crack (unclimbed).

Wootton Lodge Crags

O.S. Ref. SK095435 Altitude: 125m a.s.l.

These crags, which consist of two main buttresses, lie overlooking the JCB test track on a wooded hillside 2 miles along the lane running from Farley to Ellastone. The old Wootton Lodge gates, which the crags lie beyond, have now become overgrown. They are invisible. Security guards patrol the site and you will be turned away.

Conditions & aspect
Good, pebbly rock, steep, and while some of it is crumbly, the majority of it is very good.

Routes & bouldering
The crag consists of two separate main buttresses that offer a host of excellent bouldering, more so than the routes that are described. For the most part both buttresses are undercut and the rock solid.

Parking & approach
Follow the road from Farley, running behind Alton Towers, past the Towers itself and down into a hollow. Continue along this road until the gates can just be made out on the right-hand side of the road. Locate a public footpath sign, park near it and follow the track through the gates. The cliffs will be seen on the left 150m along this track.

Access
The land hereabouts is owned by JCB and climbing over recent years has become actively discouraged. The left-hand crag is covered in 'No Climbing' signs and is overgrown.

Left-Hand Buttress

On the far left is a smaller buttress that gives minor fare. On the main buttress:

1 Ungodly Groove E1 5b   1970
9m The hanging groove on the left-hand side of the first buttress. Strenuous.

2 Central Route VS 4c   1970
12m The steep wall just to the right leads rightwards to a ledge. Move right to a crack and finish up this. Worthwhile.

3 Pull John E5 6a   1971
15m The nasty crumbling arête to the right gains a ledge on the right. Continue up the wall 5m right of the overhanging upper arête, gradually moving left towards the top.

4 Quasimodo E2 6a   1971
12m The desperate crack on the right. Finish up the crack above the ledge.

5 Cripple's Corner VS 4c   1971
11m Start at the far right-hand side of the buttress. Traverse leftwards across the wall to reach a ledge. Finish via the crack on the right.

6 Wootton Wanderer HVS 5a   1971
25m Starting from the left-hand side of the crag, traverse right to the large ledge on the arête. From the left end of this, continue diagonally rightwards to the finish of Quasimodo.

Right-Hand Buttress

Just 100m up and right, this is a clean and excellent looking crag but is in a landscape garden. You takes your own chances here.

7 The Long Traverse VD ★★   1970
34m As fine a pitch at the grade in the Lower Churnet. Starting from the left-hand side of the crag, traverse right at a height of 6m.

To the right is an obvious hanging crack.

8 A Phoenix Too Frequent E3 6a ★   1975
12m From just left of the crack, make a fingery traverse leftwards from where the easier upper wall can be gained. The line immediately left of this is **Premature Evacuation** (E2 5b, 1990s).

9 Hanging Crack HVS 5b ★   1971
9m Good strenuous climbing via the obvious crack.

To the right, walls get shorter, allowing a handful of superb problems in the V3–V6 range.

How Big are Your Pebbles?
The Essential Churnet Ticklist

Footpath Chimney   Qui Vivre
The Arête, Garston
Crusty   The Clown
The Bishop's Move   ### Overlord
Ina's Chimney
South-East Crack   *Defiance*

Cave Crack
Orange Crush   ### High Speed Imp Act
The Joker
Kneewrecker Chimney   **The Renaissance**
Helix
Special K   *All Day and All of the Night*

Kalcidoscope
Toast Rack   **DNA**
Ripples   ### Wright's Traverse
Ground Support   *Face*
Inaccessible
Alternative Start   ## Sole Survivor
Friar Muck
Sauron   **The Pride**
Brad's Chimney   ## Thumbelina
Don Quixote
Ousal High Traverse   **Knossos**
Top Brick   **One Chromsome's Missing**
Jill the Traverse   # Cornelius

Staffordshire Grit

The Churnet First Ascents

pre-1951	**Ina's Chimney, Brad's Chimney, Coelred's Crack, Chockstone Crack, Himac, One Dunne, Dead Tree Slab, Dead Tree Crack** Unknown *Himac was climbed free as Supermac by Gary Gibson on April 6th 1988.*
1951 Spring	**Original Route** Dave Penlington, Michael Harby
1951 Aug	**Cave Crack, Magenta Corner, Flake Crack, Devil's Crack** Dave Penlington, P Gardener, M Moore
1952 Spring	**Hatschek's Groove** John Fisher
1952 Spring	**Glyph** Ernie Marshall
1952 Spring	**Via Trita** Martin Ridges
1952 Spring	**Introduction, Rugosity, Footpath, Saunter, Wave, Ripple, Crest, Backwash, As You Like It, Emerald Groove, Breaks, Flake Wall, Emerald Wall, Corner Traverse, Moore's Crack, Rotandas, Oak Spur, Moss Rose, Frequency, Vereker's Venture, The Cave Crack, Palpitation, Shelf Route, Tiptoe, Diagonal Crack, The Clam, Limpet** Oread Mountaineering Club members
1952 Jun	**The Arête, Hole and Corner Crack, Feet of Strength, Skull Crack, The Chute, The Bishop's Move, Larva Wall, Left Arête, Cave Wall, Rainbow Recess, Triack** Alan Simpson, Martin Ridges
1952	**The South-East Crack, The South-West Crack, The North Face, The Helix, Titan's Wall, The Web, Fandango** Dave Penlington
1962 June	**Deadwood Crack, Deadwood Groove, Cave Rib, Cave Crack, The Flake Traverse** Midland Association of Mountaineers
1962 Autumn	**Twisting Crack, Hassell's Crack, Wigglette, Sale's Bulge, Kneewrecker Chimney** Combination of Bob Hassall, Dave Sales, Graham Martin, John Wilding
1959–63	**Hollybush Hell, Defiance, Chilton's Superdirect, Left Twin Crack, Right Twin Crack, Central Crack, Tunnel Chimney, Blunder** David Hudson and some members from Denstone College Climbing Club
1959–63	**Stonemason's Route, Sculptor's Wall, Back Side** unknown
pre-1970	**Pine Tree Wall, Footpath Climb, Solo Chimney, Pegger's Original** D Hewitt
1970 Jan	**Sauron, The Hob, Tiger's Wall, Ugly Puss** John Yates, Barry Marsden, various leads
1970	**The Gallows, Pasihpae, Daedalus, Theseus, Minotaur, Labyrinth, Long Traverse, Central Route, Tactical Weapon (1 pt.), Initiation Groove, Ground Support, Rawhide, Bloody Crack, The Renaissance, Ungodly Groove, Gladiator, Atlas (1 pt.)** John Yates, Norman Hoskins, Austin Plant, Bob Hassell, various leads *The Gallows was finished via the castle walls. Tactical Weapon climbed free by Andrew and Jonny Woodward in October 1975. Atlas climbed free by Jonny and Andrew Woodward in September 1977. Only a partial ascent of Ungodly Groove was made, a complete ascent coming from John Yates in 1971.*
1970	**Alien Wall, The Overhang, Minos** North Staffordshire Mountaineering Club
1970 Spring	**The Nose, The Cheek, Ostentation, The Impending Doom (2 pts)** Austin Plant *Impending Doom climbed free in 1970 by John Yates.*
1970 June	**The Constant Grumble** Norman Hoskins
1970 June	**Manifesto** Bob Hassall, Ralph Fawcett
pre-1971	**Miller's Melody, Spearhead** unknown
1971	**Mark, Stephen, The Brothers, Transit Crack, Stark, Zeus (1 pt.)** Norman Hoskins *Zeus climbed free by Andrew and Jonny Woodward in July 1978.*
1971 Feb	**The Prodigal, Per Rectum, The Graduate** Dave Salt
1971	**Extractum, Tre Cime, Honest John, Peakstone Crack, Stumblehead, Plebble, Afrodizzy Crack, Scoop Wall, Right Wall, Scout Wall, B.J.M., Cripples Corner, Pull John, Gentleman John (1 pt.)** John Yates, Barry Marsden, various leads *Gentleman John climbed free by Jonny and Andrew Woodward in 1978.*
1971 Apr	**Donor, Amazing Grace, The Missus, Full Frontal** Bob Hassall, Dave Salt *A new finish added to The Missus in 1978 by Steve Dale.*

The Churnet Valley First Ascents

1971	**Quasimodo (some aid used)** John Yates, Barry Marsden Climbed free by Andrew and Jonny Woodward in 1973.
1971	**Wootton Wanderer, Hanging Crack (I pt.)** Pete Ruddle, Barry Marsden, Chris Cartlidge Hanging Crack climbed free by Andrew Woodward in 1975. **Rig a Dig Dig (4 pts.)** Pete Ruddle, Dave Salt, Norman Hoskins Climbed free by Jonny Woodward in 1975.
1971 May	**The Clown (I pt.), The Joker (I pt.)** Norman Hoskins Both climbed free by Jonny Woodward in 1975.
1971	**Nosey Parker** Ralph Fawcett, Barry Marsden, Pete Harrop, Jeff Wincott
1972 Mar	**Rocking Stone Crack, Magnificat, Evensong, Psalm, Descant** Bob Hassall
1973	**Special K, Kaleidoscope** John Yates (solo)
1974	**Death Wish** Barry Marsden
1975	**Dark Star, Anthem for Doomed Youth, A Phoenix too Frequent, Much Ado About Nothing** Jonny Woodward, unseconded, or with Andrew Woodward
1976	**Pebble Drop** Unknown
1977 Sep 17	**The Height Below, Four Horsemen** Andrew Woodward, Jonny Woodward, various leads
1977	**Grumbling Wall, Indecent Exposure** Steve and Brian Dale
1977 Aug	**DNA** Steve Bancroft, Nicky Stokes
1978	**Dancing Bear, Impacted Bowl, Northern Lights, Peeping Tom** Steve Dale, Brian Dale, Barry Marsden, various leads
1978	**Crud on the Tracks, Tequila Sunrise** Ewan Murray, Sharon Tonks
1978 Oct	**Jack the Traverse, To Live Again, Down to the Elbows, Pull Jonny, Patient Weaver** Jonny Woodward, Andrew Woodward.
1978	**Runaway** Mike Hernon
1978	**Technocrat, Don Quixote, Tricky Woo, The Gateless Gate, Ivanhoe, Taming of the Shrew, Tour de Force, Qui Vive, Nom de Guerre, Battle Royal, Melancholy Man** John Codling (solo)
1978	**Pillow of Winds, One Knight Stand, All the King's Horses, The Stadium, Megalomania, Alternative Ulster** Gary Gibson (solo)
1979	**Rhody Crack, Lord's Chimney, Reverse Charge, Tope Brick, Slippery Caramel, Toast Rack, Lord's Arête (I pt.), Working Hunter, Rabbit Stew, Bright Eyes, Recess Corner, Glossy Finish, Undercoat, Grott, Roof Slab, Drop Leaf, Desert Rat, White Mouse, Dust Storm, Sandbagger, Canticle, Dance of the Flies, Austin's Chimney, Rakes Dale Chimney, Crusty, Lone Wall, Even Lonelier, Thum, Maloof, Bubble, Squeak** Steve Dale, Brian Dale, various leads Lord's Arête freed by Ian Barker in 1986. Dance of the Flies was top-roped first and named after a cloud of midges that accompanied the ascent. Some of the routes may have been climbed before.
1979	**Moto Perpetuo, Whispering Myth, Five Thousand Volts, Dimetrodon, Time's Arrow, Sauroff, Thorns, Alternative Three, Doina Da J'al, Robin Hood, Friar Muck, Hand Jive** Jonny Woodward, Andrew Woodward
1979	**Killjoy, Kudos, Knossos, Kobold, Krakatoa, The Jester, Life in the Wrong Lane** Gary Gibson, solo, or with a combination of John Perry, Kons Nowak, Mark 'Ralph' Hewitt Knossos was top-roped three times before a lead was made after an on-sight failure resulted in a frightening fall. Kons Nowak was a local lad who was led to believe that climbing was fun and was lured from college to hold the ropes. He soon changed his mind to find that music and alcohol was more fun!
1970s	**Black Widow, Palsy Wall, The Sting** Martin Boysen Palsey Wall soloed by Tony Barley, May 9, 1974, which may have been the first ascent.
1980 May	**Cave Crack, Long Lankin, Little Nikki** Steve Dale, Brian Dale
1980 May	**Konsolation Prize, Krushna, Kenyatta** Gary Gibson, solo, or with Dave Williams
1982	**Crimes of Passion** Paul Pepperday
1983 Mar	**Longstop** Steve Dale, Barry Marsden Longstop led originally with a peg for aid but climbed free by the same pair on the same day.
1983	**Mental Traveller** Paddy Gaunt
1984 May 16	**Boats for Hire** Nick Dixon, Steve Lowe
1984 May 22	**One Chromosome's Missing** Nick Dixon, Andy Popp A major addition. An impressive show of boldness on these esoteric outcrops, one of the country's first E7s. The route was flashed by Ben Tetler in 1999, having been there while friends top-roped it, although…. "Ben was there when we were

Staffordshire Grit

on it, but I don't recall him paying much attention." Surprisingly, Tetler also decided to solo it, despite the fact that protection is fairly hopeful. In the afternoon, he made the 2nd ascent of Pair O' Genes.

1984 Dec 16 **Fast and Bulbous** Brian Davison, Richard Jones, Neil Horn

1986 Jul 27 **Time Flies By** Brian Davison, Richard Jones

1986 **The Fatalist's Canoe, Face** Nick Dixon The Fatalist's Canoe climbed on-sight after many attempts in the rain.

1986 **Life in the Left Lane** Ian Dunne

1987 Apr 20 **The Brazilian** Simon Alsop (solo)

1988 Feb 15 **Hopeless Holly, Aliens, You'll Always Reap What You Sow, No Future** Gary Gibson (solo)

1988 Apr 6 **Supermac, All Day and All of the Night** Gary Gibson Supermac was a free ascent of Himac.

1988 Apr 23 **Fingers in Every Pie** Simon Nadin

1988 Apr **The Leading Fireman** John Perry, Simon Nadin

1988 Jul 21 **The Pride** Martin Boysen, Alan Hubbard Soloed ground-up by Nic Sellers in 2007 and Ryan Pasquill in 2008

1988 Sep 10 **Puppet Life** Jim Nicholls, Roger Nicholls

1988 Oct **Monk's Blues, The High Priest** Rab Carrington, Martin Boysen

1989 Apr 22 **Distant Runners** Simon Alsop, Tim Twentymen, Dave Whittles Two peg runners were used on the first ascent (names Distant Summers). The route was reclimbed without these by Jim and Roger Nicholls on 2nd August 1989. and the route renamed..

1989 **Legoland, Grounded, Lethal Weapon, Open All Hours, Miss Understood** Gary Gibson, alone or with Hazel Gibson

1989 **General Accident, Chiropodist's Nightmare, No Pegs Please, We're British, Flake Escape** Roger Nicholls, Jim Nicholls, various leads

1989 Spring **In Days of Hold, The Humble Potter** Andy Popp

1990 **Pocket Hercules, Ripples, Cherry Rare, Never, Never, Suckin' Pebbles, Motorbike** Gary Gibson, either solo, or with Hazel Gibson

1990 Apr 4 **Ina City Riot** Andy Popp (solo)

1990 Apr 22 **The Molegrip Kid, Restless Natives** Simon Alsop, Brian Edmonds, Rob Hilditch

1990 **Kangerman, Cad Cam Warrior, Ex-Lion Tamer, Here Be Dragons** Roger Nicholls, Jim Nicholls, various leads A home-made cam provided half-height protection on Cad Cam Warrior.

1990 Apr 29 **Rock Around the Chock** Mark Haselgrove

1990 May 1 **The Clumsy Too** Simon Bartram (solo)

1990 Jul 10 **My Mother is a Rhinoceros** Colin Cheetham (solo)

1990 May 31 **Old King Cole** Andy Popp, on sight

1990 Jul 22 **Henry Hothead ...** Simon Alsop

1990 Oct 7 **EMS** Mike Grinder, Lee Swinson, John Emery

1991 Sep/Oct **Legosaurus Rex, Duplo Magic, The Plastics Factory, Stickle Brick Wall, Raiders of the Lost Bark, Castles of Sand** Gary Gibson (solo)

1991 Sep 9 **No Veranda** Roger Nicholls (solo)

1992 Sep 13 **Overlord** John Yates, Martin Boysen

1992 **Simple Simon** Andy Brown, Kelvin Grice, Lucy Ellis

1994 Sep **Unnamed (Wootton Lodge)** Justin Critchlow

1999 **Pair O' Genes** Sam Whittaker Second ascent by Ben Tetler, 1999. See One Chromosome first ascent note.

1990s **Moov Over, Pull the Udder One, Black and White, Curd be Cheese, Inaccessible, My Arse** Simon Nadin

1990s **John's Route** John Perry, Simon Nadin

1990s **Big Mike and the Dead Lift of Doom, Shepherd's Delight** Julian Lines

1990s **The Boyson-Carrington Route** Martin Boysen, Rab Carrington

1990s **Premature Evacuation** Justin Critchlow, Julian Lines

2002 **Travelling Light, Travelling Bag, Rocket to 'em, Prowler, Death Mask, Your Own Undoing, Sole Survivor** Gary Gibson

2003 **The Tantrum** Stuart Brooks

2007 **Little Maia** Rob Mirfin

2007 May 12 **Thumbelina** Andi Turner Climbed ground-up by Adam Long and Keith Bradbury in 2008, and others since.

2007 Aug 22 **The Warp** Andi Turner

The Churnet Valley Dimmings Dale

2008 Aug	**Cornelius**	Rob Mirfin	Climbed ground-up by Keith Bradbury and Ben Bransby in 2008/09
2009	**Cornelina**	Peter Whittaker	
2009	**Pie Hard**	Rob Mirfin	

The Churnet Bouldering First Ascents

Albatross Rob Mirfin, 2007
Allen's Fingers Allen Williams, 1986
Bhodi Mick Adams
Billy Bunter, Sid the Sexist Roger & Jim Nicholls, 1989
Bizarre Stuart Brooks, 2001
Blu-Tac, Bowcock's Chimney, Cabana, Charlie Farley, Doubloon, Golden Sovereign, Hot Dog, Hush Puppy, Marsden's Eliminate, Meninges, Mr Grogan, Peep Show, Pieces of Eight, Puffed Wheat, Raven, Spirella, Stickfast, Underhung Chimney Combination of Steve Dale, Brian Dale, Barry Marsden, John Yates,1973
Bond It Jonny Woodward, 1981
Breathe Stuart Brooks, 2003
Calyx Rob Mirfin, 2007
Cannabis Arm Ian Dunn, 1986
Cloverfield Rob Mirfin, 2009
Davros Rob Mirfin, 2007
Duck-Billed Platypus Stuart Brooks, 2007
Fat Slags Gary Gibson, 2002.
Fifty Pence Problem Dave Kettle, 2006
Fingers in Every Pie Simon Nadin, 1988
Genetix, Pebblesville, Rusks and Rye Gary Gibson, 1979
Grasshopper Stuart Brooks, 2006
Heavenly Action Stuart Brooks, 1998
High Speed Imp Act Martin Veale. *Also claimed as Ungentlemanly Conduct by Gary Gibson.*
Inaquality Gus Hudgins.
Jacquimo Rob Mirfin, 2008
Johnson'sville Ian Johnson, 1979
Keith Sharp Holds Rob Mirfin, 2007
Limp Lizard Richard Cole, 2009

Lisa Lust Jim Nicholls, 1990
The Last Post Gary Gibson, 1978
Martin's Mono Problem Martin Deardon, 2005
Mindbenderjelly Rob Mirfin, 2009
Moon Jumper Dave Parkin, 2009
Motorbike Gary Gibson, 1990
Out There and Back Stuart Brooks, 2002
Pegasus Tom Churchman, 2009
Push Stuart Brooks, 1999
Roger Melly, Billy the Fish Jim & Roger Nicholls, May, 1989
Rocket Ride Stuart Brooks, 2006
Sam Tan Mick Adams, 2005
Short Ride Jonny Woodward, 1979
Simple Simon Andy Brown, Kelvin Grice, Lucy Ellis, Oct. 6, 1992
Spooky Arête Stuart Brooks, 2006
Strenuosity, Pocket Wall Steve Dale, Brian Dale, 1979
Tyler Mick Adams, 2005
Warchild Mick Adams, 2005
The Whirling Pit Simon Alsop, 1991
White Widow Justin Critchlow, 2001
Wright's Giza Rob Mirfin, 2000
Wright's Unconquerable Rob Mirfin, 2007

5 Outlying Crags

including **Windgather**, **Castle Naze**, **Oldgate Nick, Bosley Cloud, Knypersley Area, Heighley Castle** and more besides

In an effort to do something new, Alf Bridge set out straight from work one Saturday lunchtime [in 1927]. His plan was to make a climbing and walking excursion of the Peak...

...It was 6.30 p.m. before he arrived at Castle Naze and could gaze down at the promised land of Chinley. The A.P. Chimney seemed much harder than usual, and blistered heels forced a gingerly tread across The Scoop. For the final climb of the weekend he had planned to do Castle Naze Crack, but realised that in his worn out condition it was beyond him, so instead he struggled wearily up the safe but clinging cleft of Deep Chimney.

From *High Peak*, by Eric Byne

Catherine Pettener bombing up the final jugs on the glorious North Buttress Arête Indirect, S (page 342).
Photo: Martin Kocsis.

Windgather

by Martin Kocsis

O.S. Ref. SJ997783 Altitude: 400m a.s.l.

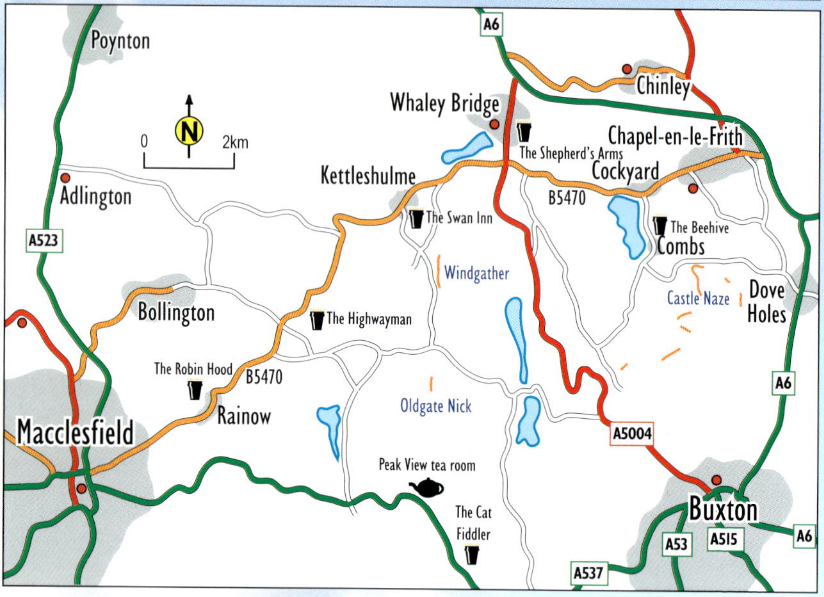

Outlying Crags Windgather

This is a beginners' crag *par excellence*, where the number of good quality, low-grade climbs on steep, juggy rock is unmatched throughout the Peak District. The crag, which sits on the Shining Tor ridge, commands an excellent view over much of the Goyt Valley. Great for soloing too.

Conditions & aspect

The name tells you pretty much all you need to know about the weather conditions around here! The rock is very clean and sound, and is quick drying. Being west-facing, it gets the sun from the afternoon, and is a suitable venue for year-round climbing.

The climbing

Superb. Seventy routes, mainly from Diff to VS. The crag is friendly, and the holds are juggy where it matters. In fact, it probably has some of the steepest easy routes anywhere! As an inevitable result of its great character, Windgather nearly always has a team or two on it, and this has contributed to the smooth nature of some of the holds. Stoney Middleton though, this isn't, and there's very little reason why a foot should slip, other than as a result of the usual 'Elvis' impersonation at moments of extreme stress!

Parking & approach

See map opposite. Tractors and other agricultural car-wreckers use the lane beneath the crag, so you're advised to park well into the lay-by. There's space for a dozen cars, eight minibuses, or three coaches (not a pretty sight). Approach only via the two stiles and the fenced-in alley. See access note.

Access

After opposition to climbers using the crag from a previous owner, the crag is now owned by the Peak Park Planning Board, and must ONLY be approached via the two stiles and the fenced alley. Climbers have access to the area within the fences above and below the crag, and they are asked not to damage them or the walls which limit the access area at either end of the crag. The lower fence, denoting the boundary, runs south under the crag towards the quarry to meet one of these transverse walls. **Please do not climb over this fence.** There is a stone stile giving access to the quarry hidden a little higher up the slope. The base of the crag is owned by the PDNPA whilst the top is owned by United Utilities. In practice this brings no problems as both are pro-access.

Advice for groups.

This crag is very popular for group use as well as for individuals climbing and bouldering. In recent years the practice of reserving routes by leaving ropes in place has become too prevalent. Please do not use this 'towel on the sunbed' practice and be accommodating to all users.

Staffordshire Grit

Left-Hand Rocks

Lots of bouldering can be had along the first low rocks. These little buttresses are almost the same size as some of the crags they climb on in North Yorkshire! The problems start far to the left, where the path that skirts the base of the crag bends up, through a pair of old gateposts and onto the top of the crag. This is about 20m right of the boundary dry stone wall.

The first few problems to the right of the gateposts are obvious. They take a variety of slabs, ribs and cracks in the lower grades starting with a buttress with a projecting 'gun' at its top. The gun itself is split by a crack: this is an excellent but exposed 5a, whilst the face to the right is about 5b. To the right is an easy crack at VD, then a narrow, bulging buttress. The direct is a steep 4c. Just right again is a low cave. Climbing out of its left side and up the face above apparently involves a dyno and comes in at about 5a. All these V0. Direct through the lip is 5c (V1), and up and out of the right-hand side is 5a. Just right of this buttress is a short crack through a low roof: **Pure Crackling**, is a frustrating 5b (V1) that sticks purely to the crack and which will, most likely, spit you out several times!

Further right is a quarry. The north-facing wall is fingery, steep and green. The left and right lines are 4c, whilst the central one is V0 (5b). Not far right are some small undercut slabs, with jamming cracks in the middle. The right-hand slab is 4c and the left-hand one is 5a. Forty metres right there is a steep face with a niche near the top. The right-hand side of the face is a fingery 4c. Direct to the niche is 5b, the jinking crack to the left is 4b and the scooped face left again is a tricky 5c. All V0–V1. Other, harder eliminates up to 6a are possible.

The first routes start from two small grassy bays almost opposite a dry stone wall running up to the road on its other side. To the left, there is a concave wall above the first grassy bay. Climb the shallow angle at its centre, moving left at the bulge. **Bay Wall** (S 4a★). Worthwhile. **Christmas Nose** (VS 5a) goes up the staircase on the left, then moves gymnastically over the nose. **Red Nose Route** (D) climbs the corner on the left. Best done in the wet (and at night) for full satisfaction. **Christmas Arête** (HVD★) climbs a short wall on the right-hand side of the second grassy bay to a ledge, then the sharp arête on satisfying holds. The traverse across the short wall, using the obvious sloping shelf is a short but hard 5c (V2). Down and right of this bay is a small bulging buttress. A fun V0– (5a) problem tackles the most bulging line. Further fillers-in lie in the next 10m.

Christopher Hughes on Heather Buttress, VD (page 342). Photo: Martin Kocsis.

Staffordshire Grit

North Buttress

The first major buttress lies 40m right of Christmas Arête, and 100m left of the access point to the crag.

1 The Rib VS 5a
9m A hard step off a block leads directly up the centre on small crimps. Tricky to protect. Use of the arêtes makes it 4c.

2 The Rib Right-Hand S 4a
9m Start at the same point as The Rib, but climb up and right to a small flake. Use this to gain the side face of the buttress, and climb it until you can step round onto the front face about ten feet below the top.

3 Staircase M ★
9m A fine beginner's lead with both good moves and good protection.

4 Green Slab S ★
9m Start just to the left of the wide flake-crack (or cheat up the crack). Make an awkward but well-protected move off the flake and go up the wall above.

5 Black Slab S ★
9m A tricky start leads to more steep climbing. Cross the bulge, then go up a flake to finish 1m left of Green Crack.

6 Green Crack S 4a ★★
9m A thrilling lead, with great three dimensional climbing on steep rock. Follow the steep groove to the wide, leaning upper crack.

7 North Buttress Arête VS 4c ★★
9m A steep and bold climb, but with great holds. Surmount the undercut left side of the arête (rumoured to be 5a), then continue up the left-hand side of the arête. A Windgather classic.

8 North Buttress Arête Indirect S 4a ★
9m Follow the arête on its right side, pulling round left onto the front face near the top. Exposed: *see photo on page 336*.

9 Chimney and Crack HVD
9m Climb to the ledge and move up leftwards into the chimney, to finish with some difficulty up the wide crack on the left.

10 Heather Buttress VD ★
8m This route lies 15m right of North Buttress. Climb the arête and the wall above the overhang. Opinions about the grade vary considerably; consequently *perhaps* a soft touch at this grade: *see photo on page 340*.

Outlying Crags Windgather

Middle Buttress

This is the next blocky buttress 15m right of Heather Buttress. Tricky descents are possible on either side of it.

11 Taller Overhang VS 5b
8m This takes the double overhangs as centrally as possible. More technical than strenuous, and as hard as Portfolio but nowhere near as entertaining.

12 Small Wall S 4b

13 The Other Corner M
8m The obvious corner. Stepping out of it leftwards onto the platform gives an easy way up (or down).

14 Portfolio HVS 5b ★
8m A steep local testpiece. Avoiding the holds on Wall Climb, ascend direct to the overhang. This is surmounted via a crucial series of strenuous pulls. Be careful of the polish on the initial slab.

15 Wall Climb VD
9m Strangely named… Climb the parallel cracks (polished) to the final chimney. This is steep, deep and exciting.

16 Central Route HVD ★
9m Start below a thin crack in the crag top and climb direct to it. For **Slant Start** (VD) climb diagonally to the top crack from the start of Chockstone Chimney.

17 Chockstone Chimney D ★
9m The ragged crack gives a well-protected lead.

18 Mississippi (or Straight) Crack S 4a ★
9m The fine bottomless crack is long and sustained, and a good first Severe lead.

19 Mississippi Crack Variant VD ★★
9m Start up The Medicine and traverse left under the overlap to join the Mississippi crack above its crux. An excellent, sustained combination.

20 The Medicine HS 4a ★
9m Take the juggy bulges direct. Poorly protected and with some worryingly long reaches: testing!

21 M.B. Arête D
9m Climb up to an awkward move into a corner. This leads to the broad platform. Step left and climb the right edge of the face above.

Staffordshire Grit

High Buttress

This is the next buttress along, with its prominent brown, slightly sandy 'footprint' halfway up the face. This is the most popular buttress hereabouts.

22 Bulging Arête S 4a
9m This climb takes the small overhang on its right. Demanding on the arms and with a serious feel, until you find the hidden hold.

23 The Corner D
9m A route to consider as both an early lead and an introduction to the delights of polished holds!

24 Toe Nail VD ★
9m Go directly through the 'toes'. Protection is a little distant above the bulge.

25 Zigzag D
9m Start as for Toe Nail and climb diagonally right to a position above the nose, then finish direct. A long route on this little crag.

26 Footprint VD
9m Climb direct through the heel of the footprint.

27 Nose Direct HVD ★★
9m Start at the small recess just left of the arête, and climb direct to the nose. Pull over it, step left, and continue direct. A problematic route, but with great protection. Climbing 1m to the right gives the myopic **Director**, (VS 4c).

28 High Buttress Arête D ★★
9m Start at the foot of the arête and follow it almost direct. An excellent route at this grade, perhaps one of the best in the Peak.

29 Heather Face HVD ★
9m Similar in nature to Side Face (poor gear and rounded holds) and with an excellent (but protected) 'sting in the tail' at the overlap. **Broken Cracks** (HD), the climb just right, is better protected, but vegetated and loose.

Buttress Two

This is the nearest buttress to the road.

30 Rib and Slab M
9m Clean climbing just left of the gully.

31 Buttress Two Gully M ★
9m A very traditional climb (for your first lead!)

32 Leg Stump D
9m The easiest (but unprotected) line up the slab.

Outlying Crags Windgather

33 Middle and Leg D
9m Good climbing and protection.

34 The Centre VD
9m Fine climbing but unprotected until near the top.

35 Squashed Finger VD ★
9m Good climbing; quite stiff but well-protected.

36 Struggle HS 4b ★
9m The crack through the nose. A hard but well-protected little problem that gives 'full value' at this grade.

37 Corner Crack VD ★
9m The crack. The one in the corner.

38 Aged Crack HS 4a ★
9m Climb direct to the crack. Moving into the crack from Corner Crack makes the route VD.

39 Traditional HS 4a ★
9m Step off the block and climb directly past the blunt flake. Small cams are useful.

40 The Broken Groove in the Arête D
9m Steep and well-protected: a great first lead.

41 Cheek VS 5a
9m Start from a block below the sidewall and climb up to meet the arête at the top. Short and sharp. The protection is there for those with the cunning.

Windgather

is a very popular crag for top-roping on. However, it should be remembered that, for those new to the game, there is no finer place to learn one's leading skills.

In the text, every effort has been made to point out less well-protected routes that inexperienced leaders may wish to avoid. Also, a list of well-protected routes is given here:

- **Staircase**
- **Slant Start**
- **Chockstone Chimney**
- **Mississippi Crack**
- **The Corner**
- **High Buttress Arête**
- **Buttress Two Gully**
- **Squashed Finger**

All these routes can be well-protected with a modest beginner's rack, consisting of a set of nuts, a few larger hexes, a couple of slings and a few quickdraws. Once you are comfortable with these, then check out the suggestions for beginners on the Roaches, then the list of advanced beginner's routes at Hen Cloud and Ramshaw. After that, you will be a skilled leader ready for anything.

Staffordshire Grit

Buttress One

The next compact buttress past broken rocks.

42 Face Route 2 M
9m Follow the broken cracks.

43 Face Route 1 VD
9m Easy climbing but gearless where it matters the most. Pull over the small overhang, then climb more easily up the face.

44 First's Arête HD
9m Follow the right-hand side of the arête.

45 Side Face S
9m Climb directly up the right-hand side face on sloping holds and limited gear, keeping to the left of the holly. Poor gear and rounded holds.

The small walls within the next 30m offer many problems and possibilities. The flat, quarried face in the middle of these walls offers blinkered eliminates at about Severe.

South Buttress

Thirty five metres to the right of the entrance to the crag is a large undercut buttress with a cave at the right-hand end and a pulpit at about the same level under its left-hand end.

46 Overhanging Arête VD
9m Hard moves lead from the gully on the left of the buttress. Move rightwards to join and follow Leg Up.

47 Leg Up HVS 5a
9m From the pulpit, make a bold and strenuous pull over the nose. A strenuous problem, and easily protected, although this is not initially obvious. If you stray too far right then the problem is almost two grades harder due to a broken hold.

48 Route 2 VS 4b ★
9m From the pulpit, step right and climb the steep crack through the overhang. Quite hard considering its shortness.

49 Route 1.5 HVS 4c ★
9m A route with adequate protection, if you have the strength and cunning to place it.

50 Editor's Note VS 5a
9m Pull out and up to join and follow Route 1 on rapidly improving jugs. Small wires may help for the one and only hard move.

51 Arête Direct E1 5b ★
9m A fun climb with very good moves but effectively a solo, as the finish is much easier. Stretch from the ledge for good holds on the lip left of the arête and cut loose. If you are unsure, side-runners can be placed on the right wall from the ledge, reducing the climb to HVS 5b. Some locals will tell you that even heel hooking on the right is cheating!

52 Route 1 S 4a ★★
9m Climb part way up South Crack, and then traverse leftwards round the arête onto a ledge above the cave. Pull past blocks and continue to the top. **Variation:** The left-hand side of the arête, from the right-hand side of the ledge, is VS 4c.

Outlying Crags Windgather

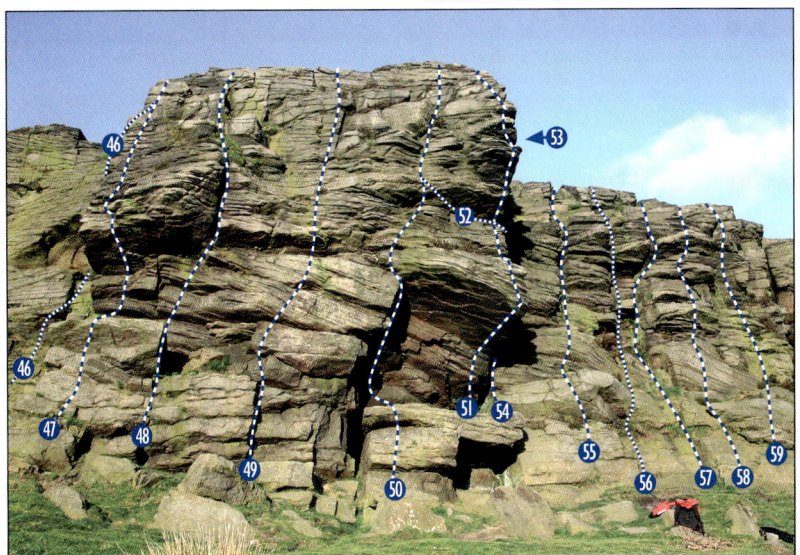

53 Route I Direct HVS 5a
9m The right-hand side of the arête, followed direct. Bold and rounded and thought by some to be the hardest climb on the crag.

54 South Crack M
9m Wide crack climbing in the corner.

55 Left Triplet Crack D
9m The leftmost of the three close-together cracks to the right of the corner. Not as easy as it looks.

56 Middle Triplet Crack HVD 4a
9m The middle of the three twins.

57 Right Triplet Crack HVD 4a
9m The left-hand crack. Ha ha, got you. It is actually the rightmost of the three cracks.

58 Overlapping Wall HS 4b
9m The small bulging buttress just to the right.

59 Discontinuous Rib and Groove M
9m Any way up the easy rock to the right.

The Quarry 100m to the right of the main crag is an excellent and sheltered venue for both amenable boulder problems and steady traverses. There are many, many variations and so nothing is described, just find out for yourself!

Oldgate Nick

by John H Bull

O.S. Ref. SJ996764　　　　　　　　　　　　　　　　　　　　　Altitude: 400m a.s.l.

This pleasant isolated buttress, also known as Cat's Tor, is visible from the road junction about half a mile south of Windgather Rocks. Approach from the junction via the path that leads along the to ridge to Cat's Tor proper and Shining Tor. The two ribs to the left are **Stilted** HVD 4a (2000) and **Jilted** HD (2000).

1 Nick Slab M ★　　　　　　　　　　traditional
10m A fun romp straight up the left side of the slab.

2 Rib and Slab HVD 4b ★　　　　　traditional
10m A great little big climb. Climb the bouldery rib on the left of the crag to gain the slab above. Meander right as low as possible, in fine position, to finish up the arête.

3 Nine Tales VS 4c　　　　　　　　　　　　2000
10m Under the left side of the main overhang is a bulging flake at 4m. Climb direct to the bulging flake, and hand-traverse it steeply leftwards to join the slab. Finish direct. A variant below is S.

4 Original Route HVD 4a ★　　　　　pre-1990
12m Climb up a rightward-leaning groove to a ledge under the roof. Traverse awkwardly rightwards to gain twin cracks, and finish up these with reverence.

5 Catapult E5 6a ★　　　　　　　　　　　2003
12m A committing traverse of the vertical tiered face under the roof. Climb to the ledge under the right-hand side of the roof, and reach from a wobbly flake to good incuts above. Follow holds leftwards under the roof until, feet on the flake of Nine Tales, it is possible to pull onto the slab.

6 Crime Gene VS 4b　　　　　　　　　　　2000
10m Climb a steep rib to gain the ledge of Original Route. Pull around the right side of the overhang just left of the twin cracks of Original Route, and steal up the stratified face directly.

7 The Cat Inside HVD　　　　　　　　　　1997
12m Start up a hole-studded groove and carefully traverse the face above the overhang to the arête.

8 Little Roof V1 (5b)
Great powerful moves over the widest part of the roof just right. To the right another juggy gem takes the smaller recessed overlap, **Twin Cracks**, V0- (4c) and two more V0- 5a problems are right again.

Hello! It's Lynn Robinson on Nick Slab, M. Photo: Steve Clark

Castle Naze

by Martin Kocsis

O.S. Ref. SJ054785 Altitude: 400m a.s.l.

Highly underrated for many years, Castle Naze has often been dismissed as a beginners' crag, perhaps next on the syllabus after Windgather. This is something of a misconception, for while it may be true that it is a beginners' crag, there are enough routes in the Extreme category to interest and baffle any competent leader.

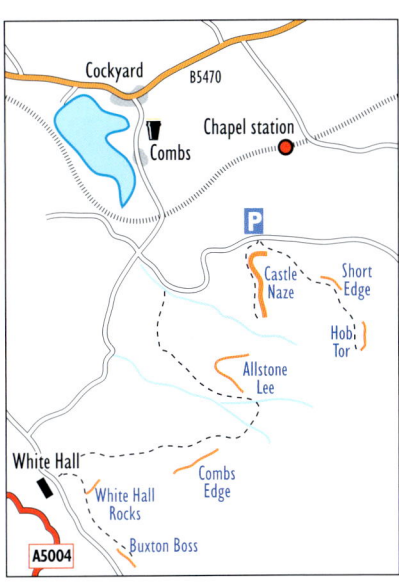

Conditions & aspect

The crag faces west, is fairly sheltered, and is consequently clean and quick drying. It is also an excellent evening venue with great views and a reasonably sheltered nature.

Routes & bouldering

Best suited to the low- and mid-grade leader. Many of the VS and HVS routes are less than easy, and have been known to cause both broken bones and damaged egos. Routes up to VS are also generally regarded as 'good value' (whatever that may mean). The quarried section at the right-hand end is home to some suspect rock above the routes, but the routes themselves have been well-cleaned and are as solid as you could expect. Belays are occasionally hard to find, though assorted metal stakes and fence posts are more than adequate in most cases. Not a great crag for bouldering, although there are a few problems.

Parking & approach

The Naze is on the moorland above the High Peak village of Combs, reached by a minor road off the B5470 between Whaley Bridge and Chapel en le Frith. From The Beehive pub in Combs (excellent for food, beer and a warm fire) follow the road towards the crag, seen above the village to the east. The road is narrow and steep in places. Once the road levels out at the top of the moor, two laybys will be obvious with spaces for about six cars. If they're full please go elsewhere, since wing mirrors are, on occasion, easily removed by passing tractors.

If you're coming from Buxton, turn left in Dove Holes ("Twinned with Siberia", according to infamous local graffiti) down Station Road, following signs to the railway station. Go over the railway bridge, and a couple of hundred metres later, turn left up Cowlow Lane. After a couple of miles, the lay-bys previously mentioned will be seen. There's an obvious, but strangely exhausting, path up to the rocks. 5 minutes.

Access

Castle Naze crags are now in Open Access land which begins part way up the hillside on approach. The path to the crags is a concession one but you have a right of way. The Coombes Moss moor at the top is owned by a shooting syndicate, so keep your head down.

Staffordshire Grit

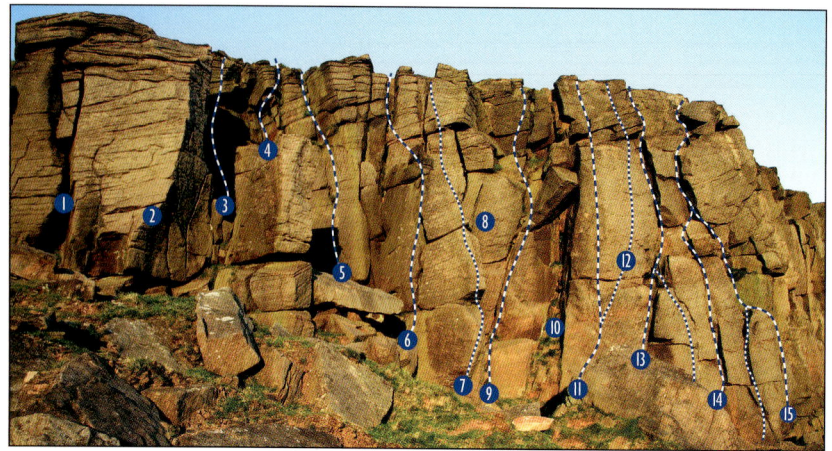

Left Hand Section

The first rocks, with lots of good little climbs packed closely in.

1 Double Crack D   pre-1913
4m Climb the crack. The face to the right, avoiding the crack and arête, is an exciting V0 (5a).

2 The Arête HS 4a   pre-1913
4m The fine slabby arête. A small cam protects the easier but still exposed finish. Climbing the arête on its right is V1 (5c).

3 Easy Corner D   trad
5m The wee corner in the left of the bay just right.

4 Easy Cracks D   trad
5m The crack system a couple of metres right.

5 Right-Hand Crack D   trad
5m Another shorty up the crack and quick groove.

Warning: The pinnacle to the right has some unattached, wobbly and very heavy blocks. Please exercise caution on the next four routes.

6 Pinnacle Crack VD   pre-1913
5m Climb the wide crack left of the arête then the easier crack above.

7 Pinnacle Arête VD   pre-1913
5m Climb the outer edge of the pinnacle to the summit. The top block is wobbly.

8 Sheltered Crack S 4a ★   pre-1913
5m This crack is behind and right of the pinnacle. Avoid use of the pinnacle for the full tick. **Bow Crack** (S, 1984) starts as for this, but breaks out rightwards to a perched block.

9 Slanting Crack S   1960s
5m Climb a crack passing to the left of the jammed triangular block then finish direct.

10 Overhanging Chockstone Crack
VD   pre-1913
6m A good traditional tweed-wrecker. Start up the gully, and somehow climb over the huge chockstone. You may also wish to do the through route for full value at a slightly easier grade.

11 The Fifth Horseman HVS 5a ★   1984
6m Take the easiest line up the left-hand side of the wall. Quite bold for its size.

12 Icebreaker E2 5b   2002
6m This takes a bold but enjoyable line up the slab right. You should head for, and use, the obvious big pebble. A small wire provides limited protection for the few short moves on the slab. Reachy.

Outlying Crags Castle Naze

13 V-Corner S 4b   pre-1913
4m Awkward thrutching or precarious layaways gain the ledge via the short corner. Take the left-hand crack above. The alternative start just right is **Thin Crack** (4c, 1960s).

14 Muscle Crack HVD   pre-1913
4m The blocky crack leads to the ledge. Climb the flake on the right.

15 Block Crack Left-Hand S 4a   1960s
6m The thick crack leads to the ledge. Take the flake above. **Bloody Crack** (S, 1960s) is the well-named alternative start up the fist-crack to the left.

16 The Nose HS 4b   1960s
12m Technical and committing bridging leads up the recess, and then into the sentry box. Go back up and right from there.

17 The Nithin S 4a   pre-1913
12m The steep right-hand crack of the recess leads strenuously to the ledge. Finish up the chimney crack.

18 Flake Crack HS 4a   pre-1913
12m Start in the corner to the right, and climb the obvious crack to the ledge on The Nithin. Layback the propped flakes to get to a leftwards finish.

19 Main Corner S 4a   1960s
12m A deeply traditional struggle.

20 The Fly Walk S 4a   pre-1913
10m The well worn crack right of Main Corner.

21 The Niche S 4a ★★   pre-1913
10m Steep jamming on good rough rock. Leave the niche via jams and the jammed block.

22 Niche Arête VS 4c ★★   pre-1913
10m Rounded, bold and satisfying. Climb the arête directly via long reaches and a pull up or two.

Staffordshire Grit

23 Orm and Cheep E1 6a ★   1989
10m The right slanting groove is climbed to a ledge (V3). Climb the wall above directly via several shallow pockets. Side-runners sometimes used.

24 Studio HS 4a ★   pre-1913
9m Climb the major crack.

25 Nursery Arête HVS 5b ★   2003
10m The hanging arête. Step off a boulder and make tricky moves to a ledge. Climb the arête above using the breaks (but not the right-hand wall). Surprisingly independent.

26 A.P. Chimney S 4a ★   pre-1913
10m A classic chimney that needs no description. The AP stands for Absolutely Perpendicular.

27 Pod Crack E1 5c ★   1984
11m The thin crack with the pod halfway up it. Criminally undergraded… if you cruise this, go straight past 'Regent Street' and on to something much harder.

28 Pilgrim's Progress HS 4b ★   pre-1935
11m Climb the crack at the right end of the wall. Use of the right arête will not be frowned upon.

Pitoned Crack (HVS 5b, 1960s) is the barely independent crack to the left. If you stick to the crack, award yourself a pat on the back, but it's very hard to keep a hand or foot out of Pilgrim's Progress.

29 Little Pillar HS 4b   pre-1913
11m Climb the crack in the right hand side of a rib. From the platform above, climb the continuation of the crack to the top.

30 Ledgeway HVS 5a   1970s
11m Climb to the ledge any way you chose, then use a flake on the back wall to reach a left slanting crack. **Short and Sweet** V3 (6a) climbs the arête to the left of the start.

31 No Name HVD 4a   pre-1948
11m Climb the awkward crack to reach the ledge. Continue directly.

32 Keep Buttress HVS 5a   1970s
11m Climb the crack in the rib to the right and then finish up the right-hand side of the rib above.

33 Keep Corner HVD ★   pre-1913
11m A good route up the corner right of Keep Buttress.

Pilgrim's Progress. HS 4b (opposite page) one of the many fine cracklines at the Naze. Photo: Mike Hutton.

Staffordshire Grit

Scoop Buttress

The next buttress is home to the 'world famous' Scoop. Originally, bare feet were considered appropriate for an ascent; these days, a blizzard of chalk and a load of sliding around on the first few moves seems more usual!

34 Keep Arête VS 4b ★   pre-1948
11m After some good steep moves, follow the arête of the buttress as closely as you can.

35 Scoop Direct HVS 5a   1970s
11m Gain the left-hand end of the scoop (as for Scoop Face), and continue directly via a thin crack.

36 Scoop Face HVS 5a ★★   1914
13m An inspirational achievement for the year it was climbed. Start 3m right of Keep Arête, and using polished holds and clean technique, climb into the scoop above. Traverse delicately up and right to a useful pocket and thin crack. Go up and left to finish.

37 Scoop Direct Start V2 (E1 5c)
Step off a little ledge 3m right of the normal start, and gain the scoop via the obvious pocket below the centre of the scoop itself. Various other 'directs' have been done, all at about 6a.

38 Scoop Wall E1 5b   1988
11m Climb directly to the right edge of the scoop. From there, take a more or less direct line to the top. You might have to turn the bulge slightly on the left.

39 Footstool Left S   pre-1913
11m The corner is a bit of a struggle.

40 Piano Stool E1 5b   1988
11m The arête to the right is a bold undertaking, not helped by pointy boulders beneath.

41 Footstool Right VD   1964
11m Another struggle up the corner on the right side of the arête.

42 Layback VD   traditional
11m The short layback flake to join the last climb.

43 Combs Climb S   traditional
11m The fingercrack.

It may no longer be the hardest route in the Peak, but it is still one of the finest VSs in the area. Ronan Browner climbing The Crack (see overleaf). Photo: Niall Grimes.

Staffordshire Grit

The Crack Area

The gully to the right is an easy scrambling way down. The next routes start on the wall to the right. The first, **The Two-Step** (VD, 1960s) is a poor route up the left side of the ridge. **Fat Man's Chimney** (M, pre-1913), is a short but entertaining problem up the first chimney. The next face contained what was, for nearly 30 years, the hardest route at the Naze.

44 Come On Eileen E2 5c   1999
9m A bouldery and committing route up the left side of the wall. Climb to the porthole, and use the arête to climb to the top.

45 Plankton E4 6a   1984
9m A serious and artificial line up the centre of the wall, finishing rightwards.

46 Assorted Pond Life HVS 5a   1997
9m Climb directly up the face just to the left of Deep Crack. Quite independent, and not all that easy.

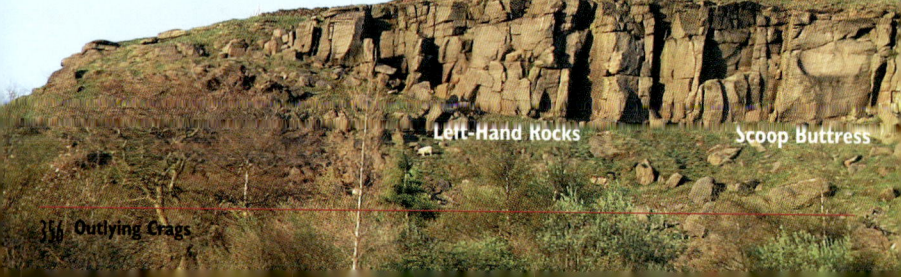

Left-Hand Rocks   Scoop Buttress

Outlying Crags Castle Naze

47 Deep Crack VD — 1984
9m Guess where this goes…

48 Deep Chimney VD — pre-1913
9m The next fissure to the right. If you cruise this without raising a sweat, head for The Beehive and a cream tea (or two).

49 Birthday Climb HVS 5b ★ — 1968
16m Follow The Crack to its sentry box. Leave this by climbing up and left to the base of a flake, then follow this to the top. Underrated.

50 The Crack VS 4b ★★ — pre-1913
14m Once one of the hardest routes in the Peak. From the sentry box, follow the alluring crack through the overhang: *see photo on page 355*.

51 Nozag VS 4c ★★★ — pre-1948
14m Testing climbing in a superb position. Climb a crack until a step left leads onto the bold face. Climb this directly using the thin crack and all your bottle.

52 Zigzag Crack HS 4b ★ — pre-1913
16m As for Nozag, but follow the crack to a wider crack and an easy finish.

53 Zig-a-Zag-a D — 1984
14m A long and easy climb. Follow a corner system and wall above.

54 Long Climb VD — pre-1913
16m Take the easiest direct line to the top.

55 Central Tower VD ★ — pre-1913
16m Better than it looks! Follow the green corner to the terrace. Move back right again and climb the left-hand groove to the top.

56 Atropine HS 4b ★ — 1977
16m A good sustained route. Right of Central Tower, is a projecting flake. Climb over this to a bay, then climb a ramp and crack near the left end of the bay to ledges. From here, take the tough flake to the right-hand finishing crack.

57 Belladonna E1 5c ★ — 1977
17m A good route, despite the strangeness of the line. Follow Atropine to the ledge and continue up the right side of the arête above, until an overlap is reached. Go right beneath this and then up to the next overlap. From here, traverse back left to the upper part of the original arête and an excellent finish. **Belladonna Direct** (E3 5c★, 1990), climbs the short section of arête avoided by Belladonna.

58 The Ugly Bloke E3 6a — 1997
16m Follow the Belladonna to the rightwards traverse and flake-crack above. Step left and move directly up the wall above, finishing via a blind pocket. Very bold, needing great care and cunning to place adequate gear.

59 The Green Crack S 4a — pre-1913
16m Take the series of corners. The top is somewhat dodgy, so take care. **The Blusher** (HVS, 1984), climbs rocks down and to the right. Always loose and utterly dangerous: try tiger baiting as a safer alternative.

Staffordshire Grit

The Quarry

The next routes are in the quarried section. The routes are quite good but the rock is a bit hollow.

60 Morocc'n Roll E1 5b ★   1986
14m A good route. After a tricky start, follow the right-slanting crack to join Syringe Benefit.

61 Syringe Benefit E1 5c   1986
14m The obvious, harder crack to the right.

62 Columbal Convenience VS 4b   1986
14m The unappealing chimney. Loose.

63 Chamonaze Blues E4 6b ★   2003
14m The first crack in the face ends its usefulness at half height. From there, hard crimping, technical moves and some very small wires may be of some use.

64 Peg Crack E1 5c ★   1960s
14m A good route up the crack in the middle of the face. The start is the hardest part of the climb.

65 Iron Age Fortitude E4 6b ★★   2003
14m The striking crack-line. Hard moves will get you to the first jam; from there only determination will see you to the top. Well-protected and extremely good value.

66 Keith George: The Movie E1 5b ★   2003
14m Climb directly to the niche at the right end of the quarried face, and then make a couple of hard pulls up and left from a scary undercut onto the face. Finish up the thin crack above. Like Keith, better than it looks.

67 Stoke the Engines E1 5b ★   2003
14m Just to the right of the previous route, climb easily into the corner. From here, step up and left onto the base of the clean slab, and boldly climb it to a steeper finish.

There are some slightly loose lines to the right. The two chimneys are both S while the crack just right is **Oversight Crack**, HVS 5b (all trad).

Herford's Girdle Traverse
HS 4b ★★   1910–1912

Seigfried Herford's ultra-historic traverse of the crag is still well worth doing, and not as easy as you might imagine. The route starts at Double Crack, and finishes, some time later at the top of Overhanging Chimney. Many variations can be done to either raise or lower the difficulty.

Right-Hand Rocks

About 15m right of this last route is a short, natural buttress. It has a fine collection of short routes, which are of very different character to the main face, on weathered, heavily-featured sound rock. One of the biggest problems of climbing here is the exposed start positions where belays are a sensible idea, especially if there is any dampness around. The rock is good, weathered moorland grit, and although the climbs are very short, they are good problems nonetheless. There is an exposed but easy grassy descent slope on its left, which requires care in wet conditions, especially given the steep slope below. The first route is **Hodgkinson's Chimney** (M, pre-1913), the easy chimney in the left wall of the buttress. **South Crack** (D, 1986) is a right slanting crack just right. **South Buttress** (D, pre-1913) climbs the steps of the buttress from a lower level, finishing up the V-groove in the headwall. **V-Chimney** (D★, pre-1913) is a quality route taking the obvious major groove containing two flakes. **Southern Arête** (HS 4a, 1986), is the right arête of V-Chimney.

Across the descent gully is an enticing, rippled buttress. **Bubbly Wall** (HVS 5a, 1970s) climbs the sidewall of the buttress, just left of the right arête. **Vanishing Crack** (HVD 4a★, pre-1913) climbs the V-shaped corner and crack above. Another good little route. **The Vice** (S 4a, pre-1948) is broken crack to the right, finishing up the cleft. **Struggle** (HS 4b, 1950s) is the final route, up the chimney and twin cracks.

Ten metres right of the last route is a small cluster of ribs and grooves. There are three short lines here that have somehow acquired route status: **Boomerang** (M) is the obvious wide crack on the left of the first rib; **Boomerang Buttress** (VS 4b) is the arête to the right with a grim landing; **Overhanging Chimney** (VD) is, well… All pre-1913.

Beyond these routes are further areas of assorted ribs, corners and arêtes. It feels so 'remote' here that it has become known as Australia Buttress! A great place to solo in the last of the evening's light. Most routes are about 4 or 5m in height. **Duck-Billed Platypus** (HS 4c) is the arête right of Overhanging Chimney climbed with blinkers. **Koala** (M) is the chimney gully to the right, which is worthwhile despite some vegetation. **Wombat** (VD) is the hanging corner crack right again. **Kangaroo** (VS 5a) is a very good micro-route up the steep prow using sidepulls on both sides to finish on jugs. **Opossum** (D) is the cracks and chimney right again. **Tasmanian Devil** (HD) is the corner right again, preferably starting up the front of the detached block below. Better than its green appearance would suggest. **Wallaby** (S 4b) is the arête right again on good holds. **Bandicoot** (M) is the broken corner right again. **Dingo** (S 4b) is the arête right again and is a little dirty. Right again, at the end of the crag is another grassy descent that requires care.

Surrounding Crags

By John H. Bull

Dotted about on the edges of the moor are several small outcrops. For those who might enjoy the walk needed to reach them, the crags provide a smattering of mostly easy climbing in unfrequented situations, with the added attractions of Combs' excellent Beehive Inn in at the end of the day.

Western Combs OS ref. SK054780: This lies 300m south along the ridge from Castle Naze. It has some great micro-routes making it well worth the visit. It is recognisable by a prominent detached pillar at the right-hand side. The left-hand buttress contains: **Eeny** (S 4b) is the face and crack on the left of the buttress; **Meeny** (HVS 5b), a direct up the front face from the rock platform; **Inbetweenie** (S 4c, trad) is the arête on its left, tricky to jugs, trend left above; good stuff. **Miny** (D) is the right arête of the buttress. On the pinnacle, **Mo** (VS 4c) is the ragged crack up the left face. **Frank's Route** (HVS 5a) is the right arête. Photogenic, although it is a bit artifical: *see photo on page 360*. All 2003. **Let it Go** (VS 4c, trad), is the crack line right of the arête.

Frank Connell on Frank's Route, HVS 5a (previous page). One of the many good reasons to venture away from the main area of Castle Naze. Photo: Niall Grimes.

Outlying Crags Castle Naze

Allstone Lee Rocks OS ref. SK051773: The rocks are reached in about 15 minutes from Castle Naze. Follow the edge of the moor south, past the deep gash of Pyegreave Brook. Just past Pyegreave Brook is a tiny outcrop (O.S. ref SK054777), set in the slope between two minor stream gullies. **Insects from Hell** (VS 5a) climbs the striking crack. Further along the edge, pass some minor north-facing outcrops with scrambling possibilities, to reach the far side of a moorland promontory. The crag comprises several south-facing buttresses that bask in any available sunshine. The first is the most substantial and is characterised by a steep arête above a flat grassy ledge. **Waggledunce** (VD) is the minor arête a few metres left of the main buttress. **Bees** (VD) climbs the crack and face 1m left of the arête past a small ledge, while the more substantial **Honeycomb** (S 4a) ascends the central crack system past some steep moves. At a lower level, **Thorax** (D) climbs the stepped crest. The remaining buttresses are small but interesting, comprising several easy micro-routes and some bouldering that is currently rather friable. The best feature is **Cyber Insekt** (HS 4b), an alluring crack set into the prow of a left-hand arête. All trad.

Buxton Boss OS ref. SK041757: Some small but pleasant natural rocks, south-west facing, with micro-routes and problems from Mod to the low V grades; worth a quick visit and a nice picnic spot. From White Hall or the A5004, walk up the old Roman road and take the obvious footpath just north of the crag across to the edge (20 mins). The best of the problems are on the highest two-tier section: **Respectable Street** (VS 4c), is the tricky thin crack on the left of a bulge, and the flake above; **Geography of Power** (HS 4b), the wider crack just right, and flake; and **Crushed Pagan God** (V0 5a), the excellent undercut slab to the right with numerous variations (all trad). The south of Combs Moss has several other scattered sections of crag but no named routes. These include the large but loose **White Hall Rocks** (OS ref. SK036763) and the extensive **South-West Combs** (OS ref. SK040764).

Short Edge OS ref. SK060782: Short Edge is situated 600m to the south-east of Castle Naze. Follow the footpath along the moor edge until the crag, consisting of three small north-facing buttresses, comes into view (10 minutes). The main buttress is the most visible, and is set at a slightly lower level. The crag suffers more than most from vegetation. **Flies of Ambition, Windshields of Fate** (HVD, 2000) climbs the crack 10m left of the main buttress. On the main buttress itself, **Earthquake Crack** (VS 4c★, 1984) with a tough pull into the crack system from a ledge opposite or traverse in from higher up the gully at S 4b. **Richter 5** (HVS 5b, 1984) climbs an overhang just right at its centre to the easy slab above. **Off The Scale** (HVS 5a, 1988) ascends the short corner 2m to the right. Finish up the arête. **Quaking All Over** (HS 4a, 1984) is the right-hand arête direct. Set back to the right is the unmistakable if unappealing **Corner Crack** (HVD 4a, 1988). The slab to its right of the corner gives **Framed** (VS 5a, 1988), and **Shockwave** (HVS 5b, 1988) is the green groove and flake to the right. Another 30m to the right is a square-cut buttress at a higher level (stake belays above). Although small, the routes start above a steeply sloping hillside that drops away alarmingly as height is gained, giving a good sense of exposure. The first route is **Slanting Crack** (HS 4b★, 1988), a lovely problem using laybacking, wide crack technique or both. **Fat Man Burger Overdose** (E1 5b, 2000) is based on the clean arête to the right (rather friable) that has yet to be led direct. This route climbs the face right of Slanting Crack (side-runner) to get started until a swing right around the arête can be made to finish. **Seismic Wall** (HVS 5a, 1984) gains the broad sloping ledge in the centre of the wall, then quakes upwards on holds that are very overgrown. **Inspector Remorse** (E1 5c★, 1993) is the rippled arête to the right of Seismic Wall giving a worthwhile climb on unhelpful holds. Start on the right past a tiny crack. Very small cams are useful higher up. The corner-crack just to the right (**Andy's Crack** HVD 4a, 1984) features some interesting plant life. **Short Arête** (S, 1984) is the appealing arête to the right. The next buttress 15m to the right has a large overhang on its front. **Carpet Crack** (HS, 1984) is the overhanging block-filled crack 2m from the left-hand end of the wall. **Hooverville** (HVS 4c, 1988) ascends the broken wall and makes worrying moves, just to the left of a big jug, over the obvious overhang. **Tremor** (VS 4c, 1984) climbs the slabby wall on the right-hand side of the buttress, moving left at the top.

The Hard Obscurist?

Westies Ahoy! Alright heads, having warmed up on the list of obscurities for beginners on page 283, this is an itinerary of just as obscure, but much harder climbs to test your dedication to the cause. So, slip a note under the pillow, pack your sandwiches and slide down knotted bedsheets. The asylum will never know you're gone.

- **Heart of Gold** E2 5c, Hen Cloud   A local classic on a far and forgotten end of Hen Cloud to ease you in.
- **Titan** E2 6b, Miriam Farm Rocks   A tough tick to be sure as the owners don't let you on to the crag. One to test your bargaining skills.
- **Bridge of Sighs** E3 5c, Hanging Stone   Another tricky ticky on a naughty no-no crag.
- **Gib** E2 6b, Gib Torr   Such a lowly little grade, only E2 – be prepared to curse, grunt and grapple on this seldom-succeeded-on desperate.
- **The Clown** E3 6a, Belmont Hall   A lovely journey down an idyllic dale for this testing little tipple. Bring your soft brush and your RPs.
- **Pillar of Judgement** E4 5c, Nth Cloud   Despite being very close to the main Roaches and Clouds area, the Nth Cloud still manages to preserve an isolated demeanour. Savour it on this fine bold route, the best at the crag.
- **The Phantom** E4 5c, Gradbach   Pronounced Grad-*back* if you want to annoy the locals. A local testpiece with a local history; bolts, ghosts and boyscouts. It's all there.
- **DNA** E4 6a, Harston   As good a reason as any to visit the mythical pinnacle with solid seventies-style boldness and exposure. A classic.
- **Crystal Voyager** E3 6a, Bosley Cloud   Reckoned by one local Bosley-obsessed slab devotee to be the best route in Staffordshire.
- **Inaccessible** E5 6a, Ina's Rock   Bunter madness blasting up a steep bubble- and pebble-besplatted wall giving pumpy but well-protected cranking.

The last exam – for your black belts, go forth and conquer: **The Pride** (Stoney Dale), **Sole Survivor** (Stoney Dale Quarry), **One Chromosome's Missing** (Harston), **Thumbelina** (Ina's), **Slender Thread** (Bosley), **Ray's Roof** (Baldstones), **Catapult** (Oldgate Nick), **Judge Dread** (Nth Cloud), **Fingers in Every Pie** (Wright's), **Knossos** (Sharpcliffe).

Hob Tor   O.S. ref. SK063778: This diminutive crag is reached by walking along the edge of the moor past Short Edge. Continue for a few hundred metres, passing a stone wall that eventually parts company with the moor edge, until the rocks become visible (15 minutes from the road). Facing east overlooking one of the more ravaged areas of the Peak, it nevertheless feels remote from the quarries that defile its aspect. It is probably best approached with some out-of-the-way soloing in mind, yet protection is available on most of the routes. The rock is variable, and there is copious lichen. However, the jugs are generous and the landings good.

The first small outcrop/boulder has some good problems including a V3 face, then the main buttress, upon which the unmistakable **Hob Crack** is a good landmark, is 40m beyond. The crag continues in the shape of two clusters of small buttresses lying between grassy gullies. Routes are described from right to left. **Hobjection Overruled** (HS 4b) is the juggy rib to the right of Hob Crack giving a good route on solid rock. **Hob Crack** (VS 4c ★) is the obvious splitter crack, the best line at the crag. Lunging for the enticing jug at the top is not to be recommended. **N.E. Hobbs** (HS 5b) is the undercut rib with a desperate starting sequence. **Imperfect Lichenous** (VS 4b) is the crack which leads to a grittily desperate top wall (a finish via the rib is S). Fifteen metres left is a blunt rib with a bulge at half height, taken by **Furry Green Atom Bowl** (HS 4b).

Ten metres left again is the second main buttress, characterised by 3 overhanging prows. **Hobs of Hell** (HS 4c ★) is the appealing crack between the jutting arêtes and the best route here. Gain it direct, or better, from the left. **City Hobgoblins** (VS 5a) is the undercut arête to the left of an easy gully with a tricky start. **Uncorrected Personality Traits** (D) takes the slab just left. Twenty metres left again is the final broken outcrop. **The Mixer** (D) climbs the best rock on its right-hand side, between 2 grassy gullies. **High Tension Line** (D) takes a line 2m right, on the right arête of a buttress past a grassy ledge. Better is **A Past Gone Mad** (VD), which takes a more continuous line up the left side of the buttress. The final slabby face lies a few m to the left. **City Dweller** (VD) climbs the right arête to a crack. **Rose** (S) takes the centre of the face past an overhang. **Antidote** (VD) climbs the left arête.

Crags in the Biddulph Area

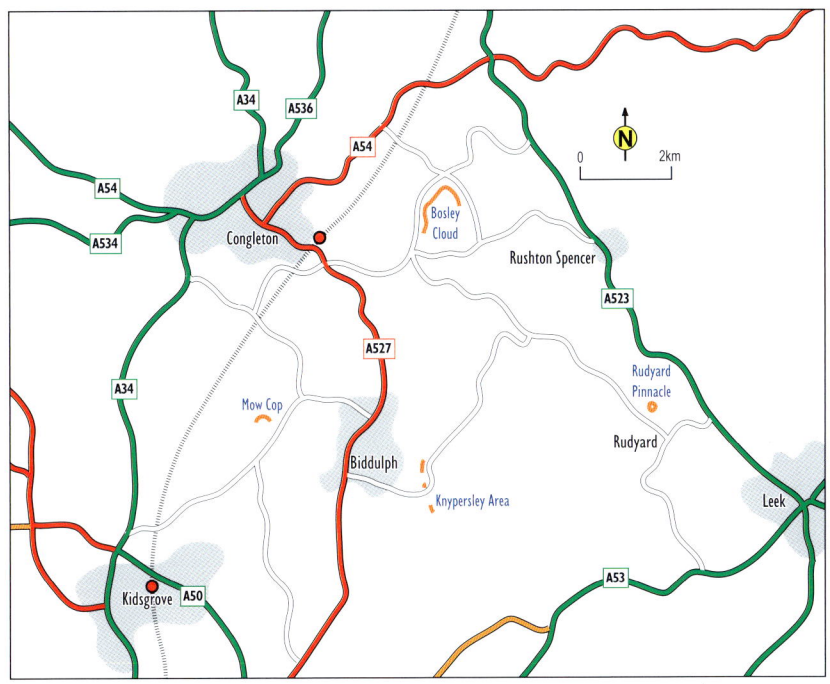

Rudyard Pinnacle

O.S. Ref. SJ945588 See map above. A tiny piece of the genuinely obscure: a 12m, north-facing, narrow prow of sculpted gritstone in the woods above Rudyard Reservoir, with a couple of worthwhile routes that through lack of traffic often revert to a natural coating of moss (easily removed with a soft brush); if clean, one route is good and the other excellent. On the B5331 to Rudyard, from the direction of Leek, turn right at the mini-roundabout, head into the village and follow the through road uphill, for a mile, to Horton St Michael's School on the left. Be considerate when parking near here. Cross the road from the school entrance to a public footpath (disguised between two houses: 'Oakwood' and 'Wit's End') and head down to a private wood at the bottom of the gardens, where the path turns sharp right and heads uphill. About 30m away in the woods, just below the path, is the well camouflaged prow (2 minutes walk). Access is clearly problematic so keep a low profile. **Moss Side Story** (E1 5a, 2003) is the left arête of the prow with good, if usually well-upholstered, holds leading to a bold and delicate finale. **Kipling Arête** (E2 5c ★, 2003) takes the steep right arête to a friendly break at half height; then moves up to a good hold (awkward protection round to the right) before balancing up the narrowing prow with a precarious move round to the left gaining a prominent hold, and a junction with Moss Side Story just below the top. Delectable climbing if clean that is easily worth a star.

Knypersley Area

by **Dave Garnett**

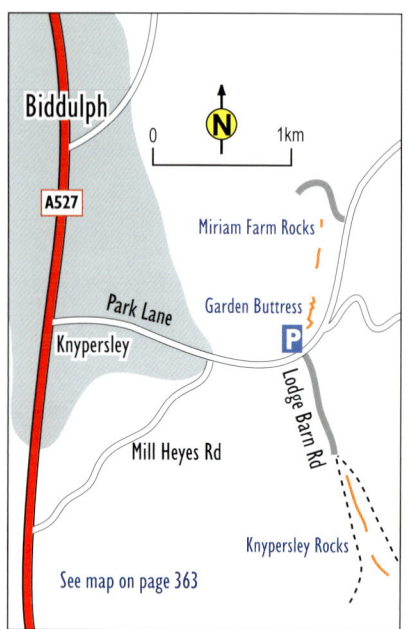

The dinosaur's spine of gritstone outcrops obvious from the Knypersley to Biddulph Moor road, 2km east of Biddulph, near the hamlet of Rock End. Composed of hard fine-grained gritstone, these buttresses give micro-routes and bouldering. Some of the crags are banned, and some are not. Some of the rock gives excellent climbing, and some does not. Still, it is surprising that they are not more popular.

There are three main areas: Miriam Farm Rocks are excellent, but suffer from an unwelcoming owner. Garden Buttress is okay and climbing is allowed as long as you ask for permission. Knypersley Rocks are generally poor although climbing is allowed.

Knypersley Rocks O.S. Ref. SJ901558

The rocks are found in a tongue of woodland on the low ridge running on from the end of the private Lodge Barn Road (off the Biddulph Moor road: Park Lane). The rock is allegedly gritstone, but hidden in the trees, it tends to be green and often overgrown, with only a few worthwhile routes. Access is not a problem providing you leave the car, fittingly, on Park Lane (heeding all the 'No Parking' signs beyond). Walk down Lodge Barn Road for 300m until it ends at three gated private drives. A footpath on the left of the central drive leads on into the woods, following the right-hand side of a dry-stone wall. After 150m some rocks up on the ridge to the right give some bouldering. Continuing through the woods for about 300m (ignoring a stile on the left at 200m) a gap in a wall is reached. Green Slab is up the hillside next to wall. This heavily camouflaged obscurity is probably best left as an ungardened offering to bryologists. For the record, **Twinkletoes** (VD) picked its way across the upholstered slab diagonally rightwards to reach the right arête, which is followed to the top. **Two Step** (S) ascended the left edge directly. **Little Slab** lies about 50m across to the right and is more or less feral. **Right It** (VD) climbed up the centre and **Left It** (VD) predictably, climbed up to the left via a ledge.

The Pinnacle: this is through the gap in the wall about 150m away and although green, it gives the best of the climbing hereabouts. It is best reached by following the path for 50m before trekking diagonally right into the woods. An overhanging front face is split by a blocky chimney feature. **Cold Shoulder** (HVS 5b, pre-1989) gains the right arête from the right by a diagonal weakness, and climbs it to the short finishing crack on the left. **The Jug Jam** (VD ★, pre-1973) gains and steeply climbs the impressive and unusual chimney feature. **Scorpion** (VS 4c, pre-1973) starts on the left wall of the buttress and traverses boldly right to gain the arête and a delicate finish. **Logos** (VS 4c, pre-1973) takes the shallow groove left of Scorpion to another bold move onto the arête, then moves slightly right and finishes direct. Across to the left from the Pinnacle is an overgrown slab that once gave a VD ramble (**Grassy Slabs**).

Hermit's Buttress: 200m from the gap in the wall, is a junction with a track and beyond this, a large boulder is perched on top of several blocks. This affords the possibility of boulder problems with lie-down starts. The extensive 'buttress' starts above this, with a natural arch bounding its right. 20m right from the first rocks is a slanting fingery crack, **Keep Left** (VS 5a). **Danera** (VD), takes the narrow ramp and juggy crack just right. **The Common Good** (VS 4b) laybacks through the overhang on flakes a few metres right again, to fight a heather cornice to the ledge. **Prometheus** (M) is the green alcove and crack to the right; not worth having your liver pecked out for. Down and right is a dismal corner and dirty crack, **Northern Lights** (D); a waste of a good route name. **Halcyone** (VD) is anything but, climbing just left of the bulge to the right to an awkward finish, whilst down a step is the appropriately unpleasant **Misogynist** (VD), a miserable chimney. Slightly more substantial, if rather nasty, is the cracked damp wall to the right: **Christmas Cracker** (HVS 5b, pre-1973). **Briar** (VS) is the cracks just left of the arch gained by slippery moves up the appalling bilious wall. The charms of the arch have been ignored so far but on the buttress to the right, **Gryphon** (VD) climbs out of the left side of an overhang to a faint crack, up this until level with the arch, then traverses right to a large ledge and steep corner.

Garden Buttress O.S. Ref. SJ898568

The best landmark is the fork in the road at the north end of Rock End. Heading north, the right-hand fork leads to Lask Edge and cars are best left here, near the junction, before walking for a few metres back up the main road towards Biddulph Moor. Garden Buttress is approached through the garden of the last house on the left (The Woodlands). Obviously, **permission to climb must always be sought at the house**, whose occupants are surprisingly co-operative as long as numbers are kept to a minimum and visits are not too frequent. Please be sensitive to this and, above all, park considerately, well away from the drive. **Access:** Climbing is permitted at Garden Buttress **BUT YOU MUST ASK FOR PERMISSION AT THE HOUSE**. The owners are friendly and usually grant permission. **The climbs are described from left to right starting with the outcrop situated at the left-hand side of the crag.**

1 Tube Snake VS 4c   pre-1989
9m The obvious jutting prow on the left arête may be gained from the left by a series of sandy pockets. Squirm painfully along the prow until it is possible to gain a standing position, then layback the huge flake above to finish.

2 Joshua HVS 5b   pre-1989
9m Four metres right is a shallow water-worn runnel below a whitish flake. Hard starting moves enable some extraordinary holds to be reached at the top of the runnel. Continue direct past the flake to an awkward move to gain the headwall. Finish straight up.

3 Cherry Hill E1 5b   pre-1989
9m The ramp 2m right is followed until it is possible to swing left under the roof. Tackle this direct using a long reach for hidden holds.

5 Brick Bank Crack VD   pre-1989
9m The wide central crack is climbed using holds on the right past a difficult section at mid-height.

6 The Friends of Eddie Coil E2 6a ★   pre-1989
9m The undercut slab right of Brick Bank Crack. Start just left of centre and move up then right to make desperate moves over the overlap, small wires, to gain easy ground above a poor pocket. Continue, stunned, to the top.

7 Hot Digital Dog HVS 5c ★   pre-1989
8m The right arête. Use pockets in the right wall to gain the arête. Balance up this to reach the top.

The crag continues farther right, but decreases in height, to give some entertaining boulder problems. The vandalised slab in the field 200m right again yields many excellent and hard friction test-pieces. The two large outcrops, which can be seen 200m farther along the ridge, are on private land and the owners have made it clear that they do not wish climbing to take place.

Staffordshire Grit

Miriam Farm Rocks O.S. Ref. SJ898572

(Previously known as ERF Rocks) At the opposite end of the chain, the largest of the outcrops is situated in a field behind and to the left of the Mitras Composites factory (but named after a previous incarnation of the factory), some 500m north, towards Biddulph Moor. See map on page 364.

Access: The owners do not wish to allow climbing and they live in the farm within sight of the rocks.

The left end wall of the main buttress is split by a deep chimney. The bulging rocks to the left give some interesting problems. The **wall** left of the chimney gives a fingery V3 (6b) up sloping scoops to ripples and the top. The **left arête** of the chimney is a worthwhile V1 (5c).

1 Beam Me Up Scotty   VD   c1992
5m The tight chimney is convenient (and easier) in descent. **Simon's Wall** V2 (6a) is the balancy wall right of the chimney via the break and a just-good-enough pocket. No sneaking onto the arête.

2 Farmer Barlimow   VS 4b   c1992
5m From the slab just right of the arête, pull over the bulge on good holds.

3 Enterprise   HVS 5c   pre-1989
6m Climb the overhanging scoop just to the right on disappearing flakes to a bold pull onto the slab above. The finish is currently rather dirty.

4 Titan   E2 6b ★★   pre-1989
7m The innocuous-looking roof-crack provides a short but intense problem for all but the very tall. A sharp start leads to a desperate struggle to gain improving jams in the unfriendly crack. Ramshaw awaits successful applicants!

5 Up to the Elbows   HVS 4c   pre-1989
7m The gruesome orifice to the right requires a baffling combination of laybacking, bridging, arm-barring and body-jamming, as well as industrial-sized cams to protect it.

An excellent sustained **low traverse** leads from Farmer Barlimow to Up to the Elbows at V5 (6b).

6 Spiderman Meets the Carlsberg Club   VS 5b   2003
7m The steep rounded arête to the right. An entertaining start leads to a blinkered finish up the slab directly above.

7 The Fruit Palace   VS 4b ★★   pre-1989
7m The excellent, but unprotected, pocketed slab on the right. The starting moves are hard, but persevere to reach the easier-than-it-looks slab and climb it direct.

8 Way Purple Splat Balloon   VS 4b   2003
8m The rib bounding the Fruit Palace slab on the right.

The traverse of the lowest break across the Fruit Palace slab is a satisfying V3 (5c).

9 Harvest Moon   HS 4a   pre-1989
6m The gritty groove to a precarious exit.

10 Sickle Moon   HVS 5a ★   pre-1989
8m A worthwhile eliminate taking the right-hand of two sickle-shaped flakes, over the bulge just to the right, starting with a mantel and pulling over using a good finger flake.

11 The Blackpool Trip   S 4a ★   pre-1989
8m Roll up and try your luck on the towering crack. Perfect jams make it a pushover.

12 Bilberry Slab   S ★   pre-1989
8m Amble up the centre of the large slab to the right.

13 Desert Head   HS   pre-1989
8m The bottomless vertical crack halfway along to the end of the crag.

Around the corner, the slabby end wall gives some good balancy problems, including the tenuous groove, **V3 (6a)**.

Mow Cop

by Gary Gibson and Dave Garnett

O.S. Ref. SJ858576　　　　　　　　　　　　　　　　　　　　　　　　　　　　　　　　Altitude: 330m a.s.l.

This craggy outcrop is a prominent feature on the Cheshire-Staffordshire border and is clearly visible from miles around. The Folly Castle is a well-known local landmark some 7 miles north of Stoke-on-Trent. However, don't let the apparent gentrification of the area and the nice National Trust car-park fool you. This is still a venue for the desperate and/or very local and transportless only. The Old Man itself is an impressive feature and might exert a deviant fascination for some. However, access to climbers is refused on grounds of alleged instability (of the Old Man). For the rest, the rock is as uninviting as the worst Knypersley can throw at you, without its compensatory sylvan charms.

Conditions & aspect: As the highest point for miles around, Mow Cop tends to attract the worst of the available weather. Faces mostly east. **Routes & bouldering:** Mostly in the middle grades, but serious and rarely repeated. Not a place for beginners, those pushing their grade, or sensitive aesthetes. No bouldering of note. **Parking & approach:** See map on page 363. Mow Cop is well-signposted from Biddulph and Kidsgrove and there is a convenient car-park on its western side. A useful landmark is the Mow Cop Inn, from which Castle Road leads up to the top of the Cop and a left turn leads to the Folly car-park. The Folly Cliff and nearby quarries lie on the eastern side of the Folly, whilst the Old Man lies 200m to the north-west, back across Castle Road and along a sign-posted footpath.

Access: The Old Man, Folly Cliff and Hawk's Hole Quarry are owned by the National Trust and the warden lives on site. Millstone Quarry ownership is unknown. Following a geological study the National Trust know that the Old Man is in a dangerous condition and therefore they do not allow climbing on it. Climbing is allowed on the small cliff alongside under the triangulation point. Climbing on Folly Cliff is not allowed because of loose rock and uncertain ground conditions beneath as well as intense public use of the area close by. Climbing is allowed at Hawk's Hole Quarry but beware of things thrown from above. Millstone Quarry can be climbed in but please respect the privacy of the residents whose premises abut the northern edge.

The Old Man of Mow

Half a dozen climbs have been described on the Old Man itself. Starting at the low platform at the back (i.e. facing the hillside) and proceeding clockwise they are as follows:

The Spiral Route (VS 4a, pre-1960) moves up left to gain a ledge at the base of a slab, leads left and down round the corner under the chin, and moves up another slab to the left shoulder. Step up, then move out right onto the forehead and finish direct. **The Direct Route** (HVS 5a, pre-1960) starts at the Old Man's feet and climbs the steep frontal groove to pull over the overhang to meet the Spiral Route. It then steps up and then left onto the face to finish as the previous route. **Alsager Route** (HVS 5a, pre-1960) trends left from the start of the Direct Route to climb direct to the left shoulder to finish up the tight groove in the arête above. **The Lee Side** (E1 5a, 1973) starts at the right-hand side of a pedestal forming the left arête of the front face of the buttress (or the outside of the Old Man's right leg in more anatomical terms). From the top of the pedestal, move out rightwards across the leaning wall and go round the arête onto the shoulder. Finish diagonally back leftwards. **Cambridge Crack** (VS 4c, pre-1960) climbs the prominent steep green crack just left, to any convenient finish. Finally, **Piton Route** (pre-1960) ascends the series of steps on the left skyline as viewed from the

Staffordshire Grit

Cambridge Crack side, to finish by the Old Man's left ear. It should be noted that descent from this pinnacle is by a very precarious abseil; not advised for the inexperienced. The geriatric summit bolt may or may not increase confidence. Numerous problems and routes of varying grades are possible in the adjacent quarry. None has any particular merit.

The Folly Cliff: Cioch Groove (VD, pre-1973) is the leaning chimney/ groove at the right-hand end of the cliff. **Crystal Voyager** (HVS 5a, 1979) is the slabby wall just left, and **Initiation Wall** (VS 4b, pre-1973) is the loose overhanging wall 3m left again. **B.S. Mow** (E1 5c, 1960s) is the once-pegged crack another 3m left again with a rightwards finish up the wall above, and **The Arête** (E3 5c, 1960s) is climbed by the sandy peg-scarred cracks. **Man Mow** (E1 5a, 1960s) starts just left of The Arête and climbs to The Arête before swinging right to and finishing directly past a Damoclean spike. **Folly Berger** (HVS 5a,1960s) moves diagonally left from the ledge on Man Mow to regain The Arête before stepping back right to finish direct. **Right Tot** (HVS 4c, 1960s) climbs the wall to the right of the scoop left of The Arête, moves left to a rotten flake and finishes up this and the wall above (bet you can't wait). Even more beguilingly, **Rot** and **Tot** lie up the wall to the left. Both should delight the connoisseur of loose rock and poor climbing. A girdle traverse is of equally fine quality.

Hawk's Hole Quarry: This the large hole slightly to the south of the castle. Its upper right wall sports two V-shaped notches, which are climbed by **Double Vee** (HS 4a, pre-1973). **Three Steps** (S, pre-1973) gains the stepped, broken corner left of Double Vee from that route. A harder start lies below, up the obvious short ramp (HVS 5a). The overhanging prow just to the left sports the dynamic aid-climbing duo, **Batman** and **Robin**. Both are A2. **Hawk's Hell** (VS 4c, 1960s) ascends the back right-hand corner of the quarry, gaining the half-height ledge via a large flake. The two cracks springing from the half-height ledge of Hawk's Hell are **Right Eliminate** (A1, pre-1973) and, spookily, **Left Eliminate** (VS 5a,1960s). **Vee Diff** (S, pre-1973!) starts just left of Hawk's Hell and climbs leftwards to reach a large ledge, to continue up the arête or the slab above. **Square Buttress** (HS 4a, pre-1973) is the centre of the square buttress 5m to the left. To the left is an obvious scooped face, which gives **The Captain's Blood** (E2 6a, 1979) up the blank-looking right-hand side, and **Captain Skyhook** (E1 5c, 1976) up the centre with a step right to finish.

Millstone Quarry

The largest, and only accessible, quarry lies round to the left again.

1 The Reach HS 4a   pre-1973
11m Climb the right arête until a step left leads to a groove and the top. Carbonel (VS 4c, 1960) goes left from this to the vegetated rampline.

2 Silent Scream E3 6a   1979
13m Start below the mid-point of the traverse of Carbonel. Climb directly up the crystalline wall by difficult moves to reach Carbonel and a finish up the shallow groove above. **Bow and Arrow** (VS 4c, 1960s) is the beautifully disgusting bird-limed crack 10m to the left. **Special Branch** (E1 5b, 1978) is the vague crack-line just left of the appalling gully.

3 Castle Crack VS 4b ★   1960s
18m Climb the conspicuous wide crack in the face to the left, gained from a small rib below. Attractive, by local standards, although falling victim to reafforestation.

4 Crystine E2 5b   1979
18m Climb the wall 3m left of Castle Crack to easy ground and finish up the arête directly above.

5 Arête and Slab Climb S   pre-1973
25m Follow a vague line 3m left again, by-passing a tricky section to the left. Move rightwards on the obvious line and finish as for the upper section of Castle Crack.

Nick I' Th' Hill   OS ref. SJ881607

There are several quarries along the crest of this ridge, 3 miles north-east of Mow Cop. Many overlook gardens (or are gardens themselves!) and are therefore not worthy of attention.

Bosley Cloud

by Simon Wilson

O.S. Ref. SJ904638 | Altitude: 310m a.s.l.

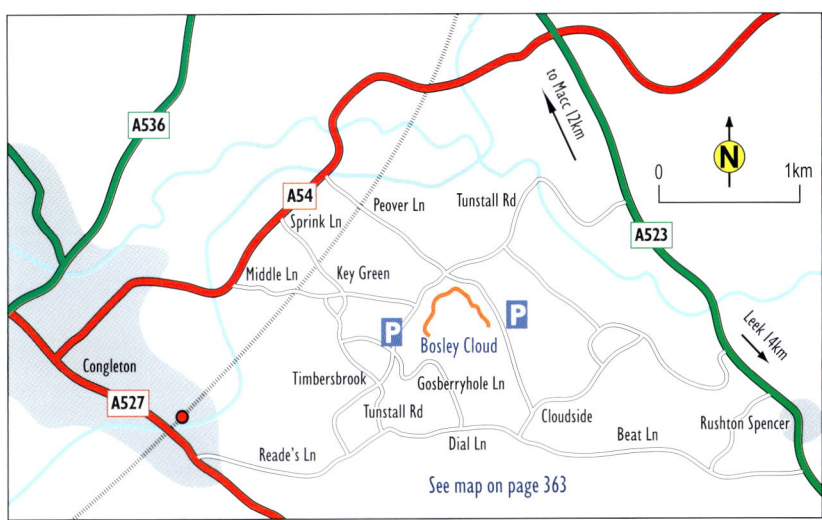

Bosley Cloud is the prominent hill 5km east of Congleton, marking the boundary between the hills of North Staffordshire and the Cheshire Plain, the boundary between the two counties running through the summit trig point. Locally famous for its dramatic skyline and the curious 'double sunset' visible from St Edward's churchyard in Leek on midsummer's day, the Cloud is less well-known to climbers, other than the local cognoscenti. The climbing is of two distinct, contrasting styles; natural and quarried rock.

Conditions & aspect

The crags line the Cloud from east to west and can be very green after a wet winter, but on a warm summer's day can be delightful. The Catstone, being west-facing, tends to be in better condition earlier in the season and is especially suitable for a sunny evening.

Routes & bouldering

Over 50 routes from rambling VDiff slabs to the serious of E7s, with an out-of-the-way atmosphere. Enough to give anyone a memorable day's climbing. A popular bouldering venue with locals with some especially good problems in the easier grades, particularly in the Summit Rocks area, plus, of course, one famous desperate.

Parking & approach

Visible from afar, the Cloud can be approached from Congleton, Bosley, or Rushton Spencer, but can be surprisingly frustrating to reach without a map. Those unfamiliar with the area will probably approach from the A523 Leek–Macclesfield road, whence the simplest approach is probably from Rushton Spencer, following Beat Lane for about two miles to a junction, where 'Cloudside' is signposted to the right. From here, the map should indicate the most convenient parking for each buttress.

Outlying Crags

Staffordshire Grit

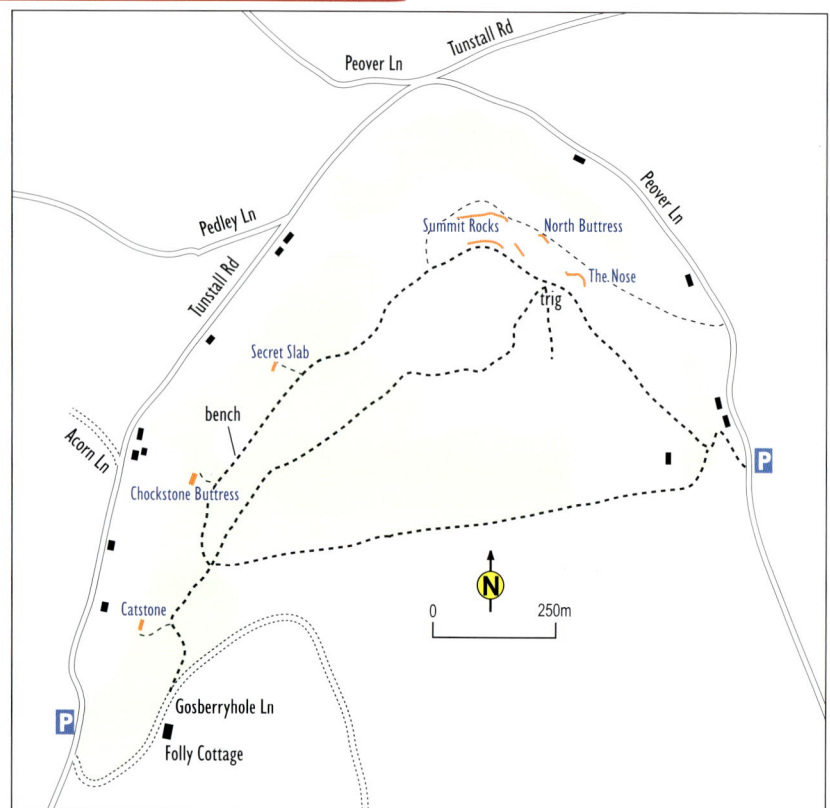

Access

Bosley Cloud is owned by the National Trust and there have been no objections to climbing. Climbers on the Catstone are asked to respect the peace and quiet of the residents of the house just below the crag, particularly on summer evenings.

Northern Crags

For The Nose, North Buttress and Summit Rocks, use the car park on the east of the rocks on Peover Lane. A large track runs to the summit from here giving access to the three crags. A smaller path leaves the road further north giving more direct access The Nose, but this is a bit overgrown. You will make your life a bit easier by taking the main path.

The Nose

The first routes lie on a buttress 50m east of, and at a lower level than the trig point, bounded on its left by a large green wall. **Corner Route** (VD, pre-1951) takes an indistinct line up the green, ledgy wall on the left-hand side of the buttress. An alternative, and better, finish climbs the right wall of the hanging groove at the top, Severe.

1 Left Nostril HVD   pre-1951
15m Picks its way up the obvious chimney, which is reached by an awkward scrabble onto the slab and a crack to a ledge.

2 Right Nostril S 4b pre-1951
15m The steep crack just to the right is sharp but short, leading to a junction with Left Nostril. The best finish takes the arête and wall left of the chimney

3 V-Chimney E1 5b ★ 1940s
15m The acute groove provides a compelling line, which would probably give excellent climbing following a good cleaning during an exceptional summer. A thoroughly untrustworthy peg runner at 8m is unlikely to be of much comfort. Finish leftwards across the overhanging wall to the top.

4 Why Kill Time When You Can Kill a Friend? E5 6a ★ 1985
14m The left arête of the imposing blank wall just to the right gives a good, but frightening, route. There is no gear until the hard climbing is completed, but a mat and spotter would make a difference.

5 Stuck Behind a Yellow Metro E6 6b † 1995
15m A bold route directly up to the shallow scoop just right of the centre of the seemingly blank wall to the right. Poor rock, unreliable protection and a dirty line all come together to make a very unattractive prospect. Very green at present.

6 Green Gully Direct HS 4a pre-1951
11m The well-named corner 6m to the right to the large grassy ledge. Step back left, up the corner and mantel on the right to the top.

The next two climbs are on a small face 50m right.

7 Envy Face S 4a pre-1951
8m Pull awkwardly into the thin crack in the wall, finishing on the left arête.

8 Mr Magoo E1 6a, 6a 1986
6m Essentially two extended boulder problems one above the other, about 15m right of Envy Face. The first is up a steep thin slab to the grass (V3) while the next continues up the upper slab to the small overhang and over this directly (V3, spotter advised). Unfortunately rather dirty.

Bosley Cloud North Buttress

North Buttress

The bigger buttress, 30m right.

9 Contraception on Demand E2 5c ★ 1985
6m A good solo up the left-most slab of the buttress, behind the rowan, to a nerve-wracking top-out. Short, but surprisingly committing - with a bad landing. Try not to fall off rightwards!

10 Fertility Rite Left-Hand E1 5c 1977
8m From the same start as the next route, trend leftwards up the slab to the finish of Contraception.

11 Fertility Rite HVS 5a pre-1973
8m The hanging corner is gained from the slab on the right and is climbed direct to a bold finish.

12 Slab Wall HVS 4c ★★ 1973
8m The steep slab left of the arête gives a delicate and rewarding route. Small wires protect the crucial middle section.

13 Kremlin Wall E4 6b ★ 1985
8m The steep flaky wall, with the aid of the arête is powerful, with a worryingly technical upper half.

14 Bulldog Flake E1 5b ★ 1963
8m Aggressive and unpredictable. Strenuous and poorly protected laybacking, and precarious unless perfectly dry.

15 White House Crack HVD 4a ★ pre-1963
8m The classic right-hand flake is a much friendlier affair. Quite reachy.... to retrieve some of the gear that is!

16 Solitaire E5 6b ★★ 1985
8m The wall to the right with the scary, insecure crux coming just below the top. Originally climbed coming in from the left, a direct start gives the line more independence.

17 Deception HS 4b pre-1973
6m A fierce little route. The undercut crack has a steep start on good flakes. Once the upper crack is gained good jams lead to the top. **Tin Tin** (HVS 6a, 1985) is the slab immediately right of the last route.

Sam Whittaker climbing the mythical Summit Arête, Bosley Cloud's famous desperate. Grades start at E2 6b.
Photo: David Simmonite.

Summit Rocks

The next climbs are on the biggest buttress on the right-hand end of the edge. The rest of this edge provides good bouldering above generally excellent landings.

18 Summit Arête E2 6b ★   1980
8m The undercut arête. From a standing start from the bank, a long slap off poor holds gains a jug, another long stretch brings a finger slot and easier climbing above: highball **V5: *see photo opposite*.** An indirect start using the left wall, dubbed **Summit Bypass** (E4 6b, pre-1991), gains the upper arête by traversing the runnel.

19 Drystone Wall E1 5a   pre-1965
9m The crack to the right is climbed by steep pulls until the blocky break is reached. Step left on big (but not entirely sound) footholds until the top can be reached.

At a much lower level and 50m to the right is a vertical rectangular wall:

20 Death Crack E2 6a   1986
6m The obvious thin crack is somehow much more technical than it should be. **Living Wall** (E3 6a, 1986) is a hard sequence on crimps and undercuts up the wall to the left.

The next buttress, 20m to the right contains one route, the prominent curving arête.

21 Big Red Rock Eater E1 5c   1984
7m The arête on the front on the buttress is laybacked with assistance from the pocket on the right wall.

Another 20m right is a bigger buttress with two grooves.

22 Death Wish E3 6a   1983
8m The shallow corner, thin and scary, leads to better holds up right. The green wall to the left is **Everdance** (HVS 5b, pre-1965), an enjoyable solo.

23 Thin Finger Corner VS 4b   pre-1965
8m The sharp corner to the right. After a ledgy introduction, make some hard moves using the left arête to get established in the groove. Finish up and left.

Bosley Cloud   Summit Rocks

24 Existentialist Arête E3 6a ★   1984
8m I crimp therefore I am. The arête to the right provides a superb series of committing moves. The climbing eases after the ledge but the rock becomes less reliable to compensate!

The quarry now becomes much larger but unfortunately the rock is very poor. There have been rockfalls in the past: a huge block came tumbling down the cliff in December 1999. Given this and the seriousness of the routes hereabouts, a Culm coast, rather than a gritstone cragging, attitude is probably wise. At the very least, an abseil inspection of the harder routes is advised. The buttress is bounded on its left by a Y-shaped crack. **The Lubricant** (VS 4b) *is the left branch, while* **Wet and Warm** (VS 4c) *is the right. Both pre-1965.*

25 The Couch Potato E7 6b   2000
15m A miscalculation is likely to result in an even more unfortunate vegetative state. From the start of the Wet and Warm, make a committing series of long reaches to gain the hanging flake on the upper wall and the dubious protection behind it. Press on to the top before strength fades. A bold route made even more serious by the nature of the rock.

26 Main Wall E5 6a   pre-1973
15m The steep crack on the right side of the wall provides a strenuous and serious route. The peg runners are now *very* old, and should probably be replaced before an ascent.

27 Impact Two E5 5c   1977
13m The soaring arête to the right is less strenuous than Main Wall but no less scary. Traverse to the arête at half height from the right. Layback the heart-stopping edge with conviction.

Bosley Cloud... the inconvenient truth.
Be warned. Some crags at Bosley Cloud are notoriously hard to find. Bear this in mind as you are planning your first visit. Allow some exploration time, and bring a soft brush to get routes into a clean state if need be.

Staffordshire Grit

Western Crags

The rest of the climbs are on the western side of the hill and at a lower level. The majority of the routes are in the trees and unfortunately this means an abundance of lichen, especially during the winter months, when the area is probably best avoided. However, when dry, the routes here are superb. They are described as they are best approached, from Gosberryhole Lane.

The Catstone

Follow Gosberryhole Lane to Folly Cottage and then the track on the left just past the buildings marked with the NT sign. This leads uphill a short distance to where it levels out at a clearing. The Catstone is below this about 30m down the hill. It is highly recommended to locate the black top of the Catstone before you descend too far. Also the lesser slab 30m north is best located from the top of the Catstone first. **Termination Crack** (S, pre-1973) is the crack left of the main face.

28 The Cat Crawl HS 4a ★★   1920s
18m The superb left arête. An easy start gains the arête from where holds on both sides of the arête lead to the exhilarating upper section.

29 Hot Tin Roof E1 5a ★★   1973
18m The centre of the buttress is magnificent, but bold. Starting up a crack to the left, traverse rightwards along parallel ledges. Continue up and place gear in the pockets and then storm confidently (or wobble!) through the crux above. Finish directly. A more direct start straight to the end of the traverse is also 5a: *see photo opposite*.

30 Mutiny Chimney VS 5a   1920s
18m The chimney to the right is gained from the lower wall, crux. Easier moves up the wide crack enable the pleasant arête above to be gained.

31 Hollybush Wall VS 4c   pre-1973
10m The thin curving crack is followed by more hard moves to get established on the sharp arête to the right, this is then laybacked. A good finish can be made up the arête of the previous route.

Thirty metres right is a buttress, which has some pleasant little slab routes.

32 The Crafty Cockney HVS 5b   1985
8m The slab on the left is climbed by committing moves on small edges. The upper arête is much easier.

33 Cool in a Crisis HVS 5c ★   1985
8m The central arête involves thin, balancy climbing to gain and leave the pocket to the right. **Crying Wolf** (VS 4c, 1985) is the crack system to the right.

34 Prescription for the Poor VS 4c   1985
8m The groove on the right of the buttress is topped by a bulge, the route tackles this direct.

Chockstone Buttress

The next buttress is best reached by going back up to the path again. This leads north-east away from the Catstone to a gap in the fence in under 100m. Take the leftmost of four paths and in 200m a bench is reached in a big clearing. From the bench back-track 30m south-west on the path and then head straight downhill for 40m for Chockstone Buttress (well hidden from above).

35 Minute Wall HS 4b   pre-1965
6m Starting 2m to the left of the crack, head for the obvious jug. An awkward move to stand up on it leads to easier climbing.

36 Key Green Crack VD ★   pre-1965
8m The central crack. Once the chockstone has been mounted, either continue up the wide crack or move left to gain a ledge. Lovely.

37 April Showers HVS 5a   1984
8m A hard start to get established on the thin wall to the right, soon leads to a double pocket. Finish up the thin slanting crack above. The **Direct Start** (HVS 5b, 1990) climbs direct to the left-hand pocket.

38 May Day HVS 5c   1984
7m A line of leftward trending pockets further right are followed until the double pocket can be gained and a common finish with April Showers.

For those willing to seek it out, the Catstone has one of the best slab routes in the area. Stephen Coughlan going for it on Hot Tin Roof, E1 5a (opposite). Photo: Ian Parnell.

Staffordshire Grit

39 Hotter Than July HVS 5c ★   1990
7m The arête just to the right is climbed on its left-hand side.

Secret Slab

Home to two of the best hard routes on the crag. From the bench (see Chockstone Buttress directions) walk 120m north east on the path to a slight clearing on the left (currently with a 2m dead tree stump) and head downhill for 50m until a holly marks the side of the buttress (which is well hidden from above). Facing the slab, contouring 40m right (south-west) is the other buttress (also with a holly on its right side). From the bench the edge of the trees is 300m or so away on the path and the summit just over half a kilometre.

40 Herbivacious E4 6a ★   1984
9m A brilliant, technical climb on pockets and undercuts with a committing high crux following the blunt left arête of slab. Bosley's own Piece of Mind.

41 Slender Thread E5 6b ★★   1979
9m The hairline crack in the centre of the buttress gives a bold and sustained route. From the top of the crack, which doesn't take protection as easily as it should, trend leftwards up the steep slab above. A variation, **Cobweb** (E4 6b, 2008), starts at the bottom of Slender Thread (very high side-runner) and tip-toes up the vague scoop to the left then swings round to join the crux of Herbivacious.

42 Crystal Voyager E3 6a ★★★   1979
9m Starting below the smooth groove, climb steadily up the slab on good edges until bold moves allow a good hold to be grasped. Place protection in the crack above before a precarious step gains the groove to the left. A superb route, on which good balance and a cool head are essential.

43 Pretentious? Moi? E1 6a ★   1984
7m The shorter wall to the right is home to a technical, bouldery route. The good landing is likely to be tested.

The next routes are on a smaller buttress 40m to the right of Secret Slab, and at the same level.

44 Slab of Meat S 4a   traditional
8m The featured slab left of the dirty corner gives a fine little pitch. The dirty corner itself gives **Birch Tree Climb** (S, pre-1965). Grovel up the dirty corner to the left of the overhang until escape is possible via some exposed moves right onto the hanging arête.

45 The Cleavers E4 6a   2008
8m The arête to the right. Jump off the knife-shaped boulder and battle up to a jug pocket. Easier balancy moves lead to the top. Would be a good highball if it weren't for the mother of all bad landings.

46 Sirloin S 4a   pre-1965
8m From the large block under the overhang make a hard move to get established on the front face, then continue up the cracks above

47 Anticlimax HVS 5b ★   pre-1981
8m The short wall to the right. A precarious rock-over from the obvious pocket provides the crux.

48 Bottle Crack S 4a   pre-1965
8m Thrash through the holly-filled gully until the sanctuary of the alcove is reached. The route finishes up the attractive but miniscule crack on the left wall.

Timbersbrook Quarry

These quarries to the south of the Cloud are no longer climbed. They are very overgrown and dangerous. Also, unsurprisingly, the landowners are not happy to allow access.

Above the lowly ridge

is a small 25 foot face, severely undercut; on this is found the Summit Climb (decidedly difficult), which finishes at the highest point of the Cloud. Owing to the undercut base the leader must have a shoulder, or, if his supporter is less than six foot in height, a head, to reach the first hand-hold.
Having once drawn himself up, so as to get a foothold the going is good, for though the face is approximately vertical, the holds are excellent.

**From Some Gritstone Climbs
by John Laycock, 1913**

Heighley Castle Quarries

by Dave Bishop

O.S. Ref. SJ774471　　　　　　　　　　　　　　　　　　　　　　　　　Altitude: 170m a.s.l.

A very useful quarry of vertical sandstone giving a great number of fingery boulder problems and routes. Traditionally enjoyed by many in the Stoke area, it is now in the possession of an uncompromising owner who refuses to permit climbing. A shame.

Routes & bouldering

Traditionally recorded as routes, but best seen as a bouldering venue — topping out on many of the awful finishes is an esoteric risk. The bouldering consists of traverses, arêtes and walls, and is very fingery on generally sound rock. There are a significant number of vital pebbles, vulnerable to misuse, that make for crucial holds on some of the problems. Thirty problems are recorded here, but more potential exists.

Conditions & aspect

The quarries can be vivid green and damp on occasions so the best times to climb are when there is no leaf cover on the trees, November through May. Unfortunately these times also coincide with the pheasant shooting and breeding season. The Fourth Quarry is usually dry at low level even on damp days. Faces east, getting some morning sun.

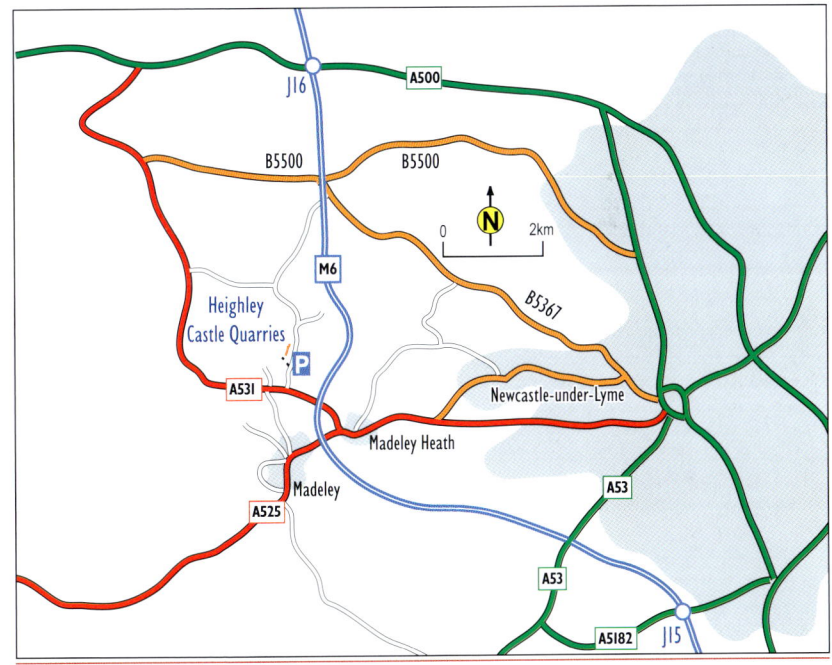

Staffordshire Grit

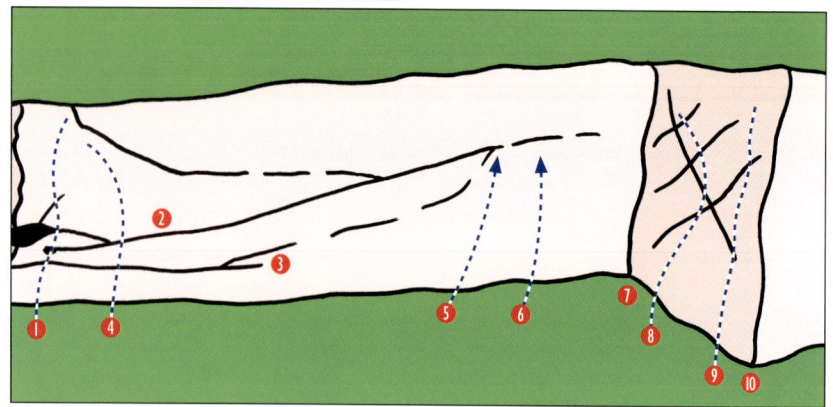

Parking & approach
On the A531, about 2km north-east of Madeley Heath, Heighley Lane cuts off north, signed towards the castle itself. Follow this road for about 700m. To park, use the three passing places on either side of the public highway beyond the farm access lane. **Do not park in this gateway entrance.** Better still is to park elsewhere and walk or cycle so as to not alert the farmer. The No 85 Bus from Chester to The Potteries stops at the Madeley turn, less than a mile away. Approach 1 minute.

Access
The farmer does not want anyone in the woods as it disturbs the pheasants. We as climbers are not prepared to pay for access to compensate any 'losses'. The owners keep a constant eye on these woods and will turn you away. As a result these excellent rocks are becoming greened and the undergrowth is spreading.

First Quarry

Characterised by a long wall with an inviting rising traverse line.

1 Ivy League V1 (5c)

2 Long Wall Traverse V2 (5c)
Follow the main, upper break. Usually done from left to right but goes either way. Can be continued around the short wall.

3 Low Traverse V4 (6b)
The much harder bottom line. Keep as low as possible, avoiding the upper line. Done left to right. It is much easier, and normal, if you move up to the higher traverse line at about one third distance, but it is still very fingery.

4 Dixon's Dart Board V3 (6a)

5 Eric the Frog V3 (6a)

6 Brian the Snail V4 (6b)

7 Little Cenotaph V0 (5b)
Cenotaph Variant traverses the foot-ledge out from the corner to the arête.

8 Right Wall V0 (5a)

9 Bill's XS V4 (6b)

10 Ecstasy I V1 (5c)

Second Quarry

This is found at a slightly lower level 10m on the right.

11 Punch Arete V5 (6b)
The corner to the left is **Gommorah, 5c.**

Heighley Castle Third Quarry

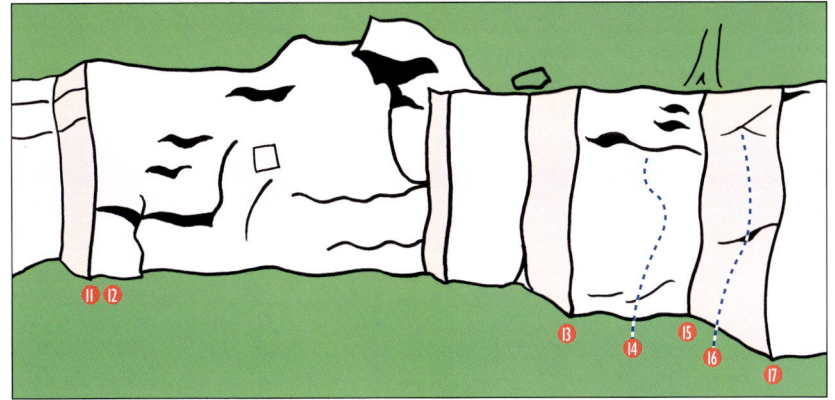

12 The Serpent V5 (6b)
Traverse right from the arête, along the obvious line, all the way to beyond Jess's Arête.

13 The Heighley Nightmare V4 (6b)

14 Killer Wall V3 (6b)

15 Jess's Corner VI (5b)

16 Alan's Variant VI (5b)

17 Jess's Arête V2 (6a)
Done on either side but easier on the left. Not using the pocket close to the arête on its right is the standard. Finishing not recommended.

Third Quarry

The next quarry lies 40m to the right.

18 Mark of Zorro V0 (5b)
Traverse the break rightwards.

19 Southern Sloper V0 (5b)
A lower traverse.

20 5b Arête VI (5b)

21 Fresher's Arête VI (5b)

22 Stepped Arête V0 (5b)

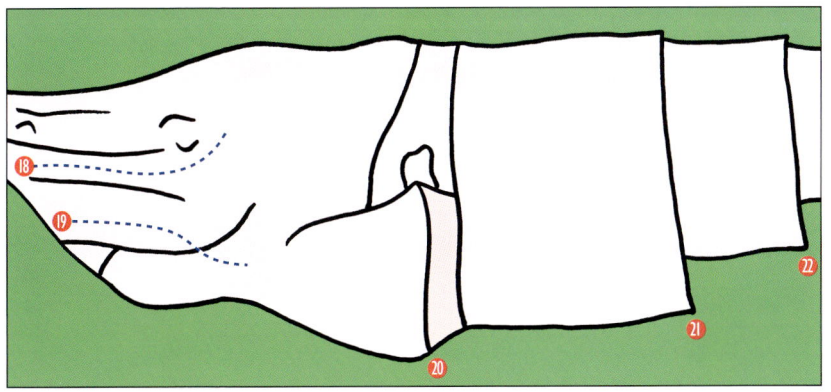

Staffordshire Grit

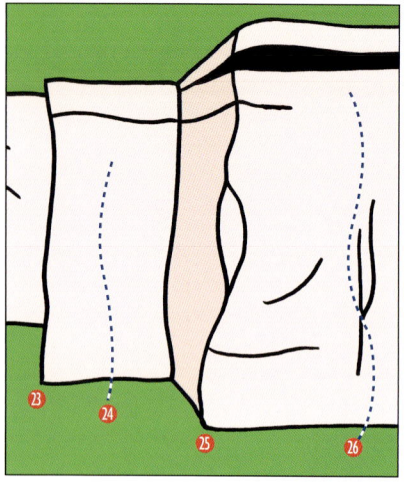

bits of all three to your own taste and ability, and to traverse in either direction. Numerous up and down problems can be deduced and the main corner of the bay provides **tough bridging** with an exit left at the first break, V4 (6b). To the right of the bay the height of the crag diminishes and the curved small bay gives entertaining traverses that get harder the more holds you miss out.

Fourth Quarry

The final quarry is another 50m right again, down a large bank. It is for big boulderers only.

23 Slim Corner 5c
E3 really, so be warned.

24 Suicide Wall 6a
The wall to the right is far too big to ever be a boulder problem. It has been led sometime before 1973, perhaps the only ascent. E5.

25 Suicide Arête 6a
The dominating arête to the right has also been led, sometime before 1973. It was recorded in a Keele University climbing guide from that year that a member of the South Cheshire Climbing Club had led the route (graded 5d). It has subsequently been led once again at E5. As such it must have been one of the hardest routes of its day.

26 Hilti Gunner 6b
The wall to the right is another E5.

There are at least three traverses at different heights moving right from Suicide Arete to the main corner of the bay. The lowest with the hands at about head height is the hardest. It is more common to combine

Outlying Crags First Ascents

The history of many of the minor crags in the area has not been meticulously maintained and in many cases the only indication of even the era in which the routes were done comes from the publication date of the first guide in which they appear and often the first ascensionists are unrecorded.

1910–1912	**Herford's Girdle Traverse** Siegfried Herford, John Laycock *'At Castle Naze Herford originated the idea of traversing horizontally along a line of cliff, so was born the Girdle Traverse.'*
pre-1913	**Pinnacle Crack, Pinnacle Arête, Sheltered Crack, Overhanging Chockstone Crack, V-Corner, Muscle Crack, The Nithin, Flake Crack, The Fly Walk, The Niche, Niche Arête, Studio, A.P. (Absolutely Perpendicular) Chimney, Little Pillar, Keep Corner, Footstool, Left Zigzag Crack, Fat Man's Chimney, Deep Chimney, The Crack, Zigzag Crack, Long Climb, Central Tower, Green Crack, Hodgkinson's Chimney, South Buttress, V-Chimney, Vanishing Crack, Boomerang, Overhanging Chimney** Stanley Jeffcoat and friends
1914	**Scoop Face** Stanley Jeffcoat
1915 Jun 13	**The Crack** HM Kelly (first descent) *'Most exhilarating and exciting and taxes the climber's powers to the uttermost.'*
1924	**Castle Naze Girdle Extension** Patrick Monkhouse, M de Selincourt, Miss R Monkhouse
1920s	**Mutiny Chimney, The Cat Crawl** Morley Wood, Fred Piggott, Harry Kelly
1930s	**Pilgrim's Progress** Morley Wood and Rucksack Club friends
pre-1948	**No Name, Keep Arête, Scoop Face Direct Start, Nozag, The Vice, Boomerang Buttress**
1940s	**V-Chimney** Eric Byne, M Holland
pre-1951	**Green Gully Direct, Left Nostril, Right Nostril, Corner Route** Mentioned briefly in the 1951 guidebook.
1958 Jun	**Birthday Climb**
1950s	**The Two-Step, Struggle**
pre-1960	**Spiral Route** K Maskery
	Alsager Route Harold Drasdo, K Finlay
	Cambridge Crack, Direct Route J Sutton, Harold Drasdo, Bob Downes, Tony Moulam
	Piton Route Harold Drasdo *At least one peg was used for aid but it was probably fully aided. Climbed free by persons unknown in the 1970s.*
1960	**Carbonel, Bow and Arrow** A Taylor, Paul Williams
1963	**Bulldog Flake** Ed Drummond
pre-1965	**Envy Face, Dry-Stone Wall, Thin Finger Corner, Everdance, The Lubricant, Birch Tree Climb, Bottle Climb, Minute Wall, Key Green Crack** All appeared in Peter Bamfield's notes in the Midland Association of Mountaineers club journal but were lost for the 1973 guide.
1960s	**Hawks Hell, Left Eliminate (aid), Folly Berger, Man Mow, Right Tot** P Kenway, John Amies, John Lockett
	Castle Crack
	B.S. Mow Some aid, climbed free and solo by Jonny and Andrew Woodward in 1975.
	The Arête (some aid) Climbed free by Jonny and Andrew Woodward in 1976.
	Slanting Crack, The Bloody Crack, Block Cracks, The Nose, Main Corner, Pitoned Crack, Peg Crack
pre-1973	**Cioch Groove, Initiation Wall, Double Vee, Three Steps, Right Eliminate, Vee Diff, Square Buttress, The Reach, Oak Tree Crack, The Cleft Route, The Cue, Fertility Rite, White House Crack, Deception, Wet and Warm, Main Wall (aided), Hollybush Wall, Termination Crack, Right It, Left It, Twinkle Toes, Two Step, Jug Jam, Scorpion, Logos, Grassy Slabs, Gryphon, Briar,**

Staffordshire Grit

	Christmas Crack, Misogynist, Halcyone, Northern Lights, Prometheus, Common Good, Danera, Keep Left Main Wall free in 1978 by Jonny and Andrew Woodward.		**Earthquake Crack, Quaking all Over** Malc Baxter, Al Parker, Andy French
Andy's Crack Andy French, Al Parker, Malc Baxter
Carpet Crack, Tremor, Short Arête Al Parker, Malc Baxter, Andy French
Richter 5, Seismic Wall Malc Baxter, Al Parker
1973	**Hot Tin Roof, Slab Wall** Paul Williams, John Amies, P. King
The Lee Side	1985	**Solitaire, Contraception on Demand, Kremlin Wall** Ian Dunn (solo)
Tin Tin Ian Dunn, Claudie Dunn **Why Kill Time…** Nick Dixon, Ian Dunn
1976 Jun	**Captain Skyhook** Andrew Woodward (solo)	1985 Dec 21	**The Crafty Cockney, Prescription for the Poor, Crying Wolf** Keith Ashton, Malc Baxter
1977 Jul	**Plankton, Belladonna** Al Evans
"Plankton was practised on a rope every time I went up to The Naze. Finally I had it wired one day and soloed it straight after a top rope ascent. I guess these days you'd call it a 'headpoint'."		**Cool in a Crisis**
Malc Baxter, Keith Ashton
1977 Jul	**Atropine** Lew Hardy and friend	1986 Apr	**Death Crack** Nick Dixon, Mark 'Face' McGowan, Simon Oaker, Denise Arkless, Allen Williams
1977 Oct	**Fertility Rite Left-Hand, Impact Two, Death Wish** Jonny Woodward		**Living Wall**
Nick Dixon, Allen Williams
1978	**Special Branch** John Holt		**Mr Magoo** Simon Oaker, Nick Dixon, Allen Williams
1978 May	**Feed the Enemy** Gary Gibson (solo)	1986 Sep 14	**Morocc'n Roll, Syringe Benefit, Columbal Convenience, South Crack, Southern Arête** Jim Rubery, Dave Gregory
1979	**Slender Thread, Crystal Voyager (Bosley)** Jonny Woodward, Andrew Woodward **Silent Scream** Andrew Woodward	1988	**Shockwave** Malc Baxter, Al Parker
Slanting Crack Al Parker (solo)
Framed Keith Ashton, Peter Frame
An earthquake had recently occurred in the area
1979 Sep	**Crystal Voyager** (Mow Cop), **The Captain's Blood, Crystine** Gary Gibson (solo)		**Hooverville, Off The Scale, Corner Crack** Keith Aston
Piano Stool, Short but Sweet Malc Baxter
1970s	**Ledgeway, Bubbly Wall, Scoop Wall, Keep Buttress, Scoop Direct**	pre-1989	**Cold Shoulder, Tube Snake, Joshua, Cherry Hill, Brick Bank Crack, Friends of Eddie Coil, Hot Digital Dog, Enterprise, Titan, Up to the Elbows, Fruit Palace, Harvest Moon, Sickle Moon, Blackpool Trip, Bilberry Slab, Desert Head**
1980	**Summit Arête** Jonny Woodward First free ascent. Originally graded E2 6b but given E5 7a in the last guide. The discrepancy was partly down to the start used.	1989 May	**Orm and Cheep** Al Evans "Orm and Cheep were stars in a kids' TV programme around the time of the first ascent. James was crying in his buggy as Andrea belayed me, so she sang the theme tune to it. That did the trick long enough for me to get the hard bit done!"
pre-1981	**Anticlimax** probably Jonny Woodward		
1984 Apr 30	**April Showers** Mark Stokes, John Allen
May Day John Allen, Mark Stokes		
1984 May 31	**Big Red Rock Eater, Pretentious? Moi?** Allen Williams (solo)
Existentialist Arête
Andy Popp (on-sight solo)
Herbivacious Nick Dixon (solo)
A very productive day!	pre-1990	**Original Route** (Oldgate Nick)
1984	**Double Crack, The Arête, Bow Crack, The Fifth Horseman**
Jim Rubery, Dave Gregory
Pod Crack Jim Rubery, Dave Gregory
Scoop Direct Alastair Ferguson, Jim Rubery
Footstool Right, Combs Climb, Deep Crack, Zig-a-zag-a Dave Gregory, Jim Rubery
The Blusher Jim Rubery, Dave Spencer	1990	**Belladonna Direct**
Malc Baxter, Jim Perrin, Harry Venables

Outlying Crags First Ascents

Also claimed as Primadonna by Joe Bawden in 1977.

1990 May 3 **April Showers Direct** Dave Whittles (solo)

Hotter Than July Simon Allsop (solo)

pre-1991 **Summit Bypass** Mike Cluer (solo)

1991 Jul 27 **Sleeping with Sarah** Tim McLean

c1992 **Beam Me Up Scotty** Justin Critchlow (solo) *Very likely to have been done before, but then Justin was destined for greater things!*

Farmer Barlimow Antony Hall (solo)

1993 **Fat Man Burger Overdose, Inspector Remorse** Keith Ashton, Dave Whitely.

1994 Spring **Stuck Behind a Yellow Metro** Ed Jackson *The route was named with reference to the frustrating journey to the crag.*

1995 May 7 **Come on Eileen** Malc Baxter, Harry Venables, Matt Rhodes

1997 **The Cat Inside** Ben Tye

1997 **The Ugly Bloke** Joe Bawden, Paul Knowles

Primadonna Joe Bawden, Paul Knowles *Essentially the way Belladonna should have gone* **Assorted Pond Life** Sandy Sanderson, Tony Knowles

2000 **Flies of Ambition, Windshields of Fate** John H Bull, Karen Dalkin (solo). *Routes on Buxton Moss, Hob Tor and Allstone Lee Rocks recorded by John H Bull, although some will have been climbed previously.*

2000 Jul 19 **The Couch Potato** Ed Jackson, Dan Taylor *E7 reaches Bosley Cloud in the form of an utterly serious route. "Dubious protection is available behind the flake, at two thirds height, but it creaks when you pull on it so I didn't bother on the first ascent. I first top roped it in the winter of '94 but couldn't climb it in one go." Repeated October 2000 by Chris Hutchins.*

2001 **Simon's Wall** Simon Wilson

2002 Jun **Ice Breaker** Paul Fitzsimmons, Helena Garnard

2003 Apr 6 **Spiderman Meets the Carlsberg Club** Dave Garnett (solo), John H Bull (solo) *The local under-age drinking club were very easily impressed*

Way Purple Splat Balloon John H Bull (solo)

2003 **Nursery Arête** Paul Messenger, Rob Moran *Climbed (whilst Paul's son was at nursery) after a chance conversation with the crag writer revealed this overlooked line.*

2003 **Stoke the Engines** Laurie Carefoot, Martin Kocsis

Keith George: The Movie Martin Kocsis, Laurie Carefoot *Named after a local climbing legend who's catchphrase is "If that's not a jug, I'm off!" usually in extremis, usually with rising concern in his voice. There may, or may not, be a hidden jug on this route!*

Iron Age Fortitude Neil Foster, Graham Hoey, Clare Reading, Martin Kocsis *Enticed to the crag by the promise of tea and cakes once the route was in the bag, Neil lost more blood on this route than on any other in the previous six months!*

Chamonaze Blues Olly Allen, Martin Kocsis *The final line on Castle Naze falls to a leader jaded from three months of hard alpine climbing and even harder Chamonix living.*

2003 Jul 12 **Kipling Arête** Dave Garnett, John H Bull *A birthday ascent powered by celebratory chocolate orange*

Moss Side Story John H Bull, Dave Garnett

2003 **Nine Tales, Crime Gene** John H Bull, solo or with Karen Dalkin *Some, if not all, had certainly been done before.*

Catapult Andrew Healey, Simon Wren, both solo

2003 **Eeny, Meeny, Miny, Mo, Frank's Route** Frank Loftus, John Jones, Ken Wilson, Martin Kocsis, Niall Grimes

2008 **Cobweb, The Cleavers** Col Allott

It's hard to believe that lines as prime as Night Prowler, E6 6a (page 184) have been opened only in the last few years. Mark Sharratt on the lonely crux. Photo: David Simmonite.

Graded List - Routes

E8
Skin and Wishbones
Cornelius
Final Destination
Ultimate Sculpture
Young Pretender
Doug
Judge Jules

E7
Obsession Fatale
Clippety Clop
Moov Over
Logical Progression
A Little Peculiar
Catharsis
Cornelina
Paralogism
Boom Bip
Pair o' Genes
The Driven Bow
B4 XS
Ray's Roof
The Couch Potato
Never Never Land
Dangerous Crocodile Snogging
One Chromosome's Missing

E6
Thing on a Spring
Against the Grain
Pull the Udder One
Myxi
Piece of Mind
Destination Earth
Fingers in Every Pie
Night Prowler
Miss Understood
Master of Reality
Arêtenophobia
Art Nouveau

A Fist Full of Crystals
National Acrobat
Painted Rumour
Judge Dread
Northern Comfort
The Pride
Barriers in Time
Bloodspeed

E5
Gillted
Knossos
Nature Trail
Jean the Bean
Justin Time
Mandatory
The Warp
Sole Survivor
Solitaire
Caricature
Antithesis
Patient Weaver
Slender Thread
Mirror, Mirror
Apache Dawn
Inaccessible
Bloodstone
Leethal Weapon
The Thin Air
Entropy's Jaw
Counterstroke of Equity
Old Fogey Direct
Catastrophe Internationale
Track of the Cat

E4
Crystal Voyager, Nth Cloud
Fast Piping
Scrumptious
Ramshaw Crack
DNA
Chameleon
The Super Girdle

Space Probe
The Impending Doom
Secrets of Dance
Bareback Rider
Caesarian
Borstal Breakout
All Day and All of the Night
Icarus Allsorts
Metaphysical Scoop
Willow Farm
Trepidation
Iron Age Fortitude
The Phantom
Licence to Run
The Death Knell
Acid Drop
The High Priest
Gypfast
The Pillar of Judgement
Wings of Unreason
Anthrax
Cloudbusting

E3
A Phoenix Too Frequent
Corinthian
Hunky Dory
Traveller in Time
Comedian
Crystal Voyager, Bosley Cloud
The Better End
Old Fogey
Ascent of Man
Bordello
Waiting for the Lions
The Clown
The Swan
The Joker
Appaloosa Sunset
Carrion
The Bridge of Sighs
Entente Cordiale

Qui Vive
The Sorcerer
The Undertaker
San Melas
Smear Test

E2
Gib
Electric Chair
Gallows
The Leading Fireman
Elegy
Gumshoe
Commander Energy
Titan
Walleroo
Ruby Tuesday
Topaz
Enchanted Forest
Atlas
Don Quixote
Heart of Gold
Boysen's Arête
Wombat
Sauroff
Crack of Gloom
Sense of Doubt
The Perp
Original Route, Baldstones

E1
Pod Crack
Brown's Crack
The Fox
Enigma Variations
Shortcomings
Hawkwing
Safety Net
The Untouchable
Tower Face
Chicken
Keith George: The Movie
The Press
Dorothy's Dilemma

Slowhand
Drain the Main Vein
Ripples
Hypothesis
Morocc'n Roll
Hot Tin Roof
Round Table
Tequila Sunrise
Wild Thing
Ground Support
Encouragement
Tactical Weapon
Kaleidoscope
Double Overhang

Hard Very Severe
Masochism
Teck Crack
Bengal Buttress
Tally Not
Hen Cloud Eliminate
The Gape
Alcatraz
Delstree
Eye of Japetus
Boysen's Delight
The Mincer
Bachelor's Left-Hand
The Sloth
The Helix
Don's Crack
Matinee
Rubberneck
Second's Advance
The Great Zawn
Saul's Crack
Valkyrie Direct
Portfolio
Prostration
Libra
Cave Crack (Skyline)
Baldstones Arête
Roscoe's Wall
Scoop Face
Sauron
Fifth Horseman
Slab Wall
Crispin's Crack
Special K

Toe Rail
Kneewrecker Chimney
En Rappel

Very Severe
Crabbie's Crack
Perverted Staircase
Valkyrie
West's Wallaby
Central Climb Direct
Bachelor's Buttress
The Crank
Pincer
Reunion Crack
Rainbow Crack
Pinnacle Face
Niche Arête
Bachelor's Climb
Main Crack
Devoted
Condor Slab
Hedgehog Crack
Battle of the Bulge
Smun
The Crack, Castle Naze
North Buttress Arête
Via Dolorosa
Keep Arête
Baldstones Face
The Fruit Palace
Bollard Edge
Aqua
Cave Crack (Belmont Hall)
Defiance
Little Crack
Nozag
Rhynose
The Neb Finish
Roof Climb

Hard Severe
Kestrel Crack
Gibbon Wall
Billiard Table
Central Climb
Jeffcoat's Buttress
Calcutta Crab Dance
Runner Route
Technical Slab

Damascus Crack
Herford's Girdle
  Traverse
Sifta's Quid
Honky Tonk
Struggle
Little Giraffe Man
Skull Crack
Final Crack
Modern
Tricouni Crack
South–East Crack
Traditional
Zig-Zag Crack
Ogden Arête
Hazel Barrow Crack
Thin Crack, Back Forest

Severe
Crack and Corner
Via Dolorosa Variation
Crab Walk
Chockstone Crack,
  Gradbach
The Cat Crawl
Ina's Chimney
Slab and Arête
Calcutta Crack
Hollybush Crack
Fledgling's Climb
Portcullis Crack
Rib Chimney
The Niche, Castle Naze
Right-Hand Route
K2
The Blackpool Trip
Great Chimney
Thompson's Buttress
  Route I
Black and Tans
Hazel Barn
Green Crack, Wydgather
Route I, Wydgather

Hard Very Difficult
Fern Crack
White House Flake
Yong

Rib and Slab
Original Route,
  Oldgate Nick
Black Velvet
The Arête, Hen Cloud
The Arête, Garston
Keep Corner
Pedestal Route
Cave Arête
Pseudo Crack

Very Difficult
Beckermet Slab
Maud's Garden
Squash Balls
Squashed Finger
Perambulator Parade
Brad's Chimney
Lighthouse
Central Tower, Castle Naze
Camelian Crack
Jeffcoat's Chimney
Prow Corner
Boomerang
Right Route, Upper Tier
Prow Cracks
Jug Jam

Difficult
Inverted Staircase
Mild Thing
Footpath Chimney
Mantelshelf Route
Raven Rock Gully
Flake Chimney, Lower Tier
Steeplechaser
High Buttress Arête
Chockstone Chimney,
  Windgather

Moderate
Buttress Two Gully
Staircase

Graded List – Bouldering

V12
Inertia Reel Traverse (LT)

V11
Columns (5CL)
War Child (WRI)

V10
Mushin' (LT)
Turbo (LT)
Maurice Gib (GIB)

V9
The Fogey Prow (RAM)
Tetris (5CL)
Mansize (RAM)
Thumbs (WRI)
Grand Theft (UT)
Micro Diddy 'Ole (UT)
Monologue (RAM)
Who Needs Ready Brek? (5CL)
Crank Cuffin (BST)
Another Nadin Traverse (DXY)

Note: Due to a large amount of problems falling into the V8 range, a grade that encompasses approximately two grades of the Fontainebleau system, this section of the graded list has been broken down into Font 7b and 7b+.

V8 (Font 7b+)
Boba Fett (SPR)
Fielder's Wall (BST)
Melvin Bragg (RAM)
Dialogue (RAM)
Sheep Shit (UT)
Higginson's Arm (UT)
Ram Air (RAM)
Cube Direct (CUB)
Baldstones Low (BST)
Pegasus (OUS)
Limp Lizard (DIM)
Crystal Voyager (NTH)

V8 (Font 7b)
Sam Sam Tan (WRI)
Adam's Arête (OUS)
California Screamin' (RAM)
Wrong's Traverse (WRI)
Parental Duties (LTB)
Point Break (WRI)
Simple Simon (WRI)
Wright's Traverse (WRI)
Staying Alive (GIB)
Dirtnap (UT)
Leather Joy Boys (NST)
Fifty Pence (DIM)
Crack Eliminate (WRI)
Gibbering Wreck (GIB)

V7
Inertia Reel (LT)
Spring Slab (SPR)
Nadin's Traverse (UT)
S&M (NST)
Rock Climbing in Britain (RAM)
Sidepull Wall (ART)
Baldstones Traverse (BLD)
The Hard Arête (5CL)
Bancroft's 6b (UT)
Bhodi (WRI)
Drowning Pool (DXY)
Tierdrop Sit Start (RAM)
The Gutter (LT)
Milky Buttons (5CL)
Simon's Slab (HC)
Throwball (BLD)
The Fink (GIB)
Broken Wing (UT)
Clever Skin (BLD)
The Rumour (SPR)
The Green Streak (GBH)
Undercut Dyno (LTB)

V6
Starlight and Storm (HC)
Fingers Start (WRI)
C3PO (SPR)
Be Calmed (RAM)
Simple Simon Indirect (WRI)
Glued Up (UT)
Ousal Low (OUS)
Stall Arête (GIB)
Tierdrop (RAM)
The Hanging Slab (5CL)
Dignity of Labour (LT)
Heavenly Action (SDQ)
High Speed Imp Act (DIM)
Ant Lives (LT)
Limbless Limbo Dancer (UT)
Too Drunk (UT)
Particle Exchange (SPR)
Cottaging (OUS)
The Crack (WRI)
Stallone Arête (NST)

V5
Summit Arête (BOS)
Sheep Shit Crack (UT)
Teck Crack Direct (LT)
The Cube (CUB)
Martin's Problem (GIB)
The Nose (UT)
Elephant's Ear Sit Start (BLD)
Epilogue (RAM)
Gibbering Right (GIB)
Sleeping with the Flowers (UT)
Collywood (RAM)
Blue Nunn (SDQ)
Stretch and Mantel (LTB)
Drunk Enough (UT)

Left Pine (OUS)
Night of Lust Start (RAM)
The Fin (GIB)
Gibby Haines (GIB)
The Boss (UT)

V4
Gentleman John (DIM)
Teck Crack Direct (LT)
Niche Traverse (WRI)
Smoothment Traverse (RAM)
Calcutta Crimp (UT)
Left Groove (UT)
The Grind (SPR)
The Lurch (RAM)
Undercut Traverse (LTB)
The Pinches (RAM)
Buster (POM)
Right Pube (CUB)
Staffordshire Flyer (DXY)
Virgin Wall Traverse (DIM)
Press Direct (RAM)
Fireman Section (WRI)
Starlight Left (HC)
Finger of Fate (5CL)
Jill the Traverse (DIM)
Fielder's Corner (BST)
The Uppercut (LTB)
Elephant's Eye (BST)
Gibbering Left (GIB)
Swivel Flakes (NTH)
Itchy Groove (NST)
Ride My Pimp (CA)
Inner Tube (VFB)
Brown Wall (GBH)
Stretch Left (LTB)
Low Traverse (DIM)
Long Boulder Mantel (UT)

V3
Midge (RAM)
Charlie's Overhang (NST)

Staffordshire Grit

Alternative Start (WRI)
Greener Traverse (LTB)
Oik (UT)
Ousal High (OUS)
Mistral Start (UT)
Rippler (UT)
Sly Stallone (NST)
Baldstones Dyno (BST)
The Undercutter (LTB)
Persistence (5CL)
Cooper's Traverse (UT)
Pine Wall (OUS)
Three Pocket Slab (LTB)
Wildy's Right (POM)
Sprung (SPR)
Crack and Arête (ART)
Matchbox Arête (5CL)
Swivel Finger (NTH)
Spankasaurus Does Chicago (NTH)
Sneezy (OUS)
Joe's Arête (UT)
Ossie's Bulge (RAM)
Ripple (NST)
Hazel Traverse (NST)
Sauroff Sit Start (WRI)
Hazel Groove (NST)
Baldy (BST)

V2

Nose Section (WRI)
Pebbles and Seam (SPR)
Magic Arête (RAM)
Bow Crack (LTB)
Wild Thing Start (SKY)
Right Vein (HC)
The Jams (POM)
Right Slot (RAM)
Pink Wall (UT)
Cottage Arête (POM)

Touched (HC)
Right Groove (UT)
Off Work (POM)
Last Wrights (WRI)
The Break (UT)
Left Vein (HC)
Sign Start (UT)
Calcutta Traverse (UT)
Peace Traverse (SDQ)
Blind Flake (DXY)
Cake (RAM)
Ninestein (5CL)
Fourth Arête (5CL)
Sketchy Rib (SPR)
Roll Off (RAM)
Sly Superdirect (NST)
Traverse of Man (LT)
Matchbox Slab (5CL)
Itchy Fingers (NST)
Flake and Arête (POM)
Reachy Wall (CA)
Impotence (SPR)
Hammy (NST)
Juggy Groove (UT)
Sly Traverse (NST)
Square-Cut Face (NST)
The Clanger (NST)
Violence (SPR)

V1

Seconds Out (SPR)
Staircase (UT)
Chips Ahoy (POM)
Last Drop (RAM)
Bombay Overhang (UT)
Pink Flake (RAM)
Blister Slab (LTB)
Barley (UT)
The Scoop (RAM)
Winger (UT)

Fielder's Indirect (BST)
The Green Greenie (LTB)
Crocodile Slot (RAM)
Tier's End (RAM)
Risky Runnel (UT)
Calcutta Rib (UT)
Babbacombe Start (UT)
Bog Standard (SPR)
Little Groove (WRI)
Harry Patch (VFB)
Thorns Section (WRI)
Boo Meringue (SPR)
Flight Exam (VFB)
Martin's Traverse (NST)
Jamless (RAM)
Hob Traverse (WRI)
Tyrannosaurus Hex (NST)
Ganderhole Crack (BST)
The Arête (GBH)

V0+

Nose Arête Right (UT)
Flakes and Chips (UT)
The Wafer (OUS)
Blister's Sister (LTB)
Pine Slab (LTB)
The Squirm (CA)
Don's Crack (UT)
Long Traverse (UT)
Notch Slab (CUB)
Sprat (SPR)
Soup Dragon (NST)
Gobble (GIB)
The Yawn (GBH)
Billy Bunter (OUS)

V0

Little Rib (OUS)
Big Block Arête (LTB)
Pine Martin (LTB)

Classic Arête (LTB)
Boss Slab (LTB)
Pine Arête Right (LTB)
Right Ramp (HC)
Bridget (NST)
Sail Rib (POM)
Slippery Groove (UT)
Flaky Romp (ART)
Sail Arête (POM)
Static (5CL)
Dreadful (NTH)
Shark's Fin (RAM)
Left Crack (NST)
Yo Clam (NST)
Elephant's Ear (BST)

V0-

Black Nook Arête (LTB)
Pine Arête (LTB)
Joe's Portholes (UT)
Bog Slab (SPR)
Jobby (POM)
The Rammer (RAM)
Big 'Oles (UT)
Thorns Start (WRI)
Popper (UT)
Prehistoric Offwidth (NST)
K2 (CUB)
Summit Arête (SPR)
Bog Arête Left (SPR)
Poxy (SPR)
Sail Slab (POM)
Pinkies to Perkies (VFB)
Practice Chimney (RAM)
Crusty (OUS)
The Hob (WRI)

5CL – Five Clouds
ART – Art Nouveau Boulders (Skyline)
BST – Baldstones
CA – Cellar and Attic
CUB – The Cube
DIM – Dimmings Dale

DXY – Doxey's Pool (Skyline)
GBH – Gradbach Hill
GIB – Gib Torr
HC – Hen Cloud
LT – Roaches Lower Tier
LTB – Roaches Lower Tier Boulders

NTH – Nth Cloud
NST – Newstones
OUS – Ousal Dale
POM – Piece of Mind Boulders
RAM – Ramshaw
SDQ – Stoney Dale Quarry Area
SKY – Skyline

SPR – Spring Boulders
UT – Roaches Upper Tier
VFB – Very far Boulders (Skyline)
WRI – Wright's Rock

Justin Critchlow working his magic on Bancroft's 6b, V7 (page 96). Photo: Adam Long.

Meilee Rafe about to do the mother of all heave-hos on the brutal starting moves of Wild Thing, V2 (page 133), one of the fondest routes in Staffordshire. From here boulderers can jump back to the deck but few will be able to resist the easier but sublime groovelet that leads to the top of the buttress (E1). Photo: David Simmonite.

Index of Climbs

2K 110
39th Step 122
5b Arête 379
5c Wall 208
5c Wall 251
7 of 9 179
99% of Gargoyles Look Like Bob Todd 89

A

A Day at the Seaside 78
A Fist Full of Crystals 53
A Fist Full of Freshers 270
A Little Peculiar 64
A Past Gone Mad 362
A.M. Anaesthetic 113
A.P. Chimney 352
Abdomen 207
Abstract 118
Acid Drop 118
Ackit 51
Acne Arête 127
Action Trousers 268
Adam's Arête 304
A Flabby Crack 171
Afrodizzycrack 322
After Eight 199
Against the Grain 60
Aged Crack 345
Ageing Adolescents 155
Aiguillette, The 167
Alan Whicker 171
Alan's Variant 379
Albatross 311
Alcatraz 205
Alien Wall 325
Aliens 325
All Day and All of the Night 318
All the King's Horses 289
Allen's Fingers 281
All-Stars' Wall 245
Alpha 123
Alpha Arête 123
Alsager Route 367
Alternative Start 314
Alternative Three 312
Alternative Ulster 285
Always Dreaming 140
Amazing Grace 327
Anaconda 175
Ancient 181
Andrei's Route 182
Andy's Crack 361
Annie's Egg 71
Anniversaire 259
Another Nadin Traverse 124
Ant Lives 51
Anthem for a Doomed Youth 325
Anthrax 171
Anticlimax 376
Antidote 362
Antithesis 90
Apache Dawn 49
Ape, The 175
Aperitif 105
A Phoenix Too Frequent 330
Apocalypse Now 95
Appaloosa Sunset 145
Appocaliss 191
Approaching Dark 225
April Showers 374
Aqua 78
Arch, The 44
Arête and Crack 214
Arête and Slab Climb 368
Arête Direct 346
Arête Wall (Hen Cloud) 181
Arête Wall (Ramshaw) 220
Arête, The (Hen Cloud) 179
Arête, The (Ramshaw) 201
Arêtenophobia 185
Armstrain 271
Army Route 219
Art Nouveau 132
Arthur Scargill's Hairpiece is Missing 215
As You Like It 285
Ascent of Man 49
Ascent of Woman 49
Aspirant, The 49
Assegai 215
Assembled Techniques 201
Assorted Pond Life 356
Atlas 327
Atropine 357
Attempted Moustache 78
Austin's Chimney 320
Automatix 117

B

B.S. Mow 368
B4XS 179
Babbacombe Lee 100
Babbacombe Start 99
Baby Groove 208
Bachelor's Buttress 82
Bachelor's Climb 184
Bachelor's Left-Hand 184
Back Crack 110
Back Forest Gâteau 268
Back Side 322
Back Slab Right 42
Backwash 285
Bad Joke 170
Bad Poynt 116
Bad Sneakers 115
Bakewell Tart 145
Baldstones Arête 242
Baldstones Dyno 243
Baldstones Face 242
Baldstones Low 243
Baldstones Traverse 243
Baldy 243
Bancroft's 6b 96
Bandicoot 359
Bantam Crack 171
Barbecue Corners 155
Barbiturate 259
Bareback Rider 49
Bareleg Wall 245
Barley 102
Barriers in Time 51
Bastion Corner 269
Bastion Face 269
Batman 368
Battery Crack 64
Battle of the Bulge 204
Battle Royal 291
Bay Wall 340
Be Calmed 221
Beak, The 95
Beam Me Up Scotty 366
Beckermet Slab 75
Bed of Nails 90
Bees 361
Belladonna 357
Belladonna Direct 357
Bender, The 146
Bengal Buttress 57
Bernie 137
Better End 172
Between the Lines 75
Between the Tiles 106
Beware Coconuts 48
Bewhiskered Behemoth 192
Bhodi 315
Big 'Oles 94
Big Block Arête 43
Big Block Gully 43
Big Flake 147
Big Mike and the Deadlift of Doom 327
Big Red Rock Eater 373
Big Richard 222
Bilberry Slab 366
Bilberry Traverse 120
Bill's XS 378
Billiard Table 256
Billy Bunter 304
Billy the Fish 297
Birthday Climb 357
Bishop, The 260
Bishop's Move 289
Bitch, The 259
Bitching 182
Bizarre 303
BJM 318
Black and Tans 86
Black and Tans Variations 86
Black and White 323
Black Eyed Dog 170
Black Nook Arête 42
Black Nook Slab 42
Black Pig 116
Black Ram 128
Black Ram Arête 128
Black Slab 342
Black Velvet 86
Black Widow 285
Blackbank Crack 245
Blackpool Trip 366
Blazes 314
Blister Slab 42
Blister's Sister 42
Blizzard Buttress 172
Blob, The 71
Block Crack Left-Hand 351
Blockbuster 211
Blood Blisters 170
Bloodspeed 63
Bloodstone 63
Bloody Crack (Ina's) 329
Bloody Crack (Castle Naze) 351
Blow Hard 268
Blue Bandanna 147

391

Staffordshire Grit

Blue Nunn 296
Blunder 325
Blu-Tac 278
Boats for Hire 290
Boba Fett 41
Bobarête 41
Boboon 190
Body Pop 201
Bog Arête Left 40
Bog Arête Right 40
Bog Monster 40
Bog Slab 40
Bog Standard 40
Bollard Edge 269
Bombay Overhang 108
Bond It 278
Bone Idol 123
Boo Meringue 40
Boom Bip 219
Boomerang (Ramshaw) 215
Boomerang (Castle Naze) 359
Boomerang Buttress 359
Booze 302
Boozy Traverse 53
Bordello 191
Border Skirmish 191
Borstal Breakout 175
Boss Slab 44
Boss, The 92
Boston Strangler 141
Bottle Crack 376
Bounty Killer 122
Bow and Arrow 368
Bow Buttress 182
Bow Crack (Castle Naze) 350
Bow Crack (Lower Tier Boulders) 43
Bowcock's Chimney 278
Bowrosin 215
Boysen's Arête 190
Boysen's Delight 143
Boysen-Carrington Route 286
Brad's Chimney 325
Brag, The 225
Brazilian, The 298
Break, The 98
Breakfast Problem 123
Breaks 285
Breathe 305
Breathless 112
Brian the Snail 378
Briar 365
Brick Bank Crack 365
Bridge of Sighs 266
Bridget 238
Broken Arrow 175

Broken Cracks 344
Broken Groove 203
Broken Groove in the Arête 345
Broken Slab 76
Broken Wing 95
Brothers, The 324
Brown Wall 260
Brown's Crack 206
Bruno Flake 112
Bubbly Wall 359
Bulger, The 64
Bulging Arête 344
Bulldog Flake 371
Bulwark 168
Bumper Cars 268
Burnham Crack 266
Burning Pete 243
Burrito Deluxe 48
Buster 71
Buster the Cat 171
Buttress Two Gully 344

C

C3PO 41
Cabana 277
Cad Cam Warrior 298
Caesarian 172
Cake 206
Calcutta Buttress 106
Calcutta Crab Dance 106
Calcutta Crack 106
Calcutta Crimp 108
Calcutta Rib 108
Calcutta Traverse 108
Calf Path 133
California Screamin' 225
Calyx 316
Cambridge Crack 367
Camelian Crack 211
Candy Man 238
Cannabis Arm 278
Cannon, The 205
Cannonball Crack 55
Canticle 297
Capitol Climb 74
Capstan's Corner 118
Capstone Chimney 269
Captain Lethargy 68
Captain Quark 241
Captain Skyhook 368
Captain's Blood 368
Caramta 225
Caricature 183
Carpet Crack 361
Carrion 65
Castle Crack 368
Castles of Sand 320
Cat Crawl 374
Cat Inside 348

Catapult 348
Catastrophe Internationale 49
Catharsis 173
Cave Arête 118
Cave Crack (Skyline) 117
Cave Crack (Belmont Hall) 281
Cave Exit 110
Cave Overhang 311
Cave Rib 281
Cave Wall 289
Cedez le Passage 214
Ceiling Zero 226
Cellar Dwella 103
Cellar Slab 1 103
Cellar Slab 2 103
Central Climb 179
Central Climb Direct 175
Central Massif 78
Central Route (Back Forest) 270
Central Route (Wootton Lodge) 330
Central Route (Windgather) 343
Central Route (Upper Tier) 89
Central Tower (Hen Cloud) 188
Central Tower (Castle Naze) 357
Central Traverse 115
Centre, The 345
Chalkstorm 67
Chameleon 185
Chamonaze Blues 358
Charlie Farley 278
Charlie's Overhang 234
Chasm Arête 102
Cheek 345
Cheek, The 285
Cheesy Moon 98
Cherry Hill 365
Cherry Rare 310
Chiaroscuro 184
Chicane 117
Chicane Destination 113
Chicanery 112
Chicken 169
Chicken Run 73
Childhood's End 226
Chilton's Superdirect 325
Chimney and Crack 342
Chips Ahoy 70
Chiropodist's Nightmare 298
Chockstone Chimney (Ramshaw) 204
Chockstone Chimney

(Windgather) 343
Chockstone Corner 143
Chockstone Crack (Hen Cloud) 172
Chockstone Crack (Gradbach Hill) 259
Chockstone Crack (Peakstone Inn Amphitheatre) 318
Choka 66
Christmas Arête 340
Christmas Cracker 365
Christmas Nose 340
Chronicle 128
Chunky 260
Chute, The 289
Cioch Groove 368
Circuit Breaker 66
City Dweller 362
City Hobgoblins 362
Clam 286
Clammy Hands 241
Clanger, The 241
Classic Arête 43
Cleavers, The 376
Cleft Route 256
Cleg 205
Clever Skin 247
Clever Skin Left-Hand 247
Clippety Clop 211
Clive Coolhead Realises the Excitement of Knowing You May Be the Author of Your Own Death is More Intense Than Orgasm 64
Cloud Nine 140
Cloudbusting 144
Clover Field 309
Clown, The 280
Clumsy Too 310
Cobweb 376
Coelred's Crack 325
Cold Blood 63
Cold Bone Forgotten 59
Cold Shoulder 364
Cold Sweat 187
Cold Wind 205
Coldfinger 76
CollyWobble 207
Collywood 207
Columbal Convenience 358
Columns 144
Coma Sutra 129
Combs Climb 354
Come On! 120
Come On Eileen 356
Comedian 183
Comedian, The 211

Index

Commander Energy 67
Communist Crack 151
Condor Chimney 113
Condor Slab 113
Connector 117
Constant Rrumble 283
Contraception on Demand 371
Contract Worker 271
Contrary Mary 76
Cool Fool 183
Cool in a Crisis 374
Cooper's Traverse 95
Corinthian 183
Cornelina 327
Cornelius 327
Corner Crack (Ramshaw) 205
Corner Cracks 67
Corner Traverse 285
Corner, The 344
Cornflake 78
Cottage Arête 70
Cottage Slab 304
Cottaging 304
Couch Potato 373
Counterstroke of Equity 135
Crab Walk 206
Crab Walk Direct 206
Crabbie's Crack 146
Crabbie's Crack Left-Hand 145
Crack and Corner 100
Crack Indirect 99
Crack of Gloom 57
Crack Start 99
Crack, The 316
Cracked Arête (Skyline) 113
Cracked Arête (Ramshaw) 221
Cracked Arête (Ramshaw) 219
Cracked Gully 219
Crafty Cockney 374
Crank Cuffin 243
Crank, The 203
Credit Crunch 297
Creep 214
Crenation 74
Crest 285
Crime Gene 348
Crimes of Passion 281
Crinkles Wall 71
Cripple's Corner 330
Crippler, The 222
Crispin's Crack 190
Crocodile Slot 208
Croissant Groove 70

Crud on the Tracks 329
Crumble in the Jungle 297
Crumble Roof 311
Crushed Pagan God 361
Crusty 304
Crying Wolf 374
Crystal Grazer 53
Crystal Tipps 220
Crystal Voyager (Nth Cloud) 154
Crystal Voyager (Bosley) 376
Crystal Voyager (Mow Cop) 368,
Crystine 368
Cube Crack 110
Cube Traverse 110
Cube, The 110
Cue, The 256
Curd be Cheese 323
Curfew 223
Curiosity Kitten 117
Curvature 133
Cyber Insekt 361

D

Daedalus 324
Damascus Crack 76
Dan's Dare 215
Dance of the Flies 299
Dancing Bear 318
Danera 365
Dangerous Crocodile Snogging 211
Dangler 128
Darkness 219
Dave's Traverse 311
Davros 311
Dawn Piper 76
Days Gone 123
Days of Future Passed 49
Dazed and Confused 109
Dazzler 128
Dead Banana Slab 185
Dead Tree Crack 318
Dead Tree Slab 318
Deadwood Crack 281
Deadwood Groove 281
Death Crack 373
Death Knell 66
Death Mask 324
Death Wish (Flintmill) 283
Death Wish (Bosley) 373
Deceiver, The 188
Deception 371
Deep Chimney 357
Deep Crack 357
Deep in Mystery 126
Defiance 325

Definitive Gaze 122
Delectable Deviation 220
Delstree 173
Delusion 187
Demon Wall 73
Descant 297
Desert Head 366
Desert Rat 320
Desperado 185
Destination Earth 55
Destination Venus 102
Devil's Crack 285
Devotoed 123
Diagonal Crack 286
Diagonal Route 188
Dialogue 221
Diamond Wednesday 86
Dignity of Labour 52
Dimetrodon 322
Director 344
Dirtnap 108
Dirty Wee Rouge 64
Discontinuous Rib and Groove 347
Dish Grab 108
Distant Runners 281
Dixon's Dart Board 378
DNA 287
Dog-Leg Corner 271
Dog-Leg Crack 271
Doina Da J'al 298
Don Quixote 289
Don's Arête 95
Don's Crack (Ramshaw) 207
Don's Crack (Upper Tier) 95
Don't Go Down to the Woods Today 126
Donor 327
Don't be Strangers 297
Dorothy's Dilemma 55
Double Chin 202
Double Crack 350
Double Overhang 266
Double Vee 368
Doubloon 279
Doug 53
Dougie Returns Home 68
Doug-less 41
Down To The Elbows 324
Downpipe, The 103
Drain the Main Vein 238
Dreadful 154
Dream Fighter 201
Dreamer 140
Drifter's Escape 266
Driven Bow 182
Drop Acid 118
Dropsy 71

Drowning Pool 124
Drunk Enough 109
Drystone Wall 373
Duck Billed Platypus (Dimmings Dale) 305
Duck-Billed Platypus (Castle Naze) 359
Duck Soup 190
Duplo Magic 320
Dusk 219
Dust Storm 320

E

Early Retirement 225
Earthquake Crack 361
East Face 199
Easy Come 181
Easy Corner 350
Easy Cracks 350
Easy Exit 243
Easy Gully 181
Easy Gully Wall 100
Easy Slab 235
Eclipsed Peach 145
Ecstasy 1 378
Editor's Note 346
Elastic Arm 144
Elastic Limit 211
Elastic Wall 208
Electric Chair 170
Electric Savage 217
Electrofly 308
Elegy 64
Elephant's Ear 247
Elephant's Ear Sit-Start 247
Elephant's Eye 247
Emerald Groove 285
Emerald Wall 285
EMS 287
En Rappel 172
Encouragement 179
English Towns 215
Enigma Variation 120
Ensign, The 254
Entente Cordiale 128
Enterprise 366
Entropy's Jaw 133
Envy Face 371
Epilogue 221
Eric the Frog 378
Escape 222
Eugene's Axe 60
Even Lonelier 303
Even Smaller Buttress 181
Evensong 297
Everdance 373
Evil Crack 226
Existentialist Arête 373
Ex-Lion Tamer 297
Extended Credit 225

393

Staffordshire Grit

Extended Torrture 254
Extractum 325
Eye of Japetus 268

F

Face 281
Face Route 1 346
Face Route 2 346
Face Value 187
False Chicane 112
Fandango 286
Farmer Barlimow 366
Farmhouse Arête 226
Fast and Bulbous 325
Fast Piping 183
Fat Man Burger Overdose 361
Fat Man's Chimney 356
Fat Old Nick 256
Fat Old Sun 173
Fat Slags 297
Fatalist's Canoe 290
Feet of Strength 289
Fern Crack 73
Fertility Rite 371
Fertility Rite Left-Hand 371
Fielder's Corner 247
Fielder's Indirect 247
Fielder's Wall 247
Fifth Cloud Eliminate 140
Fifth Horseman 350
Fifty Pence Problem 308
Filler In 269
Fin, The 251
Final Crack 175
Final Destination 68
Finger of Fate 151
Finger, The 102
Fingers in Every Pie 312
Fingers Start 314
Fink, The 251
Fire Down Below 191
Fireman Indirect 314
Fireman Section 315
First's Arête 346
Five Thousand Volts 322
Flake Chimney 66
Flake Crack 351
Flake Escape 281
Flake Museum 98
Flake Slab 236
Flake Traverse 281
Flake Wall 285
Flakes and Chips 96
Flaky Romp 132
Flaky Wall Direct 219
Flaky Wall Indirect 219
Flap Dancer 98
Fledgling's Climb 64

Flexure Line 181
Flies of Ambition 361
Flight Exam 137
Flimney 66
Flour Wall 185
Flourescent Squid 188
Flower Power Arête 146
Flowtation 309
Fluorescent Stripper 67
Flutterbye Grooves 129
Fly Walk 351
Fly, The 38
Fogey Prow 226
Folly Berger 368
Foord's Folly 223
Footpath 285
Footpath Chimney (Hen Cloud) 185
Footpath Chimney (Dimmings Dale) 305
Footprint 344
Footprints 305
Footstool Left 354
Footstool Right 354
For Tim 256
Force Nine 221
Forking Chimney 245
Formative Years 123
Four Horsemen 325
Four Purists 217
Fourth Arête 144
Fourthright 144
Fox, The 240
Foxy Lady 140
Framed 361
Frank's Route 359
Frayed Nerve 183
Freak Out 73
Fred's Café 53
Frequency 286
Fresher's Arête 379
Friar Muck 298
Friends of Eddie Coil 365
Front Crack 258
Fruit Palace 366
Full Frontal 283
Furry Green Atom Bowl 362

G

Gain Entry to Your Soul 298
Gallows, The (Hen Cloud) 170
Gallows, The (Castle Crag) 324
Ganderhole Crack 247
Gape, The 259
Gaping Void 266
Garlic 109

Gary's 5c 253
Gateless Gate 291
Gates, The 103
General Accident 299
Genetix (Upper Tier) 106
Genetix (Sharpcliffe) 278
Gentleman John 309
Geography of Power 361
Gib 254
Gibber Crack 252
Gibbering Left 251
Gibbering Lip 251
Gibbering Right 251
Gibbering Wreck 254
Gibbet, The 254
Gibble Gabble Slab 253
Gibbon Take 252
Gibbon Wall 254
Gibby Haines 252
Gibe Turkey 254
Gibe, The 252
Gibeonite Girdle 254
Giblet Crack 254
Gibling Corner 254
Gibraltar 254
GibTorrture 254
Gillted 88
Ging 76
Ginger Biscuit 192
Gingerbread 192
Gladiator 327
Glass Back 144
Glory Hole 304
Glossy Finish 310
Glued Up 95
Goats Gruff 98
Gobble 252
Gold Rush 243
Golden Sovereign 279
Goldsitch Crack 243
Gollum 263
Gommorah 378
Gorgonzola 278
Graduate, The 324
Graffiti 55
Grand Theft 92
Grasper 270
Grasper, The 44
Grasshopper 305
Grassy Slabs 365
Great Chimney 185
Great Scene Baby 222
Great Zawn 202
Green Chimney 153
Green Corner (Hen Cloud) 170
Green Corner (Ramshaw) 217
Green Crack (Ramshaw) 201

Green Crack (Back Forest) 268
Green Crack (Gradbach) 256,
Green Greenie 44
Green Gully Direct 371
Green Shaker 270
Green Slab 44
Green Streak 260
Greenerête 44
Grenadier 153
Grind, The 39
Grinding Sloper 235
Gritstone Pimple 127
Gromit 152
Gromit Arête 152
Groovy Baby 222
Grott 307
Ground Support 329
Grounded 325
Grumbling Wall 283
Gryphon 365
Guano Gully 63
Gully Arête 203
Gully Wall (Upper Tier) 105
Gully Wall (Hen Cloud) 215
Gumshoe 204
Gurning Bulldog 247
Gutter, The 59
Gypfast 83

H

Hal's Ridge 190
Halcyone 365
Hallow to our Men 122
Hammy 236
Hand Jive 297
Handrail 214
Handrail Direct 214
Handy Wall 102
Hanging Around 86
Hanging Crack 208
Hanging Slab 144
Hanging Stone Crack 266
Hangman's Crack 102
Hank's Horror 115
Happiness from Outer Space 153
Hard Arête 144
Harry Patch 137
Harvest Moon 366
Hassall's Crack 281
Hatscheck's Groove 286
Hawk's Hell 368
Hawkwing 65
Hazel Barn 236
Hazel Barrow Crack 236
Hazel Groove 236

Index

Hazel Traverse 236
Headless Horseman 65
Heart of Gold 188
Heather Buttress 342
Heather Face 344
Heather Slab 74
Heavenly Action 298
Hedgehog Crack 183
Heighley Nightmare 379
Height Below 325
Heinous Mantel 43
Helix, The 287
Helter Skelter Finish 184
Hem Line 207
Hen Cloud Eliminate 183
Hens Dropping 179
Herbivacious 376
Here Be Dragons 283
Herford's Girdle Traverse 358
Hey Diddle Diddle 308
Higginson's Arm 96
High Buttress Arête 344
High Crossing 102
High Energy Plan 192
High Girdle 266
High Priest 296
High Speed Imp Act 309
High Tensile Crack 171
High Tension Line 362
Hilti Gunner 380
Hippo 238
Hob Crack 362
Hob Knob 316
Hob Traverse 316
Hob, The 316
Hobjection Overruled 362
Hobs of Hell 362
Hodgkinson's Chimney 359
Hole and Corner Crack 289
Holly Tree Niche Left Route 268
Holly Tree Niche Right Route 268
Hollybush Crack 87
Hollybush Hell 325
Hollybush Wall 374
Honest John 325
Honest Jonny 202
Honeycomb 361
Honking Bank Worker 225
Honky Tonk 128
Hooverville 361
Hopeless Holly 325
Hot Digital Dog 365
Hot Dog 277
Hot Tin Roof 374
Hotter Than July 376

Hour Glass 256
Humble Potter 325
Humdinger 83
Humpty Dumpty 308
Hunky Dory 67
Hush Puppy 277
Hypothesis 55

I

Icarus 324
Icarus Allsorts 146
Icebreaker 350
Impact Two 373
Impacted Bowel 303
Impending Doom 286
Imperfect Lichenous 362
Imposition 219
Impotence 38
In Days of Hold 281
In Passing 111
Ina City Riot 329
Ina's Chimney 327
Inaccessible 327
Inaquality 329
Inasense 329
Inbetweenie 359
Incognito 242
Indecent Exposure 283
Inertia Reel 52
Inertia Reel Traverse 51
Inexplicably Anonymous 154
Initiation Groove 329
Initiation Wall 368
Inner Tube 137
Insects from Hell 361
Inspector Remorse 361
Inspiration Point 136
Inverted Staircase 73
Iron Age Fortitude 358
Iron Horse Crack 219
Iron Pebble 311
Itchy Fingers 238
Itchy Groove 238
Ivanhoe 291
Ivy League 378

J

Jack the Traverse 308
Jacquimo 329
Jamless 221
Jean the Bean 179
Jeffcoat's Buttress 86
Jeffcoat's Chimney 86
Jeffcoat's Chimney Variations 86
Jelly Roll 100
Jellyfish 188
Jess's Arête 379

Jess's Corner 379
Jester, The 280
Jetez le Pantalon 192
Jill the Traverse 308
Jilted 348
Jimmy Carter 151
Jobby 71
Joe Public 78
Joe's Arête 94
Joe's Portholes 95
Jog 76
John's Arête 259
John's Route 268
Johnny Pooh Poohed 113
Johnny Utah 314
Johnny's Groove 208
Johnny's Indirect Rear Entry 245
Johnson'sville 278
Joiner 117
Joker, The 281
Josephina 152
Joshua 365
Juan Cur 205
Judge Dread 155
Judge Jules 155
Jug Jam 364
Jug Up 95
Jug Wall 311
Juggy Groove 96
Jump 110
Just for Today 51
Just Thirteen 185
Justin Time 171

K

K.P. Nuts 49
K2 (The Cube) 110
K2 (Hen Cloud) 179
Kaleidoscope 279
Kangaroo 359
Karabiner Chimney 118
Karabiner Slab 118
Keep Arête 354
Keep Buttress 352
Keep Corner 352
Keep Face 269
Keep Left 365
Keeper, The 268
Keith George: The Movie 358
Keith Sharp Holds 310
Kelly's Connection 90
Kelly's Direct 90
Kelly's Shelf 90
Kenyatta 279
Kestrel Crack 65
Key Green Crack 374
Kicking Bird 63
Kill a Friend 371

Killer Wall 379
Killjoy 279
King Harold 226
King Swing 117
Kipling Arête 363
Klangerman 298
Kneewrecker Chimney 281
Knossos 278
Koala 359
Kobold 279
Konsolation Prize 278
Krakatoa 279
Kremlin Wall 371
Krushna 278
Kudos 279

L

Labyrinth, The 324
Ladies' Route 226
Laguna Sunrise 145
Larva Wall 289
Last Banana Before Sunset 245
Last Drop 207
Last Post 289
Last Wrights 315
Late Night Final 75
Laughing all the way to the Blank 90
Lawnmower Man 297
Layback 354
Layered Cake 297
Lazy Trout 136
Leading Firemen 312
Leaky Traverse 153
Leap 214
Leather Joy Boys 234
Lechery 225
Ledgeway 352
Lee Side 367
Leeds Crack 202
Leeds Slab 202
Leek Hills 137
Left Block Crack 141
Left Eliminate 368
Left Fin 251
Left Groove 96
Left It 364
Left Nostril 370
Left Pine 305
Left Slab 42
Left Triplet Crack 347
Left Twin Arête 236
Left Twin Crack 114
Left Twin Crack 185
Left Twin Crack 325
Left Vein 182
Left-Hand Crack 266
Left-Hand Route 105

395

Staffordshire Grit

Leg Stump 344
Leg Up 346
Legends of Lost Leaders 151
Legoland 321
Legosaurus Rex 320
Lenin 151
Let it Go 359
Lethal Weapon 329
Letter Box Cracks 115
Letter Box Gully 115
Levitation 173
Libra 78
Licence to Lust 59
Licence to Run 59
License to Kill 59
Licensed to Fill 113
Lichenthrope 99
Life In The Left Lane 280
Life in the Wrong Lane 280
Lighthouse 114
Lightning Crack 52
Limbless Limbo Dancer 108
Limp Lizard 309
Limpet 286
Lintel, The 98
Lisa Lust 297
Little Cenotaph 378
Little Chimney 64
Little Crack 154
Little Flake 147
Little Giraffe Man 226
Little Groove 315
Little Maia 327
Little Nasty 217
Little Nikki 299
Little Perforations 78
Little Pillar 352
Little Pinnacle Climb 168
Little Prow 208
Little Rib 302
Live Bait 74
Living Wall 373
Loaf and Cheese 201
Lockit to the Pockit 309
Logical Progression 65
Logos 364
Lone Ascent 78
Lone Wall 303
Loner, The 137
Long and the Short 175
Long Boulder Mantel 95
Long Climb 357
Long Lankin 298
Long Traverse 98
Longstop 299
Looking for Today 122

Loose Fingers 181
Lord's Arête 307
Lord's Chimney 307
Louie Groove 201
Lout 39
Lubricant, The 373
Lucas Chimney 64
Lucid Reams 247
Lum, The 171
Lung Cancer 112
Lurch, The (Ramshaw) 208
Lurch, The (Lower Tier) 38
Lust Left-Hand 222
Lybstep 76

M

M.B. Arête 343
Mad Lines 191
Magenta Corner 286
Magic Arête 221
Magic Child 100
Magic Crossing 98
Magic Roundabout 220
Magic Roundabout Direct 220
Magic Roundabout Super Direct 220
Magnificat 297
Maid Marion 298
Main Corner 351
Main Crack 173
Main Wall 373
Man Mow 368
Man oh Man 169
Mandatory 169
Mandrake, The 169
Mandrill 169
Manifesto 283
Mansize 208
Mantel and Pocket 70
Mantelshelf Route 143
Mantelshelf Slab 120
Mantis 122
Mantrap 222
Mark 325
Mark of Zorro 190
Mark of Zorro 379
Marsden's Crack 259
Marsden's Eliminate 278
Martin's Problem 252
Martin's Traverse 236
Martin's Mono Problem 308
Marxist Undertones 151
Masochism 203
Master of Puppets 169
Master of Reality 169
Matchbox Arête 110
Matchbox Slab 140
Matinee 59

Maurice Gib 252
Max 136
Maximum Hype 204
May Day 374
Mayhem 153
Mean Ol' B'stard 95
Meander 141
Meander Variation 141
Medicine, The 343
Meeny 359
Mega Traverse 309
Megalomania 286
Melaleucion 123
Melancholy Man 287
Melvin Bragg 202
Meninges 278
Mental Traveller 307
Metaphysical Scoop 155
Mick's Metaphor 190
Micky 71
Micro Diddy 'Ole 98
Microcosm 129
Middle and Leg 345
Middle Triplet Crack 347
Middleton's Motion 115
Midge 205
Mild Thing 133
Milky Buttons 143
Miller's Melody 283
Mincer, The 63
Mindbenderjelly 309
Mindbridge 168
Minipin Crack 245
Minos 324
Minotaur 324
Minute Wall 374
Miny 359
Mirror 143
Mishmash 259
Misogynist 365
Miss Understood 325
Miss You Already 296
Mississippi (or Straight) Crack 343
Mississippi Crack Variant 343
Mistaken Identity 118
Mister Coconut 236
Mistral 106
Mistral Start 108
Mixer, The 362
Mo 359
Modern 181
Modesty Crack 225
Molegrip Kid 324
Mongolian Throat Singing 243
Monk's Blues 296
Monkey in your Soul 175
Monodoigt, The 98

Monologue 221
Monstrous Angel 126
Montezuma's Revenge 253
Monty 215
Moon Jumper 308
Moonshine 235
Moore's Crack 286
Moov Over 323
Morocc'n Roll 358
Morpheus 259
Morridge Top 245
Moss Rose 286
Moss Side Story 363
Moto Perpetuo 303
Motorbike 316
Mounty 102
Mousey's Mistake 63
Mr Creosote 266
Mr Decisive 133
Mr Grogan 278
Mr Left 39
Mr Magoo 371
Mr Nice 39
Much Ado About Nothing 286
Mudhopper 128
Muscle Crack 351
Mushin 52
Mustard 270
Mutiny Chimney 374
Muzzle 243
My Arse 322
My Mother is a Rhinoceros 299
Myxi 171

N

N.E. Hobbs 362
Nadin's Traverse 95
Nadin's Secret Finger 151
National Acrobat 201
National Hero 48
National Hysteria 243
Nature Trail 135
Navy Cut 112
Neb Finish 87
Never Never 310
Never Never Land 217
New Fi'nial 88
Newstones Chimney 234
Niche Arête 351
Niche Traverse 311
Niche, The 175
Nick Slab 348
Night of Lust 223
Night of Lust Start 222
Night Prowler 185
Nine Tales 348
Ninestein 140
Nithin, The 351

Index

No Future 325
No Name 352
No Pegs Please 281
No Veranda 305
Nom De Guerre 291
North Buttress Arête 342
North Buttress Arête Indirect 342
North Face 291
Northern Comfort 59
Northern Lights 318
Nose Arête Left 94
Nose Arête Right 94
Nose Direct 344
Nose Section 315
Nose, The 96
Nosepicker 113
Nosey Parker 283
Nosy 92
Not Much Further 126
Not So Central Route 270
Not So Fast 126
Not So Steep 126
November Cracks 168
Nozag 357
Nursery Arête 352
Nutcracker, The 188
Nutmeg 236
Nutmeg Groove 236
Nutted by Reality 168

O

Oak Spur 286
Oak Tree Crack 258
Obsession Fatale 68
Off Work 70
Off-Fingers Crack 137
Ogden 116
Ogden Arête 116
Ogden Recess 116
Oik 99
Old Fogey 226
Old Fogey Direct 226
Old King Cole 286
Old Sloper Problem 315
Old Son 256
Omega 123
One Chromosome's Missing 286
One Dunne 318
One Knight Stand 289
Ooze 302
Open All Hours 325
Open Bum Cleft 70
Orange Crush 304
Original Route (Baldstones) 242
Original Route (Harston) 285

Orm and Cheep 352
Ossie's Bulge 208
Ostentation 286
Other Corner, The 343
Ou est le Spit? 109
Ousal High 303
Ousal Low 302
Out There and Back 310
Outdoor Pursuits Cooperative 151
Outflanked 206
Overdrive 202
Overhanging Arête 346
Overhanging Chimney 359
Overhanging Chockstone Crack 350
Overlap 206
Overlapping Wall 347
Overlord 307
Oversight 116
Oversight Crack 358

P

Painted Rumour 88
Painter's Rock 310
Pair O' Genes 286
Palpitation 286
Palsy Wall 286
Pants on Fire 242
Parallel Lines 184
Paralogism 90
Parental Duties 43
Parrot and the Balaclava 133
Particle Exchange 41
Pasiphae 324
Patient Weaver 325
Paul's Puffer 115
Paul's Wall 271
Peace Traverse 296
Peakstone Crack 322
Pebbledash 60
Pebbles and Seam 40
Pebbles on a Wessex Beach 115
Pebblesville 277
Ped X-ing 100
Pedestal Route 88
Peep Show 277
Peeping Tom 283
Peg Crack 358
Pegasus 309
Pegger's Original 299
Pepper 109
Per Rectum 325
Perambulator Parade 242
Perched Block Arête 117
Perched Flake 220

Period Drama 110
Perp, The 155
Persistence 144
Perverted Staircase 73
Pete's Back Side 188
Peter and the Wolf 183
Phallic Crack 205
Phantom, The 256
Piano Stool 354
Pie Hard 312
Piece of Mind 68
Pieces of Eight 279
Pile Driver 222
Pilgrim's Progress 352
Pillar of Judgement 155
Pillow of Wind 289
Pincer 63
Pinch, The 173
Pinches, The 221
Pindles Numb 53
Pine Arête 44
Pine Arête Right 44
Pine Crack 44
Pine Martin 44
Pine Slab 44
Pine Wall 305
Pink Flake 202
Pink Wall 95
Pink Wall Eliminate 94
Pinkies to Perkies 137
Pinnacle Arête (Skyline) 120
Pinnacle Arête (Castle Naze) 350
Pinnacle Buttress 268
Pinnacle Crack (Skyline) 120
Pinnacle Crack (Castle Naze) 350
Pinnacle Face 187
Pinnacle Rib 187
Pinnacle Slab 120
Pinnacle Start and Shaun's End 155
Pip 258
Pipe Entry 103
Piston Groove 169
Piton Route 367
Pitoned Crack 352
Pixie 95
Plankton 356
Plastics Factory 320
Plebble 322
Plumb-Line 155
Pluto's Ring 192
Pocket Hercules 318
Pocket Wall (Ramshaw) 226
Pocket Wall (Cottage

Rocks) 304
Pockets Arête 42
Pod Crack 352
Pod 'n' up 38
Poems and Promises 181
Point Break 315
Pointless Arête 147
Pointless but Pumpy 173
Poison Gift 65
Poisonous Python 55
Ponsified 238
Poodle Vindaloo 118
Pop Art 129
Popper 98
Porridge at Morridge Top 252
Porridge Wall 252
Port Crack 221
Portcullis Crack 268
Portfolio 343
Pot Black 256
Potty 70
Poxy 40
Practice Chimney 221
Prayers 181
Praying Mantel 235
Prehistoric Offwidth 241
Prelude to Space 135
Prelude to XB 243
Premature Evacuation 330
Prescription for the Poor 374
Press Direct 222
Press On Regardless 175
Press, The 222
Pretentious? Moi? 376
Pride, The 297
Prism, The 225
Private Display 143
Probably Boysen's Arête 190
Problem Arête 271
Proboscid, The 222
Prodigal, The 324
Prometheus 365
Prostration 206
Prow Corner 67
Prow Cracks 67
Prowler 202
Prowler 303
Psalm 297
Pseudo Crack 269
Pube, The 110
Public Enemy Number One 78
Puffed Up 238
Puffed Wheat 278
Pug 171
Pugilist, The 111

397

Staffordshire Grit

Pull John 330
Pull Johnny 324
Pull the Udder One 323
Punch 66
Punch Arete 378
Puppet Life 310
Pure Crackling 340
Push 305
Pussin' Boots 127
Pyeclough 247

Q
Qantas 175
Quaking All Over 361
Quasimodo 330
Qui Vive 291
Quickbrew 78

R
Rabbit Stew 310
Raid, The 172
Raiders of the Lost Bark 321
Rainbow Crack 185
Rainbow Recess 289
Rakes Dale Chimney 321
Ralph's Direct 114
Ralph's Mantelshelves 114
Ram Air 208
Rammer, The 221
Ramphole of the Roaches 38
Ramshaw Crack 217
Rash Challenge 225
Rassp! 115
Raven 278
Raven Rock Gully 57
Raven Rock Gully Left-Hand 57
Rawhide 327
Ray's Roof 245
Reach, The 368
Reachy Wall 102
Recess Chimney 170
Recess Corner 310
Recess Wall and Arête 114
Red Nose Route 340
Reg 95
Renaissance, The 325
Requiem for Tired Fingers 270
Reset Portion of Galley 37 76
Respectable Street 361
Restless Natives 324
Reunion Crack 173
Reverse Charge 307
Rhodren 66

Rhody Crack 307
Rhynose 238
Rib and Slab 344
Rib Chimney 183
Rib Crack 183
Rib Wall 105
Rib, The 105
Richter 5 361
Ride My Pimp 103
Ride the Lightning 140
Riding the Gravy Train 245
Rig A Dig Dig 324
Right Block Crack 141
Right Bow 266
Right Eliminate 368
Right Groove 96
Right It 364
Right Nostril 371
Right Pine 305
Right Pube 110
Right Ramp 182
Right Route 90
Right Route Right 90
Right Slot 208
Right Tot 368
Right Triplet Crack 347
Right Twin Arête 236
Right Twin Crack (Hen Cloud) 185
Right Twin Crack (Park banks) 325
Right Vein 182
Right Wall 318
Right-Hand Crack 350
Right-Hand Route (Upper Tier) 105
Right-Hand Route (Skyline) 122
Ripple 236
Ripple 285
Ripple Arête 92
Rippler 92
Rippler, The 205
Ripples 318
Risky Runnel 102
Robin 368
Robin Hood 298
Rock Around The Chock 318
Rock Climbing in Britain 206
Rock Room Slab 71
Rock Trivia 203
Rocket Ride 311
Rocket to 'em 297
Rocking Stone Crack 297
Rocking Stone Gully 68
Rocking Stone Ridge 271
Rodeo 123

Roger Melly 297
Roll Off 206
Rollercoaster 219
Roman Candle 143
Roman Nose 143
Roof Climb 175
Rooster 72
Roscoe's Wall 100
Rosehip 238
Rostrum, The 268
Rotondas 286
Rotunda Buttress 82
Rotunda Gully 82
Round Table 102
Route 1 346
Route 1 Direct 347
Route 1.5 346
Route 2 346
Rowan Tree Crack 154
Rowan Tree Traverse 115
Rubber Crack 219
Rubberneck 145
Ruby Tuesday 86
Rugosity 285
Rumour, The 41
Runaway 289
Runnel Entry 223
Runnel Rouser 102
Runner Route 76
Rusks And Rye 278
Ruth's Septic Trench 268

S
S&M 234
Safety Net 115
Sail Arête 70
Sail Rib 70
Sail Slab 70
Sale's Bulge 281
Sally James 118
Sam Sam Tan 314
Sam's Left Hand 207
San Melas 123
Sand Castles 170
Sandbagger 320
Sands of Time 144
Sanitarium 192
Sapling Bugle 304
Saucer Direct 269
Saul's Crack 83
Saunter 285
Sauria 185
Sauroff 311
Sauroff Sit Start 311
Sauron 311
Scab 71
Scallop 98
Scarlet Wall 105
Schoolies 57

Scoop Direct 354
Scoop Direct Start 354
Scoop Face 39
Scoop Wall (Peakstone Inn Amphitheatre) 318
Scoop Wall (Castle Naze) 354
Scoop, The 208
Scooped Surprise 219
Scorpion 364
Scout In Situ 219
Scout Wall 318
Scrabble 188
Scrack 102
Scratch Arête 238
Scratch Crack 238
Scratchy Scoop 41
Screwy Driver 223
Script for a Tear 133
Scrumptious 171
Sculptor's Wall 311
Seams Green 253
Second's Advance 183
Second's Retreat 183
Seconds Out 39
Secrets of Dance 60
Sedition and Alchemy 191
Seismic Wall 361
Sennapod 122
Sennapod Crack 122
Sense of Doubt 259
Serpent, The 379
Shark's Fin 225
Shaun's Other End 153
Sheep Shit 99
Sheep Shit Crack 99
Shelf Route 286
Sheltered Crack 350
Shepherd, The 137
Shining Path 141
Shockwave 361
Shoe Shine Shuffle 188
Short 'n Sharp 169
Short and Sweet 352
Short Man's Misery 190
Short Ride 297
Short Trip to a Transylvanian Brain Surgery 78
Shortbread 192
Shortcake 192
Shortcomings 114
Shrug 117
Sickle Moon 366
Sid the Sexist 304
Side Face 346
Sidepull Wall 132
Sidewinder 57
Sifta's Quid 68

Index

Sign of the Times 106
Sign Start 108
Silent Scream 368
Simon's Slab 167
Simon's Wall 366
Simpkins' Overhang 73
Simple Simon 312, 314
Simple Simon Indirect 314
Simple View 271
Sirloin 376
Skallagrigg 76
Sketching Wildly 206
Sketchy Rib 41
Skin and Wishbones 90
Skinned Rabbit 39
Skull Crack 289
Skydivin' 52
Skytrain 118
Slab 2 42
Slab and Arête 118
Slab and Crack 71
Slab of Meat 376
Slab Wall 371
Slanting Crack (Five Clouds) 153
Slanting Crack (Castle Naze) 350
Slanting Crack (Short Edge) 361,
Sleeping with the Flowers 108
Sleepwalker 259
Slender Thread 376
Slim Corner 380
Slim Groove 259
Slimline 183
Slippery Caramel 307
Slippery Groove 96
Slippery Jim 49
Slips 118
Slipstreams 168
Slither 128
Sloth, The 88
Slow Hand Clap 225
Slowhand 168
Sly Corner 241
Sly Direct 241
Sly Mantelshelf 240
Sly Stallone 240
Sly Superdirect 240
Sly Traverse 240
Small Buttress 182
Small Wall 343
Smear Test 63
Smoothment Traverse 206
Smun 141
Snake, The 240
Snap, Crackle and Andy Popp 49

Sneeze 203
Sneezy 302
Soggy Bottom Crack 124
Sole Survivor 299
Solid Geometry 182
Solitaire 371
Solo Chimney 303
Something Better Change 55
Something Biblical 83
Songs of Praise 181
Sorcerer, The 170
Sorcerer's Apprentice 117
Soup Dragon 241
South Crack 347
South-East Crack 291
Southern Arête 359
Southern Crack 199
Southern Sloper 379
Southpaw 111
South-West Crack 290
Space Probe 184
Spacepube 192
Spandau Ballet 99
Spanish Fly 215
Spankasaurus Does Chicago 154
Spare Rib 116
Sparkle 105
Spearhead 283
Special Branch 368
Special K 279
Spectatorship of the Proletariat 106
Spectrum 115
Spiderman Meets the Carlsberg Club 366
Spirella 278
Split Personality 120
Spooky Arête 309
Spotter's Pop 127
Spotter's Slop 127
Spragbach 259
Sprat 41
Spring Roll 41
Spring Roll Left 41
Spring Slab 41
Sprite 41
Sprung 41
Square Buttress 368
Square Chimney 114
Square-Cut Face 235
Squarepusher 309
Squash Balls 144
Squashed Finger 345
Squeezer's Spots 127
Squirm, The 102
Stadium, The 289
Staffordshire Flyer 124

Staircase 342
Staircase 95
Stalin 151
Stall 253
Stall Arête 252
Stallone Arête 240
Starboard Crack 221
Stark 325
Starlight and Storm 167
Starlight Left 167
Static 141
Staying Alive 252
Steeper 202
Steeplechase Crack 128
Steeplechaser 128
Stephen 117
Stephen 325
Stepped Arête 379
Steps 57
Stickfast 278
Stickle Brick Wall 321
Stilted 348
Sting, The 286
Stoke the Engines 358
Stokesline 182
Stolen Days 66
Stone Loach 171
Stonemason's Route 310
Stop… Carry on! 106
Straight Crack 66
Strain Station 115
Stranglehold 141
Strenuosity 304
Stretch and Mantel 43
Stretch Left 43
Struggle 345, 359
Stuck Behind a Yellow Metro 371
Studio 352
Stumblehead 322
Sublime, The 74
Substance 114
Suckin' Pebbles 318
Suicide Arête 380
Suicide Wall 380
Summit Arête (Bosley) 373
Summit Arête (Lower Tier) 40
Summit Bypass 373
Sumo Cellulite 67
Sunday at Chapel 51
Super Girdle 69
Supermac 318
Suspended Sentence 266
Swan Bank 63
Swan, The 60
Swinger 57
Swinger, The 223
Swinger, The 40

Swivel Finger 153
Swivel Flakes 153
Syringe Benefit 358

T

T'rival Traverse 203
Tactical Weapon 329
Taller Overhang 343
Tally Not 204
Taming of the Shrew 286
Tantrum, The 303
Tasmanian Devil 359
Tasmanian Tendencies 243
Teacup, The 70
Technical Slab 88
Technician, The 286
Technocrat 289
Teck Crack 52
Teck Crack Direct 52
Teck Crack Super-Direct 52
Tequila Sunrise 289
Termination Crack 374
Tetris 144
The Blusher 357
The Common Good 365
The Crack 357
The Letter T 202
The Missus 283
The Notch 169
The Rib Right-Hand 342
The Thin Air 68
The Witch 238
The Yawn 260
Theseus 324
Thin Crack 270
Thin Crack 351
Thin Finger Corner 373
Thing on a Spring 60
Third Degree Burn 78
This is My Church 263
This Poison 183
Thompson Twins 187
Thompson's Buttress Route One 187
Thompson's Buttress Route Two 187
Thorax 361
Thorns 312
Thorns Section 315
Thorns Start 314
Threapwood Arête 311
Threapwood Bulge 311
Three Pocket Slab 42
Three Steps 368
Three Tier Buttress 126
Throwball 243
Thrug 117
Thrutch 153
Thud 52

399

Thum 303
Thumbelina 327
Thumbs 314
Tier's End 207
Tierdrop 207
Tiger's Wall 316
Tim Benzadrino 147
Time Flies By 325
Time Out 221
Time to be Had 113
Time's Arrow 322
Tip Toe 144
Tiptoe 286
Tip-Toe Arête 258
Tit Grip 206
Titan 366
Titan's Wall 286
Tittersworth Rib 70
To Live Again 324
Toast Rack 307
Tobacco Road 113
Toe Nail 344
Toe Rail 269
Too Drunk 109
Top Brick 307
Topaz 115
Torture 205
Totally Unprecedented 154
Toucan 99
Touch 188
Touched 187
Tour De Force 291
Tower Chimney 117
Tower Eliminate 117
Tower Face 117
Tower of Bizarre Delights 74
Toxic Socks 113
Track of the Cat 135
Traditional 345
Transcendental Medication 129
Transit Crack 324
Trap Door Finish 170
Traveller in Time 201
Travelling Bag 307
Travelling Light 307
Traverse of Man 49
Traverse, Girdle 69
Traverse, The Greener 44
Traverse, The Undercut 43
Tre Cime 325
Trebia 102
Tree Chimney 187
Tree Corner 128
Tree Grooves 128
Tremor 362
Trepidation 240
Triack 289

Tricky Woo 289
Tricouni Crack 219
Trio Chimney 114
Triple Point 133
Triptych Groove 127
Triumph of the Good City 188
Trivial Traverse 203
Trouble at t'Mill 191
Tube Snake 365
Tufa 304
Tunnel Chimney 316
Tunnel Vision 187
Twin Cracks 202
Twin Thin 268
Twinkletoes 364
Twisted Crack 70
Twisting Crack 281
Two Pocket Slab 136
Two Step (Knypersley) 364
Two-Step (Castle naze) 356
Tyler 315
Tyrannosaurus Hex 241

U

Uchimata 325
Ugly Bloke 357
Ugly Puss 316
Ultimate Sculpture 203
Ultra Direct 220
Uncorrected Personality Traits 362
Undercoat 310
Undercut Dyno 43
Undercut, The 315
Undercutter, The 43
Underhung Chimney 278
Underpass, The 69
Undertaker, The 202
Ungodly Groove 330
Unseen Face 271
Untouchable, The 205
Up Chips 44
Up The Swanee 63
Up to the Elbows 366
Up Your Slip 215
Uppercut, The 43
Uppermost Traverse 235
Upright 92
Uzi Lover 302

V

Valkyrie 59
Valkyrie Corner 59
Valkyrie Direct 59
Valley of Ultravixens 240
Valve, The 75
Vanishing Crack 359

Varicose 235
V-Chimney 371
V-Corner 351
Vee Diff 368
Vereker's Venture 286
Very Connoisseurish 133
Via Dolorosa 59
Via Dolorosa Variations 59
Via Trita 287
Vice, The 359
Victory 169
Violence 38
Virgin Wall Traverse 308
Vixen, The 240
Voila 3 67

W

Wad Man Slang 116
Wafer, The 304
Waggledunce 361
Waistline, The 102
Waiting for the Lions 204
Walking on Sunshine 145
Wall and Groove 201
Wall Climb 343
Wall Past Mono 235
Wallaby 359
Wallaby Wall 122
Walleroo 75
Wander 141
War Child 315
War Wound 105
Warp, The 312
Wart, The 247
Watercourse, The 215
Wavelength 187
Waxwing 146
Way Purple Splat Balloon 366
We're British 281
Weathered Corner 271
Web, The 285
Wellingtons 203
West's Wallaby 75
Wet and Warm 373
Wheel of Misfortune 222
Wheeze 112
Whilly's Whopper 205
Whirling Pit 297
Whispering Myth 329
White House Crack 371
White Mouse 320
White Widow 289
Who Needs Ready Brek? 144
Whose Line is it Anyway? 256
Why Kill Time When You Can 371

Wick Slip 215
Wicked Wind 122
Wigglette 281
Wild Thing 133
Wildy's Arête 70
Wildy's Right 71
Willow Farm 136
Windshields of Fate 361
Wine Gums 204
Wing Wing 64
Wing Wong 95
Winger 95
Wings of Unreason 135
Winter in Combat 141
Wipers 78
Wisecrack 55
Wolfman of the KGB 109
Wombat 359
Wombat 74
Woody 260
Wootton Wanderer 330
Working Hunter 310
Wraparound Arête 235
Wrestle Crack 269
Wriggler 214
Wright's Traverse 312
Wright's Giza 310
Wright's Unconquerable 311
Wrong Way Round 74
Wrong's Traverse 314

X

X Marks the Spot 256

Y

Yankee Jam 151
Yo Clam 241
Yong 55
Yong Arête 55
You'll Always Reap What You Sow 325
Young Pretender 190
Your Own Undoing 299

Z

Zeus 324
Zig-a-Zag-a 357
Zigzag 344
Zigzag Crack 357
Zoom Wall 168

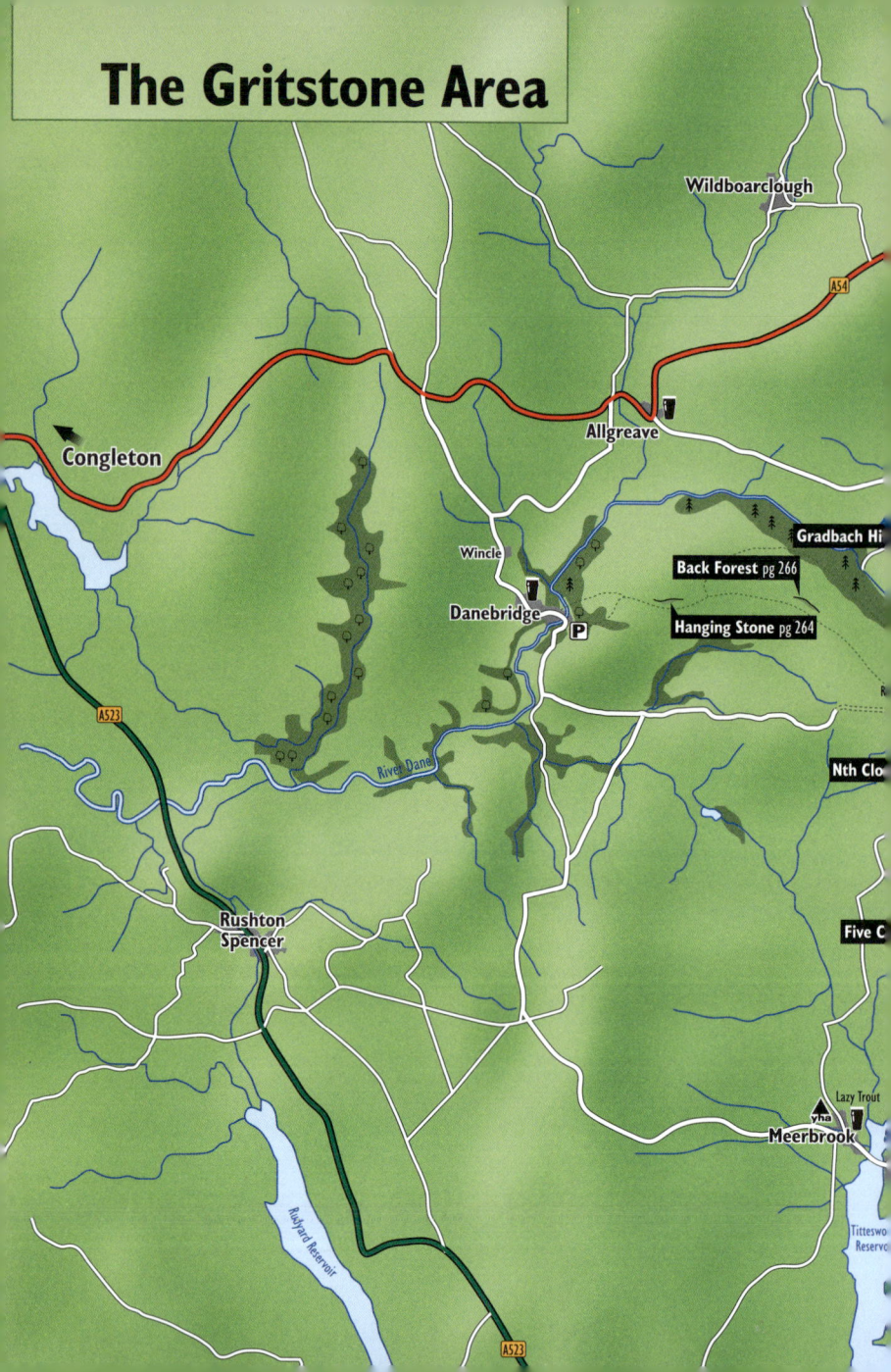